T0211604

Enterprise Mac Administrator's Guide

Second Edition

■■■

Charles S. Edge Jr.

William Smith

Apress®

Enterprise Mac Administrator's Guide, Second Edition

ISBN-13 (pbk): 978-1-4842-1705-4

ISBN-13 (electronic): 978-1-4842-1706-1

Managing Director: Welmoed Spahr
Lead Editor: Louise Corrigan
Technical Reviewer: James Graham
Editorial Board: Steve Anglin, Louise Corrigan, Jim DeWolf, Jonathan Gennick, Robert Hutchinson,
    Michelle Lowman, James Markham, Susan McDermott, Matthew Moodie, Jeffrey Pepper,
    Douglas Pundick, Ben Renow-Clarke, Gwenan Spearing
Coordinating Editor: Jill Balzano
Copy Editor: Kim Wimpsett
Compositor: SPi Global
Indexer: SPi Global
Artist: SPi Global
Cover Designer: Anna Ishchenko

Distributed to the book trade worldwide by Springer Science+Business Media New York, 233 Spring Street, 6th Floor, New York, NY 10013. Phone 1-800-SPRINGER, fax (201) 348-4505, e-mail orders-ny@springer-sbm.com, or visit www.springer.com. Apress Media, LLC is a California LLC and the sole member (owner) is Springer Science + Business Media Finance Inc (SSBM Finance Inc). SSBM Finance Inc is a Delaware corporation.

For information on translations, please e-mail rights@apress.com, or visit www.apress.com.

Apress and friends of ED books may be purchased in bulk for academic, corporate, or promotional use. eBook versions and licenses are also available for most titles. For more information, reference our Special Bulk Sales–eBook Licensing web page at www.apress.com/bulk-sales.

Any source code or other supplementary materials referenced by the author in this text is available to readers at www.apress.com. For detailed information about how to locate your book's source code, go to www.apress.com/source-code/.

To my little Emerald, with oh so much love

—*Charles S. Edge Jr.*

*To the brilliant Mac admin community
and Dean for putting up with me :-)*

—*William Smith*

Contents at a Glance

Contents

About the Authors

Charles S. Edge Jr. is a product manager at JAMF Software and the former CTO of 318, which at the time was the largest consultancy for Mac in the enterprise. Charles maintains the Bushel blog at `blog.bushel.com` as well as a personal site at `krypted.com`.

Charles is the author of a number of books on Mac OS X Server and systems administration topics going back to OS X 10.3, including a number of books from Apress for Mac OS X. He has spoken at a variety of conferences including DefCon, Black Hat, LinuxWorld, Macworld, MacSysAdmin, X World, ACES, the Penn State Mac Admins Conference, and the Apple WorldWide Developers Conference. Charles is the developer of the SANS course on Mac OS X security and coauthor of its best practices guide to securing Mac OS X. Charles now lives in Minneapolis, Minnesota, with his sweet little daughter, Emerald.

William Smith is a senior solutions architect at 318, Inc., where he has provided consulting and training services on behalf of partner organizations such as Apple and JAMF Software as well as supporting many wonderful customers. William is co-owner of OfficeforMacHelp.com and occasionally speaks his mind on his personal site Remember the Human at `talkingmoose.net`.

William is also a Microsoft Most Valuable Professional (MVP), supporting Office for Mac users and Mac admins, and is a cofounder of Twin Cities Mac Admins, a community supporting all things Apple from education to enterprise. He has spoken at JAMF Nation User Conference (JNUC), MacIT at Macworld, and Penn State Mac Admins Conference. William lives with Dean, his partner of 15 years in Minneapolis, Minnesota.

About the Technical Reviewer

Jim Graham received a bachelor of science in electronics with a specialty in telecommunications from Texas A&M University in 1989. He was published in the International Communications Association's 1988 issue of *ICA Communique* ("Fast Packet Switching: An Overview of Theory and Performance"). He has worked as an associate network engineer in the Network Design Group at Amoco Corporation in Chicago, Illinois; as a senior network engineer at Tybrin Corporation in Fort Walton Beach, Florida; and as an intelligence systems analyst at both 16th Special Operations Wing Intelligence and HQ US Air Force Special Operations Command Intelligence at Hurlburt Field, Florida. He received a formal letter of commendation from the 16th Special Operations Wing Intelligence in 2001.

Acknowledgments

We'd like to first thank the OS X community. This includes everyone from the people who design the black box to the people who dissect it and finally the people who help others learn to dissect it. We truly stand on the shoulders of giants. Of those at Apple who need to be thanked specifically are Schoun Regan, Joel Rennich, Greg Smith, JD Mankovsky, David Winter, Stale Bjorndal, Cawan Starks, Eric Senf, Jennifer Jones, and of course the one and only Josh Wisenbaker.

The Apple community is an exceptional group. Of those in that community who deserve thanks, it starts with Allister Banks, Adam Codega, Andrina Kelly, Ben Clayton, Ben Toms, Bill Smith, Bryson Terrell, Calum Hunter, Clayton Bureson, Ed Marczak, Eldon Ahrold, Emmanuel Lauhan, Emily Nykto, Eric Holtam, Erik Gomez, Gary Larizza, Graham Gilbert, Graham Pugh, Greg Neagle, Hannes Juutilainen, James Barclay, Jeremy Reichman, John Kitzmiller, Joseph Chilcote, Justin Rummel, Karl Kuehn, Marcus Jaensson Wahlstam, Michael Lynn, Mike Solin, Mles Leacy, Nick McSpadden, Patrick Fergus, Pepijn Bruienne, Per Olofsson, Randy Saeks, Rich Trouton, Richard Purves, Tim Sutton, Sam Marshall, Sean Kaiser, Shea Craig, Stéphen Sudre, Steve Yuroff, Vanessa White, Victor Vranchan, Yoann Gini, and of course the co-authors of the first edition of this book: Zach Smith and Beau Hunter.

I thank the crew at JAMF Software for their hard work. Without you (Bryson and Michael for starters, but oh so many more), I would never have been able to complete this book! Bill thanks his recent Apple mentors David McKee, John McMahon Jr., and Pete Markham as well as his fellow Twin Cities Mac Admins steering committee members Brad Schmidt, Brian LaShomb, Bryson Tyrrell, and John Wetter.

And a special thanks to the late and great Michael Bartosh.

Finally, a special thanks to the fine staff at Apress for tuning this book to be a well-oiled machine of prose and code. Thanks also to my coauthor, Bill Smith, for tirelessly working with me to meet our deadlines—it was a fun ride!

—Charles S. Edge Jr.

Introduction

In the beginning was the command line. You can automate anything and everything in OS X, but knowledge of the command line will be required to fully automate your deployment and integrate Mac OS X in the enterprise while maintaining a low total cost of ownership. This isn't to say you can't integrate OS X into a large organization en masse without using the command line—you can. However, from automation to troubleshooting, opening up a terminal window will be key to keeping your sanity, if only from time to time. But don't fear the terminal, and know that the fundamental tasks required and the fundamental methodologies with Windows deployments are the same as with OS X.

If you are reading this book, then you are likely charged with integrating Macs into your environment, whether kicking and screaming (which we hope this book will change) or as the sponsor. The message that you take away from this book is ideally that you can do anything you want to with OS X, from deploying 10,000 machines overnight to building a petabyte worth of storage to house all sorts of data for your Macs, provided you are not averse to learning a little bit of the command line to achieve your goals. The power and flexibility of OS X along with the best of the open source community is right at your fingertips to help along the way.

The first question many in IT ask when told about the need to use the command line is, "But isn't OS X supposed to be easy to use?" It is. But we're not talking about just using the Mac. We're talking about building and managing a complicated IT infrastructure, which at some point requires staff who is tooled with the mastery of the internals of each platform for which they are tasked as the steward. As such, the more you learn about internals, the more you learn about the basics, the more you can automate, the more you learn about what goes on under the hood, the more you can master management en masse, and, ultimately, the more appropriately you will be able to address issues and concerns on an enterprise-wide scale as they arise. To take this a step further, the more you learn about managing a second platform (no matter what the platform is), the better you will be at managing others. But drastic reduction in total cost of ownership is possible with OS X compared to other platforms for a variety of reasons. And since users are typically happier on a Mac, who wouldn't want a happier user base combined with lower recurring costs?

Paradigm Shifts

Just as when enterprise computing was young, you will need to rethink some of your strategies to accommodate for a wider variety of platforms, resulting in a paradigm shift of sorts. But luckily you are not alone, and the jump is not as bad as many seem to think. There are a number of resources to help you through the process. From web sites to books, from Apple engineers to third-party providers/channel partners, from e-mail lists to user groups, you are not on an island. And while it is not fully open source, the Mac platform is a largely community-driven affair. One of our contributions to that community is this book, where we take on the lofty task of bridging the gap between your enterprise and your Mac.

The fundamentals of designing a Mac-based enterprise are the same as with any other platform—the specifics are not. In any enterprise organization you will need to perform a mass deployment, whether all at once or a refresh cycle performed on an ongoing basis. Every enterprise will also need centralized servers that provide a number of services to hosts on the network, including directory services, shared storage, groupware, and application servers. But the software that provides the needs of an enterprise is often different with the Mac than with other platforms. This isn't to say that the functionality of solutions already in use in many organizations cannot be extended to cover OS X. But in some cases it is going to garner a higher return on investment to prop up an entire infrastructure to support the Mac while in others you are best to leave your existing solutions in place and extend them to the Mac.

OS X is a standards-compliant operating system—to a point. Given the support of a number of standards, OS X can be integrated into a primarily Microsoft environment. This includes support for Active Directory, Exchange support (either through Entourage or natively with ActiveSync), DFS, SMB/CIFS, and NFS. Many Microsoft-centric solutions will work out of the box. But when compared to the features available to Windows-based users, you may find yourself frustrated with integrating systems on a large scale. Users may also be frustrated with certain features that are missing when moving from Mac to Windows. Ultimately some of these features can even result in needing to purchase a third-party solution, deploying a thin client-based solution, or using virtualization solutions to ease the pain of integration, be it temporarily or permanently.

None of these obstacles is insurmountable. Through each release of OS X, the system has become more and more enterprise friendly. And with each subsequent release you can expect that trend to continue. But don't expect to be able to do business as usual; expect to slightly alter your way of thinking to a more open model of computing. That shift toward openness, once you get right down to it, will make the process far easier and far more rewarding and in the end will lead you to a new paradigm in how you deal with enterprise computing.

Measure Twice, Cut Once

This likely goes without saying, but here goes: Before you deploy and integrate on a large scale, test. Before you test, plan. The more you plan, the less work you will ultimately have to do. What do you need to plan for? In our experience, it all starts with directory services. This is why the first chapter of the book jumps into directory services, and from there we cover further integration in the same order that most organizations build out that infrastructure. It varies between environments, but if you go through each chapter and take into account the technologies introduced, then you will be able to plan more holistically.

OS X is a great platform and suitable for a bevy of uses but not the right fit for providing a number of network services. Therefore, throughout the book you will find information for integrating with existing infrastructure that may or may not be more suitable given your shift in platforms (however extensive that shift may be). Aside from infrastructure, the Mac systems you are planning to deploy and support require users to be productive on them, something they may not be able to do within the confines of OS X. The book ends with virtualization and thin client solutions that can be leveraged to provide services that otherwise would not be available to the Mac platform.

Application Availability

While the book covers virtualization, the best deployments are going to be those that don't require any applications to be virtualized. If your organization has invested in leveraging a consumer model—a mixture of using cloud services and migrating client-based software into intranets—then the Mac is more likely going to be able to take on your software with ease. But if you are using a number of proprietary products that do not come with an OS X client, then you may need to use some form of virtualization to bridge the gap.

Long term, though, you need a plan to migrate to applications that are cross-platform to keep the costs for your OS X clients at a minimum. There are a number of sites available to help you find software for the Mac, most notably Versiontracker.com. But there will be times when the Mac software is not as advanced or well-kept as the Windows versions. This can lead to frustration from end users who possibly once championed the platform. In this case, you may have to virtualize the software or an entire operating system to achieve parity. But this is where testing on a per-group basis will become key to planning your deployment.

When testing, make sure each user in your pilot thoroughly tests each piece of software. Find the biggest power users in a group and ask them to be your testers. Their voices will often be heard the loudest when things don't go well. But if you can keep them involved in the process and communicate with them along the way, once you achieve success, you will often have the best proponent you could ask for.

How This Book Is Organized

Sandwiched between chapters on directory services and virtualization, there are a variety of other topics that have been near and dear to organizations big and small as they grapple with integrating OS X. We have broken these topics down into a number of chapters, each playing a critical role and requiring specialized planning. Here is a summary of the chapters, aimed at guiding your planning and deployment:

Chapter 1: Directory services are a critical aspect of OS X integration. In this chapter we cover how to set up a directory services environment using Open Directory, Apple's own directory service solution. Whether you are working in an Active Directory environment, with eDirectory, or in some other variant of a supported directory service, you will need to become acquainted with the fundamentals of implementing Open Directory. Additionally, Open Directory can be leveraged to work with Active Directory, providing a compelling framework for policy management.

Chapter 2: Directory services clients are as critical as directory services themselves. In this chapter, the focus is on how to configure the directory services client from the command line, allowing you to deploy complex and automated binding scripts. The script examples provided with Chapter 2 will, at a minimum, help to get any mass deployment of OS X in motion, saving a considerable amount of time and giving a glance into best practices that can be applied to further automation topics that will arise throughout the book.

Chapter 3: Active Directory deserves a dedicated chapter. Why? The binding process, while part of the directory services framework, is considerably different from that of the other directory services modules. The third-party solutions, requirements, and roadblocks to a successful integration, and the methodology are just that different from the other directory services modules. These differences should show the considerable amount of development taken on by Apple to provide such a feature-rich Active Directory solution.

Chapter 4: Storage administration is a fundamental administrative task, but today's storage includes drive capacities on thumb drives that use to be reserved for high-end workstations five to ten years ago. And it includes cloud storage, which not only introduces new levels of risk with higher needs for security but the ability to work anywhere on any device. We'll cover network, cloud, and local storage with an emphasis on securing data while at rest and in transit.

Chapter 5: Messaging and groupware mean productivity. In this chapter, we look at the options for typing your OS X clients into shared groupware services hosted on Microsoft Exchange, Google Apps, and Office 365. We also look into implementing groupware-oriented policies in the environment and automatically configuring groupware applications as part of your deployment process.

Chapter 6: Whether it's imaging, deploying the image, or automating the tasks that enable you to be closer and closer to the one-touch image, this chapter is all about providing a step-by-step process to accomplishing these tasks. However, over the past few years a number of solutions have emerged to make mass deployment infinitely easier for administrators. Therefore, of the tasks we follow through the steps, we will use a different solution for each, allowing you to see a spectrum of options.

Chapter 7: OS X has a rich client management framework. In this chapter, we look at local and directory services–based deployments of policies and explore the options for extending existing solutions to cover client management.

Chapter 8: By automating administrative tasks, you as an IT professional (or the manager of an IT professional) will be freed up to take on enhancing how your business interacts with technology (or you'll learn to fish, sleep nights, etc.). In this chapter, we take a deep look into scripting and other forms of automation. This is where mastery of the command can become absolutely critical.

Chapter 9: You just can't do everything on the Mac that you can do in Windows 10, Linux, or any other operating systems you can think of. Therefore, we give you a whole chapter of virtualization and thin client best practices and deployment techniques to ease the burden of your now doubled operating system footprint if you embark on this convoluted journey.

Chapter 10: Open source technologies are part of many Mac deployments. There are a lot of Mac admins out there, pushing the boundaries of what's possible and bridging the gaps between what Apple builds, what third-party vendors build, and what administrators actually need. In this chapter, we lay out a tool chain that can be used in environments where you cannot afford the proprietary tools or when you need access to source code not always available with third-party vendors.

Chapter 11: Apple provides a number of services used during large deployments. In some cases, these services are obviously good, and in other cases they can be a huge challenge because your security team will have big problems with these technologies. This chapter addresses some misconceptions with Apple deployment programs so you can deploy the correct strategy with regard to Apple programs.

Chaos Theory

There is no magic bullet for your deployment. Most environments are going to be different in some way, shape, or form from every other environment out there. But provided there is industry-standard infrastructure (and most vendors have long since moved into providing industry standards), then rest assured that there is some way to make your Mac clients integrate fairly seamlessly into the enterprise. Therefore, while we don't have a magic bullet to offer, we do have a plethora of options for a given situation, options you can use to cut costs, reduce required human capital, and free up IT staff for creating value to businesses rather than living in the IT cost center.

## Chapter 1

Directory Services

A *directory service* is the software that stores, organizes, and provides access to information in a directory or a database of users, groups, computers, and network devices such as printers. The directory service supplies that database to client computers. In most enterprise, educational, and larger institutions, common directory service implementations range from Microsoft's Active Directory (AD) to Apple's Open Directory (OD) to Novell's eDirectory, as well as the open source OpenLDAP. Most modern directory services are based on open standards developed in the public forum.

The publication "The Directory: Overview of concepts, models and services" defines the most common standard architectural guidelines for the X.500 model, which is the publicly developed standard for electronic directory services. While the concepts and roots of most directories are complex, by their nature they share the simple goal of facilitating unified user management, authentication, and authorization. Directory servers with different origins thus share many commonalities in their structure and accessibility. The Lightweight Directory Access Protocol (LDAP), which nearly every major directory service system utilizes, is a testament to this need for accessibility, as we will discuss later in this chapter. Put simply, any system engineered for large-scale centralized information storage must inherently allow disparate clients to participate; otherwise, it is doomed to a finite growth potential.

In OS X, a number of plug-ins allow it to leverage a variety of directory services. Each computer must at minimum contain a local directory service database to establish a baseline of system-critical data, such as users, groups, and even some configuration data. If every Mac sold required an enterprise directory service just to log in, Apple stores would not be popping up like Starbucks in cities around the world. Local directory databases are a cornerstone of all modern operating systems and often the gateway for small and medium businesses to grow into larger directory systems over time. A common misconception is Apple's *Open Directory* terminology refers only to its enterprise-class network authentication services. In reality, the same term refers to OS X's local directory services too. In fact, earlier operating systems had the same technology running on Open Directory masters, such as Mac OS X 10.2's netinfod and Mac OS X's 10.3 Password Server. This concept of architecting miniature directory servers into the base operating system allows for later migration to larger network directory systems with little re-education of entry-level system administrators. The best example of this is Apple's parental controls system, which utilizes the same technology managing thousands of OS X systems in enterprise environments every day. Because of such forethought, clients can also be configured out of the box to access a variety of external directories; Apple provides support for several network-based directory service systems without installing any additional software.

This chapter starts with an explanation of how the local directory service works. Once we have covered how to manage local users, we will move on to discuss LDAP, the industry-standard directory database protocol used to access directory services. Next, we will cover various types of directory service bindings for OS X that let end users log in to their computers using a centralized username and password. Finally, we will look at building external accounts and show how to build a directory service based on Apple's Open Directory.

Local Accounts

System Preferences in OS X is similar to the Control Panel in Windows; it allows you to configure a wide range of settings. The information you set in its panes is stored in files throughout the operating system. Local directory service configuration is accessed through the Users & Groups preference pane, which provides the ability to add local user accounts. You can add accounts to groups, assign them a type, and set a few other options.

To access a System Preferences pane, choose System Preferences from the Apple menu (•) in the top-left corner of the screen or launch the application directly from the Applications folder. This displays all the available preference panes. Next, click Users & Groups to view the list of local accounts on the left side of the pane. As you click through each one, the options for that account appear on the right side of the pane. To make changes, you must first authenticate to System Preferences by clicking the Lock button in the lower-left corner of the System Preferences window. This requires a user who is a member of the local directory service's admin group.

Tip   The /private/var/db/auth.db SQLite database is used to determine which groups can perform a variety of system changes. In a standard OS X environment, users in the admin group can obtain escalation for all authorization rights, and an administrator can modify this file to provide very granular administrative access. For instance, to allow a nonadmin group to manage users via the Users & Groups pane, an administrator would add the group's name under system.preferences.accounts in the database using the security command-line tool.

Creating Accounts

To add an account, first click the Lock button in the Users & Groups pane of System Preferences; then click the plus sign to create an account. In the New Account sheet, you'll see the five options shown in Figure 1-1. These are the basic account types for OS X.

- *Administrator*: Administrative user accounts can elevate themselves to root privileges, unlock System Preference panes, and perform most tasks.

- *Standard*: Standard user accounts cannot unlock System Preferences panes and cannot perform any administrative tasks unless an administrator has authorized those privileges.

- *Managed with Parental Controls*: These are standard user accounts with administrative policies applied to them.

- *Sharing Only*: These are user accounts that cannot log onto the local system but can access resources via a network.

- *Group*: This is a group of user accounts that simplifies assigning privileges and permissions to multiple users.

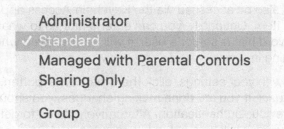

Administrator

✓ Standard

Managed with Parental Controls

Sharing Only

Group

Figure 1-1. Menu of account types

Once you have selected an account type, enter a name in the Full Name field and a short name in the Account Name field. For example, the full name might be John Doe, and the short or account name might be jdoe. By default, the account name is generated from the full name in lowercase with spaces removed. The full name is primarily used for display purposes and can be changed at will. The account name has additional system-level functions. Notably, it is used as the user's home folder name when first created, though that directory can be moved to a different location that does not correspond to the short name (such as a mystuff folder on an external drive).

The account name is used for other purposes as well, such as establishing a primary mailbox for the user or for linking scheduled items through cron. Because of this, setting the initial account name demands some consideration. It's also worth noting the account name cannot easily be edited in the prominent user interface, and though right-clicking a user account and choosing Advanced Options allows you to edit this name (as shown in Figure 1-3), doing so has other repercussions, such as the possible loss of group membership (such as admin), possible loss of preference data if an application stores configuration data based on the account name, or disassociation of the user's home folder. In most cases when you plan to modify a user's account name, you will also want to rename the user's home directory to coincide. This is merely for cosmetic reasons and is not a necessity. You can change account name jdoe to psherman and still utilize the original home directory stored at /Users/jdoe. If you do change the home directory field to /Users/psherman, you should make sure you rename the user's home folder on the file system to match the new path specified (in this case, from the original home directory value /Users/jdoe to /Users/psherman).

Next, enter your Apple ID in the iCloud ID field and the password from your iCloud account will be used to authenticate to the system. Or you can use the Use Separate Password option and enter the password in the Required field and again in the Verify field. Clicking the small key button in this dialog will reveal the Password Assistant, an interface that assists users with choosing strong passwords by supplying them with visual feedback. This functionality is available as a stand-alone program using third-party applications available on the Internet and can also be accessed via the Keychain Access application when you create a new password item. Optionally, you can enter a hint as to what the password is in the Hint field. If a password hint is set for a user, it will be displayed when the user fails to authenticate when logging in.

When you are satisfied with your settings, click the Create User button. You have now created your first OS X user. If you are done making changes, you should click the Lock button to forget your previous authentication. Alternatively, if you forget to click the Lock button, the elevated privileges will time out in five minutes.

Granting Administrative Privileges

As noted earlier, you can choose to make a user an administrator of the local computer when you create an account. To elevate an existing account to an administrative account, you can simply check the Allow User To Administer This Computer check box, as shown in Figure 1-2. To set up basic policies for an account, you can click the Open Parental Controls button and enable them for any nonadministrator account. (We will cover more in-depth policies on local and network directory services accounts in Chapter 7.)

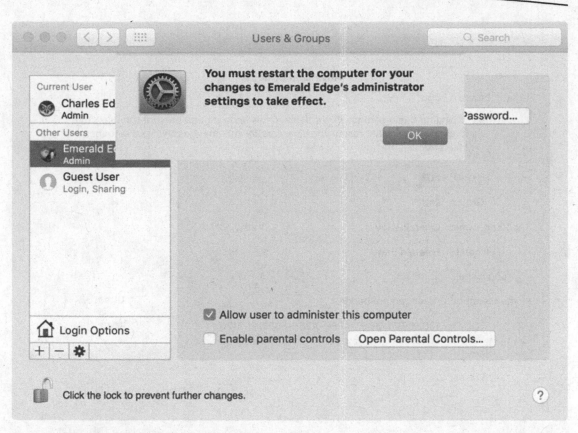

Figure 1-2. *Making a user an administrator*

As mentioned previously, you can also edit some slightly more advanced settings from within the Users & Groups pane in System Preferences. These settings are accessible by Control-clicking the account name and choosing Advanced Options to display a screen similar to the one in Figure 1-3. This screen lets you change the values for various attributes of the accounts, including account name (aka short name), user ID, group, path to the home directory (where the user's home folder is stored), login shell, and UUID for the account. You can also add aliases by clicking the plus button; this allows the same account to authenticate using multiple short names in the authentication dialogs throughout the operating system. We will discuss these attributes later in the chapter.

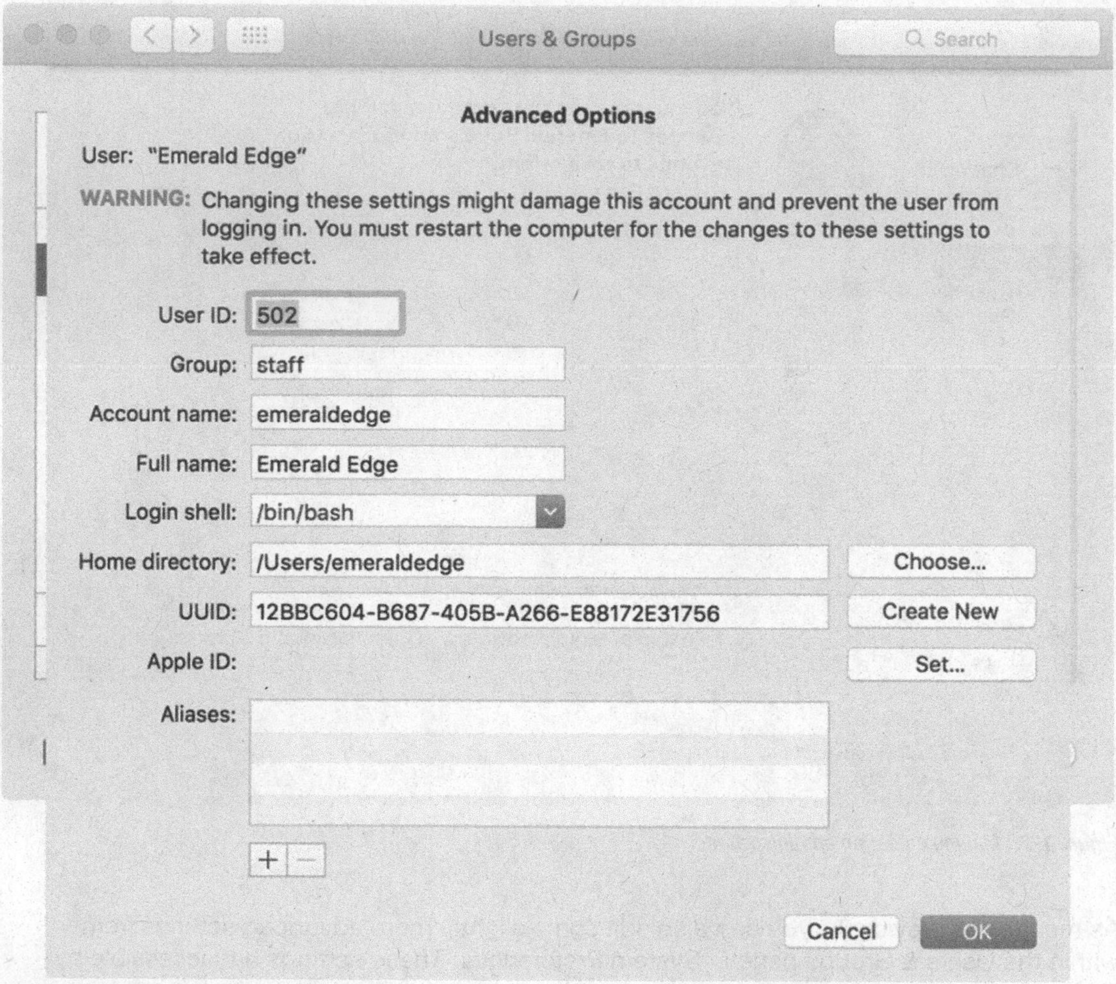

Figure 1-3. Advanced account options

The Root Account

In Unix, BSD, and other *nix environments, the root account can do things even standard administrators typically can't do. It can be a security risk, which is why Apple has disabled it by default. You should rarely, if ever, need to enable the root account.

If you find you have that rare need to enable the root account, open the Directory Utility application in the /System/Library/CoreServices/Applications folder. As with most secure operations in OS X, you will need to click the Lock button to authenticate to perform this action. Then choose Enable Root User from the Edit menu, as shown in Figure 1-4. Next, enter the password that will be assigned to the root user and click the OK button.

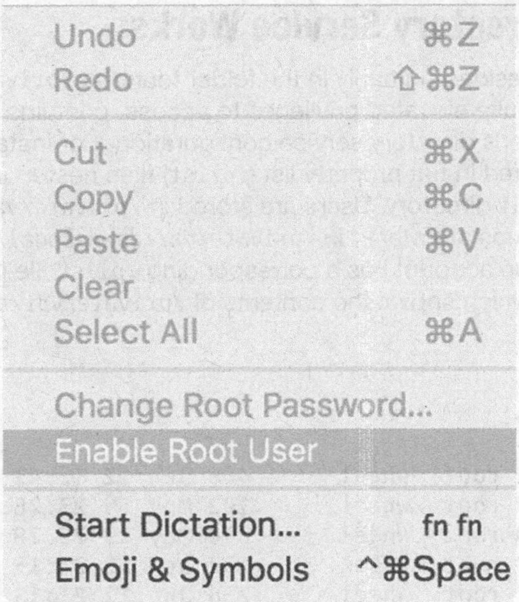

Undo	⌘Z
Redo	⇧⌘Z
Cut	⌘X
Copy	⌘C
Paste	⌘V
Clear	
Select All	⌘A
Change Root Password...	
Enable Root User	
Start Dictation...	fn fn
Emoji & Symbols	^⌘Space

Figure 1-4. Enabling root in Directory Utility

You can also enable the root account using the dsenableroot command-line tool. To enable root, enter the following:

dsenableroot

First you will be prompted for the current user password; this user must be an administrative account. You will then be prompted twice, first for a password to assign the root account and then to verify the password. On success you'll see the following success code:

dsenableroot:: ***Successfully enabled root user.

To disable the root account, enter the following:

dsenableroot -d

> **Tip** It is best to leave the root account disabled when you do not need it. If you do enable it, do so only temporarily.

How the Local Directory Service Works

The local directory data resides primarily in the folder found at /private/var/db/dslocal. This folder, which will require elevated privileges to access, contains numerous files pertaining to the computer's directory service configuration. For instance, accounts for users and groups are stored in flat property list (.plist) files nested in the /private/var/db/dslocal/nodes/Default directory. Users are stored in /private/var/db/dslocal/nodes/Default/users, while groups are stored in /private/var/db/dslocal/nodes/Default/groups. Every local user and group account has a corresponding .plist file in these directories, as shown in Figure 1-5, which shows the contents of /private/var/db/dslocal/nodes/Default/.

```
bash-3.2# ls -al
total 5768
drw-------    12 root  wheel       408 Jun 12 12:41 .
drwxr-xr-x     3 root  wheel       102 May  9 23:28 ..
drwx------    10 root  wheel       340 May  9 23:28 aliases
drwx------     3 root  wheel       102 Jun 12 21:15 computers
drwx------     7 root  wheel       238 Jun 12 21:15 config
drwx------   124 root  wheel      4216 Jul  4 22:01 groups
drwx------     3 root  wheel       102 May  9 23:28 networks
drwx------     9 root  wheel       306 Jul  4 16:37 sharepoints
-rw-------     1 root  wheel    364544 Jul  4 12:54 sqlindex
-rw-------     1 root  wheel     32768 Jul  2 01:33 sqlindex-shm
-rw-------     1 root  wheel   2554432 Jul  4 22:30 sqlindex-wal
drwx------    91 root  wheel      3094 Jul  4 22:30 users
bash-3.2# ▮
```

Figure 1-5. Contents of a dslocal node

Each folder will contain a plist file for each respective user, computer, or group in the local directory. Accounts that begin with an underscore (_) are hidden service users and groups. For example, the web server uses the _www account, which obtains user settings from the _www.plist file. The _www user can't log in because the account has no shell or password. If you created a new user in the previous section, look in the /private/var/db/dslocal/nodes/Default/users directory, and you should see a plist file with a name that corresponds to the new user's short name.

A plist stores a number of attributes listed as key-value pairs containing data about a given user or group. Looking at local users and groups from a Microsoft Windows perspective, files in the OS X local directory node resemble registry keys for local accounts. Use the defaults command in the Terminal application to read a plist file.

```
defaults read /private/var/db/dslocal/nodes/Defaults/users/jdoe.plist
```

Examine the .plist file for the user created earlier and look for the key called creationTime to see when the account was created in epoch time.

```
dict>
    <key>creationTime</key>
    <real>1419634669.1759779</real>
    <key>passwordLastSetTime</key>
    <real>1419634670.2535181</real>
</dict>
```

In the user's plist file, you will also see keys that are not in the standard XML format, such as a generateduid key, which is used to track the user account even if the short name is changed. Generated UIDs are based on a standard called the *universally unique identifier* (UUID), which is a complex, programmatically generated string of characters that will never be duplicated. A user's UUID is unique across time and space. You can see it using the plutil command to view keys rather than having them in binary, with the -p option, as follows:

```
plutil -p /private/var/db/dslocal/nodes/Default/users/cedge.plist
```

The data from the account property lists can be managed by modifying the text files directly, provided you convert the files first using plutil. For example, if you want to change a user's picture, you could alter the picture key. However, editing property lists directly can be pretty cumbersome, so Apple has provided a host of commands that can be used to manage and query data from the local directory node and other directory services plug-ins without having to read raw XML-style property list data. Some commands have GUI equivalents, while others do not. Here are some of the commands:

- dscacheutil: Looks up information stored in the directory services cache and flushes various caches.

- dscl: Used to edit and browse directory services settings, such as user accounts, group accounts, and search policies (the order in which OS X looks up account information in each directory service). The closest GUI equivalents would be Users & Groups in System Preferences and Directory Utility. This command is covered in more depth in the next section.

- dseditgroup: Used to edit, create, and delete groups and add or remove group members.

- dsenableroot: Manages the root user account (enables, disables, and resets the root password). The GUI equivalents are the Change Root Password and Enable Root User or Disable Root User options in the Edit menu of Directory Utility.

- dserr: Prints a description of directory services–related errors, such as dserr 14090. Once you have the error code, you can use the man page for opendirectoryd to look up the meaning of each error (or Google for more information on the specific errors, but quote errors if there is a dash [-] in front of the number).

- dsexport: Exports directory services data.

- ■ dsimport: Imports directory services data. Similar functionality is available using the Import feature of Workgroup Manager, although Apple has deprecated this tool and no longer encourages its use. Today, you can use Server.app to import objects, although with limited options.

- ■ dsmemberutil: Looks up UUIDs and group information and flushes group cache, as in dsmemberutil flushcache.

- ■ id: Looks up a user identity, including group memberships, as in id cedge.

You can learn more about these commands by viewing their manual pages using the man command-line program. For example, the following command looks up the manual page for the dscl tool:

man dscl

> *For more information about this and other command line tools, use their manual pages—that is, "man command".*

In many enterprises, one of the first differences that cross-platform administrators notice is by default domain administrators from a directory service are not administrators of local OS X client computers (although, as illustrated in Chapter 3, with Active Directory, you can make Enterprise Admins or any other Active Directory group administrators of OS X clients). To mimic this functionality, it is possible to nest a network directory service group inside the local Administrators group, thereby granting local administrator rights to all network members of that group. This is handy in large environments where administrator access may need to be limited to subsets of administrators. This technique is covered in more detail in Chapter 7.

Network administrators should use their own unique network credentials for administrative tasks, but you should also maintain at least a single dedicated local administrative account on OS X systems to ensure administrative access to your local client nodes. To create these local administrative accounts, you can use Setup Assistant or Users & Groups in System Preferences. This is a common practice in monolithic imaging environments (imaging is covered further in Chapter 6), but it's not entirely scalable in most cases. You can also use dscl as part of scripts.

dscl

For a number of tasks, dscl (the Directory Service command-line utility) is the gateway to directory services. Use it to view existing information in local or network directory services, augment settings for the local directory service node, or alter how the directory services daemon functions, including prioritizing domain lookups.

From an enterprise management perspective, perhaps the most useful aspect of `dscl` is its ability to automate account creation and editing. To create a local account using the command line (and thus be able to script the process), `dscl` is the preferred command. `dscl` is an interactive tool that can, in its simplest form, be used by simply typing `dscl` at a command-line prompt. To see all the directory services plug-ins enabled on the system, type `ls` at the prompt.

```
> ls
Active Directory
LDAPv3

Local
Contacts
Search
```

Any admin or standard user can use `dscl` if he is interested only in reading account information. However, to alter the contents of a database, he will need elevated privileges. To invoke `dscl` with elevated privileges, prepend the command with `sudo` as follows:

```
sudo dscl
```

You can prepend the `sudo` command to any command to force it to run with root privileges. When using `sudo`, you will be prompted for your password, and you must be an administrator. The `sudo` command will cache credentials for five minutes after successful authentication, so if you have recently authenticated, you will not need to retype your password.

At this point, you should be in an interactive command-line environment and see a > on the screen, so we'll prepend each command with a > to match what you see. The first step in the process of creating a new account is to add a user to the database, which will create a new plist file for the account. Use the `create` `dscl` command followed by the path to the record being created. In the following example, we will create an basic account called `corpadmin`:

```
> create /Local/Default/Users/corpadmin
```

A property list consists of dictionaries containing keys and values. In the previous example, we did not specify any keys. The `dscl` command created the record, and, therefore, a file in the form of the `corpadmin.plist` file has manifested in `/private/var/db/dslocal/nodes/Default/users`. For the corpadmin account to be viable, we now need to create a number of properties or key-value pairs that tell the directory services daemon about this user. These properties are the attributes for the account. Table 1-1 lists commonly used user attributes.

Table 1-1. Basic User Attributes

Attribute	Purpose
UniqueID or uid	An integer ID unique to this user
PrimaryGroupID or gid	The primary group of the user
GeneratedUID or generateduid	A universally unique identifier for the user
NFSHomeDirectory or home	Absolute path to the user's home directory
RealName or realname	The user's full name
RecordName or name	The user's short name
UserShell or shell	Absolute path to the user's default shell

To create your own user by hand, you will need to assemble the required attributes. You add the `realname` key in `dscl` to specify the user's full name as you'd type it in the New Account dialog in Users & Groups. You will use the `create` command to do this. And because the full name contains a space, let's put what will go into the record in quotes.

```
> create /Local/Default/Users/corpadmin realname "Corporate Administrator"
```

Next, you'll give the user a user ID using the `uid` key. This ID should be unique (as the name implies), so no other accounts will have the same ID. You will again use the `create` command.

```
> create /Local/Default/Users/corpadmin uid 1500
```

Now you'll set up a default group ID (GID), which has an attribute of gid. You'll set the gid to the Staff group, which has a group number of 20.

```
> create /Local/Default/Users/corpadmin gid 20
```

> **Caution**   As with most things that happen at the command line, `dscl` is unforgiving with regard to typos, including spaces. But it does support tabbed autocompletion, which is awesome.

You also need to give the account a default shell to use if it is going to do anything meaningful. The default shell is the shell Terminal uses when first opened. The attribute for a default shell is `shell`. The contents of this key should be any shell on the system, including `/bin/zsh`, `/bin/tcsh`, or the default with OS X, `/bin/bash`. To prevent users from utilizing a shell account, assign `/usr/bin/false` as their shells, which will immediately terminate any attempts at a shell session, as well as disable access to the Terminal application. This also prevents an account from logging in via `loginwindow`, in which case `/usr/bin/true` is a completely acceptable substitute. To set the `shell` attribute, create the `shell` key using the following command:

```
> create /Local/Default/Users/corpadmin shell /bin/bash
```

Every user needs a home directory. Even the root account has one (`/private/var/root` by default). The home directory doesn't need to reference a path that currently exists because the first time the user logs into a system, the home directory will be created and assigned appropriate permissions. The attribute for the home directory is home.

```
> create /Local/Default/Users/corpadmin home /Users/corpadmin
```

Because you're creating an administrative user, you also need to add the account to the admin group. Here, you'll use the append command rather than create because you're augmenting an existing key rather than creating one. You'll follow it with the relative path of the admin group and then the attribute that you'll be editing and finally the payload of the actual edit. To add the corpadmin user to the administrative users group, use this:

```
> append /Local/Default/Groups/admin GroupMembership corpadmin
```

> **Tip** If you know the value of an attribute, it is best to use the merge option here; if you don't, you can use append.

Next you'll give your new user a password using the passwd command, typing a password once the following command is run:

```
> passwd /Local/Default/Users/corpadmin
```

By now, the account should be listed in the local directory service. To make sure, you'll use the list command.

```
> list /Local/Default/Users
```

Once the account has been recognized by the local directory services node, you can look at information that was not in the original property list, such as the GeneratedUID, using dscl.

```
> read /Local/Default/Users/corpadmin GeneratedUID
```

The dscl command is also useful in troubleshooting. In the previous command, you were looking for a specific attribute, but if you wanted to see all the attributes for the new corpadmin account, you could simply run the following:

```
> read /Local/Default/Users/corpadmin
```

Changing Accounts en Masse

If you have ssh or Apple Remote Desktop (ARD) access, you can push out a variety of changes to an account. Once an account has been created, any of the attributes can be changed en masse, using dscl. For example, if you wanted to reset the corpadmin password to MYSECRETPASSWORD, the following command could be sent to each machine in your enterprise:

```
sudo dscl . -passwd /Users/corpadmin MYSECRETPASSWORD
```

> **Note**   If you change the password as a nonadministrative user, you need to enter the actual user's password to do so.

Or if you wanted to move the user's home folder into the /private/var directory (so it can live with and be friends with root), you could use the following (assuming you put the original home folder into /Users/corpadmin):

```
sudo dscl . -change /Users/corpadmin NFSHomeDirectory /Users/corpadmin/var/corpadmin
```

Notice that in the previous command you used the –change command rather than -edit. Also notice in both of these examples, you used dscl along with the . operator rather than using dscl interactively. By using the . operator, you used a different relative path to the user record; it is a shortcut to the Local/Default node. The attribute then appears as follows:

```
NFSHomeDirectory: /private/var/corpadmin
```

Account Creation Scripts

Scripts can also create new accounts. These scripts will use dscl along with the . operator (no point in complicating things by trying to script against an interactive command-line environment). To get started, let's create a script called adduser.sh on the desktop and then take the commands you used in the previous section to create your user attributes and put them into a script, replacing the > with dscl . and removing /Local/Default:

```
#!/bin/bash
user="corpadmin"
dscl . -create /Users/$user
dscl . -create /Users/$user RealName "Corporate Administrator"
dscl . -create /Users/$user UniqueID 1100
dscl . -create /Users/$user PrimaryGroupID 20
dscl . -create /Users/$user NFSHomeDirectory /Users/corpadmin
dscl . -create /Users/$user UserShell /bin/bash
dscl . -passwd /Users/$user 'MYSECRETPASSWORD'
exit 0
```

The previous script has a serious problem: it contains the administrative password in plain text. To avoid this and make setting the password more secure, you can also create an account by copying the user account plist file, which contains the hashed password, directly to the client system.

Parachuting Accounts onto Clients

You'll perform a *file drop* to create a user account. File drops are when you simply copy files into appropriate directories to achieve a task. In this example, we'll show how to copy an account you have created on your own system, using either the command line or the Users & Groups pane in System Preferences, to another Mac. You'll simply copy this file to the /private/var/db/dslocal/nodes/Default/users directory. Once copied, the new account is available immediately. The first time someone logs In to the account at the login window, OS X will create the home folder from the user template in /System/Library.

If you copy an administrator account to another computer, it's not automatically an administrator there. Instead, it's a standard user. That's because admin privileges aren't stored in the account's plist file but rather the /private/var/db/dslocal/nodes/Default/groups/admin.plist file. To make the copied user an admin, you use dscl to append the user to the local admin group.

```
dscl . –append /Groups/admin GroupMembership corpadmin
```

Hiding Administrative Accounts

Hiding an administrative account can help keep users in organizations from tampering with or disabling user accounts and can help maintain a secure channel for administrators to remotely administer the system. There are a variety of ways to obscure the presence of an administrative account in OS X. For example, if you have multiple admin accounts, you can suppress them from the login window by adding them to the HiddenUsersList array in com.apple.loginwindow.plist, using the following command:

```
sudo defaults write /Library/Preferences/com.apple.loginwindow HiddenUsersList -array-add ↵
mysecretadmin
```

You can also simply file drop a preconfigured com.apple.loginwindow.plist file into /Library/Preferences/com.apple.loginwindow.plist.

But these methods simply suppress viewing an admin account in a list of users at login and don't truly hide the account. Here's another way to hide the accounts. You can set any user's account (either existing or new) with a unique ID of any integer below 500. To create a new admin user, you can copy an existing user from /private/var/db/dslocal/nodes/Default/users and alter the NFSHomeDirectory, RealName, and UniqueID keys to be unique (not that a home directory has to be unique, but it should be. And, as noted, the new UniqueID should be an integer below 500 to be hidden). You could also create a new account called secrethiddenuser with a password of secrethiddenuserspassword using dscl, with the following script:

```
#!/bin/bash
dscl . -create /Users/secrethiddenuser
dscl . -create /Users/secrethiddenuser RealName "Hidden Admin"
dscl . -create /Users/secrethiddenuser NFSHomeDirectory /Users/hidden
dscl . -create /Users/secrethiddenuser UserShell /bin/bash
dscl . -create /Users/secrethiddenuser UniqueID 150
dscl . -create /Users/secrethiddenuser PrimaryGroupID 20
dscl . -passwd /Users/secrethiddenuser 'secrethiddenuserspassword'
exit 0
```

Although this will create a new, hidden user account, it is fairly straightforward to view the contents of the /private/var/db/dslocal/nodes/Default/users directory and look for files that are neither listed in the account's System Preferences pane nor included with a default install of OS X (including _amavisd, _appleevents, _appowner, _appserver, _ard, _assetcache, _astris, _atsserver, _avbdeviced, _calendar, _ces, _clamav, _coreaudiod, _coremediaiod, _cvmsroot, _cvs, _cyrus, _devdocs, _devicemgr, _displaypolicyd, _distnote, _dovecot, _dovenull, _dpaudio, _eppc, _ftp, _gamecontrollerd, _geod, _iconservices, _installassistant, _installer, _jabber, _kadmin_admin, _kadmin_changepw, _krb_anonymous, _krb_changepw, _krb_kadmin, _krb_kerberos, _krb_krbtgt, _krbfast, _krbtgt, _launchservicesd, _lda, _locationd, _lp, _mailman, _mbsetupuser, _mcxalr, _mdnsresponder, _mysql, _netbios, _netstatistics, _networkd, _nsurlsessiond, _nsurlstoraged, _ondemand, _postfix, _postgres, _qtss, _sandbox, _screensaver, _scsd, _securityagent, _serialnumberd, _softwareupdate, _spotlight, _sshd, _svn, _taskgated, _teamsserver, _timezone, _tokend, _trustevaluationagent, _unknown, _update_sharing, _usbmuxd, _uucp, _warmd, _webauthserver, _windowserver, _www, _wwwproxy, _xserverdocs, daemon, nobody, root, and the default user applications).

You can choose to create a hidden user account in an entirely separate directory services node. Do this by copying the current directory services node (/private/var/db/dslocal/ nodes/Default) into a new folder located in /private/var/db/dslocal/nodes and then restarting the computer. After restarting, use Directory Utility to specify a custom search path, and then add the new node. You can also do this using dscl to alter the /Search node. The downside of creating a new directory services node is that it is fairly straightforward to find the node's information using Directory Utility, and if you are attempting to be a stealthy admin, you have just increased the surface space of your hidden account.

Raw Mode

If you edit a directory services domain while a Mac is not booted (for example, if you're scripting against a bare-metal system for future imaging), you will need to use dscl's raw mode, specified by the -raw option along with the -f option to specify a nonlocal path. Raw mode allows you to specify the location of the directory services domain you will be modifying, which is useful when working against any nonbooted systems programmatically. Thus, the script to create a new user on a nonbooted Mac is as follows:

```
#!/bin/sh
VOL=/Volumes/newimagehd
dscl -f "$VOL/private/var/db/dslocal/Nodes/Default" -raw . -create /Users/corpadmin
dscl -f "$VOL/ private/var/db/dslocal/Nodes/Default" -raw . -create RealName "Corporate Admin"
dscl -f "$VOL/ private/var/db/dslocal/Nodes/Default" -raw . -create NFSHomeDirectory
/Users/corpadmin
dscl -f "$VOL/ private/var/db/dslocal/Nodes/Default" -raw . -create UserShell /bin/bash
dscl -f "$VOL/ private/var/db/dslocal/Nodes/Default" -raw . -create UniqueID 1500
dscl -f "$VOL/ private/var/db/dslocal/Nodes/Default" -raw . -create PrimaryGroupID 1500
dscl -f "$VOL/ private/var/db/dslocal/Nodes/Default" -raw . -passwd corpadmin
MYUBERSECRETPASSWORD
exit 0
```

Create Additional Local Directory Nodes

The local directory service is not limited to one directory tree to store property lists. You can have a number of different directory trees, much like you can bind to a number of different directory services. This opens up the ability not only to hide an administrative user from the GUI but also to hide that user from those who might not realize how to traverse multiple local directory nodes. Moreover, it allows you to store a directory node on a shared volume or external disk (which would, of course, err when it is not reachable and lacks the flexibility of an actual network-based directory service).

First, you'll make a copy of the local Default directory services information store. For the following example, you'll copy it into the same nodes folder OS X uses by default, but rather than call the node Default, you'll call it NEW:

```
sudo cp -prnv /private/var/db/dslocal/nodes/Default /private/var/db/dslocal/nodes/NEW
```

The accountsd daemon will look in the nodes directory for any newly created nodes when it starts. Restart the computer. If you restart the accountsd process, this will cause the node to appear, but it takes a while for it to show up.

Now open Directory Utility and click the Search Policy tab, click the Lock button to authenticate, and then change the Search pop-up menu to "Custom path," as shown in Figure 1-6.

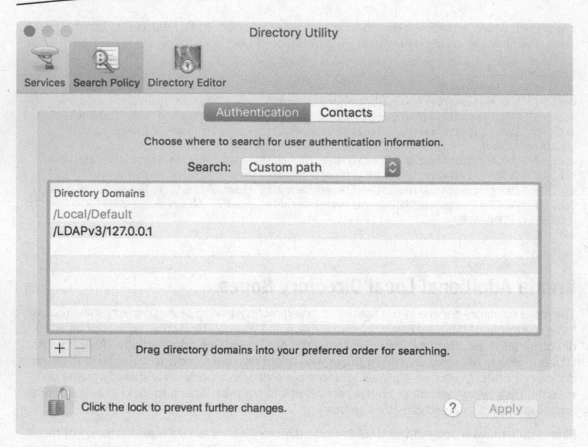

Figure 1-6. Changing the search path

Next, click the plus button and then add /Local/NEW from the list of available directory domains. The Default node will always be first in the search path and can't be removed. If accounts with the same name exist in multiple nodes, accounts that exist in the higher nodes of the search policy authenticate first. Therefore, if you have an account called corpadmin in your Default local directory service node, one in Active Directory (which we will cover in Chapter 3), and one in your secondary local directory service node, OS X uses the one in the Default directory service node for lookups and authentication; it will never consult the other accounts in the lower nodes.

Open Directory

Open Directory is the network directory services implementation native to OS X. OS X Server incorporates a number of open source products with a little bit of Apple's special sauce to form Open Directory. Open Directory provides client systems with a centralized location for accounts, passwords, mount points, and the like.

Like the Flexible Single Master of Operation (FSMO) roles in Windows Server's Active Directory, Open Directory consists of a number of parts. Open Directory utilizes LDAPv3 to store data, Kerberos to provide single sign-on, Apple Password Server to securely store passwords, and Simple Authentication and Security Layer (SASL) to provide authentication integration with other services. Each of these components is accessible using standard protocols, and each can therefore be integrated with other standard directory services such as Active Directory and Novell's eDirectory, typically using what is commonly referred to as a *triangle topology*. Historically, the most common triangle configuration was represented by the client system, Apple's Open Directory, and Active Directory. In such a setup, Active Directory was used for authentication, while Open Directory provided management capabilities. Modern triangle topologies replace Open Directory with a Mobile Device Management (MDM) server such as Profile Manager.

> **Note**   Although the term Mobile Device Management includes *mobile* in its name, that doesn't mean it's just for mobile devices. MDMs manage desktop computers too.

As an alternative to a triangle setup, augmented local records can virtually extend a single service's capabilities. A triangle is most useful when not all of the attributes needed by OS X for policy management are available by the primary directory service (the `NFSHomeDirectory` attribute, for example).

LDAP

A directory is a logically grouped collection of objects with attributes organized in a hierarchical fashion. LDAP directories track anything from users and groups, computers, printers, and mount points on servers. The LDAP implementation for OS X Server is `slapd`. The `slapd` process uses a number of schema files, located in the directory `/etc/openldap/schema`, to define the structure of the directory services database. These schema files include the object classes and attributes that the LDAP server presents to LDAP clients. Attributes are the same as those located in property list files, as noted earlier in this chapter. An `ObjectClass` is a set of attributes.

You can add new schema files, thus extending the functionality of LDAP and therefore Open Directory. You can also augment schema files to include new attributes. Enhancing the metadata stored for objects in LDAP is typically referred to as *extending* the schema.

Kerberos

Kerberos is the gold standard with regard to single sign-on. Active Directory, Open Directory, and a variety of other solutions use Kerberos. OS X clients also run a Kerberos server to secure peer-to-peer networks. With Kerberos, users and servers verify one another's identity, which helps to prevent a number of sophisticated (and some not so sophisticated) exploits when users are attempting to authenticate to services.

Kerberos makes use of a key distribution center (KDC) that consists of two parts, an authentication server (AS) and a ticket granting server (TGS). Kerberos works through the use of tickets and principals. A ticket is a session-based key used to obtain various service principals to provide access to a respective service. The KDC maintains a database of three types of principals: user, host, and service. These principals are sensitive, shared only between the KDC and the device, service, or user who corresponds to the principal. Upon requesting access to a particular server service (SS), say file services over Apple Filing

Protocol (AFP), the user must first obtain what is referred to as a ticket granting ticket (TGT). He obtains the TGT by properly authenticating with the authentication server. Once a user has a TGT, he can present it to the TGS to obtain service tickets; in this case a user would request the afpserver service ticket. Once the TGS grants the user this ticket, he presents it to the afpserver, which validates the ticket and the session. After successful validation, the server then grants the user access to the service. The ability to provide the TGT proves an entity's identity. By default, the TGT has a lifetime of ten hours, which renews without re-authenticating. Once the ticket expires, the user must re-authenticate to obtain a new TGT and active service principals.

Apple's implementation of the MIT Kerberos KDC is krb5kdc. Apple has modified Kerberos to handle communication with the Apple Password Server, which is responsible for building and replicating the Kerberos database. Clients using Open Directory for authentication (known as *binding*) are automatically configured to use Kerberos using special entries provided and updated by the LDAP server. You can manually initiate this autoconfiguration by using the kerberosautoconfig command. Apple developed the Active Directory service plug-in to provide interconnectivity with Microsoft's Active Directory and also supports Kerberos autoconfiguration for bound client using DNS entries known as service (SRV) records. This automatically generated configuration file is stored at /Library/Preferences/ DirectoryService. You can manually edit /Library/Preferences/OpenDirectory, /etc/krb5. keytab, and /etc/krb5.conf files by removing autogeneration comments from the top of the file. You can learn more about Kerberos clients in Chapter 2.

Users can specify multiple Kerberos realms by editing the Kerberos files, or using the Ticket Viewer application, located in /System/Library/CoreServices. Using Ticket Viewer, click the Add Identity button and provide an identity and password, as shown in Figure 1-7.

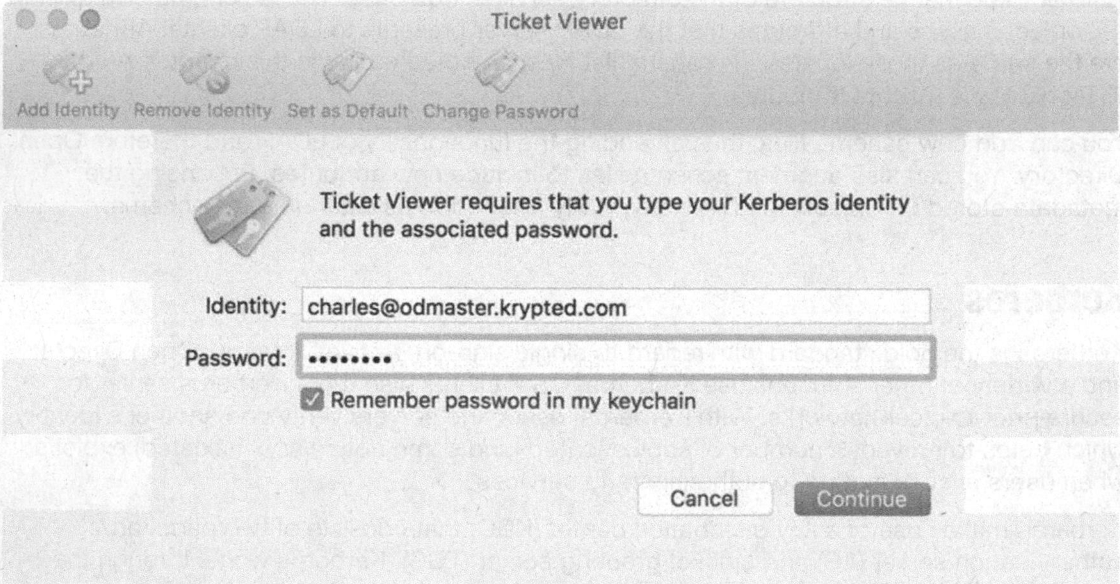

Figure 1-7. Editing realms in the Ticket Viewer application

One of the most critical aspects of Kerberos configuration is time. If a client's clock has drifted more than five minutes from its KDC server, authentication will fail. Kerberos evaluates only the minutes of the hour, not the hour itself. This allows devices to authenticate across time zones. The time value is normally best synchronized using the Network Time Protocol (NTP). You can manually install an NTP server on a Mac server or enable NTP services on a Windows server. You can then distribute this setting to Macs using scripts or management tools such as ARD (an example of changing this setting is available in the Send Unix Command Templates section of the ARD software).

Use the `systemsetup` command to set the NTP server.

```
systemsetup -setnetworktimeserver time.apple.com
```

You can configure the client setting manually in the Date & Time pane of System Preferences; note that multiple time servers are supported when separated by a space. You can manually initiate time synchronization by using the following:

```
sudo systemsetup -setusingnetworktime off
sudo systemsetup -setusingnetworktime on
```

In addition to authenticating the identity of a host in a Kerberos environment, safeguards are also put into place to protect the authenticity of each service running on a system in the form of a service principal. For a client to obtain tickets and authenticate with a daemon, the client will request a ticket using a TGT and a name in the form of `daemon/hostname:port`. This information, in the form of service principals, can be viewed in OS X by using the `klist` command from a OS X host.

To access information regarding Kerberos tickets using a graphical interface, open the Keychain Access application in `/Applications/Utilities` and choose Keychain Access ➤ Kerberos Ticket Viewer.

Configuring Open Directory

Open Directory begins with the Open Directory master. The Open Directory master houses the LDAP and the Kerberos KDC roles. It also provides a centralized repository for Open Directory replicas for synchronizing the contents of the LDAP and password server databases. Similar to Active Directory (although oddly enough, less so), Open Directory needs DNS.

> **Caution** You should not use a `.local` domain name for Open Directory. Bonjour already utilizes the `.local` domain space for zero-configuration networking/mdns. Domains utilizing `.local` name spaces require manual Kerberos configuration.

Before you install an Open Directory master, verify the server's IP address matches the information contained in your network's DNS zones for the server and vice versa. Start with the changeip command located at /usr/bin. This command utilizes a number of support scripts in the /Applications/Server.app/Contents/ServerRoot/usr/sbin directory. In its most basic form, run changeip with the –checkhostname flag to verify DNS is resolving the server's name correctly.

```
sudo /Applications/Server.app/Contents/ServerRoot/usr/sbin/changeip -checkhostname
```

The script should return success. If it doesn't, stop and fix your DNS. changeip will fail if either forward or reverse DNS resolution fails to properly map to the same respective values. Do not promote an Open Directory master that does not have perfect DNS until changeip confirms resolution.

Next, open Server in the Applications folder and mouse over the Advanced header in the main screen until *Show* appears. Click Show to display a list of advanced services including Open Directory. Click the On button (see Figure 1-8).

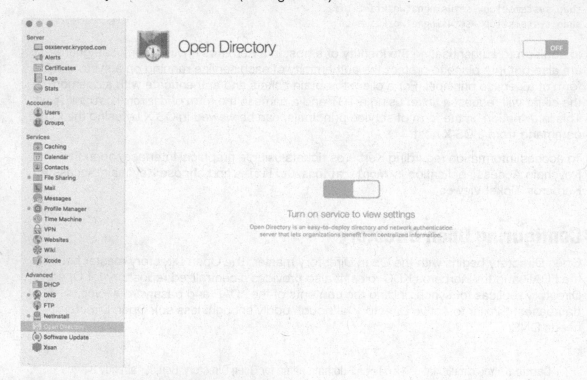

Figure 1-8. Starting the Open Directory service in Server

Starting Open Directory the first time opens the Configure Network Users and Groups Wizard. Click the "Create a new Open Directory domain" button and then click the Next button, as shown in Figure 1-9.

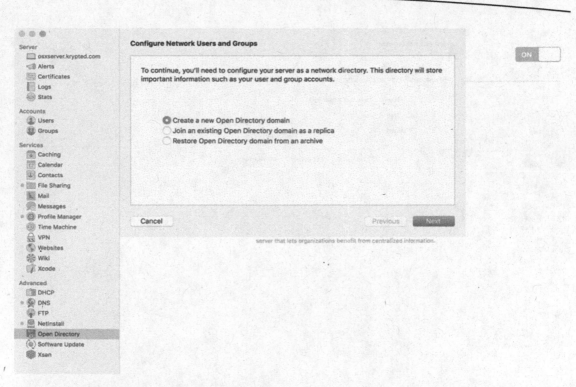

Figure 1-9. Clicking "Create a new Open Directory domain"

Specify the required information for the Open Directory administrator account. This account will administer the domain but will not have local administrative rights to computers bound to the domain. By default, the Directory Administrator account has a name of Directory Administrator and a short name of diradmin (Account Name). This information is editable, and the administrator name probably should be obscured for increased security by changing to a value specific to your environment, such as corpdiradmin. Since administrative accounts can bypass Open Directory policies, choosing a common administrator short name represents a significant chink in the armor. Once you have entered your directory account information, type a difficult -to-guess password in the Password and Verify fields, as shown in Figure 1-10.

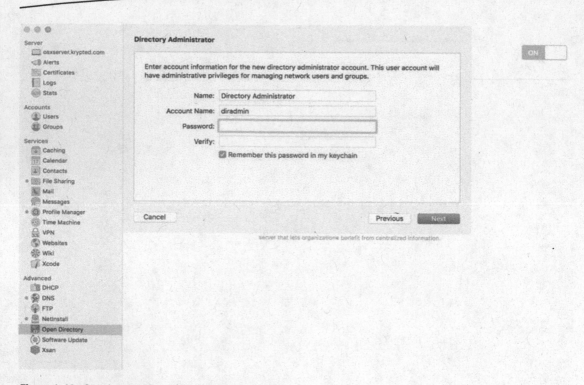

Figure 1-10. Creating the Directory Administrator account

While creating a new Open Directory master, you will need to specify the organization name (your business or school's name) and an e-mail address that will be assigned to the SSL certificate created during the promotion process, as shown in Figure 1-11. After specifying these values, click the Next button.

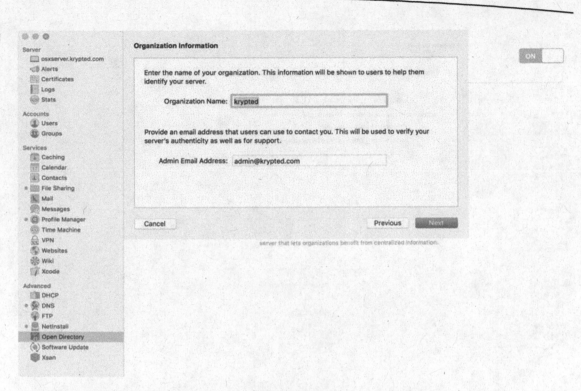

Figure 1-11. Specifying an organization name and admin e-mail address

Review your information on the Confirm Settings screen. When you are satisfied with the settings, click the Set Up button and OS X Server will finish configuring Open Directory for you (see Figure 1-12).

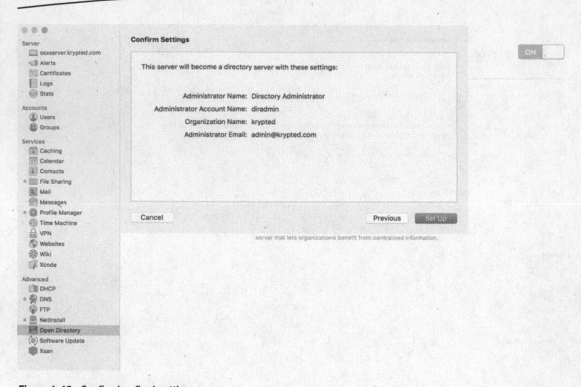

Figure 1-12. Confirming final settings

Open Directory's status should display a green dot and display Available next to your server name. Should any of the services that comprise Open Directory fail to start, consult the Open Directory logs found in Logs under Server in the sidebar. Look for any errors and make corrections as needed (see Figure 1-13).

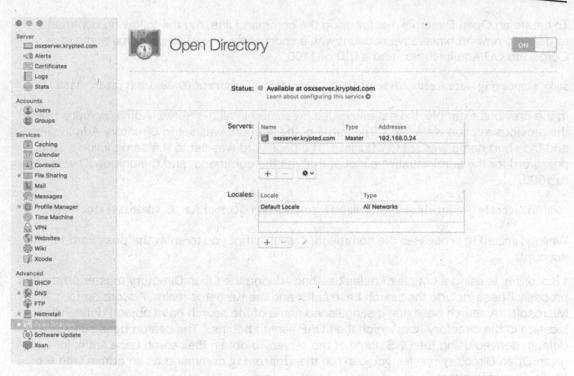

Figure 1-13. *Open Directory status*

Setting Up Open Directory from the Command Line

Setting up LDAP and Kerberos and creating a directory services administrative account could seem daunting if you were to do it manually. But as with many tasks, Apple has made setup easier if you choose to go the command-line route using the slapconfig binary (located at /usr/sbin), the same tool the Server application uses.

> **Note**   For the Active Directory guru readers, think of slapconfig as being similar to dcpromo, but with many, many more options than just promoting and destroying a directory server. In addition to promotion, slapconfig can also configure various Open Directory settings, replication, and global password policies.

To create an Open Directory master using the command line, run the following command to define a new administrative account with a short name of `corpadmin`, a full name of Corporate OD Administrator, and a UID of 1100:

```
sudo slapconfig -createldapmasterandadmin corpadmin "Corporate OD Administrator" 1100
```

In the previous example, the default values presented in all the Server Admin screens from the previous section were used. The name of the account was set to Directory Administrator, and the short name was set to `diradmin`. The password was set to the same value as the password for the administrative account that ran the command, and the unique ID was set to 1000.

```
sudo slapconfig -createldapmasterandadmin corpodadmin "Corporate OD Administrator" 1100
```

While `slapconfig` processes the command, it will prompt you to enter the password for this account.

`slapconfig` is using a couple of default settings during the Open Directory master promotion process. These include the search base suffix and the Kerberos realm. According to Microsoft, "A search base (the distinguished name of the search base object) defines the location in the directory from which the LDAP search begins." The search base suffix is, by default, derived using the DNS name of the server. To obtain the search base suffix for a given Open Directory master, you can run the `slapconfig` command as an admin with the –defaultsuffix query.

The realm is the name of the Kerberos realm. The `slapconfig` command generates this based on an enumeration of the server's host name (are you starting to put together why DNS is so important?). However, you can customize the realm during the –createmasterandadmin process.

Demoting an Open Directory Master

You can demote an Open Directory master using the command line. This can be pretty dangerous because all your users, groups, and associated settings are deleted. To demote the server using the command line, use the following:

```
sudo slapconfig -destroyldapserver
```

Setting Up an Open Directory Replica

You can configure an Open Directory replica using the Server app. Once you open the application, connect to the server you've designated for the Replica role. Under the Open Directory service, click the On button to start Open Directory, click "Join and existing Open Directory domain as a replica," and click the Next button. Enter the Open Directory master's IP/DNS name in the Parent Server field and complete the directory administrator's short name and password. The server will contact the Open Directory master and begin replicating all the relevant databases. This process takes the Open Directory master's LDAP database offline during initial setup, so plan accordingly. In a typical scenario, it will be offline for roughly a minute. As a best practice, perform this operation during nonpeak times.

If the server you're promoting to replica status is not already in the role of a stand-alone server, demote it to stand alone before you configure it as a replica. Even better, start with a nice clean server for your replica.

You can also create replicas using the `slapconfig` binary. From the replica, run the command with the following syntax:

```
sudo slapconfig -createreplica myodmaster.myco.com myodadmin
```

Removing a Replica

You should remove a replica from an Open Directory environment any time you are decommissioning a server running as an Open Directory replica. You should first attempt to do this using the Server app. Simply open Server, click the replica in Open Directory settings, and click the minus button. You will need to enter various credentials to complete the demotion and remove it from Open Directory.

For a variety of reasons, you may not be able to remove a replica from Open Directory using the Server app. When that happens, try using `slapconfig`. For example, if the replica's IP address is 192.168.53.249, the command would be as follows:

```
sudo slapconfig -removereplica 192.168.53.249
```

Using Server to Create New Users

Once Open Directory is configured, you can create Open Directory users and alter attributes for their user accounts using the Server app. When creating a user, select Local Network Directory to create that user in Open Directory. See Figure 1-14.

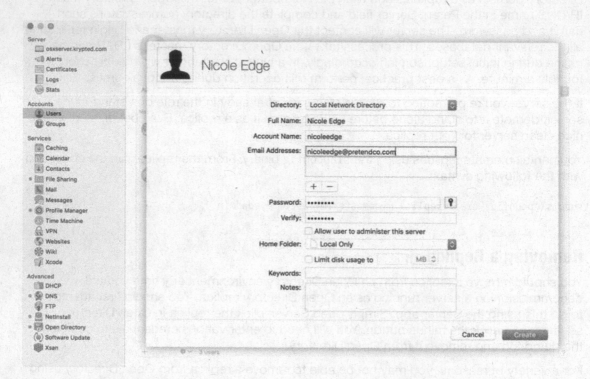

Figure 1-14. Creating Open Directory users

Provide this additional information:

- *Full Name*: Type the full name of the user (e.g., John Doe).

- *Account Name*: Type the short name of the user (e.g., johndoe, jdoe, or john.doe).

- *Email Addresses*: Type the user's e-mail address if he has one or you will create one.

- *Password*: Type a password for the new user.

- *Verify*: Re-type the password for the new user to verify it is correct.

- *Allow user to administer this server*: This allows the new user to administer Open Directory (not the actual server itself).

- *Home Folder*: This is the location for the user's network home folder if providing him server storage. Setting this to None-Services Only allows the user to use only the services hosted on the server, such as the Calendar service or Profile Manager. You'll specify other locations for home folders when creating file shares, discussed further in Chapter 4.

- *Limit disk usage to*: Use this to define a quota for the user for file shares hosted on the server, including network or portable home folders.

- *Keywords*: Add keywords to more easily locate accounts in larger Open Directory environments.

- *Notes*: Add any notes about the user such as "Intern."

Once you are satisfied with your entry, click the Create button. The user's account displays in the list of users, with a column identifying the users as Local Network User or Local Directory (on this server only), as shown in Figure 1-15.

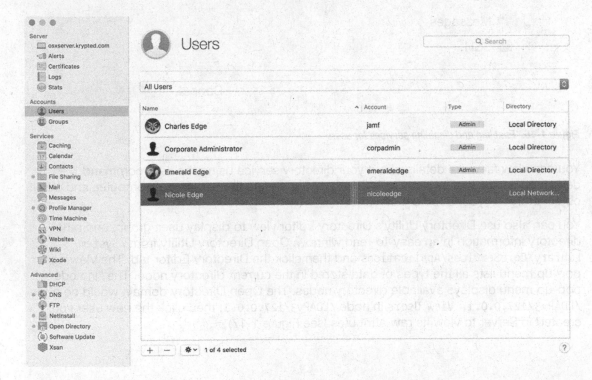

Figure 1-15. The list of users in Server

Select a user and click the Action pop-up menu labeled with a gear below the list of users. Here, you can reset a password, edit the user's account information, and define mail settings if you're using the server as a mail server. Choose Edit Access to Services. Here, you can deselect any services you won't be running or the user should not access (shown in Figure 1-16).

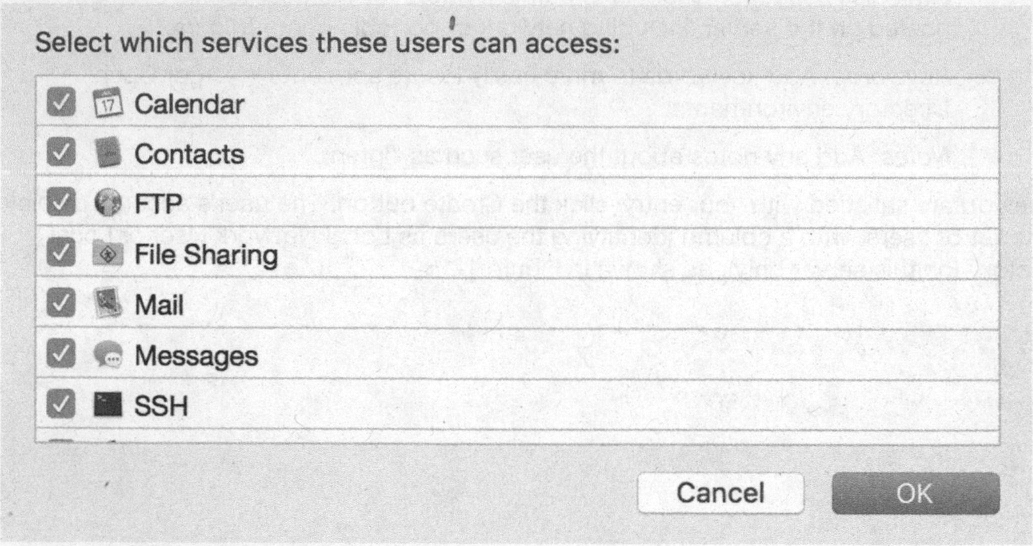

Select which services these users can access:

- ☑ 🗓 Calendar
- ☑ 📔 Contacts
- ☑ 🌐 FTP
- ☑ 🔷 File Sharing
- ☑ 📧 Mail
- ☑ 💬 Messages
- ☑ 🖥 SSH

Cancel   OK

Figure 1-16. Enabling and disabling services for users

You can view far more details about your directory service using the `dscl` command described earlier. It allows you to list each attribute of each user, group, computer, and other object stored in your directory service.

You can also use Directory Utility's Directory Editor view to display user, group, and other directory information in an easy-to-read window. Open Directory Utility from `/System/Library/CoreServices/Applications` and then click the Directory Editor tab. The Viewing pop-up menu lists all the types of data stored in the current directory node. The "in node" pop-up menu displays available directory nodes. The Open Directory domain would be node `/LDAPv3/127.0.0.1`. View Users in node `/LDAPv3/127.0.0.1`; then click the new user you created in Server to view its raw attributes (see Figure 1-17).

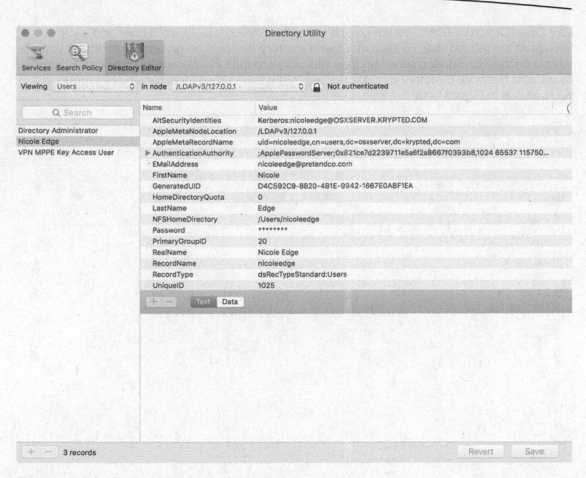

Figure 1-17. Using Directory Utility to edit Open Directory data

The Directory Editor also lets you edit objects in the directory. Be careful; you can provide settings incompatible with accounts. However, this is one of the few ways you can change home directories quickly or quickly test settings you might eventually change en masse with scripts. You can learn more about scripting these types of things in Chapter 8.

Creating Open Directory Groups

Groups allow you to organize users to better manage policies, settings, file system permissions, and e-mail. Most enterprises will have separate infrastructures for most of those tasks. But if you will be running an Open Directory environment for policies, Profile Manager, or other services, you will invariably need groups.

Like Open Directory users, create groups using the Server app. Open Server and click Groups in the left sidebar. By default, Open Directory displays no groups. Note that if you turned on the File Sharing service, Open Directory created the Workgroup group. It is listed as a Local Network Directory group, meaning that it is an Open Directory–based group, as you can see in Figure 1-18.

Figure 1-18. Viewing the workgroup group in the Server app

Click the plus sign to open a New Group window and verify you are creating your new group in Local Network Directory (see Figure 1-19). Then enter the full name or long name and a group name or short name for the group. You could use this group for mailing lists if this is also going to be your mail server. Click the OK button.

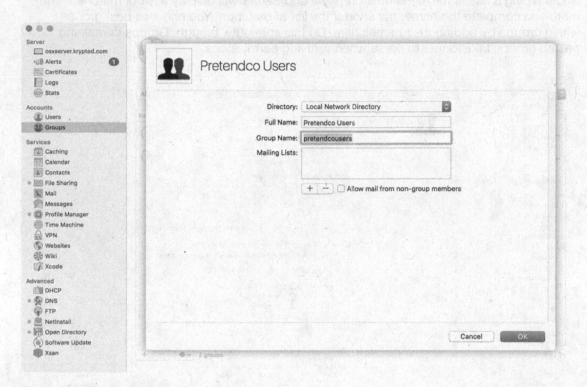

Figure 1-19. Creating a group in Server

What's the point of having a group with no members? The next step is to add users to the group. Double-click the group in the Groups list. Then, click the plus button below the Members list in the group's settings to add members (see Figure 1-20).

Begin typing a user's full name or short name and Server will display a list of matches. The more you complete the name, the shorter the list of matches. You can also nest groups within groups by adding their names here. Do this sparingly, though. Groups containing nested groups take longer to parse when verifying permissions.

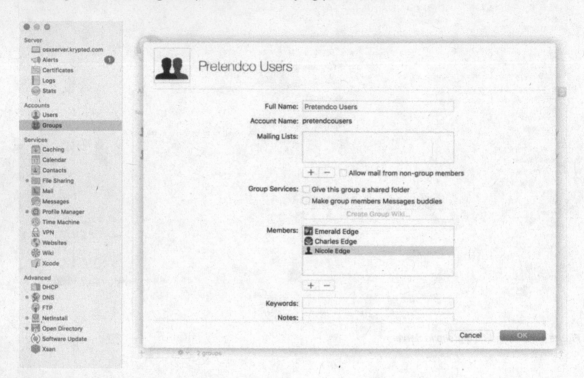

Figure 1-20. Adding members to your group

Backing Up Open Directory

In the first edition of this book, we covered creating an Open Directory backup script. However, since then, Forget Computers, a managed service provider in Chicago, has created a tool called Bender that automates this process. It's much simpler to use.

First download Bender from http://robotcloud.screenstepslive.com/s/2459/m/5322/ 1/94467-bender-automated-backup-of-os-x-server-settings and run the installer package. It will prompt you to agree to its licensing agreement and provide administrative credentials to complete the install.

As soon as you install Bender, it creates a backup of server settings and the contents of the directory service using an Open Directory archive if the server is an Open Directory master. It stores its backups at the root of the boot volume and runs each night at 10 p.m. using the local time of the server. You can modify its launchd plist in /Library/LaunchDaemons to change the backup time. And you still need a backup solution to back up Bender's data to another location.

If you will be using Time Machine to back up your server's data, then it will automatically trigger `slapconfig` to create a `sparseimage` disk backup that includes Open Directory's LDAP directory database, Kerberos configuration files, and Keychain data. It will stored these backups in `/private/var/backups` where Time Machine can later copy it to an external disk or backup server.

Troubleshooting Directory Services

Directory Services will occasionally give you problems. When this happens, it helps to have a few troubleshooting steps in your arsenal. We'll cover many of the troubleshooting steps when binding clients in Chapters 2 and 3, but for now your goal will be to troubleshoot the directory services running as part of Open Directory itself. You'll start with resolving cache issues.

The `dscacheutil` command allows you to flush cache-specific information from the cache resolver. For example, using `-cachedump` allows you to dump an overview of the cache contents. The `-cachedump` command has a slew of flags to get pretty granular with the output, such as `-entries` and `-buckets`. The `-configuration` command allows you to access detailed information about your search policy, and `-statistics` allows you to view detailed information on the statistics of calls.

Here are some examples of using these commands:

- `dscacheutil -flushcache` to empty the DNS Cache Resolver
- `dscacheutil -q user` to look up all users on a system
- `dscacheutil -q user -a name jdoe` to look up data for user `jdoe`

The `dscacheutil` tool is also one of two command-line utilities that allow you to query a group for direct membership (querying raw membership attributes with `dscl` is the other). However, this functionality is somewhat limited because `dscacheutil` does not consistently recurse through nested group membership. It does, however, work with basic membership. For instance, to list members of the group admin, you could use the following:

```
dscacheutil -q group -a name admin
```

Caches only impact your ability to find a service. Once you find the service, you'll also need to validate that users can authenticate to the service. This happens frequently when troubleshooting accounts from the server itself.

Verifying Authentication

You can test authentication in OS X multiple ways, and the exact process will vary based on the version of OS you are running. Naturally, you can verify authentication for a user by attempting to log in to a bound OS X client. The main problem with this type of testing is it is fairly inefficient; if you don't have a spare client for testing, a trip to the login window likely requires you to log out or switch users. Also, home directory problems can prevent a successful login, so this is not always an accurate test.

If the target user has a default shell, you can test authentication using the su command in any version of OS X. Simply open Terminal and type su testuser. This will prompt you to enter the user's password. If you provide the correct credentials, you will change to a shell under the new user. You can use the id tool to verify.

```
bash-3.2$ su testuser
Password:
bash-3.2$ id
uid=1078 (testuser) gid=20(staff) groups=20(staff),506(Shared),12(everyone),
61(localaccounts),702(com.apple.sharepoint.group.3),701(com.apple.sharepoint.group.2),
100(_lpoperator),401(com.apple.sharepoint.group.1)
```

Directory Services Clients

Connecting clients to directory services is one of the most important tasks in many OS X environments. Once you have a server ready, you'll want to bind systems to that server for authentication and access to services. In the next two chapters, we'll focus first on binding clients to OS X Server and then on binding clients to a Microsoft Active Directory environment.

Chapter **2**

Directory Services Clients

In Chapter 1 we discussed directory services and the various types of information a directory service provides. This chapter focuses on utilizing a centralized directory service for user and group resolution and authentication. Utilizing a centralized directory service is absolutely essential to the efficient management of your fleet of computers and eliminates the need to synchronize user and group databases across all of your computers.

Lightweight Directory Access Protocol (LDAP) is the building block for most modern directory services solutions. Whether you are using Microsoft's Active Directory or Apple's Open Directory, to a large degree the basis for their implementation lies in the LDAPv3 specification. As such, LDAP in this context consists of a communication protocol, a data scheme that is used to store directory information, and the replication infrastructure to distribute that data across multiple remote data stores. Because OS X's own local directory system is built on LDAP, it provides a myriad of options in terms of automation and management functionality to network clients whether serving using its built-in services or Server app. You will use the same LDAP structures discussed in Chapter 1 to also provide network directory services to non–OS X clients such as Microsoft Windows. We'll discuss that more in Chapter 9.

Binding is the act of joining a client to a directory services infrastructure. OS X clients join using one of two types of binding. The first is a trusted, or authenticated, bind. A trusted bind creates a representative computer object in the LDAP store that contains the same Authentication Authority record familiar to a local OS X user account. The computer itself must use a locally stored key to authenticate to the directory and receive directory data. By authenticating, the computer proves it is a member of the network and therefore has certain elevated access based on the trust relationship created during binding. Trusted binding requires a directory administrator's credentials to establish this trust. The second type of binding is an anonymous bind, which configures a client to query a certain directory server for specific types of data, such as usernames, passwords, or policies. It is not really a bind; a client computer does not have an associated computer object in LDAP with an anonymous bind.

In Chapter 1 we discussed configuring and accessing a local Open Directory service. In Chapter 2 we dive into the network Open Directory service and other non-Microsoft solutions using LDAP to provide a central directory service to client computers. First we will bind a client using LDAP. Then we will discuss deploying LDAP settings to clients en masse to realize the full potential of our directory services solution. We will conclude with Kerberos services and directory services preferences.

Access Directory Servers

OS X Server broadcasts its Open Directory services via Bonjour to make locating a server easier for network clients. Bonjour is Apple's name for zero-configuration discovery (zeroconf) of network services using TCP/IP and requires no special operator intervention or server configuration for use. It just works, provided the local network environment does not block Bonjour broadcasting. By default, routers do not pass Bonjour traffic between networks and VLANs.

To verify an Open Directory server is broadcasting on your LAN, follow these steps:

1. Open the Users & Group pane in System Preferences.

2. Click the Lock button to unlock Users & Groups. Enter your administrator credentials.

3. Click Login Options at the bottom of the left pane.

4. Next to Network Account Server, click the Join button.

5. Click the arrow to the right of the Server drop-down menu. The menu displays a list of available servers (see Figure 2-1).

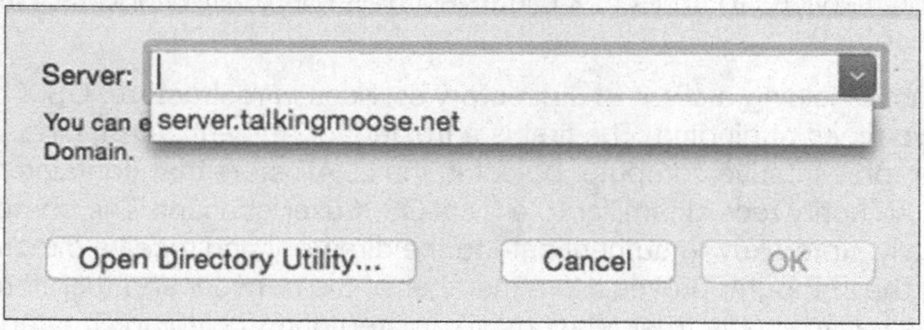

Figure 2-1. Available directory servers

> **Note**   Bonjour is a broadcast protocol for the local network and may return the local host name
> (such as `server.local`) for the responding servers if your client and server are not using the
> same DNS server. For better name resolution, verify all network computers are using the same DNS
> servers. Also, use the `scutil` command-line utility to verify your local host name matches your
> host name:
>
> ```
> $ scutil --get HostName
> $ server.talkingmoose.net
> $ scutil --set LocalHostName server
> ```

Troubleshoot Bonjour Browsing

If your search for an Open Directory server fails, use a tool such as Bonjour Browser from
TildeSoft (`www.tildesoft.com`) to find locally advertised services. After downloading Bonjour
Browser, drag the application into the `/Applications` directory and double-click to open
it. Wait for it to populate the list of hosts and services similar to those listed in Figure 2-2.
Locate the `_ldap.tcp.` entry. Bonjour Browser displays the LDAP server's IP address and
LDAP port number 389.

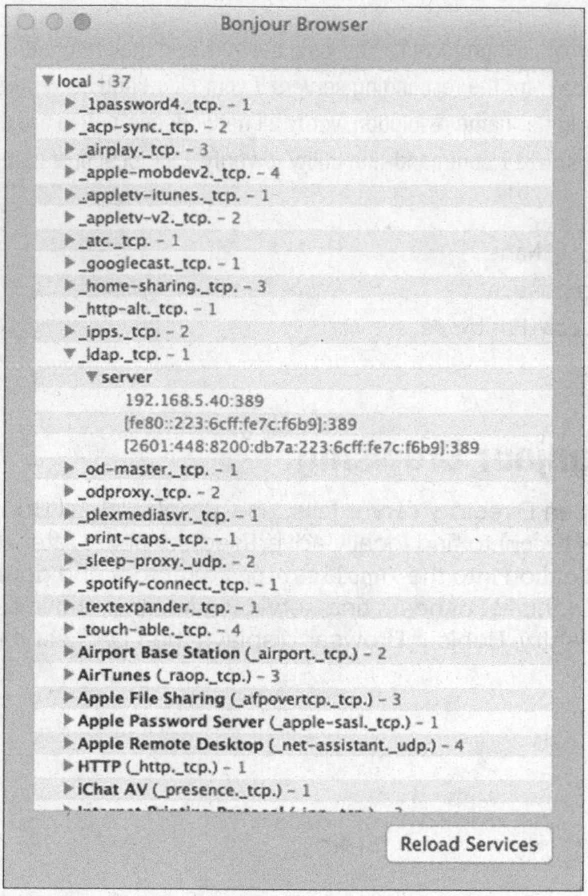

Figure 2-2. Bonjour Browser

To find an LDAP server broadcasting on your network using Terminal, use OS X's dns-sd command-line tool (DNS Service DiscoveryTest Tool). To find the instance names of all broadcasting services, run the following command:

```
dns-sd -B _services._dns-sd._udp
```

It returns a list of broadcasting services on the network, as shown here:

```
Browsing for _services._dns-sd._udp
12:17:04.413  ...STARTING...
Timestamp     A/R   Flags  if Domain   Service Type   Instance Name
12:17:04.416  Add     3    0 .         _tcp.local.    _airport
12:17:04.416  Add     3    0 .         _tcp.local.    _sftp-ssh
12:17:04.416  Add     3    0 .         _tcp.local.    _ssh
12:17:04.416  Add     3    0 .         _tcp.local.    _rfb
12:17:04.416  Add     3    0 .         _tcp.local.    _smb
12:17:04.416  Add     3    0 .         _tcp.local.    _afpovertcp
12:17:04.416  Add     3    0 .         _tcp.local.    _workstation
```

```
12:17:04.416  Add      3   0 .        _udp.local.    _net-assistant
12:17:04.416  Add      3   5 .        _tcp.local.    _raop
12:17:04.416  Add      3   5 .        _tcp.local.    _touch-able
12:17:04.416  Add      3   5 .        _tcp.local.    _appletv-v2
12:17:04.416  Add      3   5 .        _tcp.local.    _airplay
12:17:04.416  Add      3   5 .        _udp.local.    _sleep-proxy
12:17:04.416  Add      3   5 .        _tcp.local.    _ldap
12:17:04.416  Add      3   5 .        _tcp.local.    _od-master
12:17:04.416  Add      3   5 .        _tcp.local.    _apple-sasl
12:17:04.416  Add      3   5 .        _tcp.local.    _workstation
```

To display information about the specific _ldap instance name, run the following command:

```
dns-sd -B _ldap
```

It returns the name of the host system under Instance Name.

```
Browsing for _ldap._tcp
12:16:32.548  ...STARTING...
Timestamp    A/R   Flags  if Domain    Service Type    Instance Name
12:16:32.549  Add         2   5 local.    _ldap._tcp.     server
```

If neither tool returns Bonjour information, then verify the following:

- Your server is not on the other side of a router that does not pass Bonjour broadcast traffic.

- Your network administrator is not blocking Bonjour broadcast traffic.

- Your server's host name is correctly listed in DNS.

- Your client is correctly configured for DNS.

Bonjour browsing is not required to connect to a directory service. It only makes locating a server easier. If necessary, manually enter your server's fully qualified domain name (FQDN) in the Server field and click the OK button. Users & Groups will attempt to connect to your server and display a prompt for a username and password if it detects a valid LDAP server.

Verify Directory Services Connectivity

After locating your host, make sure you can communicate with the LDAP server service. By default, LDAP communicates over port 389 (636 with SSL). Verify your client is communicating with the LDAP service using one or more of the following methods.

The first method is to port scan the server using Apple's built-in Network Utility application. Open Network Utility in /System/Library/CoreServices/Applications and click the Port Scan tab. Enter the host name or IP address in the top field, enable the option to test ports between 389 and 389 only, and then click the Scan button (see Figure 2-3). A successful connection returns the following:

```
Open TCP Port:    389            ldap
```

Also test LDAP port 636 for secure communications. A successful connection returns the following:

```
Open TCP Port:    636            ldap
```

Use secure communications whenever possible.

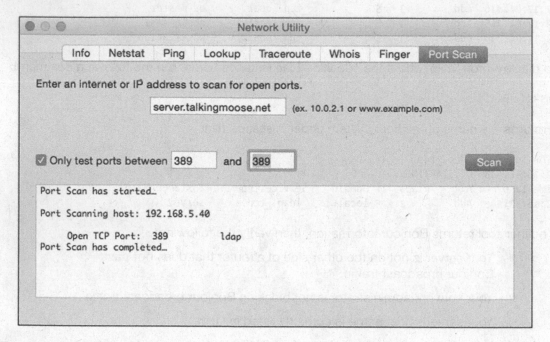

Figure 2-3. Network Utility

As part of a binding script, you can use stroke, the same command-line tool Network Utility uses to perform port scans. Launch the Terminal application and use the cd command to change directory into the Network Utility application bundle itself (one line).

```
cd "/System/Library/CoreServices/Applications/Network Utility.app/Contents/Resources"
```

Once in the Resources directory, run the stroke command with the IP address of the host server followed by a port range—entering the lower port number first, a space, and the higher port number. Use the same port number twice to test a single port.

```
./stroke 192.168.5.40 389 389
```

This returns the following:

```
Open TCP Port:    389            ldap
```

Alternatively, port scan your server using its DNS name and secure LDAP port number.

```
./stroke server.talkingmoose.net 636 636
```

This returns the following:

```
Open TCP Port:    636            ldaps
```

By using your server's DNS address during testing, you are actually verifying DNS is working correctly and you can communicate with its LDAP service in one command. If you plan to regularly scan ports using stroke, create a link to the binary in a directory specified in your environment's PATH variable. This lets you call it by name without specifying the full path to the Network Utility bundle (one line).

```
sudo ln -s "/System/Library/CoreServices/Applications/Network Utility.app/Contents/
Resources/stroke" /usr/local/bin/stroke
```

> **Note**   If scanning port 389 or 636 succeeds from the server using localhost or 127.0.0.1 but fails from a client using the server's DNS address or IP address, a network issue is likely preventing connectivity. If the server requires authentication, a prompt for username and password indicates the server is responding.

A second method to verify LDAP connectivity from client to server is the nc command (or netcat) in Terminal. The nc command is also built into OS X as part of its underlying FreeBSD UNIX foundation and is useful for testing any type of TCP or UDP connection and port such as web and SMTP services. Its advantage over other tools like the telnet command is that it is very scriptable. In Terminal enter nc -z followed by a server's DNS or IP address and a port number.

```
nc -z server.talkingmoose.net 389
```

The succeeded line verifies successful communication to the server on port 389.

```
Connection to 192.168.5.40 port 389 [tcp/ldap] succeeded!
```

A closed or inactive port on a host returns nothing.

A free third-party tool, LDapper, is a GUI front end to the ldapsearch command for viewing an LDAP server's directory data and is useful for determining correct LDAP settings for configuring Directory Utility for binding. LDapper's ability to accept different settings and quickly obtain results makes it a great tool for enumerating an LDAP environment and a helpful aid for troubleshooting connectivity problems.

Download LDapper from `http://carl-bell.baylor.edu/ReadMeFiles/LDapper.html` and drag the application into the `Applications` folder. Double-click the application and select Preferences from the LDapper menu (see Figure 2-4).

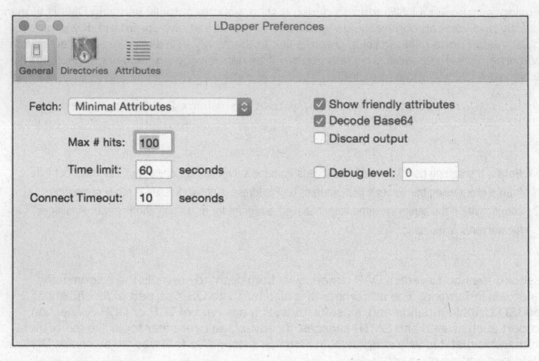

Figure 2-4. LDapper Preferences

Click the Directories button and then click the + button to add a new LDAP connection. Enter a descriptive name in the Directory Name field and then enter your server's host name or IP address in the LDAP URI field. Finally, provide a distinguished name (DN) for Search Base. A *distinguished name* is a unique path to your domain, server, or any object in your LDAP directory. For example, if your LDAP server is Open Directory, its DN is typically the FQDN of your server broken into its individual domain components (DCs) separated by commas (see Figure 2-5). The search base for a server whose host name is `server.talkingmoose.net` is as follows:

`dc=server,dc=talkingmoose,dc=net`

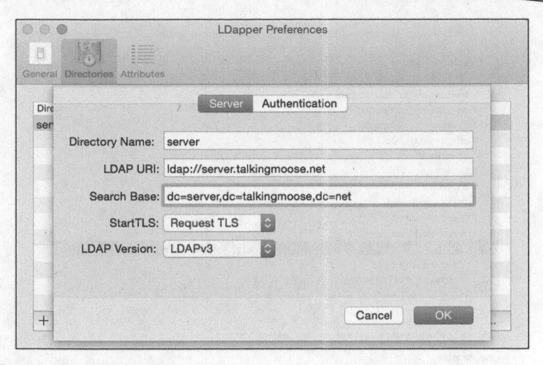

Figure 2-5. LDapper add server dialog

> **Tip**   Many LDAP implementations, including Active Directory and Open Directory, let you identify
> the search base by querying with the `ldapsearch` utility. Use the following syntax (one line):
>
> `ldapsearch -h server.example.com -x -a never -s base naming Contexts`
>
> If the server, such as Active Directory, returns multiple naming contexts, use the shortest
> distinguished name for your search base.

LDapper offers additional configuration options. To use authentication, click the Authentication
tab and enter a username from the directory in the Identification field. Anonymous
authentication also works with default Open Directory settings. Click the OK button when
finished. Click the Attributes button to enter advanced information if you have a specialized
LDAP configuration. Once you are satisfied with all your options, click the OK button. Choose
File ➤ New Browse Window and test browsing your directory (see Figure 2-6).

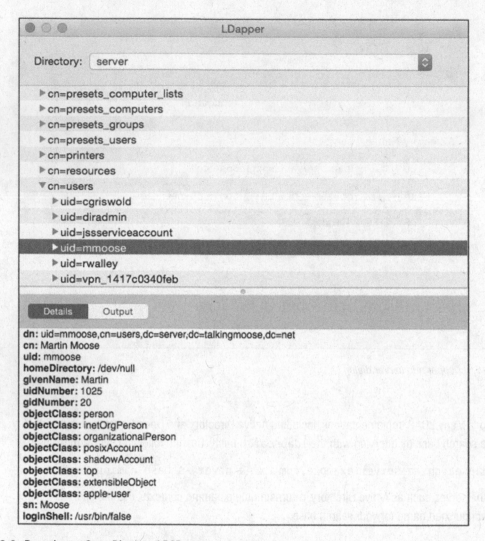

Figure 2-6. Browsing an Open Directory LDAP server using LDapper

Using the ldapsearch command directly in Terminal provides many more options such as using SASL instead of simple authentication, outputting in LDAP Data Interchange Format (LDIF), and specifying the LDAP protocol version to use.

Binding

In a trusted bind, the client computer and the directory service share a key that allows each to trust the other, and the LDAP service on the server creates a computer record in its directory database. The server grants more access to directory services information for trusted binds and less access to anonymous or nontrusted binds. For example, directory services in more secure environments allow a client system to perform LDAP queries only if it has successfully authenticated.

In an anonymous bind, the directory server does not necessarily have a record for the anonymous computer. For this type of bind to work, the LDAP server must provide anonymous access to its data store; however, a *user* can still authenticate from a computer with an anonymous bind. The client computer caches the user's credentials locally. This technically qualifies as an authenticated bind but differs from a trusted bind because the client computer and LDAP server aren't using a preshared key to establish the trust. Supplying user credentials does not qualify as computer-level authentication.

When a client is bound to a directory service, the service must allow the client to access, and in some cases update, certain records in its LDAP database. Accessible records may simply include the computer's own entry in Open Directory or an entire computer list.

In OS X, Directory Utility is the primary graphical interface for managing network directory service binds. It also includes a Directory Editor for searching, browsing, and changing directory data. Searching and browsing require an anonymous computer bind, a trusted computer bind, or an authenticated directory user. Manipulating directory data, however, requires an authenticated directory user with administrative privileges for the directory or at minimum privileges to modify one or more directory objects (users, groups, computers, and so on).

And as discussed in Chapter 1, the `dscl` command-line tool also queries and modifies the contents of directory services including *network* directory services. `dscl` plays a substantial role in communicating with directory services because it is scriptable. The `dsconfigldap` command-line tool, which actually creates the bind, is also scriptable. Management systems frequently use it for automating the bind process on individual systems or quickly binding machines en masse.

Note   Directory Utility uses plug-ins to connect to various directory service solutions. The most common are the Active Directory plug-in for binding and communicating with Microsoft's network directory service and the LDAPv3 plug-in used for Open Directory and similar network directory services. This chapter focuses on the LDAPv3 plug-in. Chapter 3 focuses on Apple's built-in and third-party Active Directory plug-ins.

Binding Combinations

Binding a client to a directory service enables the client to use it for authenticating users to the computer and for accessing user contact information. By default, OS X Server's Open Directory service allows both anonymous binding and authenticated binding. It also allows encrypted (SSL) and unencrypted communications for both the binding process and routine communications. The following are possible binding combinations from most secure to least secure:

- Authenticated and encrypted
- Unauthenticated and encrypted
- Authenticated and unencrypted
- Unauthenticated and unencrypted

Always use authenticated and encrypted binding unless your organization has a need to share its directory services to users who are not members of the directory already. For example, an internal server system may need access only to user contact information and not need authentication services. However, best practice is to still encrypt the traffic. If the Open Directory server is not configured with a third-party certificate or internal certificate for signed communications, it does at least provide a self-signed certificate. While the certificate may not verify the authenticity of the server, it will at least encrypt traffic between the client and the server.

OS X offers multiple ways to bind a client.

- Users & Groups pane in System Preferences
- Directory Utility found in `/System/Library/CoreServices/Applications`
- The `dsconfigldap` command
- Configuration profile

Users & Groups and Directory Utility are GUI methods for binding. They are useful for testing the binding process and for one-off bindings where the administrator has the time to hand-prepare Macs for users. The `dsconfigldap` command is the better tool for workflows and mass binding multiple Macs because it is both scriptable and versatile. For example, use Apple Remote Desktop's `Send UNIX Command` feature to send a one-line command to multiple Macs at the same time or create a payload-free Apple Installer package. Environments with a Mobile Device Management (MDM) server have the advantage of automating deployment by simply adding the client to the management server and letting it push a profile for binding.

Users & Groups

The simplest path for binding a single Mac to a directory service is through the Users & Groups pane in System Preferences.

1. Click the Lock button and provide administrator credentials to continue.

2. Click Login Options and then click the Join button (see Figure 2-7).

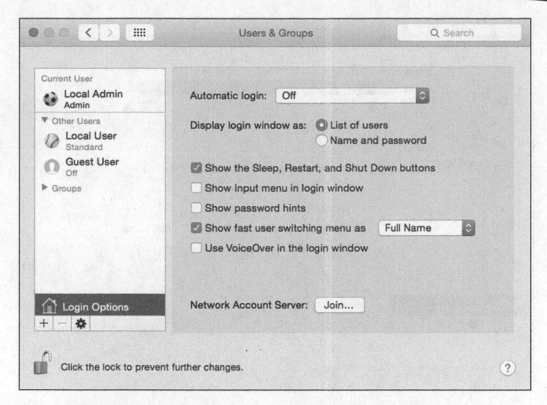

Figure 2-7. Users & Groups login options

3. Click the down arrow in the Server field to search for network
    directory servers broadcasting their services. You may need to
    manually enter the FQDN of your directory server if it does not
    appear in the drop-down list. (Your network administrator may not
    allow Bonjour traffic across routers or VLANs.) Click the OK button to
    continue (see Figure 2-8).

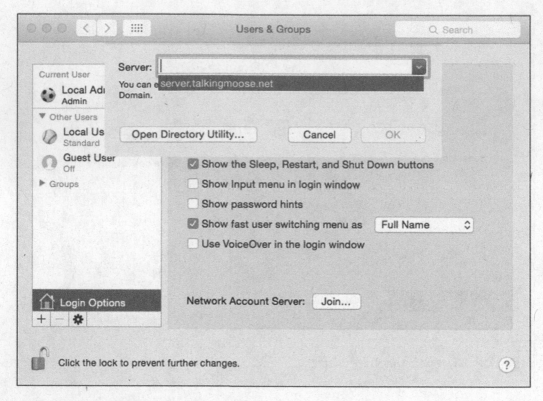

Figure 2-8. Choosing a directory server

4. If your directory server includes a self-signed certificate for encrypting traffic, it may prompt to trust the certificate. For encrypted communications, click the Trust button. For unencrypted communications, click the Don't Trust button. Clicking either button proceeds with the binding (see Figure 2-9). Best practice is to click the Trust button unless your Mac client cannot communicate with directory services on port 636.

Figure 2-9. Trusting the server certificate

5. By default, the binding uses the client's computer name as its client computer ID for Open Directory. Best practice is to keep the names the same for easier identification later; however, you can change the client computer ID if your workflow requires.

6. For an anonymous bind, leave the User Name and Password fields empty. (By default, Open Directory allows an anonymous bind.) For an authenticated bind, enter credentials for any user in the directory (see Figure 2-10). Authenticated binds do not require administrator privileges to create the bind, but they do require directory membership. Click the OK button.

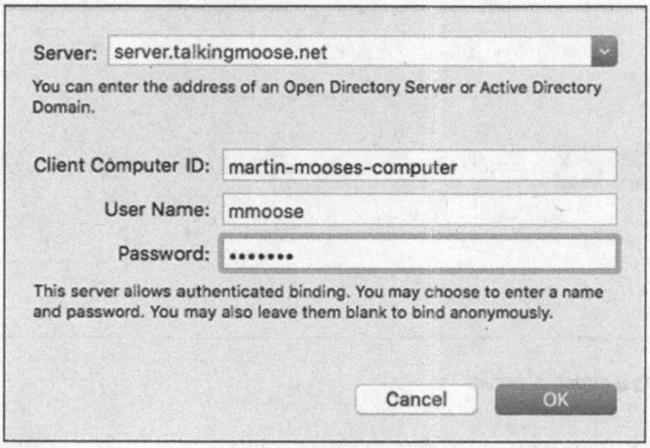

Figure 2-10. Authenticated bind

7. After a successful binding, Users & Groups displays the Network Account Server setting with a green status indicator. Green indicates the client is communicating with directory services on the server. Red indicates the client cannot access a directory server (possibly the directory service is turned off or the server itself is offline). Yellow indicates at least one directory service is accessible and another is inaccessible when the client is connected to multiple directory servers (see Figure 2-11).

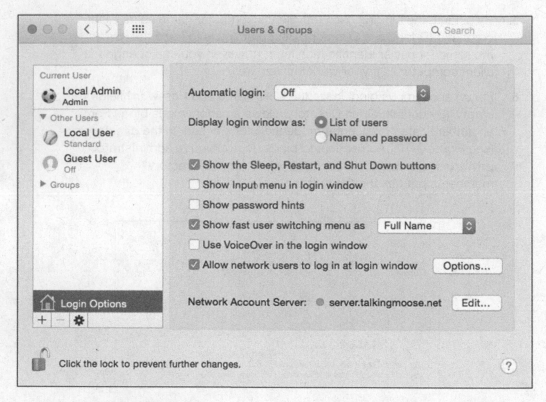

Figure 2-11. Connected to a directory server

After successful binding, the Users & Groups pane displays an extra option to allow network users to log in at the login window. Click the Options button to choose whether all network users or only specific network users may log in to the computer. Giving only specific users access to critical systems increases security for those systems.

> **Tip**   When using monolithic imaging solutions, add an unauthenticated bind to your image for easily binding en masse.

A simple method for testing the binding is to open the Contacts application, choose Directory Services in the left pane, and enter a directory member's name in the search field in the middle pane (Figure 2-12). This should return information about the user.

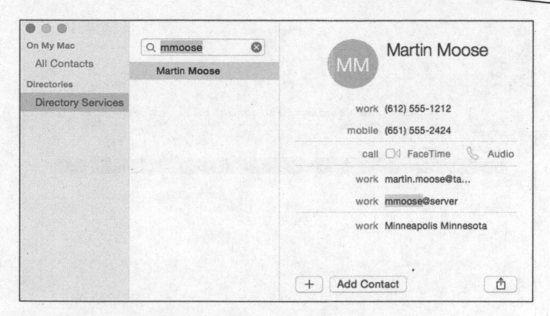

Figure 2-12. Testing directory services

Directory Utility

Binding via the Users & Groups pane provides quick and easy access to a network directory service, but binding using the Directory Utility application provides more configuration options. These options include the ability to extend timeouts, configure attribute mappings between different directory services, and increase security.

1. Open the Users & Groups pane in System Preferences.

2. Click the Lock button and provide administrator credentials to continue.

3. Click Login Options and then click the Join button (see Figure 2-7).

4. Click the Open Directory Utility button. Optionally, navigate to /System/Library/CoreServices/Applications and double-click Directory Utility to open the application.

5. Click the Lock button and provide administrator credentials to continue (see Figure 2-13).

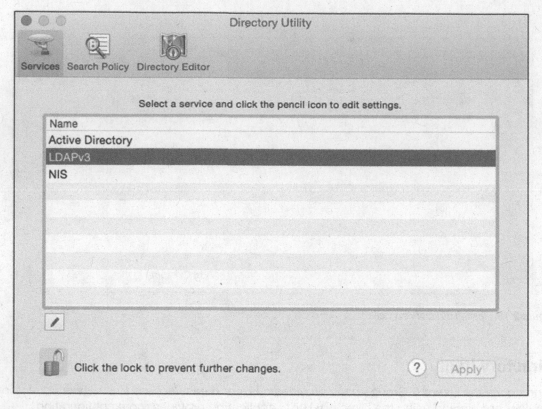

Figure 2-13. LDAPv3 plug-in in Directory Utility

6. Select the LDAPv3 plug-in and click the pencil button to configure settings.

7. Click the New button to create a new LDAP connection.

8. Enter the server name or IP address of your directory services server. Unlike the Users & Groups pane, this address field does not use Bonjour to locate available directory servers. If your server uses SSL to encrypt traffic, enable the Encrypt Using SSL option.

9. The new connection automatically enables the options to use the bind for authentication and contacts. Disable either of these if needed. Click the Continue button (see Figure 2-14).

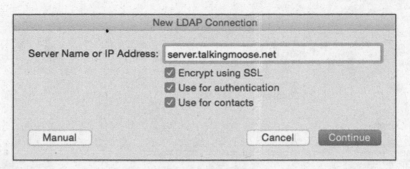

Figure 2-14. New LDAP connection in Directory Utility

10. For an anonymous bind, leave the User Name and Password fields empty. (By default, Open Directory allows an anonymous bind.) For an authenticated bind, enter credentials for any user in the directory (Figure 2-15). Authenticated binds do not require administrator privileges to create the bind, but they do require directory membership. Click the Continue button.

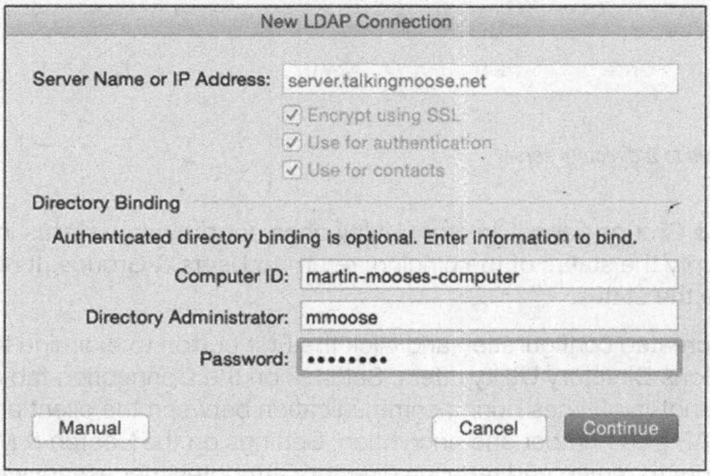

New LDAP Connection
Server Name or IP Address: server.talkingmoose.net
✓ Encrypt using SSL
✓ Use for authentication
✓ Use for contacts
Directory Binding
Authenticated directory binding is optional. Enter information to bind.
Computer ID: martin-mooses-computer
Directory Administrator: mmoose
Password: ••••••••
Manual   Cancel   Continue

Figure 2-15. Authenticated bind

11. After a successful binding, Directory Utility displays the Network Account Server setting (see Figure 2-16). Click the OK button.

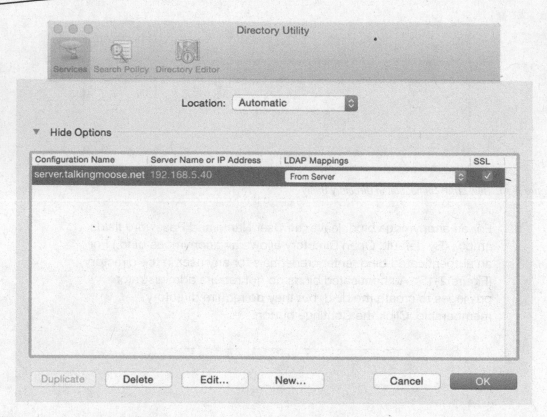

Figure 2-16. *Connected to a directory server*

Unlike the Users & Groups pane, Directory Utility does not provide a status indicator about the binding. To verify the status of the binding, return to Users & Groups. It reflects the new binding as well as the status.

Select the newly created configuration and click the Edit button to examine the additional configuration options Directory Utility offers. Settings on the Connection tab allow for more control over the lengths of times during communication between the client and the server as well as the LDAP port number and encryption. Settings on the Search & Mappings tab allow administrators to remap and redefine directory attributes, necessary when introducing systems with different directory structures (see Figure 2-17). Settings on the Security tab provide options for a strong security policy such as disabling clear-text passwords and enabling Kerberos.

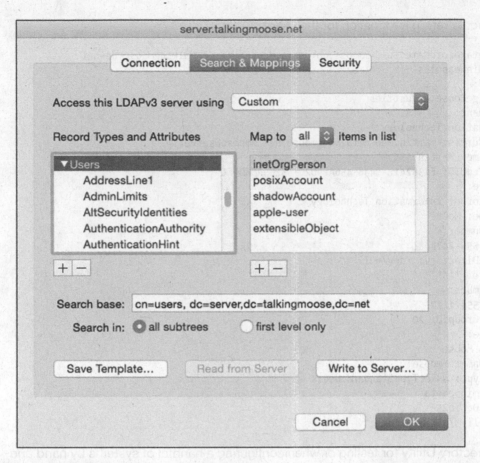

Figure 2-17. Directory Utility's additional configuration settings

Now, verify the client computer is using the new binding. In Directory Utility, click the Search Policy tab and review the Authentication and Contacts tabs. The search path for both should list Custom, and the Directory Domains list for both should include the directory server node name such as this example:

```
/LDAPv3/server.talkingmoose.net
```

Use the dscl command in Terminal to test reading the record for a known member of the directory.

```
dscl /LDAPv3/server.talkingmoose.net -read /Users/mmoose
```

This should return information for the user.

```
AppleMetaRecordName: uid=mmoose,cn=users,dc=server,dc=talkingmoose,dc=net
City: Minneapolis
Company:
 Talking Moose Industries
Department:
 Information Technology
EMailAddress: martin.moose@talkingmoose.net mmoose@server
FirstName: Martin
GeneratedUID: E138241E-5438-456A-9D2C-582C5A0BD9FC
JobTitle:
 Director of Information Technology
LastName: Moose
MobileNumber:
 (651) 555-2424
NFSHomeDirectory: /dev/null
Password: ********
PhoneNumber:
 (612) 555-1212
PrimaryGroupID: 20
RealName:
 Martin Moose
RecordName: mmoose
RecordType: dsRecTypeStandard:Users
State: Minnesota
UniqueID: 1025
UserShell: /usr/bin/false
```

Use Directory Utility for testing or when configuring a handful of systems by hand and needing to tweak LDAP settings for connection and security purposes. It is not a good tool for binding large numbers of clients to a directory service, especially if they need custom settings. For automated workflows, use the `dsconfigldap` command.

dsconfigldap

The Users & Groups pane offers simple directory setup. Directory Utility does everything the Users & Groups pane does and adds the ability to configure advanced settings. The `dsconfigldap` command-line tool does almost everything Directory Utility does with regard to adding or removing bindings. (Other tools, such as `odutil` and `ldapmodify`, handle modifying connection settings for those bindings. Ideally, any changes to attribute mappings occur on the server first so that clients can simply access the directory service using the server's configuration.)

> **Tip** When using monolithic imaging solutions, you should not deploy the image with an authenticated bind as part of the master image. Each computer needs its own record in the directory services database. You will need to script the bind as a post-imaging task in your deployment workflow. The `dsconfigldap` command is ideal for this scenario.

To use `dsconfigldap` to bind a client to a network directory service, you need just one parameter.

- ■ `-a <servername>`: Adds a directory server using its FQDN or IP address

A local administrator on the client computer must run the command using sudo to elevate privileges and must also provide a password during this interactive binding process.

```
sudo dsconfigldap -a server.talkingmoose.net
Password: enter a blind password
Certificates are available for this server.
Would you like to add them to system keychain automatically (y/n)? n
```

You can add additional parameters to the command for a noninteractive bind.

- ■ `-l <username>`: Name of a local administrator account

- ■ `-q <password>`: For the local administrator account

- ■ `-N`: Automatically accept certificates

```
dsconfigldap -N -a server.talkingmoose.net -l ladmin -q P@55wOrd
```

Because this command specifies the name and password for a local administrator account, it does not require sudo to elevate privileges. To avoid embedding credentials in the script, run it using sudo.

```
sudo dsconfigldap -N -a server.talkingmoose.net
```

This creates an unauthenticated and, therefore, untrusted bind. Creating a trusted bind requires two additional parameters.

- ■ `-u <username>`: Directory services account with privileges to bind to the service

- ■ `-p <password>`: Password for directory services account with privileges to bind to the service

```
sudo dsconfigldap -N -a server.talkingmoose.net -u diradmin -p DiradP@55
```

The following parameters are also available and more common in trusted binds:

- ■ `-n <configname>`: Configuration name for the bind

- ■ `-c <computerid>`: Client computer name for the directory service

Removing the configuration from the client computer using the `-r` parameter still requires local administrator privileges either by using sudo or by including them within the command using the `-l` and `-q` parameters.

- ■ `-r <servername>`: Removes a server configuration

Unless the `-c` parameter for the computer ID is included in the command, this procedure does not remove the computer record created in the directory service during an authenticated bind. To remove the binding configuration from the client and remove the computer record from the directory service, use the `hostname` command to dynamically include the current client computer's host name (one line).

```
sudo dsconfigldap -r server.talkignmoose.net -c $( hostname ) -u diradmin -p DiradP@55
```

For environments with preexisting machines, binding may require first removing one or more existing LDAPv3 bindings. This requires a small script to loop through the list of bindings, removing them one by one.

```
for dirservice in $(dscl localhost -list /LDAPv3)
do
  dsconfigldap -f -r "$dirservice"
done
```

Additional `dsconfigldap` parameters are available with both authenticated and unauthenticated bindings. Most are options for security and bind-time operations.

- ▪ -x: Allows you to choose an SSL connection
- ▪ -s: Enforces secure authentication only
- ▪ -g: Enforces packet signing security policy
- ▪ -m: Enforces man-in-middle security policy
- ▪ -e: Enforces encryption security policy
- ▪ -f: Forces authenticated binding/unbinding
- ▪ -v: Turns on verbose logging to `stdout`
- ▪ -i: Prompts for passwords as required

Let's put all this into a simple script for removing old bindings and adding a new one. Save the following script in a plain-text file named `bind.sh` and run the script using `sudo sh /path/to/bind.sh`:

```
#!/bin/bash

for dirservice in $(dscl localhost -list /LDAPv3)
do
  dsconfigldap -f -r "$dirservice"
done

dsconfigldap -gms -N -a server.talkingmoose.net -u diradmin -p DiradP@55

exit 0
```

Make binding scripts as basic as possible. Simple and straightforward scripts like this one are easy to troubleshoot and less likely to introduce unexpected results.

Configuration Profile

Apple introduced configuration profiles as a replacement for its Managed Client for OS X (MCX) management system. Configuration profiles are a layer of management administrators apply to an entire computer or to specific users on a computer. Unlike other methods of binding, a configuration profile is nondestructive—it does not permanently change computer settings. When an administrator removes a configuration profile, the computer reverts to its next layer of management for the correct configuration, and it even removes its computer record from the directory server with authenticated binds. Management servers such as Apple's Profile Manager commonly deploy configuration profiles as a full set of management policies; however, most any distribution method such as a script or Apple Installer package can deploy individual configuration profiles too.

Like Users & Groups, Directory Utility, and `dsconfigldap`, configuration profiles for binding to directory services support authenticated and unauthenticated binds. Simply add credentials for a directory account with privileges to bind to the directory service for authenticated binds or omit account credentials for unauthenticated binds.

Use a management server such as Apple's Profile Manager to create the configuration profile. The management server itself does not necessarily need to be actively managing devices.

1. Launch the Server app and click the Profile Manager service (Figure 2-18).

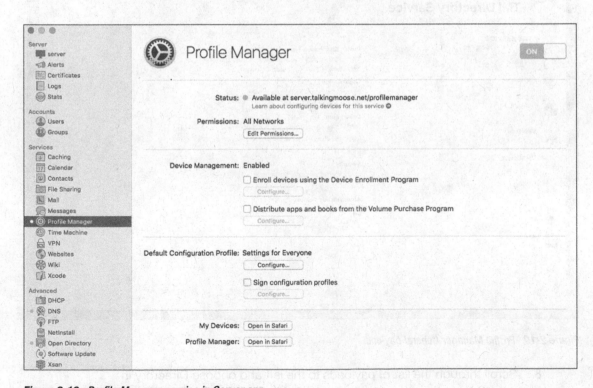

Figure 2-18. Profile Manager service in Server app

2. Turn on the service.

3. Under Settings, enable Device Management and configure any prerequisite services such as Open Directory if required.

4. At the bottom of the Profile Manager service pane, click the Open In Safari button next to Profile Manager to open Profile Manager in a web browser. Log in using administrator credentials for the server.

5. Click Device Groups under Library and click the Add Device Group button. Name the new group Directory Service and click the Save button.

6. Click the Settings tab in the new Directory Services group. Click the Edit button.

7. Complete the information in the General payload of the new configuration profile (Figure 2-19). Set the Security drop-down menu to Never to prevent the removal of the profile.

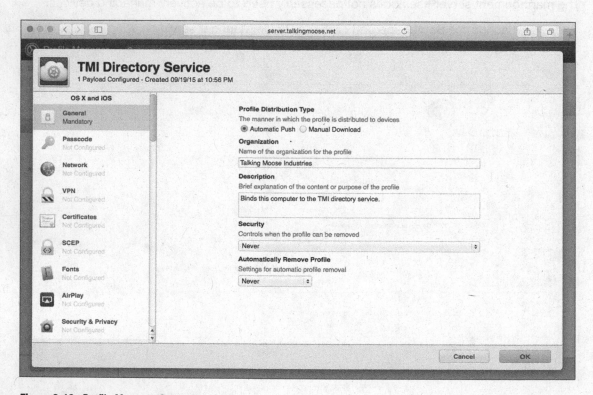

Figure 2-19. *Profile Manager General payload*

8. Scroll through the list of payloads to the left and choose Directory in the OS X section of payloads (Figure 2-20). Click the Configure button.

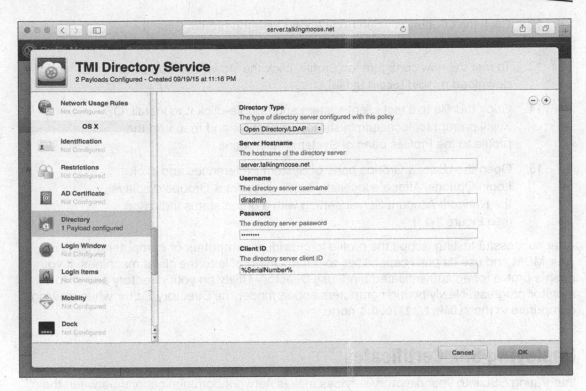

Figure 2-20. Profile Manager Directory payload

9. Enter the FQDN of your directory server in the Server Hostname field. This is the only required piece of information the configuration profile needs to bind.

10. For an authenticated bind, which also creates a computer record in the directory service, enter a username and password for a directory account allowed to bind to the service.

11. Leave the Client ID field empty to create a computer record using the host name of the client. Optionally, enter one of the following variables to bind with a different client name:

   - %ComputerName%: The computer's name, as set in System Preferences ➤ Sharing
   - %HardwareUUID%: The computer's unique identifier
   - %HostName%: The computer's DNS name, such as mac1.example.com
   - %MACAddress%: The computer's Ethernet (en0) MAC address
   - %SerialNumber%: The computer's serial number

12. Click the OK button when done configuring the profile. Click the Save button to save the new Directory Service configuration profile.

13. To test the new configuration profile, click the Download button to download a `.mobileconfig` file.

14. Copy this file to a test client system and double-click it to install. OS X will prompt for local administrator credentials and then add the profile to the Profiles pane of System Preferences.

15. Open the Users & Groups pane of System Preferences and click Login Options. After a successful binding, Users & Groups displays the Network Account Server setting with a green status indicator (see Figure 2-11).

After successful testing, scope the profile to individual computers or computer groups in your MDM and use its push capabilities to deploy the profile to the client machines. If you push a profile for an authenticated bind, use Directory Utility on your directory server to monitor progress. Newly bound computers appear under the Directory Editor when viewing computers in the `/LDAPv3/127.0.0.1` node.

Deploying SSL Certificates

Integrating SSL into your directory services makes network communications between the server and its clients as secure as possible. SSL also secures communications for other services by not only encrypting traffic but also assuring authenticity of the host system. These services include the following:

- Calendar
- Contacts
- File Sharing
- Messages
- Mail
- Websites

Securing communications is not absolutely necessary, but it is a best practice in enterprise environments, and enabling it just takes a few minutes. To use SSL on your clients, for Open Directory or any other service, each client needs to explicitly trust a security certificate signed by the server, unless it was signed by a third-party certificate authority (CA). Signed certificates from a third-party CA cost money—generally a few hundred dollars annually with established and high-quality CAs. Many administrators do not want to deal with the added cost and complexity if not required.

SSL is not difficult to implement. Since Chapter 1 covered implementation with Open Directory, we will move into managing SSL on the client side in this chapter. As with most tools in OS X, administrators can manage SSL from the GUI and the command line. The command line makes automation easier, though, so we will use this to show how to configure an SSL trust.

In newer versions of OS X, the directory services client prompts to trust an Open Directory server's certificates when using Users & Groups in System Preferences or the Directory Utility application. Clicking the Trust button downloads and installs the server's Open Directory certificate authority and intermediate CA certificates used to sign the server's SSL certificate into the System keychain. This then enables an SSL connection to Open Directory going forward. Adding the -N option when running the dsconfigldap command-line tool also downloads and installs the directory server's CA certificates.

You may have a need to reinstall the Open Directory server certificates on a client machine if they are accidentally deleted or corrupted, or you may choose to secure communications without using Open Directory. To begin, you need to export the certificate files from the server.

1. In the Server application on the Open Directory server, click Certificates and note the name of the issuer for the server's certificates (see Figure 2-21). In this example, the issuer is IntermediateCA_SERVER.TALKINGMOOSE.NET_1.

Figure 2-21. *Server certificates*

2. Open Keychain Access in /Applications/Utilities and search for the Intermediate CA issuer certificate. Double-click this certificate and click the disclosure triangle next to Details to expand the information. Make note of the common name for this certificate's issuer (see Figure 2-22). In this example, the issuer is Talking Moose Industries Open Directory Certificate Authority. This certificate is the top-level certificate, which is also known as the *root CA*. Close this window when done.

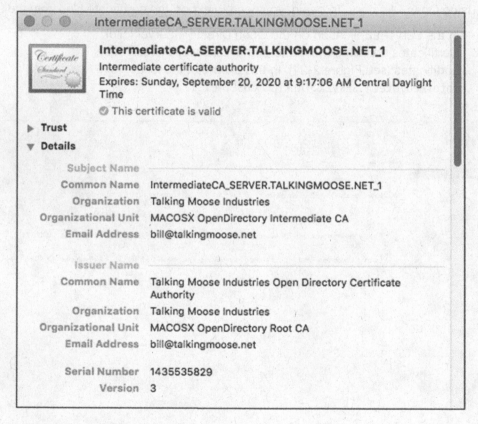

Figure 2-22. Intermediate certificate issuer CA

3. In the Keychain Access window, select the root CA certificate, choose File ➤ Export Items, and save the new file as a certificate file (.cer). In this example, the file name is rootCA.cer (see Figure 2-23). Repeat this step for the intermediate CA certificate, saving the file with a name such as intermediateCA.cer.

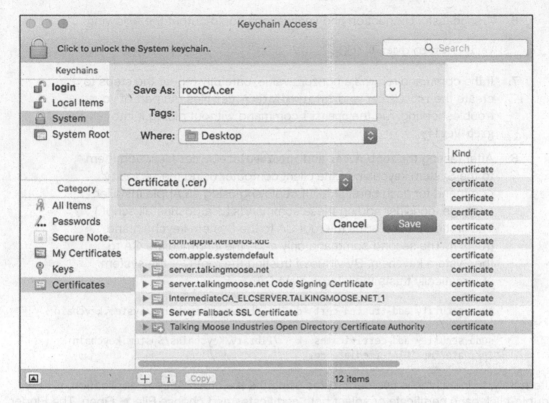

Figure 2-23. Keychain Access export items

4. Using a tool such as Apple Remote Desktop or your favorite packaging application, deploy the `rootCA.cer` and `intermediateCA.cer` files to a temporary location on each directory services client machine such as `/private/tmp`. The `/private/tmp` folder is automatically emptied at every reboot.

> **Tip** To make working with certificates in the command line easier, avoid spaces in the path to your certificate files, including the file name.

5. To validate the certificate chain in the `rootCA.cer` file against your Open Directory server, use the `openssl` command-line utility on a client machine.

```
openssl s_client -connect elcserver.talkingmoose.net:636 \
2>&1 < /dev/null -CAfile /private/tmp/ODIntermediate.cer \
-CAfile /private/tmp/ODRoot.cer | grep Verify
```

6. A successful connection and verification should output the following:

    ```
    Verify return code: 0 (ok)
    ```

7. If the command returns a nonzero value, carefully repeat the steps to create the `rootCA.cer` and `intermediateCA.cer` files. As part of your troubleshooting, run the `openssl` command without piping it into `grep Verify`.

8. After testing the `rootCA.cer` and `intermediateCA.cer` files, add them to the System keychain of the client computer using the `security` command for each certificate. (If deploying using an Apple Installer package, consider adding these commands as a postinstall script.) The first command adds the root CA to the System keychain and trusts it. The second command only adds the intermediate CA to the System keychain. By virtue of trusting the root CA, the system automatically trusts the intermediate CA.

    ```
    sudo security add-trusted-cert -d -k \ /Library/Keychains/System.keychain
    /private/tmp/ODRoot.cer
    sudo security add-certificates -k \ /Library/Keychains/System.keychain \
    /private/tmp/ODIntermediate.cer
    ```

Alternately, to install these two certificates using the Keychain Access application, simply double-click each certificate or select both certificates and choose File ➤ Open. The Finder will open the Keychain Access application and prompt for local administrator credentials to make changes. Keychain Access places these certificates into the System keychain under Certificates.

By default, OS X does not trust the root certificate. You must do this manually. Double-click the Open Directory Certificate Authority certificate and click the disclosure triangle next to Trust. Change the "When using this certificate" drop-down menu from Use System Defaults to Always Trust (see Figure 2-24). Close the certificate window and enter administrator credentials when prompted to save the change. After explicitly trusting the root CA certificate, OS X immediately trusts the intermediate CA certificate.

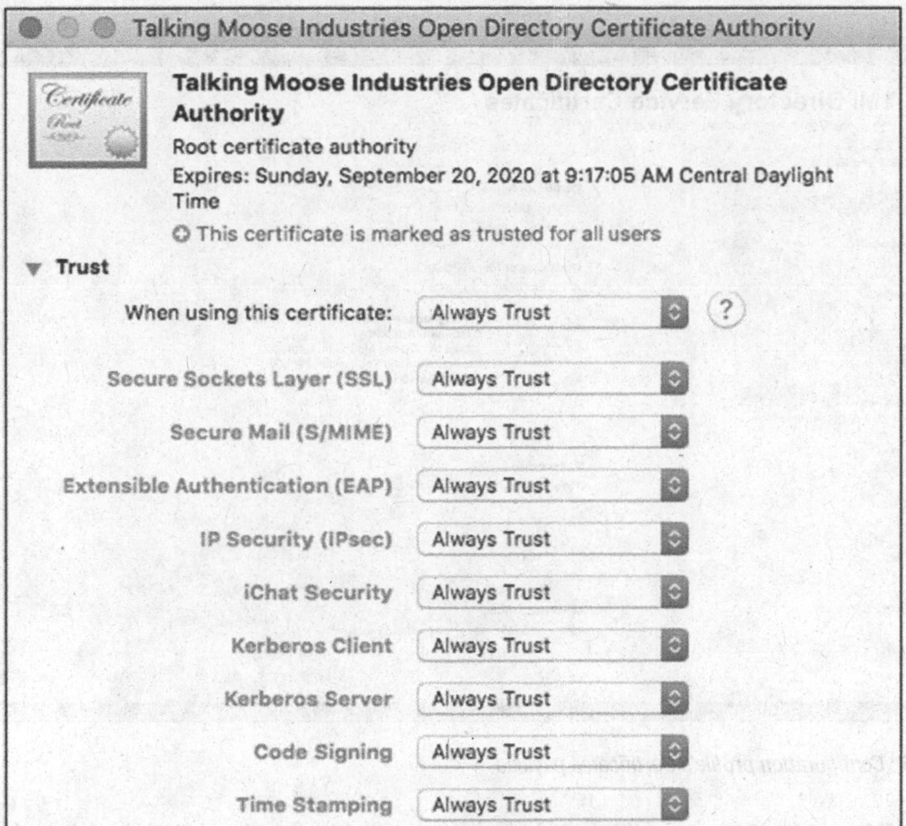

Figure 2-24. *Always trusting the root CA*

If using an MDM, the easiest way to deploy certificates is with a configuration profile. Create a new configuration profile that includes the Certificates payload and adds both certificates to the profile (see Figure 2-25). After saving the profile, download and test the `.mobileconfig` file on a client machine by double-clicking to install it into Profiles in System Preferences. During installation, Keychain Access adds the two certificates into the System keychain and automatically trusts the root CA for you (thereby creating a transitive trust for other certificates lower in the certificate chain).

Figure 2-25. Configuration profile's Certificates payload

Once the CA certificates are in the keychain, whether added during binding or installed as part of a script, package, or configuration profile, GUI applications such as Calendar, Contacts, Mail, and Safari will trust your server's SSL certificates signed by the CA.

Custom LDAP Settings

Now that you can bind to a network directory server using default settings, let's look at a way to set a little bit more information. Open Directory Utility and click the Lock button to allow changes. Next, click Services in the Directory Utility window and then double-click the LDAPv3 service. Click the New button and enter a hostname or IP address of a directory server.

Enable one or more of the following options (see Figure 2-26):

- *Encrypt Using SSL*: Select this for secure communications with the directory server.

- *Use For Authentication*: Select this to allow directory members to log on to the Mac using their directory credentials.

- *Use For Contacts*: Select this to allow user lookups on the directory server using the Contacts application.

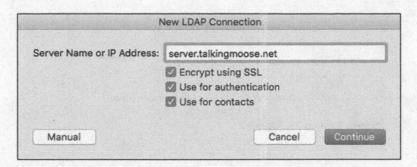

Figure 2-26. Directory Utility New LDAP Connection dialog

Click the Continue button and proceed with an authenticated bind using credentials for a directory member allowed to bind clients to Open Directory.

After binding, select the newly added configuration and click the Edit button. On the Connections tab, you'll find the following (Figure 2-27):

- *Configuration Name:* A friendly name to identify the binding. By default, this is the name or IP address of the directory server.

- *Server Name or IP Address*: IP address of the directory server.

- *Open/close times out in*: Number of seconds before the client will cancel an open or close event for the LDAP connection.

- *Query times out in*: Number of seconds the client will cancel a query for a record if the record has not yet been found.

- *Re-bind attempted in*: Number of seconds the client will wait before reconnecting to the LDAP server if it receives no response.

- *Encrypt using SSL*: Enables SSL if selected (likely set at bind time).

- *Use custom port*: Enables a custom TCP port (other than 389 or 636).

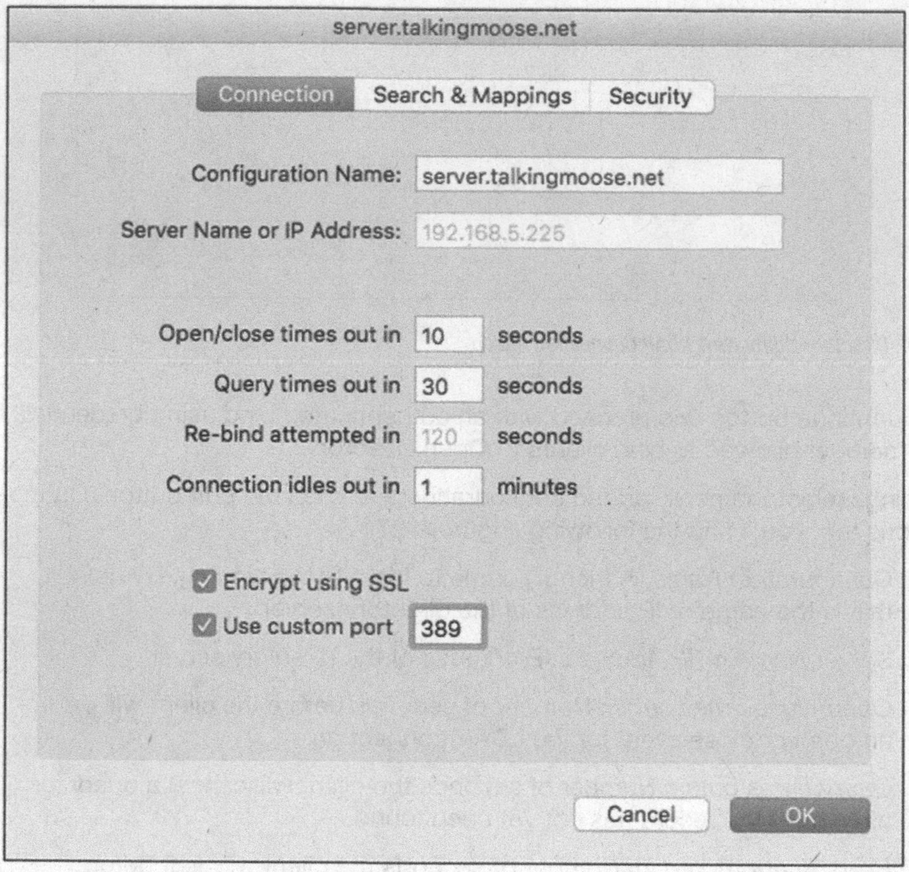

Figure 2-27. Directory Utility bind's connection settings

Note   Apple has chosen optimal default values for the timeout settings. However, fairly latent connections may require increasing the values, or saturated servers may require lowering values. Additionally, laptop users who are frequently out of the office may have a better user experience with lower values to shorten timeouts that may cause delays.

Next, click the Search & Mappings tab. This window lets administrators configure custom mappings between standard OS X attributes and those available via other LDAPv3 servers, such as a machine's ENetAddress in OS X and macAddress in another LDAP system (see Figure 2-28). Select one of the prebuilt Apple mapping schemes using the "Access this LDAPv3 server using" drop-down menu, which includes commonly used Open Directory Server, Active Directory, and RFC 2307 settings.

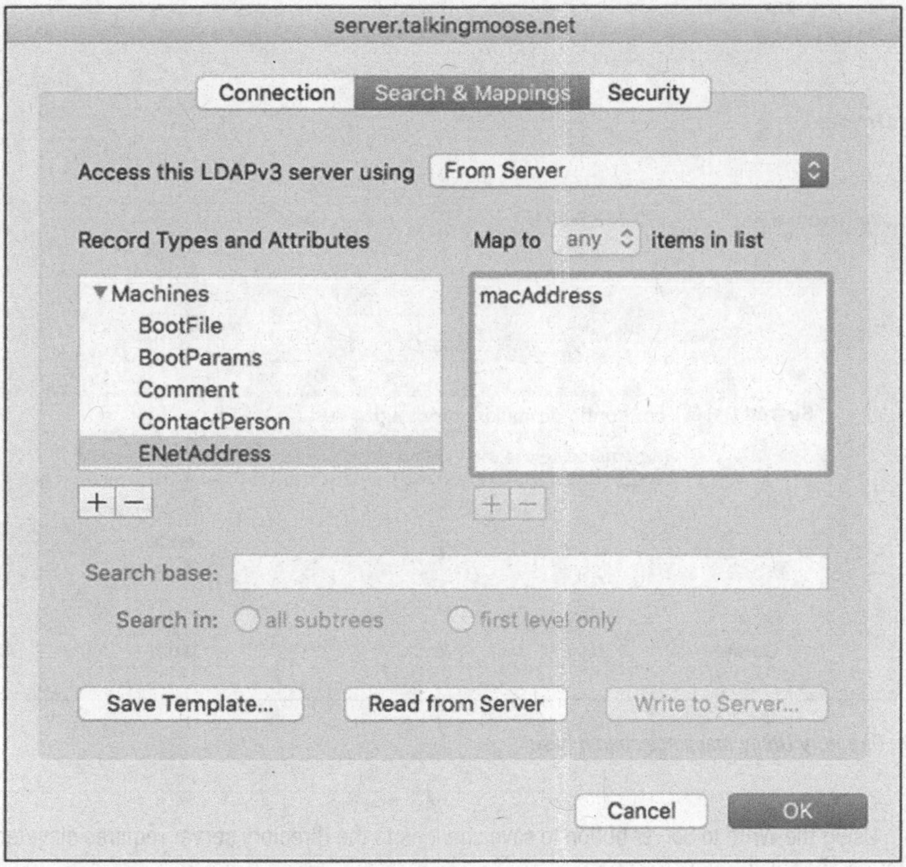

Figure 2-28. Directory Utility bind's Search & Mapping settings

RFC 2307 is a set of standards for Unix-style operating systems to map to LDAP protocol entries. Many of the attributes in Open Directory are derived from the standards presented in RFC 2307. Open Directory requires no manual mapping of fields for most LDAP entries, which are integrated out of the box. For additional information, see the following:

www.faqs.org/rfcs/rfc2307.html

Mappings allow Open Directory to store information in unused fields of other directory services to provide required fields for OS X, even if those fields do not exist in the foreign directory service. After adjusting the mappings, save them as a template using the Save Template button or write them back to the server for other clients to use them. Writing these fields back into the cn=config container saves having to set mappings on each client. Furthermore, the clients can continue to use the default From Server option from the "Access this LDAPv3 server using" drop-down list (see Figure 2-29).

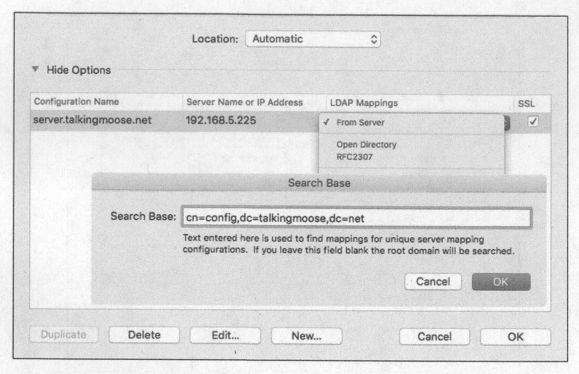

Figure 2-29. Directory Utility mappings search base

> **Note**   Using the Write to Server button to save changes to the directory server requires elevated (e.g., diradmin) privileges to the LDAP server.

Next, click the Security tab. For an authenticated bind, this window reflects the computer name (which is not actually a distinguished name as the field label suggests) as it appears in Open Directory. These settings are dimmed and unchangeable. An administrator can convert an unauthenticated bind to an authenticated bind by clicking the Bind button at the bottom of the window. The absence of a Bind button means the computer is already using an authenticated bind. This window also provides options for a stronger security policy than the default settings. Before enabling these features, verify your Open Directory server supports them. The settings shown in Figure 2-30 are as follows:

- *Disable clear text passwords*: Prevents sending unencrypted passwords over the network.

- *Digitally sign all packets (requires Kerberos)*: Enables Kerberos for signing packets.

- *Encrypt all packets (requires SSL or Kerberos)*: Encrypts all data, not just passwords using SSL or Kerberos.

- *Block man-in-the-middle attacks (requires Kerberos)*: Typically used in conjunction with the "Digitally sign all packets" option to prevent third-party servers from intercepting communications.

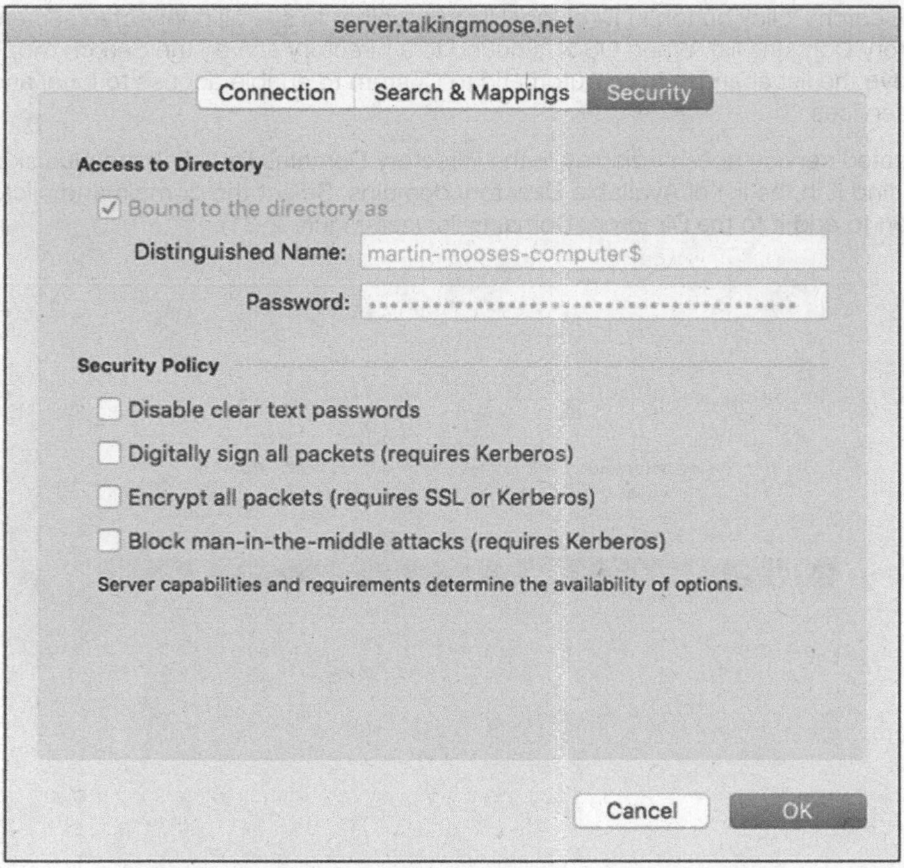

Figure 2-30. *Directory Utility bind's security settings*

After converting from an unauthenticated bind to an authenticated bind, proceed to review the search policy in Directory Utility and verify the directory service is included, as described in the next section.

Managing the Search Policy

OS X binds to multiple LDAP servers for accessing multiple directories and directory services. It uses the Search Policy settings in Directory Utility to prioritize the order of the servers for locating user accounts. The /Local/Default directory services database is always first in the Directory Domains list and has precedence over network directory services databases. Therefore, if both the local database and any bound network directory database contains the user account jcool, OS X uses the local jcool account. In addition to prioritizing LDAPv3 bindings for centralized authentication, the search policy in Directory Utility also prioritizes accessing network contacts. Re-arranging the order of directory services by dragging them up or down in the Directory Domains list is primarily useful for managing environments with multiple network directory databases.

Click the Search Policy button in Directory Utility's toolbar to see all connected servers in the Directory Domains list. When OS X is bound to a directory server, the Search drop-down menu above the list changes from Automatic to Custom to enable access to local and network services.

If a connected service doesn't display in the Directory Domains list, click the plus sign (+) button to find it in the list of Available Directory domains. Select the domain and click the Add button to add it to the Directory Domains list (see Figure 2-31).

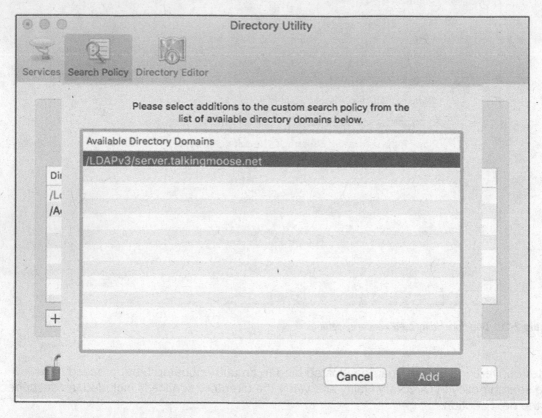

Figure 2-31. *Directory Utility's Available Directory Domains list*

Changing the priority of directory services is as easy as dragging an item in the Directory Domains list higher or lower than other items. Remember, the /Local/Default node always has the highest priority (see Figure 2-32), which is why it appears dimmed in the list.

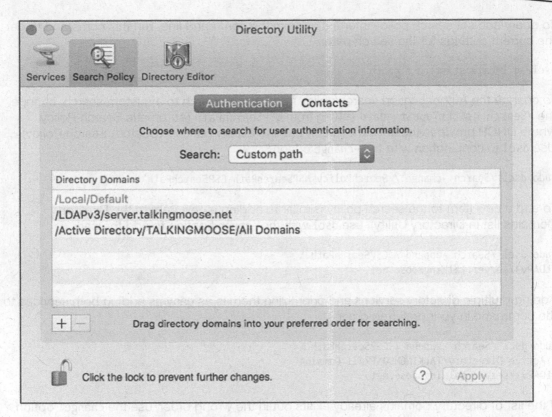

Figure 2-32. Directory Utility's Directory Domains list

> **Note**   Directory Utility treats search paths for authentication and contacts separately. Active
> Directory may be the higher-priority domain for authentication, while Open Directory may be the
> higher-priority domain for contacts. If you will not use Open Directory for authentication, removing
> it from the domains list under Authentication will actually improve performance during the lookup
> process. If a user mistypes a username, OS X will query each directory for the nonexistent name,
> which takes time, before returning an error. Likewise, if you will not use Active Directory for
> contacts, removing it from the domains list under Contacts improves lookup performance.

To manage the Authentication search policy using the command line or in a script, use the
`dscl` command-line utility. Unlike `dsconfigldap`, which is the utility for binding to a directory
service, `dscl` allows you to *manage* directory services including Active Directory services,
which we'll discuss more in the next chapter.

To query and set search policy information from the command line, run this command to get the current settings for the search path:

```
dscl -q localhost -read /Search
```

To change the Authentication search policy from a local search to a custom search, change the /Search dsAttrTypeStandard setting from NSPSearchPath (Automatic Search Policy where DHCP provides the network search path) to CSPSearchPath (Custom Search Policy). Use dscl in conjunction with the –change option.

```
sudo dscl /Search -change / SearchPolicy NSPSearchPath CSPSearchPath
```

To add a new item to the search policy (similar to adding a new item to the Directory Domains list in Directory Utility), use dscl with the –append option to add the path.

```
sudo dscl /Search -append / CSPSearchPath \
/LDAPv3/server.talkingmoose.net
```

Adding multiple directory services and prioritizing them is as easy as adding both services to the command in your preferred order.

```
sudo dscl /Search -append / CSPSearchPath \
"/Active Directory/TALKINGMOOSE/All Domains" \
/LDAPv3/server.talkingmoose.net
```

If the list of directory domains already exists but in the wrong order, use the changei option to reorder the list. First, set the preferred domain, which deletes all other domains. Then use the append option to add other domains after the first.

```
sudo dscl /Search -changei / CSPSearchPath 1 \
"/Active Directory/TALKINGMOOSE/All Domains"

sudo dscl /Search -append / CSPSearchPath \
/LDAPv3/server.talkingmoose.net
```

> **Note**   Depending on your interpretation of the man page for dscl, the changei option may not be behaving as defined. If it is supposed to change the index (change the order) of listed directory domains, then it should not delete any domains. Yet, it does. This may be a bug and subject to change in the future.

Managing the Contacts search policy is similar to the Authentication search policy but not as straightforward as replacing *Search* with *Contacts* in the previous commands. To query the search policy information for Contacts, run this command to get the current settings:

```
dscl -q localhost -read /Contact
```

To change the Contacts search policy from a local search to a custom search, change the /Search/Contacts dsAttrTypeStandard setting from NSPSearchPath (Automatic Search Policy where DHCP provides the network search path) to CSPSearchPath (Custom Search Policy). Use dscl in conjunction with the –change option.

```
sudo dscl /Search/Contacts -change / SearchPolicy NSPSearchPath CSPSearchPath
```

Note the /Local/Default node is not automatically included in the Directory Domains list for Contacts. Ordinarily, it wouldn't contain any contacts. You only need to add network directory servers to this list. To add a new item to the search policy (similar to adding a new item to the Directory Domains list in Directory Utility), use dscl with the –append option to add the path.

```
sudo dscl /Search/Contacts -append / CSPSearchPath \
/LDAPv3/server.talkingmoose.net
```

To add multiple directory services and prioritize them, add both services to the command in your preferred order.

```
sudo dscl /Search/Contacts -append / CSPSearchPath \
"/Active Directory/TALKINGMOOSE/All Domains" \
/LDAPv3/server.talkingmoose.net
```

Again, the changei option to reorder the list is buggy. Unlike the Authentication search policy, it can set each item in the Directory Domains list to the same path, or it may do nothing. Avoid using this option.

NIS

Network Information Service (NIS) is one of Sun's early attempts at providing directory services to clients. Apple maintains support for NIS in OS X for legacy purposes and provides a directory services plug-in for it in Directory Utility.

To configure OS X to access a NIS server, open Directory Utility and click the Lock button to authenticate as an administrator. Click the Services button in the toolbar and double-click NIS in the list of available services (see Figure 2-33).

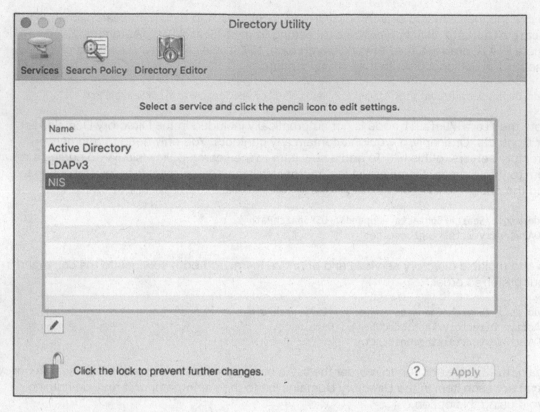

Figure 2-33. Directory Utility NIS

Enter the domain name of your NIS environment in the Domain Name field and one or more IP addresses or host names of your NIS servers in the Servers field (Figure 2-34). Because of the differences between NIS and LDAPv3, you will need to select "Use NIS domain for authentication" to populate the information for your NIS environment into the search policy of your node. Click the OK button. Follow the earlier instructions for using the dscl command-line tool to test NIS functionality and adding the domain to your Mac's search policies.

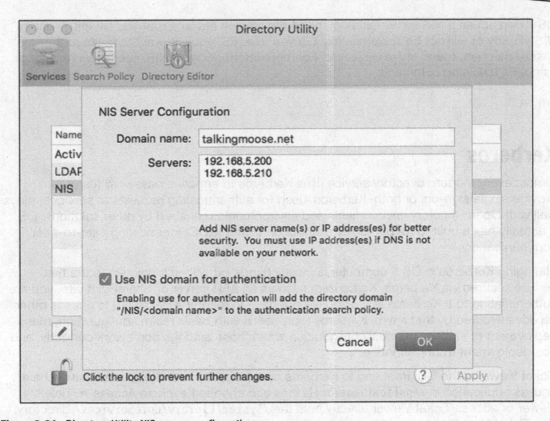

Figure 2-34. Directory Utility NIS server configuration

Command-line tools to support NIS are in the /usr/bin and /usr/sbin directories of your Mac and include the following:

- ypbind: Performs binding operations
- yppoll: Queries data from a directory server's map
- ypset: Sets which directory server to use
- ypwhich: Shows the hostname of the yp server
- ypcat: Shows all the available values in an NIS database
- ypmatch: Shows the value of a specified key in the NIS database

Note   NIS was originally named Yellow Pages; however, Sun changed the name because of trademark issues. The command-line tools to support NIS still begin with yp.

OS X can act as a NIS server, although given the age we assume that you are either using NIS already or will not be implementing it. If you use NIS, you will want to manage the `ypserv` daemon, found in `/usr/libexec`. For more information on NIS, see the yp man page using the following command:

`man yp`

Kerberos

Almost every modern directory service uses Kerberos to enhance password features, provide single sign-on, or both. Kerberos, used for authenticating requests to services, plays well with Open Directory environments and environments managed by other solutions. OS X actually has a built-in Kerberos key distribution center (KDC) for securing peer-to-peer communications.

Managing Kerberos in OS X computer is mostly hands-off. When logging in to the first service secured via Kerberos (Kerberized) such as an AFP server or SharePoint site, you are authenticating to a Kerberos realm and will not have to reenter a password to access other services secured by that realm. Kerberos tools assist with basic realm configuration, mass deployment of settings, manual configuration when those settings don't work correctly, and postdeployment troubleshooting.

Ticket Viewer is the GUI front end to Kerberos on a Mac (Figure 2-35). Open the Keychain Access application in `/Applications/Utilities` and choose Keychain Access ➤ Ticket Viewer or access Ticket Viewer directly from the `/System/Library/CoreServices/` directory. Use Ticket Viewer to browse the tickets (remember from Chapter 1 that a ticket is provided by the KDC based on the ticket-granting ticket), establish a connection to a new realm, renew tickets, destroy tickets, get more information on tickets, and change the password associated with a ticket.

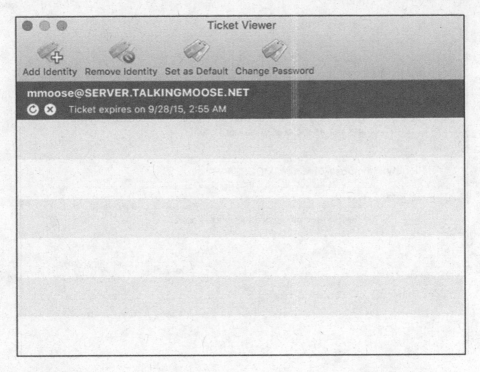

Figure 2-35. Ticket Viewer

To join a new realm, click the Add Identity button in the toolbar. Enter a user principal name (UPN) in the Identity field. A UPN looks like an e-mail address, but it is actually another method of identifying a user and associated Kerberos realm. The convention is to enter and display Kerberos realms using uppercase letters. While not necessary, this practice avoids confusing the realm with a DNS domain name. Enter the password for the user and click the Continue button (see Figure 2-36).

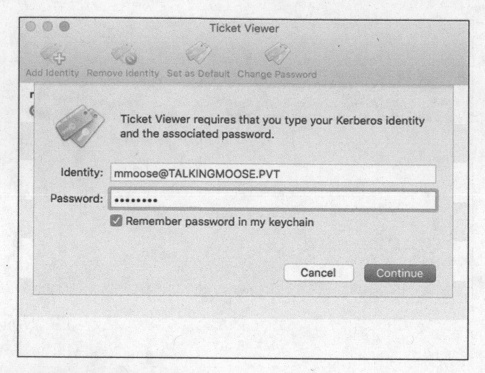

Figure 2-36. *Ticket Viewer's Add Identity screen*

The second Kerberos identity appears in Ticket Viewer below the first (see Figure 2-37). Note that only one identity is ever the default identity (identified in bold text). To change the default, choose another identity and click the Set As Default button on the toolbar.

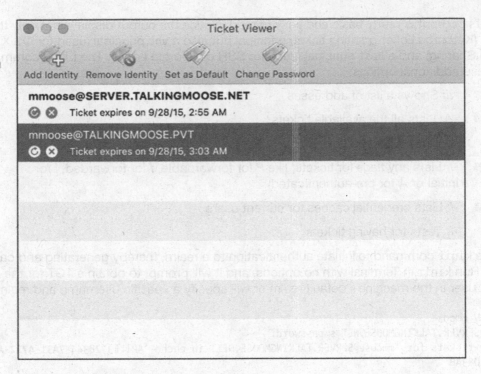

Figure 2-37. Ticket Viewer, additional identity

Every ticket expires about ten hours after its creation. To extend a ticket's expiration, hold the Shift key while clicking the Renew button to the left of the ticket. Depending on the Kerberos policy for the realm, you may need to provide credentials when renewing or the ticket's expiration may simply renew for another ten hours.

Selecting a ticket and choosing Ticket ➤ Diagnostic Information offers some additional details including creation date, expiration date, and encryption type. This corresponds to the klist command-line utility.

```
klist
Credentials cache: API:3E788ED1-B5D2-46C5-86D1-ED1306B0D443
        Principal: mmoose@SERVER.TALKINGMOOSE.NET

Issued                   Expires                  Principal
Sep 27 17:21:33 2015     Sep 28 02:55:28 2015     krbtgt/
                         SERVER.TALKINGMOOSE.NET@ SERVER.TALKINGMOOSE.NET
Sep 27 17:21:33 2015     Sep 28 02:55:28 2015     vnc/
                         SERVER.TALKINGMOOSE.NET@ SERVER.TALKINGMOOSE.NET
Sep 27 17:21:33 2015     Sep 28 02:55:28 2015     host/
                         SERVER.TALKINGMOOSE.NET@ SERVER.TALKINGMOOSE.NET
```

The `klist` output is pretty basic and easy to read. Notice the output displays not only the `krbtgt` (Kerberos ticket-granting ticket) principal but also a `vnc` principal (used for OS X Screen Sharing) and a `host` principal (used for SSH or Remote Login). The `klist` command has these additional options:

- *-a:* Shows a list of addresses

- *-A:* Lists all the available tickets

- *-c:* Shows cached tickets

- *-f:* Lists any flags for tickets, like *F* for forwardable, *f* for forwarded, I for initial or *A* for pre-authenticated)

- *-l:* Lists credential caches for current users

- *-t:* Tests for having tickets

Use the `kinit` command to initiate authentication to a realm, thereby generating and caching a TGT. Run `kinit` in Terminal with no options, and it will prompt to obtain a TGT for the current user in the machine's default realm or will specify a specific username and realm.

```
kinit -V mmoose
mmoose@SERVER.TALKINGMOOSE.NET's password:
Placing tickets for 'mmoose@SERVER.TALKINGMOOSE.NET' in cache 'API:E372B344-7A31-4722-AA89-
1391881D83AB'

klist
Credentials cache: API:E372B344-7A31-4722-AA89-1391881D83AB
        Principal: mmoose@SERVER.TALKINGMOOSE.NET

Issued                  Expires                 Principal
Sep 27 22:25:20 2015    Sep 28 08:24:38 2015    krbtgt/
                        SERVER.TALKINGMOOSE.NET@SERVER.TALKINGMOOSE.NET
```

Additional options for the `kinit` command include the following:

- *-V:* Shows verbose output

- *-l:* Defines the lifetime of the ticket in seconds when obtaining it

- *-r:* Defines the maximum renewable ticket life

- *-s:* Includes a start time (and therefore caches a postdated ticket)

- *-f :* Generates a forwardable ticket that can be used on another host

- *-f --no-forwardable:* Does not use forwardable tickets

- *-p:* Uses proxiable tickets

- *-a:* Adds a set of addresses to be put into the ticket

- *-A:* Requests ticket without a defined address

- *-v:* Tries to validate an invalid ticket

- *-R:* Renews a ticket

- *-k:* Obtains a key from a key in the local keytab file (cache) rather than from a live server

- *-S:* Gets a ticket for a service other than the local principal

The kdestroy command is fairly straightforward—to delete tickets—and has far fewer options than kinit. Its options define which tickets to delete.

- *-a* or *-A:* Destroys all tickets

- *-c:* Name of cache to delete

- *-p:* Name of principal to delete

Two other commands worth noting, kpasswd and kswitch, change a principal's password and set the cache for the default system, respectively. The kpasswd command prompts for both the old and new passwords, which is useful for troubleshooting why users are unable to reset their own passwords. The kswitch command is useful for specifying the default credential cache when authenticating to multiple realms.

The keytab file is perhaps the most critical file on an operating system to secure. Kerberos uses it to store pairs of Kerberos principals and their corresponding DES keys. In OS X, the keytab file is called krb5.keytab and is stored in the /private/etc directory. OS X stores the keytab file in binary format, which makes much of the information in the file barely readable to human eyes, much less editable. Editing the file requires using the kadmin or ktutil command-line tools. (The kadmin.local command for managing Kerberos on a KDC is deprecated. Use kadmin -l instead.)

Both Active Directory and Open Directory are *kerberized* by default, which means out of the box they are ready for single sign-on (SSO). After an administrator binds a Mac to either type of directory service, users who log in with their directory credentials automatically generate TGTs (viewable in Ticket Viewer). As users attempt to access kerberized network services in the same Kerberos realm, OS X is using the TGT to request access to the services on their behalf, and the service responds by providing its own ticket. This is all in lieu of sending passwords over the network and having a directory server authenticate users. Kerberized services may include the following:

- afp: OS X native file sharing

- cifs: Windows native file sharing

- ftp: File transfer protocol

- http: Web services

- imap: Incoming IMAP mail protocol

- ldap: Directory services

- pop: Incoming POP mail protocol

- smb: Windows file sharing for UNIX systems

- smtp: Outgoing SMTP mail protocol

- ■ ssh: Secure shell
- ■ vnc: Remote screen sharing protocol
- ■ vpn: Remote network access

The process to integrate OS X Server with another SSO instance varies based on the Kerberos implementation. For example, Apple provides `sso_util` and `krbservicesetuptools` for Open Directory. It provides the `dsconfigad` tool for Active Directory. These are the easiest directory service SSO implementations. Some of these tools may work for other directory service types, or you may need to install tools specific to those implementations.

Summary

In this chapter, we provided both a high- and low-level integration of OS X into Open Directory implementations as well as multiple directory services. We also reviewed how Kerberos automatically plays a role in Open Directory authentication and other server services.

In the next chapter, we will further explore directory services integration, with a specific focus on integrating OS X systems with Microsoft's Active Directory system.

## Chapter 3

Active Directory

Active Directory is a directory services solution developed by Microsoft. Active Directory was built using certain proprietary technologies, which (currently) runs only on the Microsoft Windows Server platform and Microsoft Azure, Microsoft's cloud platform. While many of the back-end components of Active Directory are designed for the Microsoft Windows client platform, Microsoft based much of the structure of Active Directory on open standards, such as the LDAP format known as RFC 2307 and the Kerberos v5 protocol defined in RFC 1510. Active Directory can be used to seamlessly integrate Windows systems en masse, but the real advantage of blending these technologies and open standards is that foreign operating systems can be integrated with Active Directory as well.

Integrating OS X and OS X Server with Active Directory is similar to integrating with the native directory services that OS X Server's Open Directory service can provide. The reason for this is that Active Directory supports gaining access to information within its database by using the Lightweight Directory Access Protocol (LDAP). A directory service is sometimes best thought of as a large delimited document, such as something you would create in a spreadsheet program such as Microsoft Excel. When a client attempts to use a directory for authentication and authorization, it looks up an object such as a user account via the LDAP protocol much like searching for a field in a spreadsheet. This lookup entails finding the field in the directory that matches the requested information. For example, when a user types a username, this information is stored as a key-value pair in Active Directory.

If user "cedge"logs in, then an LDAP query is started that attempts to find a user in the directory with that value. Once the user is found, the resultant set of keys that make up the user account can be accessed. For example, cedge may have a home directory that is stored on a network server. This path name will be stored in a key (homeDirectory) in the Active Directory database. Apple has two default plug-ins for communicating with LDAP servers: the LDAPv3 plug-in and the Active Directory plug-in. These two plug-ins are similar in terms of the back-end communication they use. However, Apple developed the Active Directory plug-in to supplement missing LDAP attributes that are not normally available in a standard Active Directory schema. The best example of this is the uidNumber attribute. This attribute is normally used to contain the numerical value associated with an account. On a native

Open Directory server, this value is mapped from the server's `uidNumber` attribute to the local client's `UniqueID` attribute. Without a `UniqueID`, users are not able to log in, which is because of OS X's UNIX underpinnings that require a `UniqueID` to track ownership on the file system.

If you use the LDAPv3 plug-in to authenticate to Active Directory (which is possible to do though rarely implemented), the default RFC 2307 mappings map a server attribute called `uidNumber` to a local plug-in mapping called `UniqueID`. When a user attempts to log in, they then query the server attribute `uidNumber`, and because it is unavailable but required for login, they are unable to authenticate to the login window. Apple saw this scenario and mitigated it in the design of the Active Directory plug-in. When a user logs into a workstation that is bound to Active Directory, the plug-in itself generates a numerical value based on other information in the native directory and maps it to the `UniqueID` attribute. You can think of this as a mask in front of the Active Directory server to make it seem more like a native Open Directory server.

Additionally, the Apple Active Directory plug-in will not only mask missing attributes but will also convert attributes that are in the wrong format for Mac OS X to the correct format. Let's return to the example of a home directory that is hosted on a network volume. In Active Directory, this network path is stored using the universal naming convention (UNC), or \\server\share. Despite its "universal" name, this format is not supported for connecting to URIs in Mac OS X. If you wanted to connect to \\server\share using the built-in file-sharing clients, you would format the URI as smb://server/share. This simple format difference would mean the difference of being able to log in or not using the LDAPv3 plug-in. In this instance, Apple again configures the Active Directory plug-in to read in the server `homeDirectory` attribute and then reformats and maps it to the local `HomeDirectory` attribute.

With all the supplements that are provided by Apple through the native Active Directory plug-in, it serves as an adequate tool for integration in many different environments. In the beginning of this chapter, we will cover the Apple-provided and supported tools that can be used to bind to Active Directory environments. However, depending on the needs of your environment, you may need to take advantage of some Active Directory features that cannot be facilitated using just the Active Directory plug-in. The most common needs in an enterprise environment move beyond mere authentication and into the realm of ongoing client management. For this, Apple has a robust set of management options known as *managed preferences* or MCX (covered extensively in Chapter 7). Though not natively supported by Active Directory, MCX can still be implemented alongside Active Directory via a few different methods. After reading this chapter, you will be familiar with the various options available, as well as the pros and cons of each. Today, though, note that the MCX functionality is slowly being deprecated in OS X in favor of a more iOS-like technology called *configuration profiles*, which do not necessarily require directory services.

On a native Open Directory server, these management options are stored as keys within a given object. For instance, user cedge (or more commonly a "workgroup" that he is a member of) may have a managed preference that configures his Dock to appear on the left side. These management attributes cannot be natively stored in Active Directory without modifying the Active Directory schema, a modification that is global for all objects in an organization's directory. As such, from a political aspect, extending the schema can be difficult to push through in environments with a proportionally small number of OS X workstations. For this reason, other options such as maintaining a separate supplemental Open Directory server or using a third-party Active Directory plug-in may best suit your needs. These options are covered in the following sections. Because the needs and business requirements of each environment are different, after explaining how to use the built-in Active Directory plug-in, the remainder of the chapter is dedicated to customizing the Active Directory plug-in and the common third-party add-ons.

Binding to Active Directory

When binding to an Active Directory server, keep in mind that it is an individualized process; each workstation will need a computer account named for the machine created in the directory. While it is possible to prepopulate these accounts, the Apple Active Directory plug-in will create a computer account in Active Directory at the time of binding with the correct credentials if one does not already exist. As with a Windows client account, each OS X computer account contains a unique preshared key used to authenticate that individual machine to the directory. This individualistic nature is an important aspect to consider when looking at automating the process. The process of binding a machine to Active Directory can be accomplished either through the use of a GUI interface or through a decently robust set of command-line tools. We will discuss the command-line components of this process (dscl and dsconfigad) later in this chapter. First, we will look at the manual GUI tools used to bind a Mac to Active Directory.

Directory Utility

The Apple directory service framework is a set of code allowing for modularized access to the different directory service plug-ins available (including third-party plug-ins). The graphical application for configuring the plug-ins is Directory Utility, although basic functionality is also available in the more commonly used Users & Groups pane of System Preferences. Directory Utility is bundled with all versions of OS X and can be found in /System/Library/ CoreServices/Applications (it was previously located in /System/Library/CoreServices).

As mentioned, binding to Active Directory can be done using the Login Options section of the Users & Groups preferences. From here, you can also manually open Directory Utility, rather than having to remember the path.

Once you open Directory Utility, you will need to authenticate as a local administrator to make changes to the directory services plug-in. If you are not automating this step, you will need to supply your onsite technicians with both local and directory administrator credentials to manually complete this process. You can customize the policies in your environment to supply desktop technicians with Active Directory accounts that have access only to bind computers to the domain.

To start the binding process, open the Users & Groups pane in System Preferences by clicking the Apple menu in the top-left corner of your screen, selecting System Preferences, and then clicking Accounts. Next, click the Login Options, as shown in Figure 3-1.

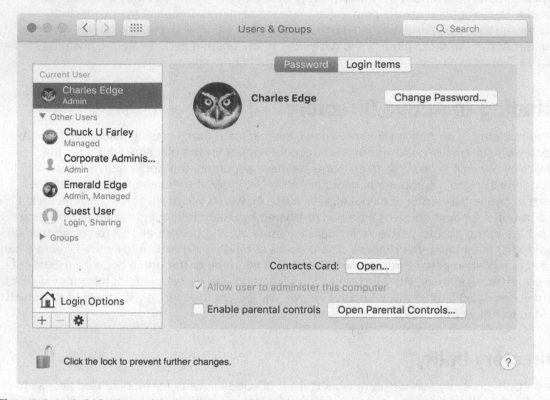

Figure 3-1. Login Options area of the Accounts preferences pane

To authorize your session to edit the system preference, locate the lock in the lower-left corner of the screen and click it to authenticate. Then click the Join button in the Network Account Server field. This will bring up a pop-up screen that simply has a field for a server. Type the name of your domain. After a time, the screen will expand so that you can enter the ID that the computer you are binding will have once it joins Active Directory, the username of an account in your Active Directory that has credentials to bind to Active Directory, and the password for that account. Supply this information, as shown in Figure 3-2, and then click the OK button.

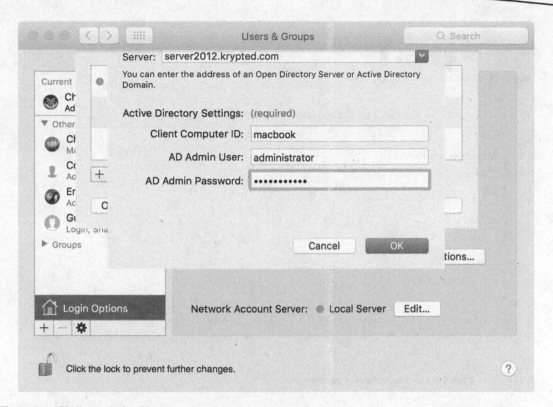

Figure 3-2. Binding to Active Directory

In an effort to simplify the binding process, Apple allows you to bind to both Open Directory and Active Directory servers from this initial screen. Keep in mind that using this screen will allow you only to bind and not to configure granular settings within either of the plug-ins, though you can do this at a later time, if necessary. To bind using a screen that allows you to configure more granular settings, click Open Directory Utility and then click Services in the upper-left corner of the screen, as you can see in Figure 3-3.

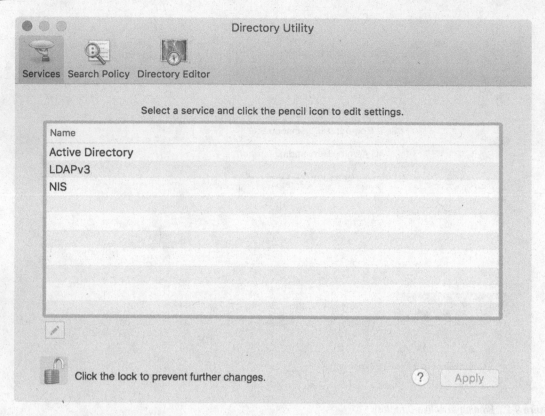

Figure 3-3. Services in Directory Utility

Use the lock in the lower-left corner of the screen to authenticate again, and then from Services in the Directory Utility toolbar, double-click the entry for Active Directory. You will then be prompted with three fields by default, which are also shown in Figure 3-4:

- *Active Directory Forest*: If there is only one forest, then the forest will be the same name as the Active Directory domain name, but check with an Active Directory administrator to confirm this is the case if you encounter binding issues.

- *Active Directory Domain*: Note that you are not connecting to a specific host but rather a domain. The Active Directory plug-in will use this domain to look up special records in DNS called *service records* (SRVs) to find the domain controller you need to connect to. This process is unique to the Active Directory plug-in and heavily relies on the client's configured DNS servers to be correctly pointing at servers that host these records or can facilitate communication to these servers; properly configured DNS is absolutely paramount for this process to succeed.

- *Computer ID:* This is the name of the computer account record as it will appear in the Active Directory domain. Note that this name also typically becomes a DNS name on the network, so if you are configuring a client named `wintermute`, the Apple AD plug-in will dynamically request a DNS record be created for `wintermute.krypted.com` if the Active Directory domain is `krypted.com` and points to all the configured IP addresses (including virtual) for that client; the specified value should generally conform to DNS standards regarding A records, as defined in RFC 1035, accessible at `www.ietf.org/rfc/rfc1035.txt`. For best results, the length of this value should be a maximum of 15 characters and should generally follow the letter-digit-hyphen (LDH) rule.

Note   For more information on resource records, see the following TechNet article: `http://technet.microsoft.com/en-us/library/cc783389(WS.10).aspx`.

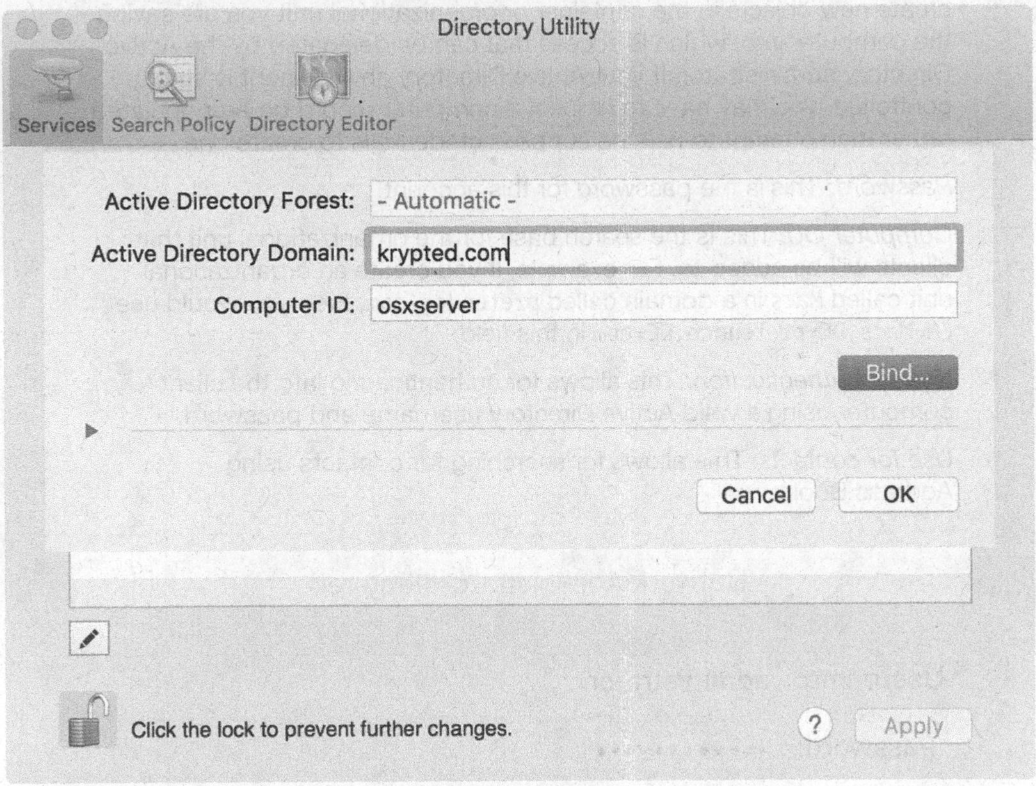

Figure 3-4. Binding to Active Directory using Directory Utility

Tip When naming OS X computers, you will generally want to follow what is referred to as the LDH rule. As defined, the LDH rule calls for the use of only ASCII alphabetic and numeric characters in addition to the hyphen (-); no other punctuation or characters are allowed. Avoid all numeric names, and with any *nix system, avoid starting a host name with a numeric character.

Next click the Bind button, and you will be asked to authenticate to the Active Directory domain using the following fields, as you can see in Figure 3-5:

- *Username*: This is any valid user account that is capable of joining computers to the domain. Additionally, this user must have rights to create new objects in the container or organizational unit you are saving the computer into, which is access that can be delegated by the Active Directory administrator. If your Active Directory environment is strictly controlled, you may have to request a computer record be prepopulated rather than attempt to use the supplied credentials to create one.

- *Password:* This is the password for this account.

- *Computer OU:* This is the search base for the organizational unit that clients will be added to. For example, if you create an organizational unit called Macs in a domain called pretendco.com, then you would use CN=Macs,DC=pretendco,DC=com in this field.

- *Use for authentication:* This allows for authenticating into the client computer using a valid Active Directory username and password.

- *Use for contacts*: This allows for searching for contacts using Address Book.

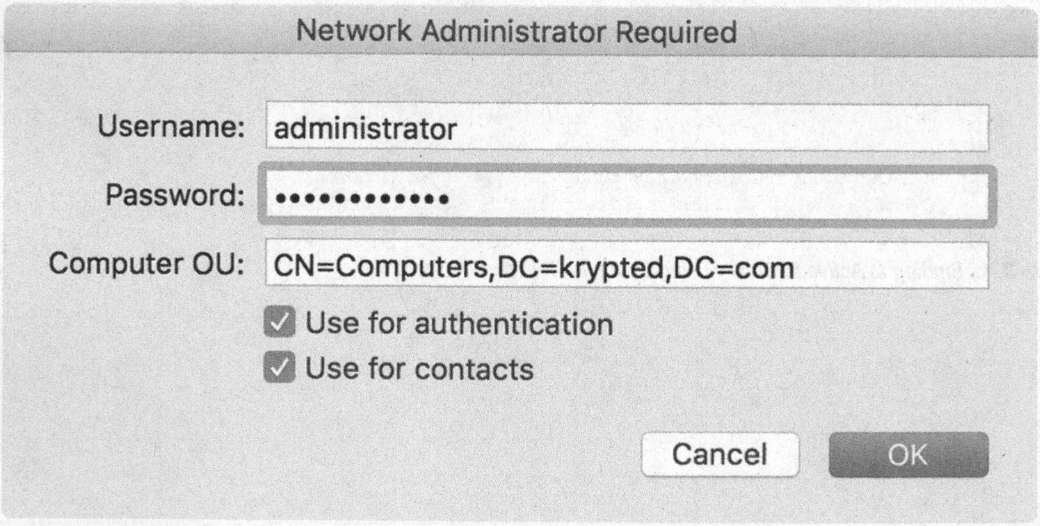

Figure 3-5. Authenticate to the Active Directory domain

The most common binding problem with Active Directory environments is that the Active Directory domain's DNS service has an incomplete set of service records. If we had a nickel for every time a Windows admin swore up and down there were no problems on their servers, only to have all problems resolved by a quick and dirty fix...! An `ipconfig /rebuildddns` command runs from a domain controller hosting the Active Directory–integrated DNS by rebuilding the required service records. Beyond DNS, a number of binding issues are caused between incompatible policies between OS X and Active Directory. For example, LDAP signing as a requirement was not supported in version 10.4.

> **Note**   As described in Chapter 1, you can use the directory services debug log and potentially `tcpdump` (which can be used to monitor port 389 to review traffic to and from your Active Directory domain controllers) to more granularly isolate binding issues.

When using the bind screen from the Accounts preferences pane, you were not prompted for the organizational unit to place the computer record in if you wanted to allow login or contact lookups. The computer record is automatically generated based on the host name of the computer you are using to bind, and the authentication and contact lookups are assumed to be used. If you have not prepopulated the computer record, your computer account will be placed in the default container, `Computers`. To continue with the previous `pretendco.com` example, organizational units are these containers, which are accessed using a convention, whereas the container is a CN followed by a DC for each part of a fully qualified domain name. Therefore, if you were to enter the `Computers` container of `mydomain.com` instead of `pretendco.com` from the previous example, you would use `cn=Computers,dc=domain,dc=com`.

Testing Your Connection

Once you have successfully bound your computer to Active Directory, you should test the connection. First, verify that the light is green beside the Active Directory service in System Preferences. A green light here is typically a pretty good indicator that everything is fine, but it's never a bad idea to test further. The most straightforward test would simply be to attempt to log in as a directory user, but logging out and then back in is not efficient, especially if there are problems resulting in login window delays. More efficiently, you can verify binding from the command line (and should test it either way). As previously referenced, an integral part of logging in on Mac OS X is a user account's `UniqueID` attribute. You can verify that user resolution is happening and view the `UniqueID` attribute using the `id` command. To do so from a command-line environment, enter the `id` command followed by the username of a directory account.

```
id administrator
uid=1763670396(administrator) gid=703907591(KRYPTED\domain users) groups=703907591↵
(KRYPTED\domain users),1842785604(KRYPTED\administrators)
```

The id command can indirectly display a local conflict. The Active Directory plug-in generates UniqueIDs, and with AD, typically these numbers have ten digits. In contrast, a standard local account, such as one that was configured using the Account preferences pane and the Setup Assistant at first boot, has an ID starting at 501, incrementing upward. Open Directory users start at 1025. This makes it possible at first glance to determine the approximate origin of an account. For example, if you saw a unique ID in the range of 600 to 1000, then you know the account was likely initially created using the Users & Groups pane in System Preferences.

If the id command fails with id: jdoe: no such user, check the account you are using for testing to see whether it exists and check that your computer is set to correctly try to search for users in Active Directory. Typically, this search path is filled in automatically for you by the Directory Utility application at the time of binding. However, if you are manually configuring or attempting to troubleshoot an automated binding, you can verify this configuration in Directory Utility. Open Directory Utility, choose Show Advanced Settings from the Windows toolbar, select Search Policy, and verify the /Active Directory/... line item is displayed. Contrary to popular belief, the order listed is not typically relevant for user and group resolution. As you will see, the local directory is always accessed first. Then typically it should be the next network directory that contains users. If you are having problems that are resolved by moving /Active Directory up in the search order, you may have a configuration problem in your other directory servers or a conflict in the namespace that users occupy.

While id is probably the easiest, the best utility for testing your directory services is dscl. The utility provides an interface for programmatically interacting with the DirectoryService application programming interfaces (APIs). This program can be run via an interactive shell or from within scripts. After first binding to Active Directory, use dscl to test that the directory is available and that user resolution (the ability to resolve user accounts) is working. While you could just log out and log back in depending on any problems encountered, you can more easily see that binding is working from the command line. From a shell prompt, use the dscl command followed by the computer or path to connect to. To establish a connection to the currently running DirectoryService daemon, we'll use localhost.

```
dscl localhost
```

The syntax for moving through the configured directory services is much like navigating a file system or FTP server from the command line. Once you have initiated your session, it will show an interactive prompt (>). Use the ls command to list the DirectoryService plug-ins. If you do not see Active Directory listed, the plug-in itself is not enabled. Even if you are bound to an Active Directory domain, you will not be able to navigate to the directory node until this plug-in is enabled (by default only the LDAPv3 and local plug-ins are enabled), although when you use Directory Utility to bind systems, the Active Directory plug-in is enabled by default.

The ls command will show you the currently enabled plug-ins (including third-party ones) in the list. In addition, you will be able to navigate into the Contacts and Search paths, which will show you the hierarchy of all configured and enabled plug-ins. You can then type cd followed by the name of any item in the list of current plug-ins.

```
Active Directory
LDAPv3
Local
Contact
Search
```

In this case, type `cd 'Active Directory'`.

> **Note**   Standard command-line conventions apply here in regard to space. Be sure to use quotes around the path when using `dscl` because Active Directory is one of the few plug-ins that has a space in the name. Alternatively, you can use the built-in Tab autocompletion to automatically quote this path for you.

Once you have changed directories into the Active Directory node, you will see the Active Directory domains and forests that were previously configured at bind time in the appropriate nesting order. The Apple Active Directory plug-in allows you to configure only one Active Directory forest at a time, and the default behavior is to allow authentication from all domains within a forest on the local machine. This is an important note because it means that depending on your organization's directory topology, you may not be able to see the users if you are in a separate forest. If you would like to restrict access to this computer (or server) to only one domain, you will need to uncheck the "Allow authentication from any domain in the forest" button in Directory Utility or run the command `dsconfigad –all domains disable`, depending on your configuration. You will see one of three things.

- All domains on Mac OS X 10.6.8 systems and earlier (e.g., `/Active Directory/All Domains`)

- Your NetBIOS domain name (KRYPTED in this case) on OS X 10.7 systems and higher when listing this value in `dscl` (e.g., `/Active Directory/ KRYPTED/All Domains`)

- Your NetBIOS domain name followed by your Active Directory domain name if you have disabled "Allow authentication from any domain in the forest" in the Active Directory plug-in in Directory Utility (e.g., `/Active Directory/KRYPTED/krypted.com`)

```
/Active Directory > ls
KRYPTED
/Active Directory > cd KRYPTED
/Active Directory/KRYPTED > ls
All Domains
```

To test that your binding worked correctly, you can change directories into the respective value and do an `ls`. If you receive an error when changing directories, your Active Directory binding has most likely failed or the current DirectoryService daemon has lost contact with your site's domain controller.

```
/Active Directory > cd KRYPTED
/Active Directory/KRYPTED > cd 'All Domains'
/Active Directory/KRYPTED/All Domains > ls
CertificateAuthorities
ComputerLists
Computers
Config
FileMakerServers
Groups
Maps
Mounts
OrganizationalUnit
People
Places
Printers
Resources
Users
```

A common procedure used to verify connectivity is to use the `dscl` command along with the read verb to view the attributes associated with a given account. This will allow you to verify that user lookup is working within the Active Directory plug-in itself and look for any potential issues, such as a missing attribute. While you could use `ls Users`, depending on the size of your organization, you may not receive all the information you are looking for. By default, the LDAP server in Active Directory will return a maximum of 1,000 results. Although many more can be enumerated, this is just a default setting for how many are shown at once. Therefore, here you will simply `cd` into the appropriate directory and then use read to view the attributes for a known good user account.

```
/Active Directory/KRYPTED/All Domains > cd Users
/Active Directory/KRYPTED/All Domains/Users > read cedge

dsAttrTypeNative:accountExpires: 456878228655687
dsAttrTypeNative:ADDomain: krypted.com
dsAttrTypeNative:badPasswordTime: 0
dsAttrTypeNative:badPwdCount: 0
dsAttrTypeNative:cn:
Charles Edge
dsAttrTypeNative:codePage: 0
dsAttrTypeNative:countryCode: 0
dsAttrTypeNative:displayName:
Charles Edge
dsAttrTypeNative:distinguishedName:
CN=Charles Edge,CN=Users,DC=krypted,DC=com
continued...
```

> **Caution**   The LDAP server in Active Directory by default will return a maximum of 1,000 results. This default setting affects user, group, computer, and computer group listings in both `dscl` and Workgroup Manager and therefore may negatively affect any scripting automations derived from this information. This is a hard limit in Windows 2000 but can be adjusted in later versions, as instructed in the Microsoft knowledge base article at `http://support.microsoft.com/kb/315071`.

One thing to keep in mind is that while using `dscl` to view data from the Active Directory plug-in directly (by changing directories into it), you can verify that you have a connection to your organization's directory services. However, simply being able to view the raw directory service data does not in fact mean that you can authenticate against it. As with `dsconfigldap` in Chapter 2, the final step is to use the information gathered about your test user and verify that your user matches in the /Search path as well.

```
/Active Directory/All Domains/Users > read /Search/Users/cedge

dsAttrTypeNative:accountExpires: 456873337655687
dsAttrTypeNative:ADDomain: krypted.com
dsAttrTypeNative:badPasswordTime: 0
dsAttrTypeNative:badPwdCount: 0
dsAttrTypeNative:cn:
Charles Edge
dsAttrTypeNative:codePage: 0
dsAttrTypeNative:countryCode: 0
dsAttrTypeNative:displayName:
Charles Edge
dsAttrTypeNative:distinguishedName:
CN=Charles Edge,CN=Users,DC=krypted,DC=com
continued...
```

If the two `read` commands return different results, you have namespace collision, which could be resolved by reprioritizing your search paths (this was covered in much more detail in Chapter 2). In some cases, it may be necessary to simply delete the conflicting user account. You can view the current search path with `dscl` along with a `read` verb, the path, and the attribute to display (in this case, `/Search SearchPath`).

```
/Active Directory > read /Search SearchPath
SearchPath:
/Local/Default
/Active Directory/KRYPTED/All Domains
```

Once you have verified that user result is functional from the DirectoryService daemon, you can verify that authentication is correctly happening (so far you have verified only that user resolution is possible). Type `exit` to end your interactive `dscl` session for localhost.

```
/Active Directory/All Domains/Users > exit
Goodbye
```

Testing Authentication at the Login Window

Once you have tested user resolution with `dscl`, you are ready to begin a login test. While you could have skipped to this step, it's normally best to test that "raw" authentication is working before trying to troubleshoot and isolate any issues encountered at a graphical prompt such as the login window, as shown in Figure 3-6.

Figure 3-6. Login window

Log out from the Apple menu and log in as your test Active Directory user account, keeping in mind that many other factors will affect this type of login compared to the command-line tests you previously performed. If all steps taken previously with `id` and `dscl` succeed without issue but you still cannot log in, then you likely have a home-directory problem.

Home Directories and the Apple Active Directory Plug-in

Home directories can be one of the more complicated aspects of integrating OS X with Active Directory. But they don't have to be. The Active Directory plug-in supplied by Apple by default creates a local home directory in the `/Users/` directory. If you do not want to synchronize data to another location using mobile homes or do want to leverage network-based home directories, then your work is made easier, and you are basically done. However, depending on your required configuration, you might have many tasks remaining. For example, a common procedure on Microsoft Windows is to redirect folders to network share points. The most common folder to be redirected is My Documents. Redirection of My Documents via a Group Policy object is not applicable to OS X, and so the fun begins.

To configure the location of a home directory for a Mac, use Directory Utility from /Applications/Utilities (10.5) or /System/Library/CoreServices (10.6 through 10.9) or /System/Library/CoreServices/Applications (10.10 and higher). Next, click Services in the Directory Utility toolbar. If you are not already operating with elevated privileges, then you will be prompted for the credentials of an account with access to add data to Active Directory. Go ahead and type that in, double-click the Active Directory plug-in, and then click the disclosure triangle to show the advanced options, as shown in Figure 3-7. Here, you will see a number of options to control the User Experience, Mappings, and Administrative options. The home directory options are stored in the User Experience tab.

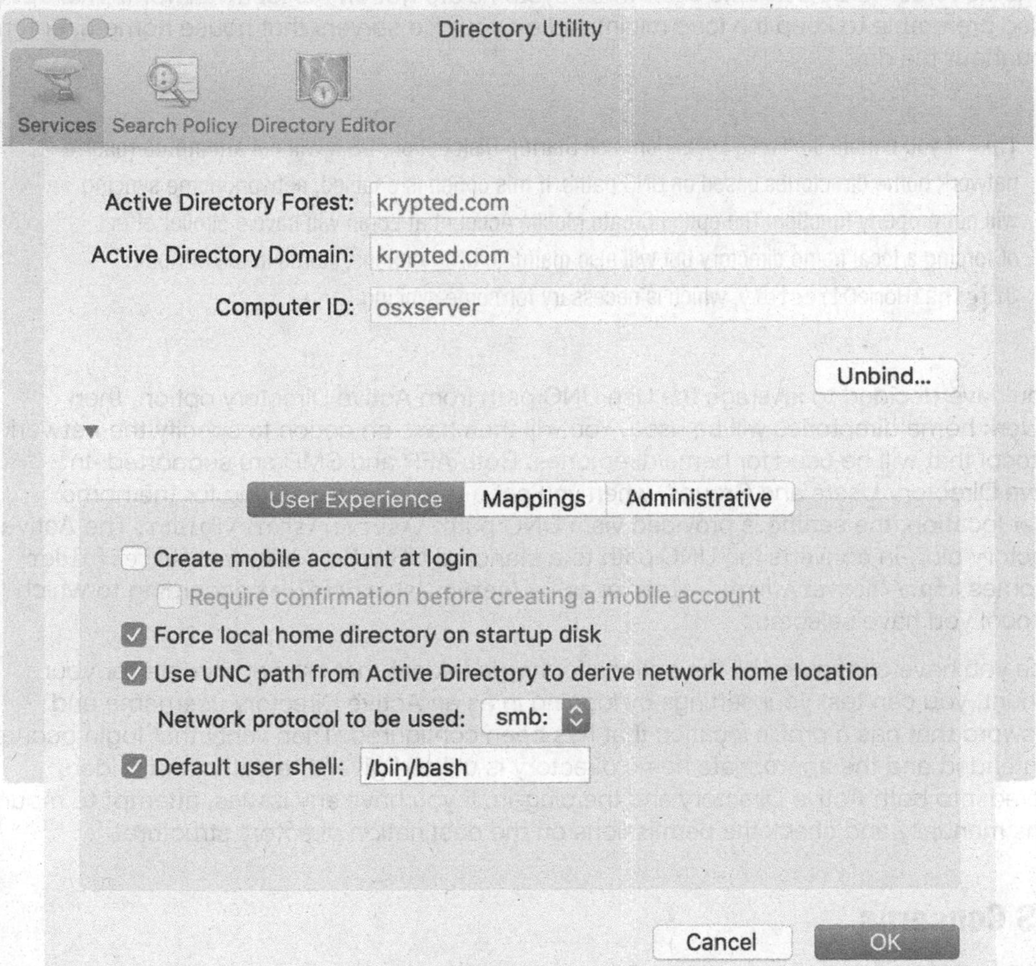

Figure 3-7. *User environment with Active Directory*

The first option is to create mobile account at login. By checking this box, you will cache an account locally, allowing login from the login window even when a system is not on your network. When a user logs in using an Active Directory account, they will now be prompted for whether the account will be a mobile account. Unchecking the box "Require confirmation before creating a mobile account" will then suppress the dialog box and simply create the account automatically.

Next, choose whether to use the UNC path from Active Directory to derive the network home location (which is a check box to enable home folders that reside on a network path). Combined with mobile accounts and OS X's home folder syncing, this option allows data in the home folder to be available even when systems are not on the local network. This option is also preferable to keep the load minimized on your file servers that house home directories throughout the day.

> **Tip**   If you enable the Force Local Home on Startup Disk option, OS X will not attempt to resolve network home directories based on UNC paths. If this option is enabled, network home syncing will not properly function. The option Create Mobile Account at Login will have a similar effect of forcing a local home directory but will also maintain UNC lookups, stored in the attribute `OriginalHomeDirectory`, which is necessary for home syncing.

If you have decided to leverage the Use UNC path from Active Directory option, then network home directories will be used. You will then have an option to specify the network protocol that will be used for home directories. Both AFP and SMB are supported. In Active Directory Users and Groups, when you set a user's profile setting for the home folder location, the setting is provided via a UNC path: `\\server\share\folder`. The Active Directory plug-in converts the UNC path to a standard URL. So, `\\server\share\folder` becomes `afp://server/share/folder` or `smb://server/share/folder` according to which protocol you have selected.

Once you have configured all the options for home folders that are appropriate for your account, you can test your settings by logging in as an Active Directory username and password that has a profile location that has been configured. Then verify that login occurs as intended and the appropriate home directory is utilized given the paths and folders entered into both Active Directory and the plug-in. If you have any issues, attempt to mount paths manually and check the permissions on the destination directory structure.

DNS Concerns

Active Directory uses sites to assign domain controllers to specific subnets on your network. The Apple Active Directory plug-in uses DNS to look up a global catalog server for your domain and subsequently queries it to find the correct domain controller to bind to. You can manually view these DNS records, which use the SRV or "service" type to hold their information within an Active Directory–integrated DNS network.

Open Terminal in /Applications/Utility, and enter the following command to do a lookup on the service record to locate the global catalog:

```
dig -t SRV _gc._tcp.krypted.com

; <<>> DiG 9.8.3-P1 <<>> -t SRV _gc._tcp.krypted.com
;; global options: +cmd
;; Got answer:
;; ->>HEADER<<- opcode: QUERY, status: NOERROR, id: 50668
;; flags: qr aa rd ra; QUERY: 1, ANSWER: 1, AUTHORITY: 0, ADDITIONAL: 1

;; QUESTION SECTION:
;_gc._tcp.krypted.com.          IN         SRV

;; ANSWER SECTION:
_gc._tcp.krypted.com. 600      IN         SRV    0 100 3268 server2012.krypted.com.

;; ADDITIONAL SECTION:
server2012.krypted.com.    3600   IN      A      192.168.0.250

;; Query time: 59 msec
;; SERVER: 192.168.53.249#53(192.168.53.249)
;; WHEN: Sat Oct 17 10:51:56 2015
;; MSG SIZE rcvd: 93
```

The answer to the question is in the answer section. Here, it is shown as server2012. krypted.com. If you do not receive the name of a domain controller, you will want to check that you are using the correct DNS servers for your site. A common error is related to using an external DNS server that has been manually configured at some previous time (e.g., 8.8.4.4). This forces your lookup to use your organization's external DNS provider, which may not match your internal DNS server, especially if you use an internal domain like .local.

Binding Local and Domain Administrators to AD

You will need two administrative usernames to bind to Active Directory: a local administrator and a domain administrator. The local administrator is used to write the configuration files to protected directories such as /Library/Preferences/OpenDirectory/Configurations/Active Directory. This administrator can be replaced with the root user when running scripts to bind to Active Directory (e.g., an Apple installer package that runs a post-flight script as root to bind to Active Directory).

In addition to the local administrative credentials, you will need a domain administrator. This delegate administrator needs to have access to join computers to the domain and also write access to the organizational unit that you specify if you are using the Services binding section of Directory Utility or the -ou option of dsconfigad. This domain administrator should be created with a small number of privileges other than domain addition, as you may need to give this username and password to your onsite IT liaisons and embed it in scripts.

The following is an example of using the `dsconfigad` command. As you can see, we are specifying the domain administrator's password right on the line, and this would result in the password potentially being available in the shell's history depending on how we run the command. You do not need to run `sudo` when running `dsconfigad` because it will effectively do the privilege request on its own and prompt for the password of the current user to escalate the privileges for the operation. Later, we will discuss using this command in a script.

```
dsconfigad -f -a mycomputername -u domainadmin -p domainadminspassword -domain mydomain.com
```

Additionally, you can set the Active Directory plug-in settings one at a time using `dsconfigad`; these options can also be set on the `joining` command. Keep in mind this ability to granularly set all plug-in options on the fly; it means you will be able to push out a change whether to create a mobile account on login using any tool capable of sending UNIX-style commands or scripts (such as Apple Remote Desktop). Like the previous command, `sudo` is never required because the `dsconfigad` command will determine admin rights on its own, though when calling the utility from a noninteractive tool, such as ARD, you will want to execute the commands with root privileges.

```
dsconfigad -mobile enable
```

One aspect common to many Active Directory deployments in imaging environments is the automation of binding. This is done because a bound system cannot be directly built into a "gold master" image because the computer ID of each imaged host will be different. For instance, if you were to bind to Active Directory within a system that was to be cloned, the Active Directory preferences would be pushed out to all machines cloned from that image. These preferences contain the machine account name and password used for authenticating the joined computer to the Active Directory domain. While this configuration initially would allow authentication in most environments, once the computer password was cycled or once the machines were unbound, then all cloned systems would stop being able to authenticate. For this reason, joining or "binding" to the directory is then performed as a post-flight operation on the cloned systems after the first reboot. Imaging tools such as Deploy Studio and Casper Suite include built-in scripts with graphical wrappers for accomplishing this purpose.

Naming Conventions and Scripting Automated Binding

One of the single most important decisions that you will make when determining the feasibility of a binding script will be your naming convention. This is because depending on your asset tag vendor, you may have to work within a specified convention that does not correspond to anything that can be queried automatically on a fresh machine. If your asset tags were consecutive numerical values or a sequence of alphanumeric values set by the manufacturer, then you will have to match that value to a specified piece of hardware manually. Getting user input for specifics, such as asset tags, will mean that, at least for your first boot, a live human being will have to be present at the time of binding to enter in this value. Most third-party imaging tools have the ability to show a dialog box that allows the imager to enter this information and have it pass to the script as a parameter. Two examples of this follow; one is Deploy Studio's workflow step, and the other is Casper

Suite's positional parameter configuration option. If you are using either one of these tools, it is suggested you consider using this functionality. However, if you are using another deployment methodology, you may need to either have your script prompt the user for information or provide this information via a prepopulated datastore, such as a CSV file.

If you are ordering a large quantity of OS X workstations from Apple directly, consider asking your rep to provide you with a delimited list of Machine Access Control (MAC) addresses. Using this list, you can pre-assign hardware addresses to your organization's asset tag system or database. However, if you are dealing with existing inventory, you may still be required to prompt your imaging team for this information or at least collate it beforehand. If you are relegated to prompting your imaging team for this information, a good technique is to store this custom name within a machine's firmware. Mac OS X provides a way of manipulating firmware variables using the /usr/sbin/nvram command. However, nvram cannot be assumed to be persistent, so it is best to maintain this data in a spreadsheet or database.

As shown earlier, the Terminal application (found at /Applications/Utilities) can be leveraged to create a simple binding script using dsconfigad. This allows you to bind to Active Directory and adds the directory to the currently configured /Search or /Contact path.

When specifying multiple advanced options, you can specify each with their own invocation of dsconfigad, or you can supply them altogether via a single command. When specifying multiple options, the command can become a bit unruly, but the same result is achieved. Each option from the GUI translates to an option (or flag, if you will) at the command-line interface. A number of other options are available, but each is likely not to be required for all cases.

These are the basic options, which are commonly used:

- -add computerid: This is the name of the computer to add to the domain (if none is specified, then the default will be the host name).

- -force: This forces the process (i.e., removes the existing entry from the Active Directory plug-in).

- -remove: This removes the computer from the domain (unbinds it).

- -localuser: This is the username of an administrative local account.

- -localpassword: This is the password of the administrative local account defined with -localuser.

- -username: This is the username of an Active Directory administrator.

- -password: This is the password of the Active Directory administrator specified with -u.

- -ou dn: This is the fully qualified LDAP distinguished name (DN) of the container for the computer (defaults to CN=Computers,DC=domain,DC=com).

- -show: This shows the current configuration for Active Directory (this option doesn't make any modifications to the directory or the Active Directory plug-in).

These are the advanced options for the user experience:

- -mobile: This enables or disables mobile user accounts for offline use.

- -mobileconfirm: This enables or disables a warning for mobile account creation.

- -localhome: This enables or disables forcing a home directory to a local drive.

- -useuncpath: This enables or disables using Windows UNC for the network home.

- -protocol: This specifies afp or smb to change the protocol used when mounting the home.

- -shell: You can specify none for no shell or specify a default shell of /bin/bash.

These are the advanced options for mappings:

- -uid: This is the name of the attribute to be used for the UNIX uid field.

- -nouid: This generates the UID from the Active Directory GUID.

- -gid: This is the name of the attribute to be used for the UNIX gid field.

- -nogid: This generates the GID from the Active Directory information.

- -ggid: This is the name of the attribute to be used for the UNIX group gid field.

- -noggid: This generates the group GID from the Active Directory GUID.

These are the advanced options for administration:

- -preferred: This is the fully qualified domain name of the preferred domain controller.

- -nopreferred: You can specify to not use a preferred server for queries.

- -groups "1,2,...": This shows a list of groups that are granted administrative privileges on the local workstation.

- -nogroups: This disables the use of groups that were specified in-groups for granting administrative privileges.

- -alldomains: You can set this to enable or disable to allow or disallow authentication from any domain in the forest.

- -packetsign: You can set this to disable, allow, or require to enable packet signing.

- -packetencrypt: You can set this to disable, allow, or require to enable packet encryption.

- -namespace: You can set this to forest or domain, where forest qualifies all usernames.

- -passinterval: Here you can specify how often to change the computer trust account password, in days.

If your environment requires customization of the Active Directory binding screens, you can use the previous options to granularly configure the options you would otherwise use in the screens in Directory Utility. You can also access a few that have not yet been added.

Map UID and GID

As previously mentioned, OS X requires certain attributes to be able to log in, such as the primary group ID and unique ID. As Active Directory does not contain the unique ID by default, this value must be generated on the fly using some other kind of unique information. One important attribute of this generation is that it cannot be completely random; it is important that every system bound to Active Directory resolves the same unique ID for any respective user. To accomplish this, Apple uses the first 32 bytes of the user's GUID to generate a numerical value used as a statically mapped value for the OS X unique ID.

As the plug-in can run the same mathematical operation on the GUID on two different machines and receive the same value, it acts as a practical substitute for manually configuring these values in your environment. Windows Server has a schema attribute called unixid, which could be used to store custom values in the directory. If your organization is already using UNIX clients that authenticate to Active Directory, then you may already have this information populated in the directory. Mapping this information on the OS X side is often beneficial only for consistency. However, it can play a vital authorization rule when using the NFS file-sharing protocol, which uses the local system's UID to map privileges on remote server shares mounted on the client's system. If your organization does have these fields populated, it is incredibly important to make sure that these fields are populated automatically when you ingest new users. Windows Server 2008 and newer can do this using ADSI or the Power Shell Active Directory command lets. Quest Software has some examples for manipulating large numbers of Active Directory fields in a programmatic fashion using this "new" language.

By default, UID and GID attributes are not mapped but rather generated when you are using dsconfigad to bind a computer to Active Directory. To map the default fields referenced previously, open Directory Utility from /System/Library/CoreServices/Applications and then click Services in the Directory Utility toolbar. Double-click Active Directory. From here, fill in the basic Active Directory binding information from earlier. Once you have done so, click the disclosure triangle to show the advanced options, and on the resultant screen, click the Mappings tab.

From the Mappings tab, enter the information for the Active Directory attribute to map UID and GID information to.

Namespace Support Using dsconfigad

By default, dsconfigad assumes that your forest name is the same as your domain name, or authentication will succeed only to the domain that was specified when the system was bound. Some environments have multiple domains. Active Directory allows two accounts with the same username (although not the same GUID) to exist with a given forest, provided they are in separate domains. Directory Utility allows you to specify either the forest or a specific domain, allowing you to control the scope in which a client system will authenticate against at bind time. When bound to a forest, the AD plug-in allows you to go a step further, providing the ability to authenticate to separate domains within a forest by adding the domain name to your login credentials.

But you don't want to have to unbind and rebind every time you log into a different domain, if you will be switching between domains often. To provide you with the option to log in using multiple domains within one forest, you can use the -namespace flag followed by domain. The -namespace flag then prefixes the domain name to all accounts that are located in the forest. If you have conflicting accounts in separate domains, then the computer should be bound into the domain with which your account resides. To enable namespace support, you can use the following command:

```
dsconfigad -namespace forest
```

Once run, you will authenticate against the forest and will need to specify the domain name in front of the username every time a user authenticates to the system. If you want to switch back to using domain namespace at a later date, you can specify the -namespace flag with the domain as the setting, and you will no longer have to enter this.

> **Note**   When run, -namespace changes the primary ID for all accounts. Therefore, any user profiles for accounts from the Active Directory domain will need to be copied/moved into the new profile that is created, which will have a different naming convention.

Active Directory Packet Encryption Options

You can configure the Active Directory plug-in to enable the encryption options Apple has developed for communications between the Active Directory plug-in and Active Directory domain controllers. These include packet encryption, packet signing, and a timeout value for setting the computer account password rotation interval with your Active Directory domain controllers. These options are configured either after or during bind time using the dsconfigad command.

A number of Active Directory environments require packet signing to block man-in-the-middle attacks and therefore to verify the authenticity of data being exchanged between the Active Directory plug-in and Active Directory, thus protecting both the domain and the client. From the Active Directory perspective, configuring packet signing requirements is a policy configured from an Active Directory domain controller. Active Directory password policies let you allow or even require packet signing from the client for LDAP traffic (the protocol over which data will be exchanged in this scenario). By default, packet signing is a required option for clients in Windows Server but is not required by client systems.

While not the default setting, it is a good practice. Therefore, many environments require packet signing for Active Directory clients. In OS X, if you want to require packet signing for the client to communicate with the server, then this would further validate that communication is signed (and therefore authentic), so you can set the packet signing setting to require as well for a more highly secure solution. If you require packet signing from either the server side or the client side, then you should verify signing is an allowed option if not required on the other, or you may run into incompatibility issues. To change the packet signing options in Mac OS X, you use the -packetsign flag with dsconfigad. Settings available with -packetsignflag include allow, disable, and require. Therefore, to configure dsconfigad to require packet signing, use the following command:

```
dsconfigad -packetsign require
```

If the change is successful, then you will see the following output:

```
Settings changed successfully
```

Packet encryption is another option in OS X and Active Directory. Packet encryption keeps the contents as secure because they are authentic by forcing data to be encrypted. To enable packet encryption, use the -packetencryption flag with the same settings available with -packetsignflag (allow, disable, and require). As with packet signing, verify that both the server and the client support encryption before setting the option to require, although for high-security environments (or most environments these days), it is a good idea to set the client and the server to require both authentication and signing. To set encryption requirements for the client, use the following command:

```
dsconfigad -packetencrypt require
```

If the change is successful, then you will see the following output:

```
Settings changed successfully
```

Every computer that is bound to Active Directory has a computer account, and that computer account in turn has a password. Active Directory rotates these passwords routinely. The Active Directory plug-in supports the rotation by using the -passinterval flag with dsconfigad. The -passinterval flag can be set and, when set, defines the password rotation intervals, in days.

```
dsconfigad -passinterval 7
```

All the settings in this section can be set or changed during bind time or following bind time and can be independent of any other settings.

Dual Directory

As we've mentioned, you can use Active Directory and Open Directory together. To some, this is called a *magic triangle* and to others a *golden triangle*, but the official terminology at Apple is a *dual directory*. Most descriptions and walkthroughs are made more complicated than they need to be. Basically, you start with a functional Active Directory environment and a functional Open Directory environment and then bind your client machines to both directories, ensuring that both appear in the client's search path. From then on, the client will query each directory sequentially in the order defined by the search path until it receives a successful return.

You may be thinking that it probably isn't as easy as that, and certainly there are additional considerations, but at its heart that is the foundation of a triangle or dual directory configuration. The first such consideration is single sign-on—both Active Directory and Open Directory utilize Kerberos for this functionality. In a dual directory setup, having two separate Kerberos realms can complicate matters, so it is typically desirable to utilize only one Kerberos realm. To integrate your Mac clients into an Active Directory environment, you will want to utilize the Active Directory Kerberos services; thus, it will be desirable to tear down the Open Directory KDC.

> **Tip**   If an OS X server is bound to Active Directory prior to promotion to an Open Directory master, Active Directory Kerberos services will be utilized, and Open Directory–based Kerberos services will not be set up.

For the purposes of this demonstration, we will use `diradmin` as the Open Directory administrative username and `p@ssword` as the password. If you have chosen to use an Open Directory administrative username other than `diradmin`, then simply change the names as needed. Since your password is likely not `p@ssword`, then please transpose that as well.

To destroy the shared Kerberos KDC on the Open Directory master, you will use the `sso_util` command. As of Mac OS X 10.5, this is typically not required, so feel free to skip this step. The `sso_util` option you will use is the `remove` option, which will remove the KDC from the host on which it is run.

```
sudo sso_util remove -k a diradmin -p p@ssword
```

Next, you bind the Open Directory master to Active Directory as you have been binding clients throughout this chapter. Because the directory services plug-ins can coexist with one another (for the most part, some third-party plug-ins cannot coexist with the Active Directory plug-in), you can do so without risking damage to other resources within your LDAP service on the Open Directory master.

Once you have bound your server to Active Directory, will want to enable the single sign-on for all supported services by using the following command, which will create service principals for each respective shared service:

```
dsconfigad -enableSSO
```

Next, open Directory Utility and verify that you can view both your Active Directory and Open Directory domains in the Directory Editor. You can alternate between directories that you are bound to (or hosting) by choosing them from the Node drop-down menu.

Next, bind a client to both Active Directory and Open Directory, using the same process outlined earlier in this chapter in the section "Binding Local and Domain Administrators to AD" and in Chapter 2. Once you have bound to both Active Directory and Open Directory from a client, click the Search Policy tab in Directory Utility to verify that both your Active Directory and Open Directory appear in the Directory Domains list. Also, make sure that Active Directory is listed above the LDAPv3 domain for authentication purposes. It might not be likely that the LDAPv3 domain will contain any users that present a conflict with users in the Active Directory domain. However, keeping your directory domains with Active Directory listed above Open Directory may save you time troubleshooting down the line and help to maintain optimal performance. In most dual-directory environments, Active Directory will contain the bulk of the data and therefore should be the first target for lookups.

Next either log out and log in to the client computer or use `dscl -authonly` to verify that you can authenticate as an Active Directory user. Then, use `dscl` to browse both the Open Directory environment and the Active Directory environment to ensure that both directories are returning data. If you can, your client is now successfully configured for use in your dual-directory environment.

Nesting

For many tasks, such as POSIX and ACL-based file system permissions, you can directly utilize Active Directory groups, and OS X clients will properly recognize this resolution. However, other functionality, most notably legacy MCX management, requires special attributes provided by Open Directory and will not function when applied to Active Directory groups. To take advantage of Open Directory functionality, you will need to create Open Directory groups and apply the settings to these groups.

At first glance, this creates a bit of a management problem, as now you must maintain user membership for both Active Directory and Open Directory groups. Luckily, this problem is largely solved through support of nested groups or, more specifically, cross-directory network groups. That is, you can actually nest an Active Directory group inside an Open Directory group and OS X clients will properly resolve the relation. This capability becomes pretty invaluable because once you set up the initial OD group and AD membership, from then on membership of the Open Directory group will be determined by that of the AD group. Administrators simply need to adjust user membership in Active Directory, and those changes will trickle down to the Mac side of the tree.

Nesting groups is a pretty simple endeavor. In this section, you will create a group called Support Users in Open Directory and nest an Active Directory group used for support users in the Support Users group.

To get started, open Workgroup Manager, which you install in Chapter 7, on the Open Directory master (or use Workgroup Manager on an administrative computer to connect to the address of the Open Directory master). Next, click the globe in the Directory Services bar and select `/LDAPv3/127.0.0.1`, which will display the contents of Open Directory. Click the Groups tab just below the bar and then click the New Group icon in the toolbar. Enter the name for the group. Because of the complexity of dealing with multiple like-named groups across multiple directories, it is recommended that you provide a designation for the directory under which the group resides. Thus, when creating an OD mirror group for the AD group Support Users, you may want to name the correlating Open Directory group Support Users OD to easily discern between the two. As you assign a full name, a short name will automatically be generated, although you can customize this as desired. As with the full name, a directory-specific identifier can prove helpful. Thus, we'll name the group od_supportusers. When you are satisfied with the group name, click the Save button.

Now click the Members tab for the group and then click the plus sign icon just to the right of the group list. This will bring out a sliding menu with the Open Directory users of your organization. Click the globe icon at the top of the menu and select the Active Directory domain; then click the Groups tab directly below it. Drag the desired group from the sliding menu to the list of members. When you are satisfied with your entry, click the Save button.

At this point, you will be able to build permissions to files and folders and generate policies for the Open Directory user groups, which have the same effective membership as the nested Active Directory group. You can nest multiple Active Directory–based users or groups in Open Directory groups in this manner to achieve a variety of results.

MCX via Dual Directory

If you have chosen to deploy a dual-directory environment, chances are you have done so to provide legacy policy management for your OS X clients and have chosen for whatever reason to not extend the primary directory's schema for such support. The primary benefit of deploying a dual-directory environment is that it allows you to utilize the schema of one directory to supplement the other, through the use of nested group resolution, providing capabilities that otherwise would not be possible. Actual management of these policies is the same in a dual-directory environment as it is in an Open Directory native environment— the majority of the work to generate policies is done in Workgroup Manager.

Managing the Dock is one of the easiest settings to manage. It is also one of the easiest to demonstrate while being fairly unobtrusive to any users who it is applied to, in the event that issues arise from the managed preference and troubleshooting must occur. To manage the Dock, open Workgroup Manager, connecting to your Open Directory master. Next, switch to the appropriate directory service (likely Open Directory) using the disclosure triangle in the directory service domain selection bar and clicking /LDAPv3/127.0.0.1 when you are complete.

To create a group, click the lock icon to authenticate into the appropriate directory domain. Once you're authenticated, click the group lists icon in the left part of the screen and then click the icon in the toolbar for New Group. Next enter a name for the group. The group name will be Dock Test with a short name of testdock; then click the Save button to create the test group for managed Docks.

Next add the Active Directory user into an Open Directory group from Workgroup Manager. Start by clicking the Members tab for the group in Workgroup Manager and then click the plus sign (+), which opens a listing of users. In the list of users, click the disclosure triangle for Directory, selecting the Active Directory domain. Then, drag the user you will be enforcing into the new group whose Dock will be managed and save the settings, as shown in Figure 3-8.

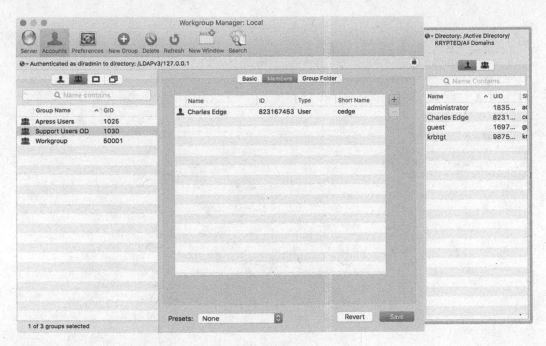

Figure 3-8. *Nesting groups with a dual-directory environment*

Once the users are created, it's time to set up the managed preference, similar to what you did in earlier sections. To get started, click the Preferences button in the Workgroup Manager toolbar. At Preferences, click Dock underneath the Overview tab and then click the Dock Display tab, using the Always radio button. Click the Right radio button and then click Apply Now to commit those managed preferences. Then move the Dock to the right side of the screen, as you can see in Figure 3-9, a setting that is inherited by objects that are members of the group.

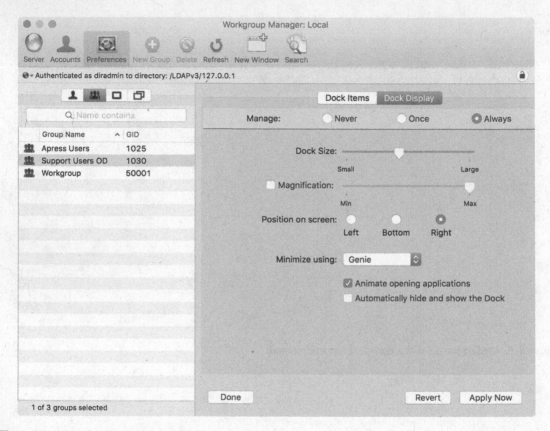

Figure 3-9. Managing the Dock in a dual directory

Finally, log in as the user with managed preferences configured, and you should see the Dock displayed on the correct side of the screen (or whichever preference you decided to set if it wasn't the Dock locale).

In an AD/OD dual-directory environment, there are some notable limitations that you should be aware of. First, without extending the Active Directory schema, OS X cannot directly utilize an Active Directory computer record for policy management. In a managed computer environment, OS X clients associate to a specific computer record via the built-in Ethernet interface's MAC address, designated by OS X as interface en0. As Active Directory computer records do not contain this information, OS X clients will not properly associate to their respective computer record when it is nested in an Open Directory computer group. To apply computer group–based management, you must create a computer record in Open Directory with the respective MAC address. This process is most easily accomplished by performing a trusted bind of your OS X clients to Open Directory, which will create the associated computer record. If you are already scripting your Directory Service binding, a trusted bind is a fairly trivial modification. Alternatively, you can prepopulate the Open Directory computer records, provided that you have documented the MAC address and computer name for your OS X nodes in the field.

MCX via Active Directory

If you can extend your Active Directory and you need to use managed preferences, then you should do so. If you can't, then you would use configuration profiles through a management system such as Profile Manager or Casper Suite, a dual directory, or a third-party solution. If you extend your schema, then you will be able to use Workgroup Manager to configure the managed preferences that you require. First, open Workgroup Manager and connect to Active Directory. You can run Workgroup Manager from any Mac client that has previously been bound to Active Directory. In this case, you will connect to 127.0.0.1 initially and then click the /Active Directory/All Domains entry in the list of available directory services (the section with the globe and the disclosure triangle), clicking the lock icon to authenticate as an administrator of your Active Directory domain when you are prompted to do so.

Directory Utility allows you to view raw attribute data no matter the directory service that you are using. For the purposes of this example, you will open Directory Utility so you can check that the managed preference has been applied and how the data appears once the record has been updated. From Directory Utility, click the Directory Editor button in the toolbar.

Click "in node" and then select your Active Directory domain. You'll then see a list of users and groups. Click one and notice all of the attributes listed. Whether or not your domain has been extended, you can now click the MCXSettings attribute to see what managed preferences are applied to the account, as shown in Figure 3-10 (assuming your Active Directory schema has been extended).

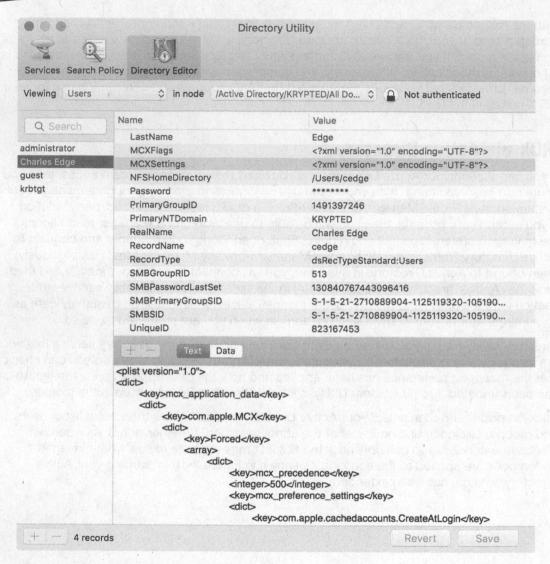

Figure 3-10. Managed preferences for Active Directory

Go back to Workgroup Manager and select the Active Directory group. Then use the Dock managed preferences as you did previously in this chapter, click Dock, and then click Always, finally removing a couple of applications from the included list for testing purposes. Then click the Dock Display tab and set the Always option by checking the Always box. Finally, highlight the radio button for Right, as shown in Figure 3-11.

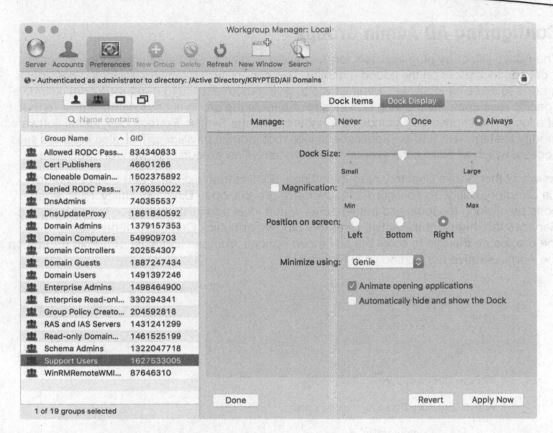

Figure 3-11. Managing the Dock for Active Directory users

When you're satisfied with your changes, click the Apply button. If you do not get any errors, you can then authenticate to a client, and the Dock should appear with the items that were defined in the list and to the right of the computer, which indicates that the managed preferences manifest has been applied as intended. If you get any errors, review the items included in your schema extension from ADAM (or the ldif file used with ldifde). MCXFlags and MCXSettings (which is an array) are the most important items to check to make sure the Mac OS X managed preferences framework is going to be functioning as intended. Items that are not being configured properly can create errors in Workgroup Manager. If the MCXFlags and MCXSettings are present on the system, you can copy their entire contents into a separate document, pasting them into mapped fields from within Active Directory.

> **Note**   When using an extended schema, similar limitations apply to computer-group and computer-based management. It is necessary that computer records have a populated MAC address field so that they properly recognize applied management settings.

Configuring AD Admin Groups

The Active Directory plug-in allows for the designation of Active Directory groups to act as local administrators on the bound machine. This capability is handy for assigning help-desk groups to serve as local Mac administrators, giving them access to numerous administrative-specific resources. This setting provides members of the group access rights similar to that of a local admin user. This includes the rights to change System Preferences, install software, modify system files, and run applications with root (admin) privileges. This also includes sudo access, which allows for the execution of command-line executables with root access.

As with other Active Directory plug-in settings, administrative groups can be configured via Directory Utility. To configure administrative groups, open Directory Utility. First, enable edits by clicking the lock, and authenticate with a local administrative user. Next, using the Services tab, highlight the Active Directory plug-in, and click Configure. If necessary, click the disclosure triangle to show the advanced options. You can find a list of admin groups on the Administrative tab, as shown in Figure 3-12.

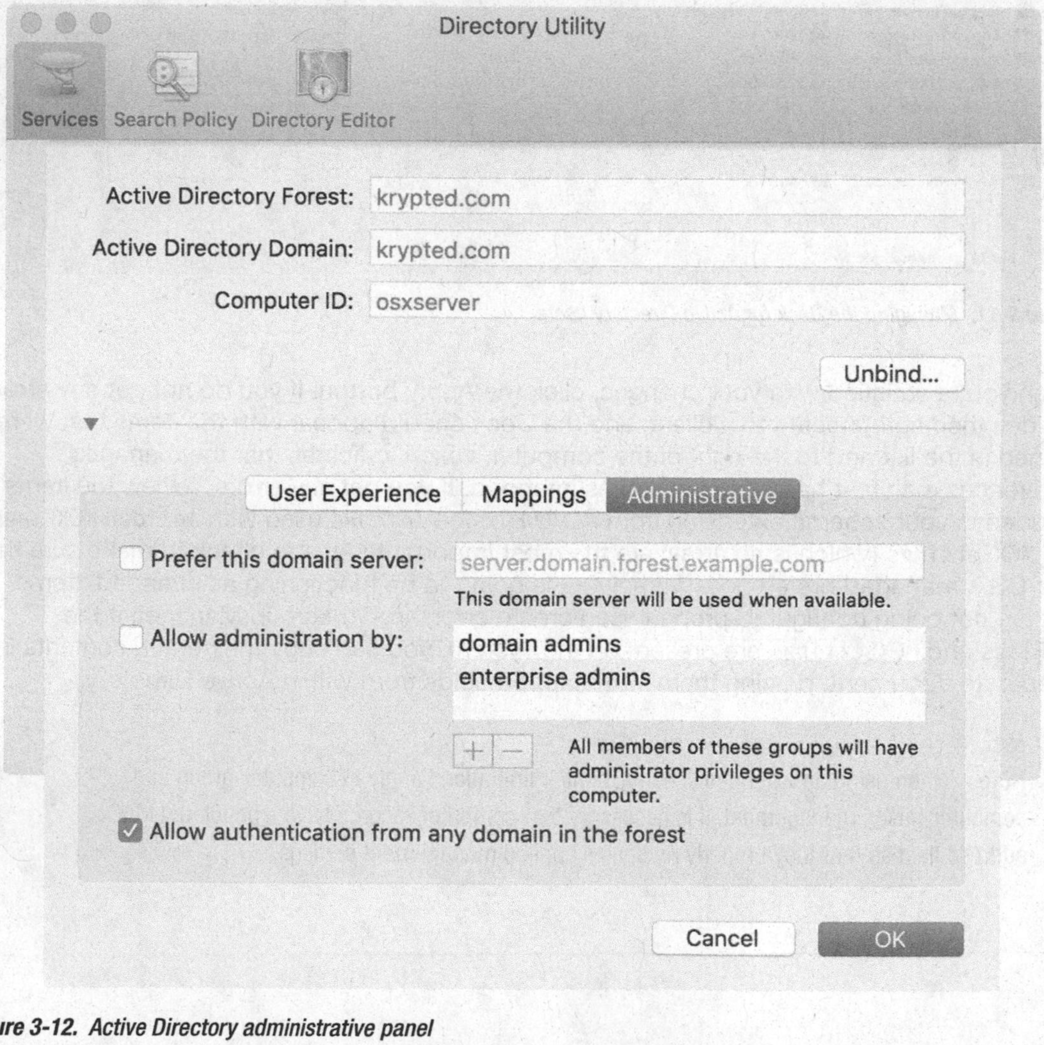

Figure 3-12. Active Directory administrative panel

To assign an administrative group, check the box Allow Administration By and specify the name of the group that contains the desired administrative users. In this case, we have created a special Active Directory group called Mac Desktop Admins, which contains a nested group of our help-desk team.

Nesting Administrators in the Local Admin Group

Many organizations provide centralized management in a decentralized environment. If you do not want to provide your support personnel access to local service accounts and you want to specify people in your organization that can administer local systems, then you can give local administrators elevated privileges by nesting those users into administrative groups. You can also accomplish this directly using the Active Directory plug-in at bind time.

To do so with nesting, though, use the dseditgroup command to nest a network group inside the local administrator group, which you can do using Workgroup Manager. However, we're going to look at doing so programmatically to ease mass deployment, especially when you are not using the stock Active Directory plug-in. To do so, use the dseditgroup command to resolve group membership.

```
dseditgroup -o read <active directory group name>
```

The -o option followed by read means to do a read operation on the specified group. If you were to run the following command, then you would read the mac_admins group:

```
dseditgroup -o read mac_admins
```

The output of the preceding read command would then give you the following output:

```
...
dsAttrTypeStandard:GroupMembership -
        KRYPTED\cedge
        KRYPTED\wsmith
...
```

The GroupMembership section lists the group members. If you do not get any output, then you should verify that there are actually members in the group by checking the domain or using the id command. Then verify that OS X can resolve group memberships with id as well. You can also use the id command to see what groups a user is in. For example, to look up the groups that an account is a member of, you could use a command similar to the following:

```
id cedge
```

Group memberships will then be output, along with the uid and gid:

```
uid=5678903(cedge) gid=45678(318\domain users) groups=45678 (KRYPTED\domain users)
```

To nest the Active Directory group, you can use `dseditgroup` with the `-o` option again, but this time leveraging the `edit` verb and using the `-a` option to indicate a group manage; use the `-t` option for the type of the group with the `-n` option indicating the location. The following code is an example:

```
sudo dseditgroup -o edit -a mac_admins -t group -n /Local/Default admin
```

You can also add a network user to the admin group by using the same command but changing the type.

```
sudo dseditgroup -o edit -a <network username> -t user -n /Local/Default admin
```

If you combine this with mobile (cached) accounts, you can provide administrative rights to local machines but then require password policies managed using server-side preferences from Active Directory. To verify the nested user has localized elevated privileges, test a local process that requires local administrative access.

> **Note**   You can also use Workgroup Manager running on a local workstation to nest groups in this same fashion.

Third-Party Solutions

For the vast majority of environments, the functionality provided through Apple's native Active Directory plug-in offers all that is needed for successful integration. However, there are numerous scenarios where functionality is needed beyond Apple's solution. Apple considers these edge cases for the most part, but if you need a feature such as multiple-forest support (rather than simply multiple-domain support, which is part of the Active Directory plug-in), then you may need to turn to a third-party solution.

Centrify DirectControl

Centrify is a third-party directory solution that includes server-side software to augment Active Directory and for OS X clients includes a custom directory service plug-in. From an OS X perspective, Centrify offers a rather elegant solution because their software directly utilizes the DirectoryService API. As such, the Centrify DirectControl client plug-in is a first-class citizen next to Apple's native LDAP and Active Directory plug-ins. From an Active Directory perspective, the server-side DirectManage Access software allows for extended functionality without the need for schema extensions. This extended functionality is then used to distribute policies to clients through what Centrify identifies as *zones*.

DirectControl Installation

To get started with DirectControl, first download the installation ISO file from Centrify, mounting the ISO on a valid Windows domain controller, preferably one in a test or lab environment for your initial installation and testing. For many environments, you may choose to have Centrify perform an onsite jump-start for your organization. But for the purposes of this chapter, we'll have you perform a basic initial installation and test, assuming that you are doing so in a laboratory environment. Before you get started, though, make sure the server you are installing the suite on is part of the Active Directory environment and that it is running IIS and the .NET 3.5 Framework.

Let's go ahead and start the installation. To begin, run the setup MSI file that is included in the ISO file on a domain controller. At the Welcome screen, click Next. You will then see the license agreement screen (Figure 3-13). Here, agree to the license agreement and click Next.

Figure 3-13. Agreeing to the license agreement

The User Registration screen needs a username and an organization name, so type those in and then click Next, as shown in Figure 3-14.

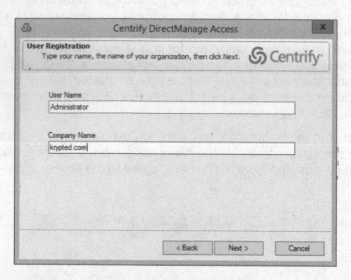

Figure 3-14. *Assigning a username and organization in DirectManage Access*

At the components screen, choose which DirectManage Access components to install. Here, click each component to determine which to install. For the purposes of this example, we'll stick with the default options, as shown in Figure 3-15.

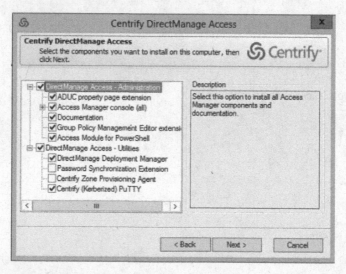

Figure 3-15. *Choosing the components to install*

Next, choose a location for DirectManage Access to be installed. At the Choose Destination Folder screen, customize the target directory or allow the installation to occur in the default directory. If you would like for the Centrify folder to be created in C:\Program Files, then click Next. Otherwise, click the Browse button, browse to the required folder, and then click the Next button.

Earlier you selected which applications in the suite to install. Now you're going to select the specific parts of DirectManage Access to install. Earlier you selected the Centrify applications, but now you are going to configure the components of each to be installed. Because this is a testing environment, you're going to look to get the full complement of options except for the extension for NIS maps, since for most environments there will not be any NIS clients. Having said this, the NIS option isn't just for administrators stuck in the 1990s. It can be practical when DirectControl is being used so that UNIX and Mac clients can authenticate through NIS into Active Directory. Either way, click Next to continue.

Open DirectManage Access Manager to get started.

Configuring DirectManage Access

When the installation is complete, you will need to set up DirectManage Access to connect to the Active Directory forest that the computer objects will be connecting to. The process starts with the Connect To Forest dialog. Before you do anything, double-check that your DNS is set appropriately and that you know the address for a system that is a domain controller for the forest. Once you have the appropriate information, enter the address of the appropriate domain controller and the appropriate credentials and click OK to begin the Setup Wizard, as shown in Figure 3-16.

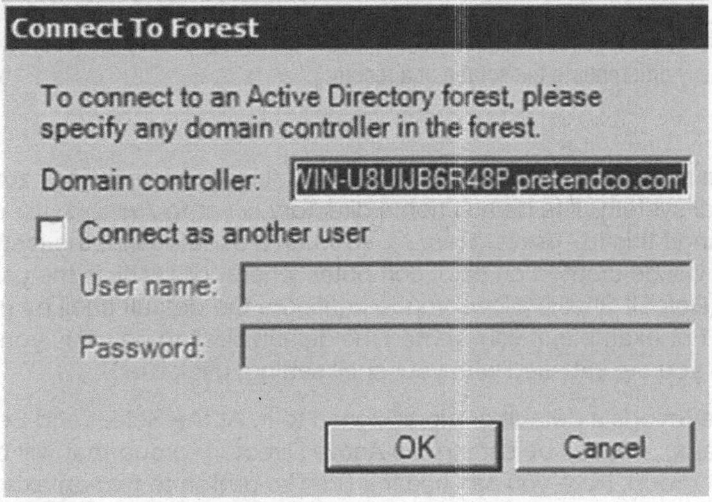

Connect To Forest

To connect to an Active Directory forest, please specify any domain controller in the forest.

Domain controller: WIN-U8UIJB6R48P.pretendco.com

☐ Connect as another user

User name:

Password:

OK   Cancel

Figure 3-16. Authenticating into a domain controller

The first few screens of the setup are innocuous. You will see the Welcome screen where you will click Next. At the User Credentials screen, enter a valid username and password for an administrative account and then click Next.

Licensing is a necessary evil. At the subsequent Install Licenses screen, select a location for your license keys. The default location is likely best, unless you have a good reason to change this location. At the Install License Keys screen, configure the keys that are populated into the default location from the Install Licenses screen. Enter the licensing key provided by Centrify and then click the Next button.

A Centrify zone is similar to an organizational unit. A zone has member objects but also allows for delegated access over the objects within the zone. Next, provide a location for your zones within Active Directory. You do not need to customize this information, so you can go ahead and click Next unless you need to do so.

In a standard Active Directory environment, when you bind to the directory, your system is stored in cn=Computers. Similarly, all objects have a default zone membership. At the Create Default Zone screen, you will supply the default zone, although most will simply leave the default setting and click the Next button.

While zones are similar to an OU, they are not an OU. In fact, a zone can be linked to an OU or a container. The default zone then will require you to enter a domain controller that has the OU or container accessible. If you did not customize the previous screen, then chances are you will not need to customize this screen either.

When you are importing data into Open Directory, one of the fields available is the first UID to use. This is similar in DirectManage Access. At the next screen, you will enter a starting UID number that will be assigned to objects. User IDs by default start at 10000, but feel free to customize this setting. Unique identification isn't just required for users; groups need unique IDs as well. Next, provide a starting GID (GroupID) space for groups to occupy (for the most part, the same rules apply as for users).

> **Tip**   It is generally recommended that you choose a range outside that provided by Apple's native solutions to easily differentiate the source of a record.

Next, set the default home directory that will be used for accounts in your zone as it would appear in the local system. The default home directory is set to /home/${user}. For OS X clients, you'll change this to /Users/${user}, so when a user logs in, the local folder /Users/USERNAME will be created on each computer, where USERNAME is the user logging in. The next screen (Default Shells) allows you to configure the default shell by using the full path to the shell. For example, if you wanted the default shell to be bash, you would use /bin/bash. When you are satisfied with your shell setting, click Next.

In OS X, each user needs a default group assigned to it. At the Select and Set the Default Normal Group dialog, you will be setting the Active Directory group that will be used for a UNIX GID for that group. Here you can use the Browse button to find an existing group. You can also use the Create button to create a new group. You will need to use the UNIX GID field if you want to use a unique identifying number for the AD group provided. While the unique number can be fairly arbitrary, do use your standard numbering scheme and organizational standards. Click Next to commit your changes, and if there are any issues with them, Centrify will bring up a screen telling you to fix the issue.

You will now see the Delegate Permissions screen, where you can set the server to be able to control settings on the workstation. When the Setup Wizard is complete, you will see the Setup Wizard's Summary page; review the settings and then select Next (or Cancel, if the setup does not match your vision of what is being installed). Finally, at the Centrify DirectControl Setup Wizard screen, click the Finish button to complete the setup wizard.

Using DirectManage Access

Once DirectManage Access is installed, it's time to get comfortable with its interface. To do so, open Active Directory Users and Computers from Administrative Tools and then open an account. Then click the newly added Centrify tab. The Domain field contains the Active Directory domain that an account belongs to, which should be populated by default with the domain name you are using. The User field has a UNIX profile in these zones and is where you configure an account's zone so that it will be managed (by default all accounts will be placed in the default zone that was specified during installation). The UID, "Login name," Shell, "Home directory," and "Primary group" fields all provide settings that are then expanded and applied by the Centrify Active Directory plug-in. If you click the Add button and select the default zone created earlier, then you will populate the remainder of the fields based on the settings previously used.

Next, look at how you can add accounts into zones from within DirectControl. To do so, open DirectManage Access Manager from Start ➤ Programs ➤ Centrify, as shown in Figure 3-17. When the window opens, click the disclosure dialog; then click Zones and Users to bring up a screen showing the account just added to the default zone. From this screen, you will not typically manage memberships—these are usually managed by Active Directory Users and Computers. Instead, you will more than likely use the DirectManage Access application itself to run reports.

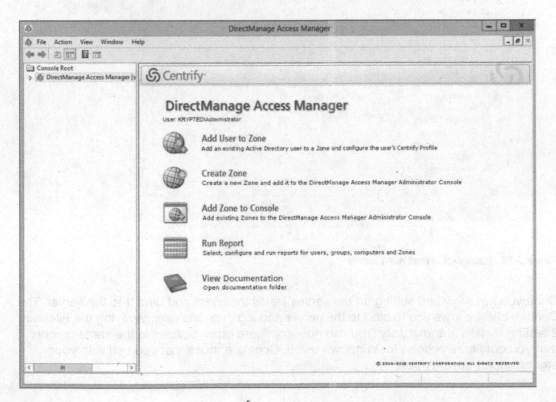

Figure 3-17. DirectControl

Next, click Create Zone and create a zone (for example, Marketing Users) that mirrors an Active Directory group. Add the Active Directory group to the Centrify group, and you are ready to set up policies. To get started, open the Group Policy Object Editor (GPOE). You will now see OS X Settings nested under both the User Configuration and Computer Configuration sections of the policy editor. You can then browse policies and configure policies for users and computers, just as you would configure Group Policy objects for Windows.

Let's look at setting up a specific policy by automatically enabling FileVault 2. To do so, browse to User Configuration, then Centrify Settings, and then Mac OS X Settings. From here, choose Security & Privacy and then double-click Enable FileVault 2 option. As shown in Figure 3-18, click Enabled and save the preference by clicking the OK button.

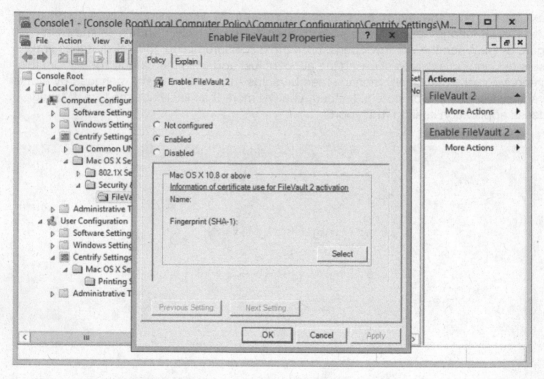

Figure 3-18. ManagingFileVault with Centrify

Once you have finished setting up the server, install the client and bind it to the server. The Centrify client allows you to bind to the server and log in as the user, verifying the FileVault 2 setting installs automatically. You can now configure other policies in the same manner that you configure policies for Windows users. Correlate those that you use with your organization's security policy.

PowerBroker

The company Likewise once made a product called Likewise Open, a tool for binding to Active Directory. Likewise was acquired by EMC, which spun off the product into what is now called PowerBroker Open. PowerBroker Open is open source software that acts as a replacement for the Active Directory plug-in. PowerBroker Open provides support for multiple-forest environments and credential caching and integrates SSH on OS X with Active Directory. It is compatible only with OS X 10.9 and earlier.

To integrate PowerBroker Open on a Mac, first download and open the package installer at `www.powerbrokeropen.org/powerbroker-open-edition-evaluation/`. At the Introduction screen, click the Continue button. At the Read Me screen, read the information provided and then click Continue. Next, at the License screen, read the license information and, provided you accept the licensing agreement, click the Continue button. When prompted to Agree, click the Agree button. At the Installation Type screen, click the Install button to install the files into the default location.

The installer will complete installing the plug-in, and provided the installer is successful, you will be greeted with the Install Succeeded screen. Here, click Close, and you will be ready to bind to Active Directory using the PowerBroker Open plug-in.

To bind to Active Directory using the plug-in, open Directory Utility from `/Applications/Utilities`. Next, if you click the Services icon in the Directory Utility toolbar, you will notice the new PowerBroker entry. Click here and then click the pencil icon to begin the GUI aspect of the Active Directory binding process.

You will now see the Join Active Directory wizard. Here, the "Computer name" field will automatically be populated with the host name of your computer. You can customize the name or enter the name of the Active Directory domain in the "Domain to join" field. If you would like to leave the system in the default `Computers` organizational unit, then you can now click the Join button. Otherwise, you can click OU Path and enter the path of the OU you would like the system to join.

You will now be prompted for the username and password of a user with rights to join the Active Directory domain. Provide the appropriate information and click the OK button. When the wizard is complete, you should see a screen indicating a successful bind to Active Directory.

From Directory Utility, you will now see a screen indicating that you have joined the appropriate domain. Finally, you can also use the command line to join Active Directory by leveraging the PowerBroker command-line interface. There are other commands as well, which can be used to perform other operations as required by Active Directory, including, of course, mass deployment.

Thursby ADmitMac

ADmitMac provides features that aren't available with the default Active Directory plug-in, such as Active Directory–based cross-realm trusts and more caching options. There is also an ADmitMac deployment tool, which reduces your reliance on manually scripting Active Directory binding and offers more options that can be used to protect your Active Directory administrative password.

Before you look at trying to mass deploy ADmitMac, you obviously need to figure out what it can do for you and which options you will use. Then you will programmatically figure out how to deploy it. To get started with your testing, you will first want to download the installer from Thursby and then run the ADmitMac installation package. Clicking Continue at the Introductions screen, at the Read Me screen, and after reading the developer's notes.

The next step in the installer package is to deal with licensing. At the Software License Agreement screen, read the agreement and click Continue. If you accept the agreement, click the Agree button in the dialog. At the License Code Entry screen, enter your username, the organization name, and the license code you were supplied with by Thursby. Then, click the Continue button.

At the Installation Type screen, click Change Install Location to select a different location to install ADmitMac or click the Install button to complete the installation process. When the installation process is complete, the ADmitMacSetup Assistant will automatically start. Here, click Continue to start the wizard.

Next, you will be prompted to set up WINS on the client computer. Most Active Directory environments no longer rely heavily on WINS support. Additionally, WINS is available using the Apple Active Directory plug-in. However, if you want to enable WINS support, you can do so through DHCP or manually. When you are satisfied with your settings, click the Continue button.

Next, configure the security policy settings, similar to the PacketSign option in `dsconfigad`. Here, select whether digital signing is required, select the bullet that most applies to your environment in terms of hashing, and then click the Continue button.

You will now be prompted to enter the name of the domain for your Active Directory environment. Enter the domain in the Domain field and click the Continue button.

Next enter the name that the computer record should be generated with into the Computer Name field and the organizational unit that the computer should reside in using the Computer OU field. Also, enter the username and password of a user who has permission to create an object in Active Directory and click the OK button.

The computer will now bind to Active Directory. When it is finished, you will have the option to use the assistant to move local accounts into Active Directory accounts. This is only for systems with existing users who need to be migrated to Active Directory users. However, if you would like to invoke the application later, you can do so using the Home Mover program that is located in `/Library/Application Support/ADmitMac`.

Now that your client is bound into Active Directory, you can use the Directory Utility application from `/Applications/Utilities` to alter any of the settings that have been previously configured and to configure shared folders on the local client using Active Directory credentials. The Directory Utility plug-in can also be used in dual-directory environments to specify exactly where to look for managed preferences.

Dell Privileged Access Suite

Dell Privileged Access Suite, as with Centrify and PowerBroker Open, is used to leverage an existing Active Directory infrastructure for providing policies for OS X. Dell Privileged Access Suite is based on the Vintela Authentication Services (VAS). Dell Privileged Access Suite will give you a new MMC snap-in for Windows Server's Group Policy Object Editor (GPOE) that will allow you to configure preference manifests and custom property list (.plist) files similar to how you would do so with Workgroup Manager. The screens look almost identical to Workgroup Manager except that policy items are formatted to fit within a GPOE screen.

Dell Privileged Access Suite adheres to RFC 2307 standards. In Windows Server domains, LDAP attributes are already part of the 2307 standard, so there is no extension of the Active Directory schema required. However, data from 2307 will need to be translated, so the client is required, which leverages the Microsoft client-side extensions (CSE). You can find more information on CSE using TechNet: http://technet.microsoft.com/en-us/library/cc736967.aspx.

To configure the VAS plug-in on a Microsoft Windows domain controller, set up a client to connect to Active Directory so that policies configured within the VAS GPOE snap-in will be applied to the client computer and run the installer.

Once the VAS installation is complete, open a GPOE screen to create your first domain policy. To do so, open a command prompt, enter **mmc** into the Open field, and click the OK button. At the Console screen, click the File menu and select Add/Remove Snap-In; then at the Add Standalone Snap-in screen, highlight Group Policy Object Editor and click the Add button.

At the Welcome to the Group Policy Wizard screen, click Browse and then select Default Domain Policy. Once you see the Finish button, then all is complete, and you can move on to the next step, which is editing policies for OS X. Use Default Domain Policy to browse to OS X Settings and select Workgroup Manager. If you have built policies for Open Directory using Workgroup Manager, then the items in the resulting list will seem familiar to you. This is because the developers of Dell Privileged Access Suite have gone through and copied the policies available in Workgroup Manager.

Once you have saved an option, verify that it has been enforced by navigating to the GPOE console again and checking that the policies are set to Yes under the column for configured preferences. Custom policies are available in Dell Privileged Access Suite, just as they are an option in Workgroup Manager on OS X Server. Policies for software that is not included by default rely on the software developer (including Apple) to create preference manifests to make their application's preference keys available for management through managed preferences. If a developer has not done so, you can also use standard property list files (.plist) to configure policies for many applications, but they are less granular in nature. Dell Privileged Access Suite provides a few common .plist files in its Preference Manifests section, including a manifest for Microsoft Office that you can use with other solutions as well. A common example of a manifest often used but not included by default is the ManagedClient options for Dashboard and Pages.

Dell Privileged Access Suite also provides a command-line interface for automating binding once you have deployed the installation package. This provides a lot more options that you can use to administer environments.

Summary

The default Active Directory plug-in should work to provide centralized authentication services for most but not all. In addition to centralized authentication, an enterprise needs its directory service to provide policies. Extending an Active Directory schema is an option for most environments looking to provide policies for OS X clients. For those where extending the schema will not be possible, a dual-directory environment should be your first thought, and, provided you fully test the environment, you should also consider the third-party products referenced in this chapter, as a last resort.

Why? Purely because of total cost of ownership. You will not be able to justify the platform if you have to bolt on too many pay-for features. Adding too many third-party solutions also dilutes ownership for troubleshooting and lateral support options. Overall, your life will be easier on a lot of different levels if you will be able to minimize the third-party solutions.

If you do bring in a third-party solution, then it should have its own total cost of ownership justification. For example, if you estimate that the cost of managing and maintaining a secondary directory service (including training, equipment, setup) for a dual directory is more than licensing Centrify for 10,000 users, especially considering that an Active Directory administrator who knows little to nothing about a Mac can manage it, then you have a clear decision in front of you at the tail end of year 1, if not sooner.

Overall, the most cost-effective method of producing managed preferences is extending your Active Directory schema. But there are still a number of cases where third-party solutions will need to be leveraged—try to use these as ways to drive down the total cost of ownership by leveraging advanced features of each solution to enable more automation for your environment. Make sure that the business cost here is known by all, especially those responsible for making these types of budgeting decisions.

Finally, keep in mind that because of the addition of profiles, other patch management solutions, such as the Casper Suite, can be a way to get policies in your environment.

## Chapter 4

Storage

How has storage changed for users over the last five years?

Not surprisingly, the size and speed of drives have come up while the cost has gone down, and Apple is strongly pushing consumers to flash and solid-state drives (SSDs) in its product lines. Today, only the low-end Mac mini and MacBook Pro models offer spinning 5400 RPM drives (7200 RPM is not an option), and only the iMac offers 5400 and 7200 RPM drives. Everything else from MacBook to Mac Pro is flash or SSD, which offers 5x the performance of 7200 RPM drives according to Apple's web site. Drives shipped with a minimum of 160 GB in 2010, compared to a minimum of 500 GB five years later.

Fusion drives, built on Apple's Core Storage technology introduced in 2012, are a relatively inexpensive upgrade for the iMac and Mac mini models that offer something in between the cheap but slower platter drives and the costly but speedy flash-based drives. They incorporate a small amount of flash capacity for frequently accessed files with roomy 1 TB drives to store the rest of a user's data.

Flash memory in smaller amounts is affordable and has caused a boon in portable markets—particularly for smartphones, cameras, and USB thumb drives. High-end smartphones contain 128 GB of storage, which is the same amount of storage as Macs with entry-level SSDs. Photographers make use of multiple microSD cards for short-term storage, while taking 20-megapixel photos or 4K resolution video. (Photographer Steve McCurry shot the last roll of Kodachrome film in 2013.) And $10 USB 3.0 flash drives with 16 GB of storage are a dirt-cheap way of booting and installing an operating system on a computer.

CD and DVD drives in Macs? Steve Jobs hinted in July 2010 that Apple would eventually abandon all optical drives when he wrote in an e-mail "Blu-ray is a big bag of hurt." In 2012 the first iMacs shipped without optical drives after Apple nixed them in Mac minis the year before. By 2013 optical drives were gone from all product lines.

But storage isn't just about what we can stick in a computer. Today, it's also about bypassing local and network storage and putting our data into the cloud. Cloud storage for some organizations is an inexpensive way of hiring someone else's IT department to manage the servers. For a monthly or annual fee, users can share documents internally and externally, access documents on multiple devices, and revert to older versions of documents in case of mistakes or changing minds. For businesses, that monthly or annual fee means employees can work from home (a high-demand job perk that helps retain employees) and—just as important—data backups.

After all the changes and advances of the past five years, though, securing data at rest and in transit has gotten more complex. If we allow users to access company data such as projected earnings on a personal laptop in a coffee shop, then we have to ensure that data is protected wherever it goes, usually while trying not to manage personal data such as family photos.

In this chapter, we will cover storage on network, cloud, and local systems with an emphasis on securing data while at rest and in transit. Security means ensuring that only the correct users can access data, other users cannot access that data, and data is available in case of mishap or disaster.

Network Storage

Our users don't care how or where we store their data. They only care it's available quickly and conveniently just like their personal systems at home. That is the benchmark for their satisfaction with our storage administration. Sometimes, they incorrectly equate enterprise-class storage with home storage and remark, "Space is cheap." They don't realize enterprise storage comes at a significant cost. Large organizations need fast servers with redundant 15,000 RPM drives that can handle dozens or even hundreds of simultaneous requests. Those servers connect to 100 GB and faster backbones using fiber, not copper, with network switches to accommodate the fast speeds. Backups for gigabytes of new and changed data every day require high-speed and high-capacity solutions that may even incorporate deduplication software to save space, time, and money. And, of course, users don't manage all of this. Good administrators who can make all that hardware sing come at a price.

The client side of network storage access is far easier to manage. Macs simply need a fast network connection, the right protocol for the need, and a good filing system.

Network Connections

Networks carry data from remote storage to Macs and comprise the low-level layers of transport. The physical layer of a network is probably the most reliable part of the connection because it has no moving parts (except for cooling fans in the switches and routers). If something is going to go wrong with the physical connection, though, it is more likely to go wrong the closer it is to the user.

A network cable running through a well-designed data center has little chance of moving for years, and server admins take great pains to avoid adding servers in crowded racks. A network cable in a wiring closet near the user's location has a higher chance of damage (or some other mishap) because telephone technicians and desktop administrators generally have freer rein to change things. And a network cable at the user's desk has the highest chance of damage with the user rolling a chair over the cord or the highest chance of disruption because of someone simply plugging it into a phone jack instead of a data jack after trying to rearrange cubicle space.

At a higher level of the network transport is how fast the data can actually move across the cabling. This is dependent on the network switches and routers as well as the grade of the cabling itself. Testing a network switch or port is fairly easy because an administrator can simply unplug a cable and move it to another port or switch. Testing cables, though, is one of the more difficult parts of a network to troubleshoot because the average Mac administrator will not have access to the tools to test and rate every connection segment. General contractors are often more than glad to have electricians run that CAT5e or CAT6 network cabling while they are installing the electrical. However, electrical-grade CAT5e is not the same as data-grade CAT5e. While it may seem to carry data just fine, it is more vulnerable to interference, which results in slower network speeds. If in doubt about certain segments of your network, have a telecom expert inspect them.

The weakest link in a chain is the first link to break under stress. So too is the weakest segment of a network. Network storage servers may plug into a high-speed fiber-optic network and then extend by fiber throughout a campus wired with CAT6e cabling in all the buildings for 1 GB connections to each desktop. But if someone uses a 25-foot CAT5 patch cable in a wiring closet because "it was convenient," the user will experience subpar performance. Furthermore, the user may not even realize how poor the connection is compared to its potential until receiving that 500 MB Adobe Photoshop file from a remote co-worker. At this point, the user perceives the server has slowed down even when nothing has really changed. Verify a twisted-pair Ethernet cable meets speed requirements by inspecting its sheathing. Avoid using cables that do not display a category rating (Figure 4-1).

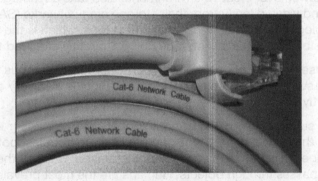

Figure 4-1. Inspect a network cable's sheathing to determine its supported speed

Be sure the length of a network cable in addition to its category rating does not exceed speed specifications (Table 4-1). Installing higher-category network-grade cabling as well as purchasing higher-category patch cables now is a good way to future-proof for tomorrow's faster machines and network equipment. You could even run both fiber and Ethernet cables.

Table 4-1. *Higher-Category Cabling Supports Faster Network Speeds*

Network Cabling Speed Specifications

	Length	Supported Speeds			
		10 MB	100 MB	1 GB	10 GB
CAT5	100 m	X	X		
CAT5e	100 m	X	X	X	
CAT6	100 m	X	X	X	
CAT6	55 m	X	X	X	X
CAT6e	100 m	X	X	X	X
Fiber	20+ km	X	X	X	X

Distance matters when evaluating speed using copper Ethernet cabling because the electrical pulses it carries degrade the farther they travel away from the source. A high-quality CAT6e cable run is great within a building where the environment remains constant but is not ideal for large distances between buildings where weather and other external forces come into play. Fiber allows us to extend those very fast network speeds over far greater distances, and it is not susceptible to electromagnetic interference like copper. High-speed production networks for creative environments also take advantage of fiber for editing photos, CAD files, and video directly from their storage area networks (SANs). For example, Apple's Xsan technology supports fiber directly to desktops, which is the fastest network storage access possible today. It rivals storage devices directly attached to computers.

You should always use fiber to connect buildings on a corporate campus. Fiber does not carry large electrical surges (e.g., via a lightning strike). Fiber is also very difficult, if not impossible, to covertly intercept data over.

Some environments support networking without copper or fiber, in other words, wirelessly. Wireless is probably the most complex type of networking to troubleshoot because signal strength changes because of distance and attenuation, which is the reduction of signal strength as it passes through objects. Humans are the most prevalent and mobile attenuators. Although today's Macs support 802.11ac Wi-Fi with a specification of 1.3 Gbps transmit speed, they will never see near that speed outside a laboratory. Wi-Fi is limited to half-duplex simply to avoid interference with itself. It does not travel well through walls and certain types of construction, and it is prone to interference from common environmental factors such as fluorescent lighting. Again, user perception may be that Wi-Fi is a great productivity booster allowing access to network storage from any location, but when the user enters the cafeteria and someone starts a microwave oven, perception will change to "the server is having problems." Resolve network storage access issues caused by Wi-Fi by plugging the computer into a physical network port.

File Sharing

Even higher in the network transport process is the language, or *protocol*, a Mac uses to communicate with a network file server. Protocols are always evolving but generally remain backward compatible with older versions. Some protocols such as the Apple Filing Protocol (AFP) or Server Message Block (SMB) are better for interactive communication. They enable Macs to connect to a file server and "mount" a share that looks like a physically connected drive. Users open, edit, and save files from the connected drive. Other protocols such as the File Transfer Protocol (FTP) or Hypertext Transfer Protocol (HTTP) are suited for transferring data only. These protocols are not meant for live editing, quick changes, or fast saves. The differences between protocols affect a user's perception of performance and speed when accessing network storage.

OS X offers multiple ways to connect to a network file server. These are the common methods:

- Finder's Connect To Server menu item
- mount_afp and mount command-line tools
- Configuration profile

AFP and SMB

AFP is *not* AppleTalk (Apple's suite of older plug-and-play protocols based heavily on network broadcasts), but technicians in network services often hold tight to the old concept that Macs are "chatty." AFP 3 communicates over TCP/IP port 548 and is the Mac's native network file sharing language. Although Apple has adopted SMB as the default protocol in the Finder, AFP seems to better support peer-to-peer file sharing communications, primarily because Apple changed from the open source implementation of SMB (Samba) to SMBX in OS X 10.7 (Lion) and later to SMB2 on OS X 10.9 (Mavericks). Its first implementations of SMB2 were challenging to use in Windows networks with older and newer versions of SMB.

Windows file sharing uses SMB, and modern Windows systems use a dialect called CIFS, which supports additional features and uses port 445 over TCP/IP. Other flavors of SMB rely on NetBIOS and run on UDP ports 137 and 138 or TCP ports 137 and 139. Similar to Apple's development of AFP, Microsoft is continually revising SMB with subsequent versions of Windows (SMB 2.0 for Windows Vista and Server 2008 and SMB 3.0 for Windows 8 and Server 2012) for increased performance and security.

Clients connect to AFP and SMB servers using the Finder, command-line utilities (mount_afp for AFP and mount for SMB), or configuration profiles provided by their administrators. AFP servers with Bonjour, Apple's implementation of a zero-configuration network (zeroconf) or multicast Domain Name System (mDNS), enable clients to discover their running services and display them in the Finder's sidebar. OS X uses Windows network browsing services to enable Macs to discover Windows computers on the local network. These services are great for local area networks but do not scale well to larger companies and enterprises with multiple networks. Directory servers best facilitate accessing resources across complex networks. Network administrators who allow broadcasts across networks for browsing resources quickly discover this is not a sustainable idea because of the amount of traffic generated by computers.

To access an AFP or SMB file server, choose Connect To Server from the Go menu in the Finder. In the Server Address field, enter the protocol `afp://` followed by the server address to access AFP servers (see Figure 4-2). (Optionally, append the specific volume name to the end of the URI to bypass the subsequent volumes selection window and connect immediately.)

```
afp://server.talkingmoose.net/Files
```

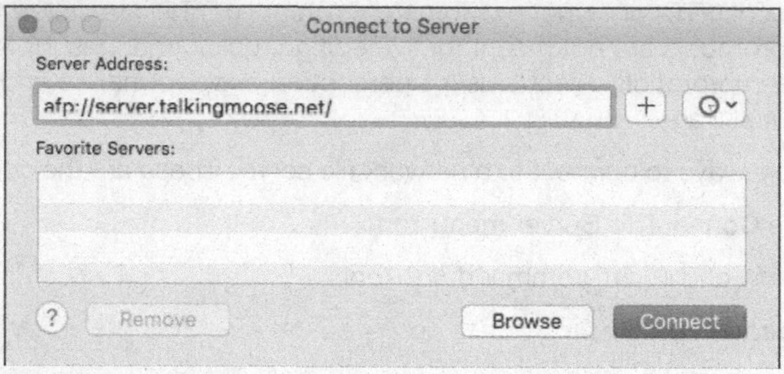

Figure 4-2. Connect to Server in the Finder

Omitting the `afp://` protocol defaults the Finder to connecting with the `smb://` protocol. Click the Connect button to initiate the connection.

```
smb://server.talkingmoose.net/
```

or

```
server.talkingmosoe.net/Files (to connect to the Files share via SMB)
```

> **Tip**   Click the plus button (+) to the right of the server field to add this address to the Favorite Servers list. Or click the clock drop-down menu to access a recently connected server from the Recent Servers list.

To connect to the server, the user must authenticate with a username and password. If the Mac is bound to Active Directory or Open Directory and the current user is logged in using directory credentials, then the user has already acquired a single sign-on (SSO) ticket from Kerberos (discussed in Chapter 2). The server will not prompt for user credentials but will immediately display a list of available *volumes*, which are the Mac equivalent to Windows shares (see Figure 4-3). Select one Mac volume or Windows share or hold the Shift or Command key to select multiple volumes or shares.

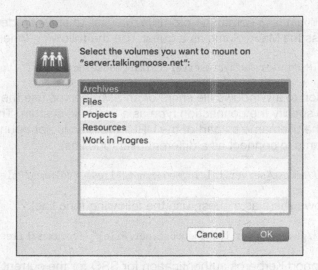

Figure 4-3. Selecting Mac volumes or Windows shares to mount

After clicking the OK button, the connected resources appear on the desktop if the Finder preferences are set to display connected servers. Additionally, connected servers appear in the sidebar of any Finder window with an Eject button to the right to unmount them.

OS X also supports connecting to Windows Distributed File System (DFS) shares and requires a slightly modified form of the SMB URI that includes the Active Directory domain name.

```
smb://talkingmoose.pvt/Files/Accounting
```

Use the `mount_afp` or `mount` command to connect to server resources via Terminal or a script and use a similar URI as the Connect to Server dialog in the Finder (including the protocol). Both protocols require the Mac volume or Windows share name as part of the URI, and both support passing usernames and passwords for authentication or using Kerberos. Each has a slightly different format, though.

Before connecting any resource, OS X needs a folder to serve as a mount point. The Finder automatically creates this folder when using its Connect to Server window. Terminal and scripts require creating the folder manually using the `mkdir` command followed with the path to the folder to create.

```
mkdir /Volumes/Files
```

While the new `Files` folder does not need to be the same name as the volume or share, using the same name makes identifying the shared resource easier. Next, initiate the connection to the file share using the `mount_afp` or `mount` command.

```
mount_afp -i "afp://server.talkingmoose.net/Files" /Volumes/Files
User: mmoose
Password: <user password>
```

The -i option in the mount_afp command prompts the user to enter credentials when connecting. To access the Mac volume as a guest, use the following (one line):

```
mount_afp "afp://;AUTH=No User Authent@server.talkingmoose.net/Files" /Volumes/Files
```

To initiate a connection to a Windows file share or an SMB server, use the mount command with the -t option to specify the connection *type* as a SMB file system. The following command requires the username as part of the URI if the Mac is not bound to a directory server or the user wants to connect as a different user (one line):

```
mount -t smbfs "smb://mmoose@server.talkingmoose.net/Files" /Volumes/Files
```

To access the Windows share as a guest, use the following (one line):

```
mount -t sbmfs "smb://guest@server.talkingmoose.net/Files" /Volumes/Files
```

AFP connections support Kerberos authentication for SSO for the current user by specifying the authentication mechanism in the URI in place of the username.

```
mount_afp "afp://;AUTH=Client%20Krb%20v2@server.talkingmoose.net/Files" /Volumes/Files
```

SMB connections support Kerberos by simply omitting the username. The following passes the user's current Kerberos credentials to the server or simply fails if the Mac is not bound to a directory server:

```
mount -t smbfs "smb://server.talkingmoose.net/Files" /Volumes/Files
```

Both commands support passing a username and password as part of the URI, which is useful when you are logged in as one directory user but need to connect as a different user or when the Mac is not bound to a directory server (one line).

```
mount_afp "afp://mmoose:Pa55wOrd@server.talkingmoose.net/Files" /Volumes/Files
```

or (one line)

```
mount -t smbfs "smb://mmoose:Pa55wOrd@server.talkingmoose.net/Files" /Volumes/Files
```

> **Tip**   Does Windows Server support AFP connections? Not anymore. Microsoft "end-of-lifed" Services for Macintosh, which included file, print, and AppleTalk services, after Windows Server 2003. However, administrators can purchase and install Acronis Access Connect (formerly Group Logic ExtremeZ-IP) to add Mac services to Windows Server 2008 and newer. Access Connect is an alternative solution for environments needing Mac file and print services in predominantly Windows environments.

Apple introduced configuration profiles as a replacement for its Managed Client for OS X (MCX) management system. Configuration profiles are a layer of management administrators apply to an entire computer or to specific users on a computer. Management servers such as Apple's Profile Manager commonly deploy configuration profiles as a full set of management policies; however, most any distribution method such as a script or Apple installer package can deploy individual configuration profiles too.

Configuration profiles support connecting users to network file shares at login including network home folders.

Use a management server such as Apple's Profile Manager to create the configuration profile. The management server itself does not necessarily need to be actively managing devices.

Launch the Server app and click Groups in the navigation pane.

1. Click the + button (plus) to create a new group named Mount Servers (Figure 4-4). Click the OK button when done.

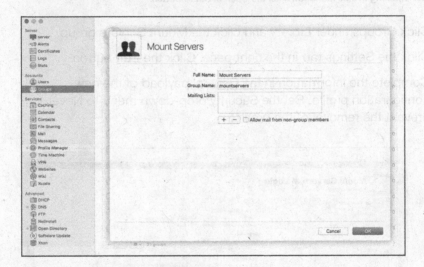

Figure 4-4. Create the Mount Servers group in Server

2. Click the Profile Manager service.

3. Turn on the service.

4. At the bottom of the Profile Manager service pane, click the Open In Safari button next to Profile Manager to open Profile Manager in a web browser (Figure 4-5). Log in using administrator credentials for the server.

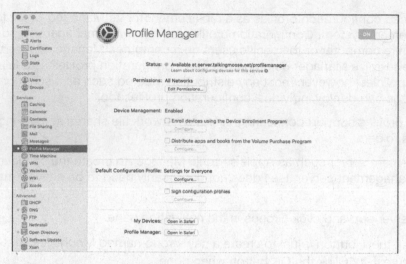

Figure 4-5. After enabling Profile Manager, click the Open In Safari button

5. Click Groups under Library and click the Mount Servers group.

6. Click the Settings tab in the right pane. Click the Edit button.

7. Complete the information in the General payload of the new configuration profile. Set the Security drop-down menu to Never to prevent the removal of the profile.

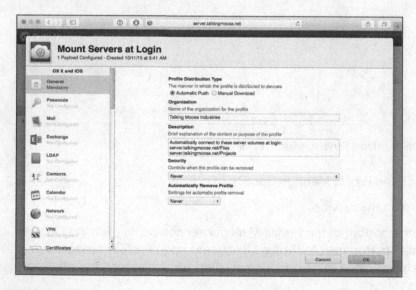

Figure 4-6. Profile Manager General payload

8. Scroll through the list of payloads to the left and choose Login Items in the OS X section of payloads. Click the Configure button.

9. To automatically connect users to their network home folders hosted on an OS X server, enable Add Network Home Share Point (Figure 4-7). This creates a new object in the Authenticated Network Mounts field.

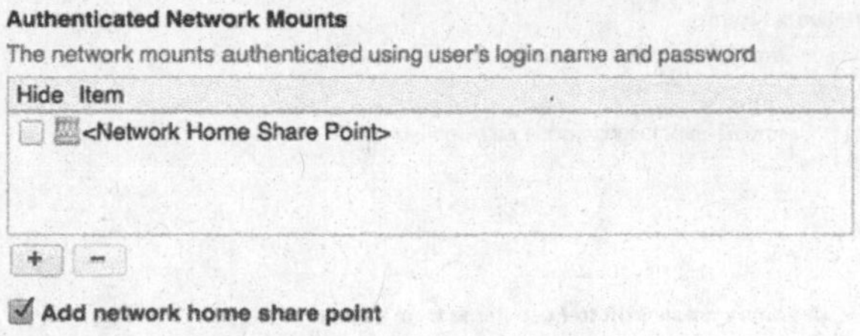

Authenticated Network Mounts
The network mounts authenticated using user's login name and password

Hide	Item
☐ 🖳	<Network Home Share Point>

+ −

☑ **Add network home share point**

Figure 4-7. Enable mounting a network home share

10. To automatically connect users to file servers using Kerberos, click the + button (plus) below Authenticated Network Mounts. Complete the information for connecting to a network file server. Click the Add button when done (Figure 4-8).

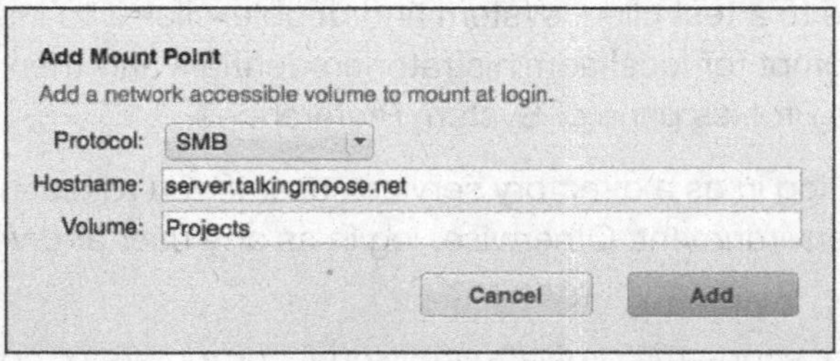

Add Mount Point
Add a network accessible volume to mount at login.

Protocol: SMB ▾
Hostname: server.talkingmoose.net
Volume: Projects

Cancel   Add

Figure 4-8. Configure a mount point

11. To automatically initiate connections for users in non-Kerberos environments (they will be prompted to enter their credentials), click the + button (plus) below Network Mounts (Figure 4-9). Complete the information for connecting to a network file server. Click the Add button when done.

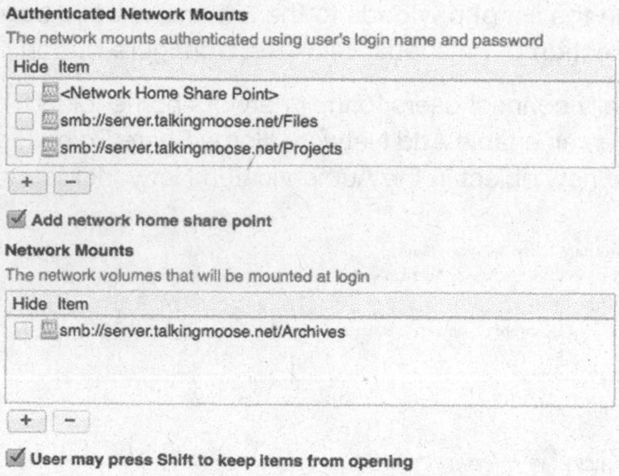

Authenticated Network Mounts

The network mounts authenticated using user's login name and password

Hide	Item
☐	🖥 <Network Home Share Point>
☐	🖥 smb://server.talkingmoose.net/Files
☐	🖥 smb://server.talkingmoose.net/Projects

[+] [−]

☑ **Add network home share point**

Network Mounts

The network volumes that will be mounted at login

Hide	Item
☐	🖥 smb://server.talkingmoose.net/Archives

[+] [−]

☑ **User may press Shift to keep items from opening**

Figure 4-9. Add authenticated network mounts

12. Click the OK button when done configuring the profile. Click the Save button to save the new Mount Servers configuration profile.

13. To test the new configuration profile, click the Download button to download a `.mobileconfig` file.

14. Copy this file to a test client system and double-click it to install. OS X will prompt for local administrator credentials and then add the profile to the Profiles pane of System Preferences.

15. Log out and log in as a directory services user if you're testing in a Kerberos environment. Otherwise, log in as any user and verify connectivity.

After successful testing, scope the profile to individual computers or computer groups in your MDM and use its push capabilities to deploy the profile to the client machines.

Cloud Storage

Users are demanding anywhere access to data, and cloud storage is an ideal solution to meet their needs. Laptops and Wi-Fi used to be a premium solution letting users unplug from their network cables to attend meetings in remote conference rooms or simply work in quiet nooks away from their cubicles. Now that portable devices are ubiquitous, users want to extend their range even further—outside the office. Internet-based cloud solutions facilitate some new demands that were not possible 5 to 10 years ago.

- Working from home, remote, and travel locations
- Accessing data on mobile devices
- Sharing data with external users
- Collaborating in real time on documents
- Offsite backing up and versioning

Cloud services are evolving quickly, and their feature sets are growing in huge spurts in this fledgling industry. Let's cover some of the broad possibilities they offer.

Work Remotely

In job fields where user demand is high but human resources are scarce, managers must make a lot of concessions to hire and retain talent. Family concerns are paramount with workers, and they want to spend less time in traffic as well as the office. One of the most successful solutions is to allow employees to work from home. Direct network connections to user homes are practically impossible because of logistics and cost, but most everyone who is able to work from home already has a high-speed Internet connection over a cable modem or DSL. Administrators only need enable secure access to company resources over the Internet.

VPN

A virtual private network (VPN) is a highly secure and dynamic method for connecting remote users to corporate networks. The *virtual* in VPN means it is building a private dedicated network between two sites without physically building the infrastructure using actual wires. VPN is prevalent with most small business-class routers and even some home network routers, and connectivity software is now standard with most major operating systems. It works by creating a "tunnel" between end points, which is a colloquial way of saying it encrypts traffic between client and server.

OS X supports four types of VPN connections.

- PPTP
- L2TP over IPSec
- Cisco IPSec
- IKEv2

Point-to-Point Tunneling Protocol (PPTP) is the oldest and least secure of these four connections, .especially if using the common Microsoft Challenge Handshake Authentication Protocol version 2 (MS-CHAPv2) authentication mechanism, which was cracked in 1998. The more secure Protected Extensible Authentication Protocol (PEAP) encapsulates the authentication using Transport Layer Security (TLS), but the infrastructure to configure and manage this is probably more effort than it is worth given other options. Also, the encryption used in PPTP still allows a hacker to modify traffic in transit. For secure communications, avoid PPTP wherever possible. The National Security Administration (NSA) more than likely decrypts PPTP traffic on a daily basis.

Layer 2 Tunneling Protocol (LT2P) .remains secure and easy to configure on both servers and clients. The "Layer 2" part of the protocol is agnostic of the traffic it's transmitting. This layer does not encrypt any traffic but rather maintains sending *data* back and forth. For security, L2TP traffic travels over IPSec, which maintains sending encrypted *traffic* between the two end points securely. Large enterprise environments should use dedicated network hardware for the server end of the connection; however, smaller businesses can take advantage of VPN services that come with servers such as OS X's Server app.

To configure OS X Server for hosting VPN clients, follow these steps:

1. Launch the Server app and click VPN in the navigation pane.

2. Turn on the VPN service. The server begins assessing whether it is available to Internet users. Ideally, it should be on a local private network and not exposed to the Internet (Figure 4-10). A router sitting between the Internet and the server should port forward all VPN traffic on UDP ports 500, 1701, and 4500 to the server. Verify the server's status displays Available.

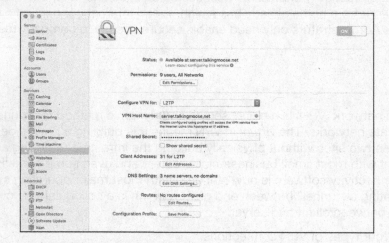

Figure 4-10. Enable VPN services in the Server app

3. Click the Edit Permissions button and verify the list of users who should have VPN access into the network. Add or delete users as needed. (Adding or removing a user here is the same as adding or removing access to the VPN service when editing user accounts.) Click the OK button shown in Figure 4-11 when done.

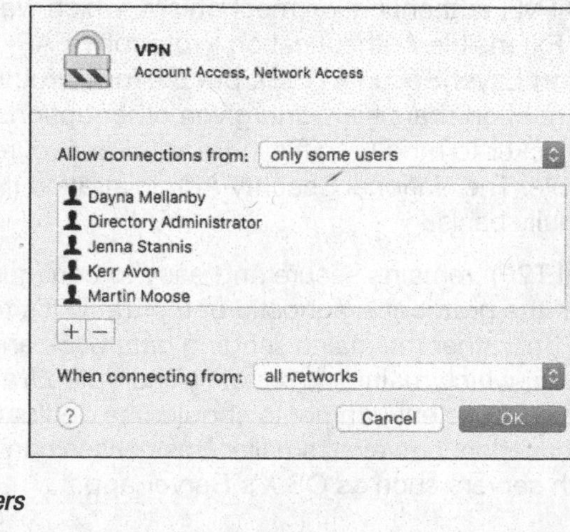

Figure 4-11. Choose VPN users

4. For stronger security, configure VPN services for L2TP only.

5. Enter the FQDN or IP address for the VPN service over the Internet. This address is used only when creating a configuration profile.

6. Enter a long and complex string of characters as your shared secret. This is a second factor in authenticating users when connecting and will not change regularly. Consider using the Keychain Access application to generate a shared secret that users must copy and paste rather than easily type (and easily remember). Here's an example:

   `*_XHPnBti1k&_3)\lIRd'kMDWcq#@m_`

7. To prevent users who have left the organization from connecting to VPN, simply disable their user accounts or change their user account passwords.

8. Click the Edit Addresses button and define an IP address range separate from the local network. To avoid potential conflicts in the future, use a different private address range. For example, if using Class A private addresses (`10.0.0.0/24`), use Class B private addresses (`172.16.0.0/16`) for your VPN connection. Also, specify the number of simultaneous VPN connections your server and Internet connections can support (Figure 4-12). This depends on server hardware and connection speed. Click the OK button when done.

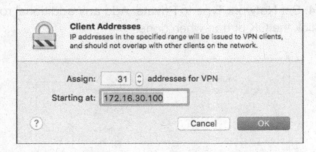

Figure 4-12. Configure the client VPN network

9. Click the Edit DNS Settings button and enter an IP address for a DNS server authoritative to the organization's internal network. This allows VPN users to locate resources by FQDN. Optionally, include one or more search domains for your organization's internal network (Figure 4-13). This allows VPN users to locate resources by simple host name such as `dc1` instead of `dc1.talkingmoose.pvt`. Click the OK button when done.

Figure 4-13. Define client VPN DNS servers and search domains

10. Click the Edit Routes button. By default, OS X Server's VPN service routes all traffic through the VPN server when users are connected. That will generate unnecessary traffic when remote users are surfing the Web or checking personal e-mail. Specifying a route has the effect of creating a *split tunnel*, sending only traffic destined for the private network over VPN and all other traffic over the user's Internet connection. Enter your organization's IP address network number (such as 10.10.100.0) and appropriate subnet mask, as shown in Figure 4-14. Set Network Type to Private. Add any additional routes if needed. Click the OK button when done.

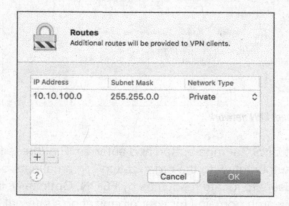

Figure 4-14. Edit client VPN routes

11. After making several of these changes, the Server app will prompt to restart the VPN service for the new settings to take effect. Restart the service if prompted.

Configuring a Mac VPN client is much easier than configuring the server; however, it's not straightforward and simple to understand for the average user. Once your VPN service settings are complete, though, Server provides a convenient option to download a configuration profile that you can deploy to individuals via e-mail or en masse via an MDM. Click the Save Profile button and save the .mobileconfig file to your computer for later.

To manually configure OS X clients to connect to your VPN server, follow these steps:

1. Open the Network pane in System Preferences.

2. If necessary, click the Lock button and authenticate as an administrator to make changes to settings.

3. Click the + button (plus) to create a new network interface. Select the following settings shown in Figure 4-15:

   Interface: VPN

   VPN Type: L2TP over IPSec

   Service Name: VPN (L2TP)

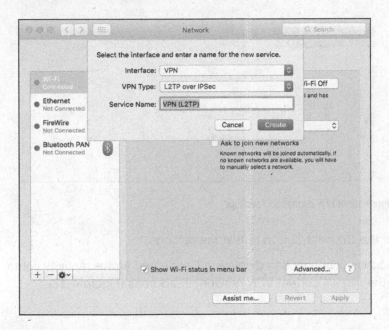

Figure 4-15. *Configure the client VPN network interface*

4. Click the Create button when done.

5. From the Configuration drop-down menu, choose Add Configuration and provide a name for the VPN connection.

6. Enter the VPN server address and provide a username.

7. Click the Authentication Settings button. Select Password for User Authentication and enter the user's account password. Select Shared Secret for Machine Authentication and paste the shared secret created in step 6 when configuring the VPN server. Click the OK button when done.

8. To save the new connection settings, click the Apply button.

9. Optionally, to make accessing the VPN network easier for the user, enable "Show VPN status in menu bar" Figure 4-16.

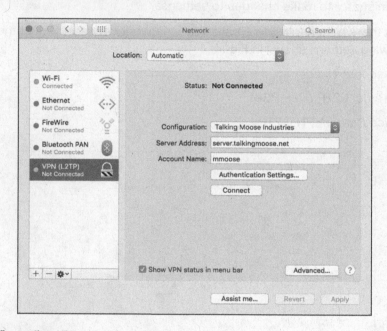

Figure 4-16. Configure client VPN connection settings

10. Click the Connect button to test the settings.

    A successful connection displays a Connected status, activity lights, and the client's current VPN network IP address (Figure 4-17).

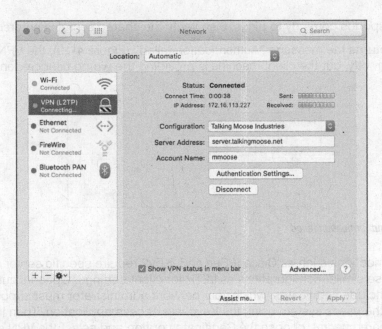

Figure 4-17. *VPN client connected*

If the service returns the message "The L2TP-VPN server did not respond" (Figure 4-18), verify the L2TP VPN service on the server is started and configured correctly. Also, verify the client computer is using the correct VPN server address.

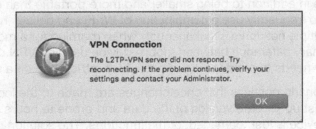

VPN Connection

The L2TP-VPN server did not respond. Try reconnecting. If the problem continues, verify your settings and contact your Administrator.

OK

Figure 4-18. *The VPN connection did not respond*

11. If the server or router allows responses to ICMP ping, use the Terminal application to ping the address by FQDN and then by IP address.

```
ping server.talkingmoose.net
ping: cannot resolve server.talkingmoose.net: Unknown host

ping 200.20.206.1
64 bytes from 200.20.206.1: icmp_seq=0 ttl=64 time=201.717 ms
64 bytes from 200.20.206.1: icmp_seq=0 ttl=64 time=201.717 ms
64 bytes from 200.20.206.1: icmp_seq=1 ttl=64 time=2.289 ms
64 bytes from 200.20.206.1: icmp_seq=2 ttl=64 time=3.368 ms
64 bytes from 200.20.206.1: icmp_seq=3 ttl=64 time=2.548 ms
```

If the server responds correctly to pings, then verify the shared secret is entered correctly.

If the service returns the message "Authentication failed" (Figure 4-19), the VPN server is responding correctly, but the client machine is providing the wrong user credentials (name or password).

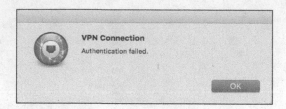

Figure 4-19. VPN authentication failed

Other VPN connections such as Cisco IPSec and IKEv2 require specific server or router hardware but use similar configurations as L2TP for client settings. Optional authentication methods may include certificates, which your network administrator must supply. Install the certificates on the user's system using the Keychain Access application. Then in lieu of a password or shared secret, choose the Certificates option and select the VPN certificate. A network administrator has the option to revoke VPN certificates when the user leaves the organization.

Mobile Devices, Collaboration, and Sharing

Laptop computers, tablets, and smartphones are mobile by nature because they require wireless connections in addition to being smaller and more portable than desktop computers. They also frequently use a combination of Wi-Fi and cellular networks to access data and access multiple networks simultaneously when roaming for a more connected user experience. The primary difference between mobile device use and VPN connectivity is that data more frequently needs to reside on the device itself rather than on a shared file server.

The problem this scenario poses is that once changes are made to the local copy of data, it is suddenly the most up-to-date version of the data and prone to hours or days of lost work if the mobile device is lost, damaged, or malfunctions. The solution to this problem lies in cloud services that specialize in keeping user data synchronized between multiple devices automatically without user intervention. These services include but are not limited to applications such as the following:

- Box
- DropBox
- Evernote
- Google Apps
- Office 365

Most cloud sync applications come with premium services to meet the higher demands of enterprise organizations, and those services generally include additional features for teams or workgroups that need to share data and collaborate with each other. Cloud storage is the easiest feature for these services to offer. On-demand access to data is the most difficult.

Established cloud sharing services offer the following benefits:

- Large amounts of data storage
- Ease of use
- Cross-platform connectivity and access to data
- Near-immediate synchronization of changes from one device to others
- Same-time collaboration

Because most cloud services offer basically the same features, users focus on ease of use and ubiquity of the service not only across devices but among other users around the world. Internet services work anywhere, but if a customer or vendor is already using the same tools as the user, then collaboration and sharing are immediately simplified because no one needs to learn a new tool. That is a compelling reason for enterprises to choose well-known over lesser-known cloud services. And because more cloud services are entering and saturating the market, developers are constantly adding new features such as same-time collaboration, broadcast presentations, remote control, and meeting services.

While users see these services as a convenience and growing necessity, enterprise administrators see them as a threat to security. Using a cloud service effectively means company data, which may be confidential, is moving to server storage that is out of the company's control. Anyone with access to the cloud servers, the hosting service, hackers (if the service is not properly secured), and even governments (for example, the National Security Administration) can gain access to this data. Unfortunately, once users begin using these services, reining them in is nearly impossible. The only option administrators have is to provide something better—not an easy and inexpensive option to develop in-house—or adopt one or more cloud services that meet their needs for data security as a company standard.

Cloud services must secure data both in transit and at rest. If they are not using modern network encryption methods such as Transport Layer Security (TLS), the successor to Secure Sockets Layer (SSL), then authentication and therefore data are at risk of being intercepted and decrypted. Data is also subject to integrity breaches by malicious hackers. Cloud servers should also store data security once received. Transferring data via the most advanced encryption methodologies is wasted if the data then sits on the server unencrypted on the hard drive or in memory.

Avoid services whose security policy effectively says, "We prohibit employees from looking at your files unless they really need to." That means someone outside your organization has access to your data. Seek services where only your organization has the cryptography keys to unlock your data. Also, request regular security auditing reports by independent agencies from the provider. Larger enterprises should hire their own third-party auditors when data integrity and security are paramount. Some of the strictest security requirements come from medical (HIPAA) and education (FERPA) customers. Cloud services certified in one or more of these security areas eliminate much of the research needed to find a reliable vendor.

Organizations should also review a service's advertised data center benefits for backups, versioning, redundancy, and availability. Basically, data should never be at risk of loss because of user error, hackers, or hardware malfunction.

After reviewing the security of a cloud service, review the security of the clients on multiple devices. Apple builds its iOS devices with hardware encryption, and so long as they are protected with a simple passcode, no one can access the data by removing the storage from the device and attempting to run analysis software. Apple computers, however, are unencrypted by default, which means Mac administrators must ensure the devices are secured with FileVault 2 or a third-party product before users copy data to the hard drives.

Backups and Versioning

Security is not only about protecting data from hackers and the competition but also protecting it from mishaps, hardware malfunctions, and catastrophes. Good security is a good backup. But better security is multiple backups in different locations. Cloud backup services such as Backblaze, Carbonite, CrashPlan, and Glacier make offsite backups not only easy to manage but easy to audit.

Similar to a user's need for automated and frequent data synchronization, administrators need automated and frequent data backups. Organizations still using tape backup face the problem that the process is slow. Running backups to tape throughout the day is impractical. But cloud backup software not only makes tiny incremental backups throughout the day easy, it sends those incremental backups off-site, which is one of the major strategies for guarding against catastrophic events such as natural disasters and forgotten sprinkler systems activating over newly installed data centers. And some backup agents include data deduplication at a block level rather than a file level for faster transfers and more efficient storage.

Important to users is that the backup software is not only protecting their current data but also protecting past data by creating versions. Just like administrators can insert a tape from two weeks ago to restore a file that was deleted or heavily edited with the wrong data, cloud backup software lets users help themselves when they need to restore older versions of files. Not only does this mean fewer calls to the help desk and storage management group but also the unique ability to restore anytime and anywhere, not just between 8 a.m. and 5 p.m. Monday through Friday at the office.

Finally, cloud backups do not need to be backups to a third-party cloud service. CrashPlan, for example, offers a professional version of its software that lets users back up to an enterprise-owned server rather than a CrashPlan server. This affords users the ability to back up and restore data on their own from anywhere while keeping company data on company-owned assets. Depending on the size of the organization, this may require a large investment in online storage and an increase in Internet bandwidth to handle all the data. However, it puts administrators back in control of the data they are responsible for protecting.

Local Storage

The closer the data, the faster and easier users can access it. Storing files locally has huge advantages with regard to editing large Photoshop files or simply expanding the amount of data at hand. If users stored all their data on network servers, they would quickly fill with working files, temporary files, and tons of personal nonbusiness stuff. Computers are like cubicles. Users want to personalize them, and the driving philosophy behind Apple and the devices it develops is to create a personal experience. Local storage facilitates personalization, and that engages employees. While administrators may not like to manage personal data, it comes along with the ride when managing the tools users need to do their jobs. Securing and protecting local storage are fundamental to securing a network.

Types of Storage

Macs are Swiss Army knives for accessing all kinds of content on numerous kinds of media. Today's common local storage media includes the following:

- Internal storage
- External connected storage
- Removable storage
- Virtual storage

Apple is vigorously transitioning how users store data on their computers. Over the past five years, it has developed more product lines with internal flash-based solid-state drives (SSDs) than any other computer manufacturer. While they do still carry products with spinning disks, those models are typically the low-end desktops. Just as Apple eliminated the floppy disk and optical drive from its product lines well before the rest of the industry, we should expect it to do the same with spinning platters. This makes sense as the cost of flash media comes down in price. The speed improvements SSDs give are already paying for the higher prices today.

No longer do we think of 256 GB of storage as adequate. Computer users today are hoarders of data. While applications may generate larger file sizes today, they do not account for the extra *stuff* we like to keep on hand such as music and videos. External storage remains our only way of collecting more stuff, and Apple has had a hand in developing technologies such as FireWire, Thunderbolt, and USB 3.0 to help us store all of it. Apart from SSD-based external drives arriving on the market, little has changed with external connected storage. External drives are simply bigger (RAID drives are more commonplace) and cheaper and ship with faster connectors.

Removable media no longer has its foothold on long-term storage now that large-capacity externally connected storage is affordable. Optical media such as compact discs (CDs) and digital video discs (DVDs) are dead to Macs. Users, however, will not give up their media collections just yet. Education users still cling to their old laptops that are slow and growing long in the tooth simply because they can play those expensive education DVDs purchased years ago with no updated replacements. Inexpensive USB thumb drives and microSD cards with gigabytes of storage for low-end models have all but replaced optical media. Their reusability, tiny physical size, and higher capacity are a far better solution than write-once read-many (WORM) media.

Disk images, which are files that behave like disks, are virtual equivalents to physical disks with some unique benefits. The Disk Utility application, for example, will convert those expensive education DVDs to disk image files with the advantage that fingerprints on the monitor will never prevent reading them. Once digitized, educators need only access the digital media and leave the optical media on the shelf. And disk images support encryption for storage sensitive files securely while on a shared computer or when transporting them on removable media.

Disk Utility

Macs need only one tool to manage all modern-day local storage—Disk Utility. It has come a long way from its Mac OS predecessor Disk First Aid, which the Mac's first disk tool. Since then, it has evolved into a multipurpose utility for checking disk health, repairing disks, partitioning disks into volumes, and securing data.

Open the Disk Utility application in /Applications/Utilities (Figure 4-20). On the left, it dynamically displays all connected disks and updates when disks, such as USB thumb drives, are ejected or inserted. For each disk, it shows both the physical disk and the volumes listed underneath it.

Figure 4-20. Disk Utility

Macs ship with the Macintosh HD volume preinstalled on the disk along with the OS X system installed on the volume. Macs also ship with a hidden Recovery HD volume with a copy of Disk Utility installed on it along with other tools such as firmware password utility, network utility, and Internet recovery tool for downloading and installing a fresh copy of OS X.

First Aid

Disk issues occur at both the disk level and the volume level, and Disk Utility includes a verify and repair tool called First Aid for checking both. A disk-level verification is much less intensive than a volume-level verification and takes only a few seconds to complete. Volume-level verifications may take several minutes, and the Mac may become unresponsive during this time.

To initiate a disk-level verification, select the internal disk in the left pane. (The disk name generally indicates the manufacturer and model of the disk, as seen in Figure 4-21.) Click the First Aid button in the toolbar. Click the Run button when prompted to begin verification and repairs. Depending on the speed of the disk, this process may complete in just a few seconds. Click the Done button when finished.

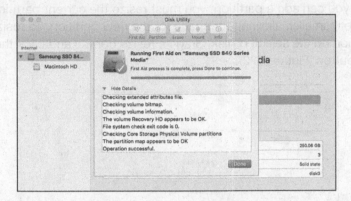

Figure 4-21. The partition map appears to be OK

OS X includes the command-line utility `diskutil`, which is the equivalent of the Disk Utility application but with many more options. To perform the same disk verification via the command line, run the following (`disk0` is the internal hard drive):

```
sudo diskutil verifyDisk disk0
```

Similarly, to initiate a volume-level verification, select the internal volume in the left pane. (The volume name is the name of the disk as it appears in the Finder.) Click the First Aid button in the toolbar. Click the Run button when prompted to begin verification and repairs. Click the Done button when finished.

The command-line equivalent for verifying a volume is as follows:

```
sudo diskutil verifyVolume "Macintosh HD"
```

Partition

Disk Utility also performs live partitioning disks, which means you can add or remove empty volumes while booted to an OS running from the disk. Multiple volumes on a single disk are useful for a few reasons.

- You can install Windows using Apple's Boot Camp.

- You can separate user home folder data from system and application data.

- You can install another OS X operating system for testing or backward compatibility.

- You can store large files such as virtual machine files to prevent filling the system volume.

To add a new volume to the current boot disk, follow these steps:

1. Select the internal disk in the left pane and then click the Partition button in the toolbar. (If you cannot click the Partition button, verify you have selected a disk and not a volume.)

2. Before you can add a partition, you must resize the current partition to make it smaller, allowing for space for the new partition. To resize a partition on the selected disk, drag its resize control and click the Apply button (Figure 4-22).

Figure 4-22. Full partition

3. Next, click the + button (plus) to add a new partition. By default, the new partition will fill any remaining free space. Drag its resize controls to resize it if needed or use the Size field to the left to enter an exact size.

4. To the right, give the new volume a name in the Partition field and choose a file system from the Format drop-down menu (Figure 4-23). OS X Extended (Journaled) is the Mac's default file system. A *journaled* file system keeps track of changes not yet committed to the file system in a data structure called a *journal* and is generally quicker to bring back online after a crash and less likely to corrupt. Other format options include the following:

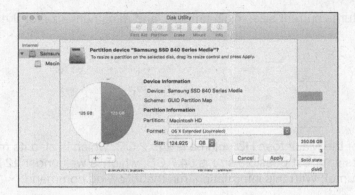

Figure 4-23. Partitioning a device

- *OS X Extended (Case-sensitive, Journaled)*: A journaled volume where uppercase and lowercase letters are considered different by the operating system (that is, File.txt and file.txt are treated as two different files).

- *OS X Extended (Journaled, Encrypted)*: Protects external hard drives with a password. This is not available for boot volumes.

- *OS X Extended (Case-sensitive, Journaled, Encrypted)*: An external journaled volume where uppercase and lowercase letters are considered different by the operating system and is protected with a password.

- *MS-DOS (FAT)*: Format for Windows volumes 32 GB or less.

- *ExFAT*: Format for Windows volumes more than 32 GB.

5. Click the Apply button when done.

The diskutil command-line tool also supports live partitioning and creating new volumes. Let's create two equal-size partitions from the original partition. First, get a list of existing volumes on the disk by running this command:

```
diskutil list disk0
```

This lists all volumes on the internal drive.

```
bash-3.2$ diskutil list disk0
/dev/disk0 (internal, physical):
   #:                       TYPE NAME              SIZE       IDENTIFIER
   0:      GUID_partition_scheme                  *250.1 GB   disk0
   1:                        EFI EFI               209.7 MB   disk0s1
   2:                  Apple_HFS Macintosh HD      249.2 GB   disk0s2
   3:                 Apple_Boot Recovery HD       650.0 MB   disk0s3
```

The identifier for the Macintosh HD volume is disk0s2. Next, determine the size limits for Macintosh HD (disk0s2) or how large and how small you can make this volume. The limits option in the command is nondestructive.

```
diskutil resizeVolume "Macintosh HD" limits
```

The command returns current size, minimum size, and maximum size for the Macintosh HD volume.

```
bash-3.2$ diskutil resizeVolume "Macintosh HD" limits
For device disk0s2 Macintosh HD:
        Current size:  249.2 GB (249199591424 Bytes)
        Minimum size:  64.7 GB (64676634624 Bytes)
        Maximum size:  249.2 GB (249199591424 Bytes)
```

The current size of the Macintosh HD volume is 249.2 GB, which is also its maximum size (the entire disk). Its smallest possible size is 64.7 GB, which is well under 124.6 GB (half the size of the full volume). With this information, run the following command:

```
sudo diskutil resizeVolume disk0s2 124.6G JHFS+ "Part 2" 120G
```

This tells `diskutil` to resize the volume identified as `disk0s2`. It resizes the existing volume to 124.6 GB and formats it as Journaled HFS+. Then it creates a second partition named Part 2 and specifies a size of 120 GB. However, `diskutil` will actually use the full remainder of the disk, 124.6 GB, for the last partition it creates.

Depending on the amount of existing data on the volume, resizing may take several minutes to complete. The `diskutil` command first runs a preliminary volume check before proceeding with relocating any data (Figure 4-24).

```
● ● ●              🗔 diskutil • sudo — 80×24
server:~ sudo diskutil resizeVolume disk0s2 124.6G JHFS+ "Part 2" 120G
Resizing to 124600000000 bytes and adding 1 partition
Started partitioning on disk0s2 Macintosh HD
Verifying the disk
Verifying file system
Using live mode
Performing live verification
Checking Journaled HFS Plus volume
Checking catalog file
Checking multi-linked files
Checking catalog hierarchy
Checking extended attributes file
Checking volume bitmap
Checking volume information
The volume Macintosh HD appears to be OK
File system check exit code is 0
Resizing
[ \ 0%..10%..20%.............................................. ] 29% 0:02:49 █
```

Figure 4-24. diskutil resizeVolume

When the command completes, it runs a quick `diskutil list disk0` command and displays the results, which shows an updated volume list that includes the new Part 2 volume.

```
Finished partitioning on disk0s2 Macintosh HD
/dev/disk0 (internal, physical):
   #:                       TYPE NAME                SIZE       IDENTIFIER
   0:      GUID_partition_scheme                     *250.1 GB  disk0
   1:                        EFI EFI                 209.7 MB   disk0s1
   2:                  Apple_HFS Macintosh HD        124.6 GB   disk0s2
   3:                 Apple_Boot Recovery HD         650.0 MB   disk0s5
   4:                  Apple_HFS Part 2              124.5 GB   disk0s4
```

The Finder also displays the new volume on the desktop and in the sidebar of any open Finder windows if those preferences are enabled. The new volume is ready for use.

Erase

Disk Utility's erase function behaves differently depending on whether you select a volume or a disk. To erase a volume, follow these steps:

1. Select the disk in Disk Utility's left pane.

2. Click the Erase button in the toolbar.

3. Optionally, provide a new name for the volume.

4. Select one of the OS X Extended or FAT formats described earlier from the Format drop-down menu (Figure 4-25).

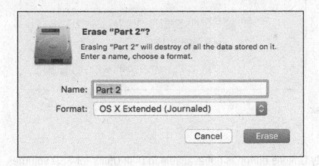

Erase "Part 2"?

Erasing "Part 2" will destroy of all the data stored on it. Enter a name, choose a format.

Name: Part 2

Format: OS X Extended (Journaled)

Cancel   Erase

Figure 4-25. Erasing a volume

5. If available, click the Security Options button and choose an erase option from Fastest (least secure) to Most Secure.

   - *Fastest*: This option does not securely erase the files on a disk. A disk recovery application may be able to recover the files.

   - *Zero out data*: This option writes a pass of random data and then a single pass of zeros over the entire disk. It erases the information used to access your files and writes over the data two times.

   - *DOD-compliant erase*: This option is a DOD-compliant three-pass secure erase. It writes two passes of random data followed by a single pass on known data over the entire disk. It erases the information used to access your files and writes over the data three times.

   - *Most Secure*: This option meets the U.S. Department of Defense (DOD) 5220-22 M standard for securely erasing magnetic media. It erases the information used to access your files and writes over the data seven times.

6. Click the Erase button. Depending on the security level you chose and the size of your drive, erasing a disk may take a few seconds or several minutes.

Erasing a disk is similar to erasing a volume; however, Disk Utility includes the option to choose the format after erasing using the Scheme drop-down menu (Figure 4-26). Format options include the following:

- *GUID Partition Map*: For all Intel-based Mac computers.

- *Master Boot Record*: For Windows partitions that will be formatted as MS-DOS (FAT) or ExFAT.

- *Apple Partition Map*: For compatibility with older PowerPC-based Mac computers.

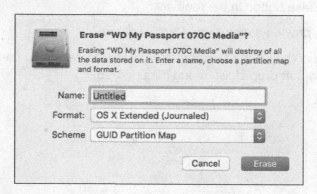

Figure 4-26. *Erasing a disk*

> **Note**   The Security Options button is not available in Disk Utility for SSD volumes. These options are not needed because recovering data from an SSD is already difficult.

Info

Finally, Disk Utility provides a simple utility for getting much of the same information about disks and volumes the `diskutil` command-line tool provides. For example, earlier you ran the `diskutil list` command to get the identifier for the Macintosh HD volume. Selecting the volume in Disk Utility and clicking the Info button displays a subset of the same information (Figure 4-27).

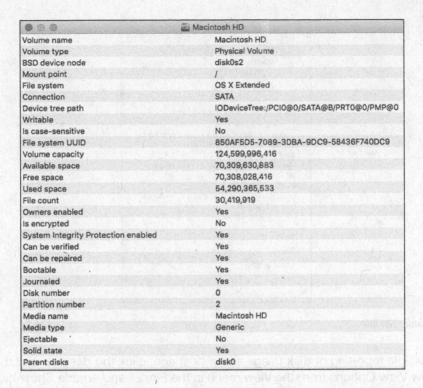

Volume name	Macintosh HD
Volume type	Physical Volume
BSD device node	disk0s2
Mount point	/
File system	OS X Extended
Connection	SATA
Device tree path	IODeviceTree:/PCI0@0/SATA@B/PRT0@0/PMP@0
Writable	Yes
Is case-sensitive	No
File system UUID	850AF5D5-7089-3DBA-9DC9-58436F740DC9
Volume capacity	124,599,996,416
Available space	70,309,630,883
Free space	70,308,028,416
Used space	54,290,365,533
File count	30,419,919
Owners enabled	Yes
Is encrypted	No
System Integrity Protection enabled	Yes
Can be verified	Yes
Can be repaired	Yes
Bootable	Yes
Journaled	Yes
Disk number	0
Partition number	2
Media name	Macintosh HD
Media type	Generic
Ejectable	No
Solid state	Yes
Parent disks	disk0

Figure 4-27. Info

Compared to the diskutil command, this information is more basic but may be enough technical information for most needs.

Disk Usage

Even with today's internal and external storage capacities, we still need to manage space. A 4 TB drive may take longer to fill, but users still manage to run out of room. Basic knowledge about drive capacity and usage are fundamental to preventing issues such as low space on system volumes or planning for expanding storage.

The Finder's Get Info command is the easiest way to assess disk usage (Figure 4-28). Select either a disk or a folder and then choose Get Info from the File menu. It displays capacity, free space, and used space.

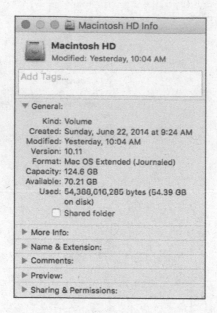

Figure 4-28. Finder Get Info

For always visible reporting of disk usage and disk space, click the desktop and then choose Show View Options from the View menu in the Finder and enable Show Item Info (Figure 4-29). You may need to arrange the label position to the right and set Grid Spacing to Maximum to fully display the information.

Figure 4-29. Finder view drive size and free space

Or open any new Finder window and choose Show Status Bar from the View menu to display free space at the bottom of every Finder window.

For detailed reporting, the du command-line utility is powerful. To get basic output of disk usage for a hard drive, run the following command:

```
sudo du -chx /
```

This recursively runs through every visible and hidden file and presents a grand total of used space in human-readable measurements. The -x option tells du to not traverse through mount points it would find in the /Volumes directory.

```
50G    total
```

Optionally, specify the usage for a specific folder as follows:

```
sudo du -ch /Applications
```

The counterpart to the du tool is df. Not only does it display disk free space, it also displays all three disk space parameters (capacity, free, and used).

```
Filesystem    Size  Used  Avail Capacity  iused    ifree %iused  Mounted on
/dev/disk0s2  116Gi  51Gi  65Gi    44% 13307131 17112788   44%  /
```

Consider using an already familiar tool, diskutil, for displaying free space and volume size.

```
diskutil info / | grep "Total Size"
diskutil info / | grep "Volume Free Space"
```

Securing Local Storage

Half of securing data is when it is in transit over network connections. The other half of securing data is when it is at rest on storage media. Security is frequently referenced as layers of an onion. No single layer is ever enough to completely protect data, but one layer will repel certain types of attacks, another layer will repel even more attacks, and so on.

Physical access to any asset is the first layer of security and generally the responsibility of facilities management. Basically, keep intruders out of the building while allowing employees to enter. But not all employees are necessarily computer users. For example, the janitorial staff responsible for emptying trash and cleaning work areas usually has free rein of the entire building except for highly secure areas such as data centers. That means they have nearly unguarded access to locked and unlocked computers and external hard drives. The easiest way to steal data is to steal the storage device. Administrators need to ensure that data is inaccessible when off-site and not the only copy of that data that exists.

Time Machine

While enterprise administrators may not consider Time Machine to be an enterprise-class backup solution, it is a solution that is easy for users to understand and support themselves. They may be using it at home to protect their personal data alongside work data they have brought home with them. Or they may be using it in the office as a personal backup "oops!" system. The first level of securing a Time Machine device is to encrypt the backups.

1. Choose System Preferences from the Apple menu.

2. Click Time Machine to open the Time Machine pane.

3. Turn on Time Machine and choose a disk for storing backups (Figure 4-30).

Figure 4-30. *Choosing a disk*

4. Enable Encrypt Backups and then click the Use Disk button.

5. Enter a strong password. Consider using the Password tool to the right of the fields to generate a random password.

6. Enter a password hint in case the user forgets the password. Avoid "my favorite…" or "Larry's Uncle" or anything that sounds related to the person. Data thieves only need to research the user online to learn about him or her.

7. Click the Encrypt Disk button (Figure 4-31). Similar to Disk Utility's format option OS X Extended (Journaled, Encrypted), Time Machine erases and formats the drive before using it to store backups.

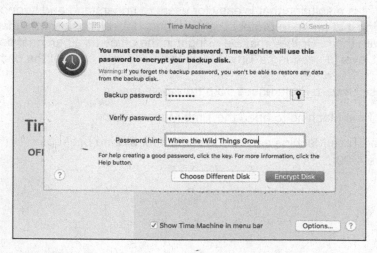

Figure 4-31. *Enabling encryption*

Remember, the data on the external drive is more valuable than the drive itself. While you can take great pains to secure the physical device, the cost and effort may not be worth the trouble. Encryption is free.

Similarly, users should secure all external storage, not just backup storage. That includes external hard drives and even those convenient little USB thumb drives for taking work home. As a best practice for organizations where security concerns are a little higher, administrators or users should use Disk Utility's feature to format all portable storage devices with encryption.

To encrypt an external storage device, follow these steps:

1. Open Disk Utility and connect or insert the external drive (Figure 4-32).

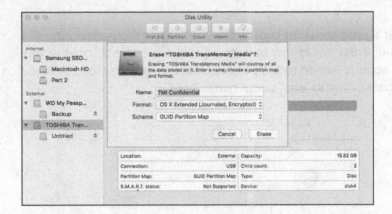

Figure 4-32. Encrypting a disk

2. If the disk is partitioned and you need to protect only one volume, select the volume in the left pane of the Disk Utility window. Otherwise, to completely encrypt the entire drive, select the disk.

3. Click the Erase button in the toolbar.

4. Name the device.

5. Choose OS X Extended (Journaled, Encrypted) from the Format menu.

6. Enter a password to access the device whenever someone inserts it into a Mac.

7. Click the Erase button.

8. When prompted, enter a strong password (Figure 4-33). Consider using the Password tool to the right of the fields to generate a random password.

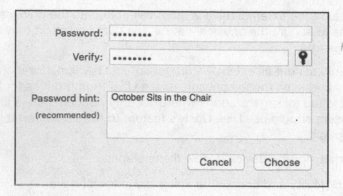

Figure 4-33. Entering an encryption password

9. Enter a password hint in case the user forgets the password
    (Figure 4-34). Avoid "my favorite…" or "Larry's Uncle" or anything
    that sounds related to the person. Data thieves only need to research
    the user online to learn about him or her.

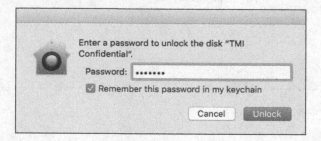

Figure 4-34. Mounting the disk image and saving a password

10. Click the Choose button. Click the Erase button for Disk Utility to
    reformat the drive using encryption and then automatically mount it
    for the user.

11. To test the security, eject and reconnect or reinsert the drive. The
    Finder should prompt for the password.

12. Enter the password and click the Unlock button. Verify the external
    drive appears on the desktop or in the sidebar of any Finder window
    if those preferences are enabled. Optionally, enable "Remember this
    password in my keychain."

Although the device may be lost or stolen, unauthorized users cannot access the data. They
can still, however, erase and reformat the drive. The only way to remove encryption is to use
Disk Utility to first erase the volume without choosing encryption and then erase the disk
without choosing encryption.

The `diskutil` command can encrypt external storage devices as well as encrypt them without having to first erase them.

1. Connect or insert the external drive.

2. Use Disk Utility to select the volume and click the Info button to get the volume's BSD Device Node. Or use the `diskutil list` command to get the volume's identifier.

3. Use `diskutil` to convert the existing volume from standard to encrypted.

   ```
   diskutil coreStorage convert disk4s2 -passphrase
   ```

4. When prompted, enter a passphrase to unlock the volume going forward. Optionally, add the passphrase in plain text to the end of the command to immediately encrypt the volume.

This process takes a while to complete depending on the size of the disk. To revert the process, use Disk Utility to get the BSD device node for the volume or `diskutil list` to get the volume's identifier. (These will be different now.) Then run the following command:

```
diskutil coreStorage revert disk5 -passphrase
```

To monitor the encryption or decryption process, run this command and note the Conversion Progress line for the node:

```
diskutil coreStorage list
```

```
Logical Volume FD27CA2D-F4C1-4A82-9D42-D9E0BC561543
------------------------------------------------------
Disk:                disk5
Status:              Online
Size (Total):        14803664896 B (14.8 GB)
Conversion Progress: 6%
Revertible:          Yes (unlock and decryption required)
LV Name:             TMI Confidential
Volume Name:         TMI Confidential
Content Hint:        Apple_HFS
```

Disk Images

What if you need to securely transfer data over an unsecured network? For example, a marketing employee may need to transfer their Black Friday price list to an external vendor, but e-mail is the quickest (and the easiest) method available. Rather than installing complicated e-mail certificates and transferring encryption keys, just use an encrypted disk image to enclose the data in a small and secure wrapper.

To create a secure and password-protected disk image, follow these steps:

1. In Disk Utility, choose File ➤ New Image ➤ Blank Image.

2. In the screen shown in Figure 4-35, set the name of the new image and set the size to 10 MB (the smallest allowed size).

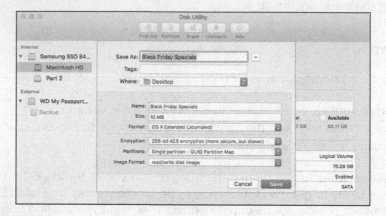

Figure 4-35. Creating an encrypted disk image

3. Set Encryption to either one of the following:

    128-bit AES encryption (recommended)

    256-bit AES encryption (more secure but slower)

4. When prompted, enter a strong password. Consider using the Password tool to the right of the fields to generate a random password. Click the Save button to save the disk image to the computer.

5. Disk Utility mounts the new disk automatically. Copy content to the disk and eject when done.

6. Copy the disk image file (.dmg) to a portable thumb drive or e-mail the file to the intended recipient.

7. Communicate the password to the disk image file via a different medium. For example, if e-mailing the disk image, call the recipient and provide the password. Never store the secured data and the password in the same location.

FileVault 2

FileVault 2 is OS X's crown jewel of disk encryption. It secures boot volumes. Although Apple touts FileVault 2 as "full disk encryption," a more correct description is "full boot volume encryption." Although administrators generally view encryption as a process that trades off speed for security, FileVault 2's implementation affects computer performance very little after the entire volume is fully encrypted, especially with spinning drives. Although you can enable FileVault 2 on computers in production, the most opportune time is just after imaging a Mac or removing it from its shrink-wrap before adding user data. It also requires OS X 10.7 or higher.

To enable FileVault 2 on a Mac (Figure 4-36), follow these steps:

1. Open the Security & Privacy pane in System Preferences. Click the FileVault tab.

2. Click the Lock button and authenticate to make changes.

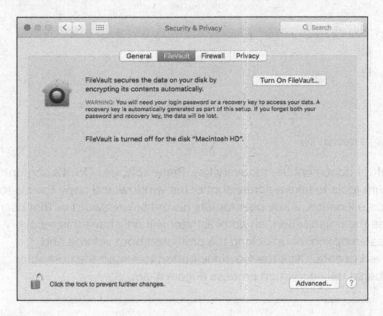

Figure 4-36. FileVault 2

3. Click the Turn On FileVault button.

4. Choose "Create a recovery key and do not use my iCloud account" and click the Continue button (Figure 4-37).

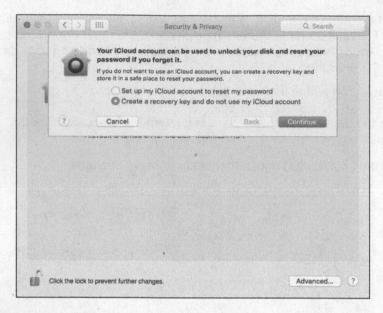

Figure 4-37. *Creating a recovery key*

5. Carefully document the recovery key. Preferably, use OS X's screen capture tools to take a screenshot of the window and copy the file to a secure location. If any user forgets his or her password or that user leaves the organization, an administrator will only have this recovery key as an option for unlocking the protected boot volume and recovering data. Click the Continue button to restart the computer and begin the encryption process (Figure 4-38).

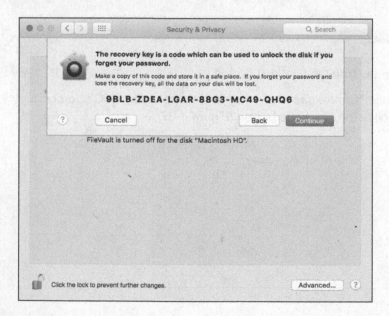

Figure 4-38. *Recovery key*

6. Once the computer reboots, it almost immediately displays a login window. FileVault 2 starts before the boot process. At this point, it requires user credentials to unlock the disk and continue the boot process. Once unlocked, FileVault 2's work is done.

7. Encryption begins just after the first boot after enabling FileVault 2 (Figure 4-39). You can monitor the progress by opening the Security & Privacy pane in System Preferences and clicking the FileVault tab.

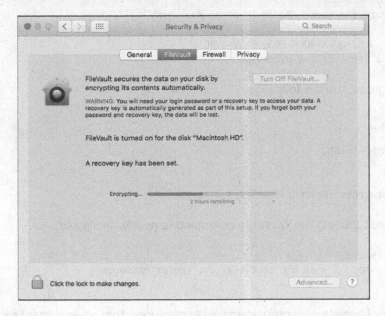

Figure 4-39. Encrypting

> **Tip** Do not enable the Guest account on FileVault 2–encrypted computers.
>
> Some administrators like to enable the Guest account in case computers are lost or stolen. Their reasoning is any user can access this account and add the computer to a network so it will phone home to their management system. This, however, completely thwarts FileVault security. Once a computer's boot volume is unlocked, accessing user data just got a lot easier for a would-be hacker.

For mass FileVault 2 management, use Apple's command-line tool fdesetup for enabling and managing encryption and escrowing recovery keys.

To get current encryption status, run the following:

```
fdesetup status
```

It returns something similar to the following:

```
FileVault is On.
Encryption in progress: Percent completed = 52.43
```

To enable FileVault 2, run the following:

```
sudo fdesetup enable
```

After authenticating, `fdesetup` interactively prompts for a username and password for an account on the Mac and provides a recovery key. Again, carefully document this recovery key. It then prompts to reboot the computer.

```
Enter the user name:mmoose
Enter the password for user 'mmoose': <enter password>
........
Recovery key = 'OL6Z-QQPA-8QPM-EGGQ-JXVV-6VRC'
Please reboot to complete the process.
```

To monitor progress, run the following:

```
fdesetup status
```

This returns the following:

```
FileVault is On.
Encryption in progress: Percent completed = 74.19
```

Disabling FileVault 2 using the `fdesetup` command is nearly as simple.

```
sudo fdesetup disable
Enter a password for '/', or the recovery key: <enter password>
...
```

The `fdesetup` tool assists with programmatically capturing that all-important recovery key for scripts or other agents to collect and escrow on a server (see CauliflowerVest in Chapter 10). This command defers the FileVault 2 setup until the next login at which point the agent can collect the recovery key. This process is useful when administrators may be handling computers that do not yet have a user account. Deferring the encryption allows the Mac's end user to log in to create the account, trigger the encryption process, and enable that user to unlock the disk.

```
sudo fdesetup enable -defer /private/var/fv2/escrow.plist
```

The simplest method, though, for enabling FileVault 2 is to use configuration profiles deployed through your MDM server solution. Use a management server such as Apple's Profile Manager to create the configuration profile. The management server itself does not necessarily need to be actively managing devices.

1. Open Profile Manager in a web browser. Log in using administrator credentials for the server.

2. Click Device Groups under Library and click the + button (plus) to create a new group called Enable FileVault 2 (Figure 4-40).

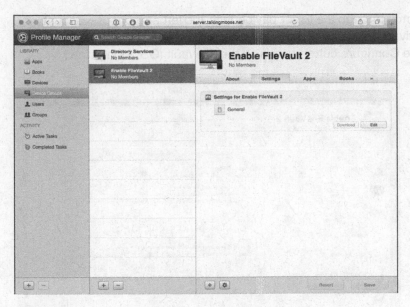

Figure 4-40. Device group

3. Click the Settings tab in the right pane. Click the Edit button.

4. Complete the information in the General payload of the new configuration profile. Set the Security drop-down menu to Never to prevent removal of the profile (Figure 4-41).

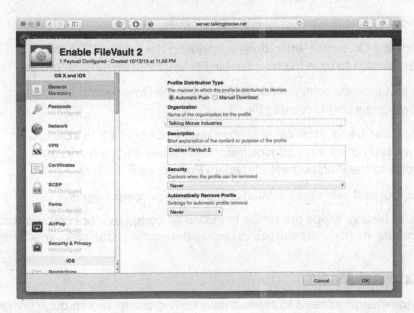

Figure 4-41. General payload

5. Scroll through the list of payloads to the left and choose Security & Privacy in the OS X and IOS section of payloads (Figure 4-42). Click the Configure button and click the FileVault (OS X Only) tab.

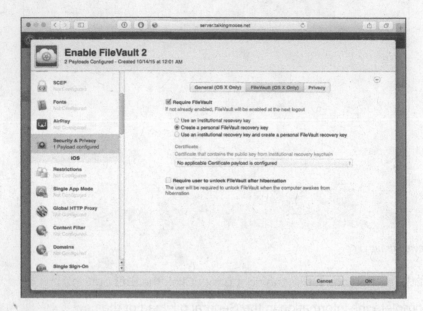

Figure 4-42. Security and privacy payload

6. Enable Require FileVault.

7. Choose "Create a personal FileVault recovery key."

8. Click the OK button when done configuring the profile. Click the Save button to save the new Enable FileVault 2 configuration profile.

9. To test the new configuration profile, click the Download button to download a `.mobileconfig` file.

10. Copy this file to a test client system and double-click it to install. OS X will prompt for local administrator credentials and then add the profile to the Profiles pane of System Preferences.

11. Log out and verify the FileVault 2 encryption process begins.

After successful testing, scope the profile to individual computers or computer groups in your MDM and use its push capabilities to deploy the profile to the client machines.

Restrict External Media

Sometimes, administrators need to prevent data leaving computers through uncontrolled media such as USB thumb drives or small portable external hard drives. Use configuration profiles to restrict access to external media or limit it to authorized users only.

Use a management server such as Apple's Profile Manager to create the configuration profile. The management server itself does not necessarily need to be actively managing devices.

1. Launch the Server app and click Groups in the navigation pane.

2. Click the + button (plus) to create a new group named Restrict External Media (Figure 4-43). Click the OK button when done.

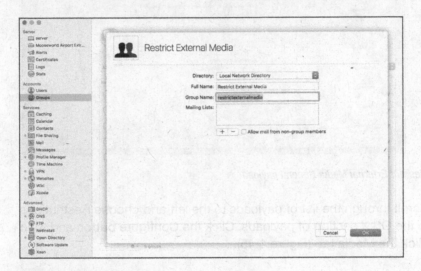

Figure 4-43. Restricting External Media group

3. Open Profile Manager in a web browser. Log in using administrator credentials for the server.

4. Click Groups under Library and click the Restrict External Media group.

5. Click the Settings tab in the right pane. Click the Edit button.

6. Complete the information in the General payload of the new configuration profile. Set the Security drop-down menu to Never to prevent the removal of the profile (Figure 4-44).

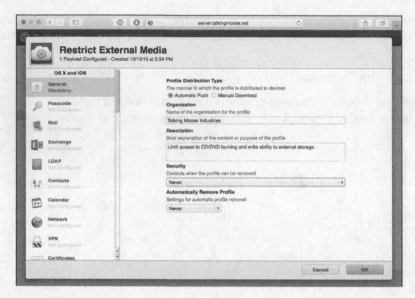

Figure 4-44. *Restrict External Media General payload*

7. Scroll through the list of payloads to the left and choose Restrictions in the OS X section of payloads. Click the Configure button and then click the Media tab (Figure 4-45).

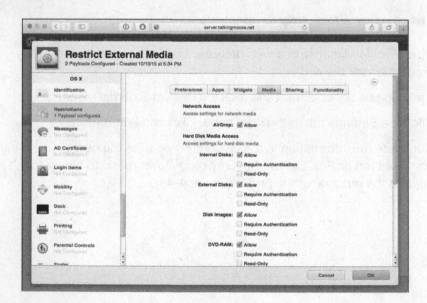

Figure 4-45. *Restrict External Media Restrictions payload*

8. Examine the available options. Note some options enable administrators to access media by denying access to standard users.

    AirDrop: Allow or deny

    Internal Disks, External Disks, Disk Images, DVD-RAM: Allow, Require Authentication, or Read Only

    CDs & CD-ROMs, DVDs, Recordable Discs: Allow or Require Authentication

    Eject at logout: Enable or disable

9. Click the OK button when done configuring the profile. Click the Save button to save the new Restrict External Media configuration profile. To test the new configuration profile, click the Download button to download a `.mobileconfig` file.

10. Copy this file to a test client system and double-click it to install. OS X will prompt for local administrator credentials and then add the profile to the Profiles pane of System Preferences.

11. Attempt to access the types of media in the restriction and verify whether the configuration profile is working correctly.

Managing Permissions

Part of discussing storage is managing access to storage. Administrators define access to network and local resources using permissions, and OS X enforces those permissions by combining *inherited* and *explicit* sets of permissions.

Inheritance means a file or folder derives its permissions from its parent folder or disk. If an administrator grants the Accounting group access to a folder named Debits & Credits, the group also has access to the folder's contents through inheritance. Explicit permissions are placed on specific files or folders to control access only to those items and their contents. An administrator can select a folder inside the Debits & Credits folder and break inheritance by defining explicit permissions. This might be to allow only managers access to sensitive files.

OS X supports two permissions schemes called POSIX and access control lists (ACLs). Although they can exist side by side, the two permissions schemes were not designed to work together for controlling access to files and folders, so applying both may display unintended results. Understanding how both work is crucial to administration.

POSIX-Based Permissions

OS X inherited its POSIX-compliant permissioning from Unix. POSIX is a simple system that defines the owner, group, and mode of a folder or file. The mode, presented as a series of numeric values such as 755 or 400, represents the object's permissions. POSIX applies access restrictions at three different user levels.

- *Owner*: User with full control of a folder or file

- *Group*: Group with privileges controlled by the owner

- *Everyone*: Users not in the group such as guests

Each user level has three possible permission levels, or *modes*:

- *Read*: The ability to see the contents of a folder or file

- *Write*: The ability to change the contents of a folder or file

- *Execute*: The ability for users to run code contained in the file or subfiles

In computer terminology, a binary digit, or *bit*, is the smallest unit of data possible. It is like two sides of a coin: heads or tails. Here are some examples:

- True or False

- On or Off

- 1 or 0 (zero)

POSIX uses three bits in a row to represent modes. The total number of possible modes with just three bits is eight, as shown in Table 4-2.

Table 4-2. Modes Are Three Bits in a Row with a Total of Eight Possible Modes

Understanding modes

Mode	Decimal	Heads or Tails	True or False	On or Off
000	0	Heads / Heads / Heads	True / True / True	On / On / On
001	1	Heads / Heads / Tails	True / True / False	On / On / Off
010	2	Heads / Tails / Heads	True / False / True	On / Off / On
011	3	Heads / Tails / Tails	True / False / False	On / Off / Off
100	4	Tails / Heads / Heads	False / True / True	Off / On / On
101	5	Tails / Heads / Tails	False / True / False	Off / On / Off
110	6	Tails / Tails / Heads	False / False / True	Off / Off / On
111	7	Tails / Tails / Tails	False / False / False	Off / Off / Off

Modes are described using binary numbers (0 and 1), but for ease of reading, we convert them to their decimal equivalents (0 through 7).

Open Terminal and run the following command:

```
ls -l
```

This command displays a list version of the current directory.

```
drwx--x--x   22 mmoose   staff    748 Oct  8 18:02 Desktop
drwx--x--x@  60 mmoose   staff   2040 Sep  3 23:04 Documents
drwx--x--x   75 mmoose   staff   2550 Oct  7 21:35 Downloads
```

```
drwx--x--x   36 mmoose   staff   1224 Jun  7 09:27 Movies
drwx--x--x   13 mmoose   staff    442 Jul  6 2014  Music
drwx--x--x  236 mmoose   staff   8024 May 17 18:09 Pictures
drwxr-xr-x    7 mmoose   staff    238 Jan 10 2015  Public
drwxr-xr-x   23 mmoose   staff    782 Jan 18 2015  Sites
-rwxr-xr-x   23 mmoose   staff    782 Jan 18 2015  script.sh
```

The beginning of each line displays the POSIX permissions for each item. with the first character denoting whether the item is a file, folder, or link. For example, a d denotes a folder, or *directory*, and a - (dash) denotes a file.

- *b*: Block special file

- *c*: Character special file

- *d*: Directory

- *l*: Symbolic link

- *s*: Socket link

- *p*: FIFO

- *-*: Regular file

The next nine characters denote the POSIX permissions for Owner, Group, and Everyone, respectively. Each character individually represents a single bit in the three-digit mode discussed earlier. The first set of three characters denotes the mode for Owner. The second set of three characters denotes the mode for Group. The third set of three characters denotes the mode for Everyone. Within each group, the first bit represents *read* permission (r), the second bit represents write permission (w), and the third bit represents executable permission (x). This is shown in Figure 4-46. When a bit is on or true, the letter of the permission appears (r, w, or x). When the bit is off or false, the position displays a dash (-).

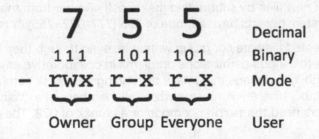

Figure 4-46. The first character denotes this is a file. The next nine characters denote permissions

A person who lacks privileges for a directory—via ownership, group membership, or public permissions—can neither list its contents nor access any file system elements it contains. Allowing read and execute privileges while denying write privileges on a directory lets users access subfolders and files and even run scripts, but it prevents them from making any changes inside the folder. Allowing write privileges while denying read privileges to a folder lets users add to its contents without seeing its contents—effectively a drop box.

Let's look at some additional modes. Run this command in Terminal:

```
ls -l /Users
```

For the enclosed Shared folder, it shows something similar to this:

```
drwxrwxrwt 13 root   wheel  442 Jun 29 23:54 Shared
```

For Everyone permissions, show rwt instead of rw- or rwx. The t is a sticky bit. When enabled on a directory, it prevents the deletion of a file in that directory by anyone other than the file's owner. Thus, if a user creates a file and gives everyone read and write privileges, other users can edit its content but not delete it. Only the Owner can delete the file. Of course, with write privileges, nothing stops other users from simply deleting the file's contents.

Assigning the sticky bit to a directory requires prepending a number to the beginning of the permissions with a value of 001. The Shared folder has a mode of 1777, with the 1 (001 binary) being the "sticky" directory. Use the chmod command to apply this mode. Run the command as root (use sudo) if you are not owner of the folder.

```
sudo chmod 1777 /Users/Shared
sudo chmod -R 777 /Users/Shared/*
```

The second command specifies the -R option to *recursively* apply the mode 777 to all contents. All files in the directory are editable by anyone, but only the owners can delete their files.

New files and folders created within a folder are owned by their creator regardless of ownership of the enclosing folder. Owner is not inherited. However, Group is inherited from the parent folder. By default, OS X ships with a umask value of 022. All newly created files default to full privileges or 777. But they are filtered by the 022 umask. Calculate the resulting privileges of new files by subtracting the umask number from the privileges number. Newly created file system objects have a mode of 755 (777-022=755) or rwxr-xr-x.

This means newly created files are *not* group writeable, even though they inherit the group, and this leads to serious permissions problems in collaborative environments. Administrators, though, can change the umask by running the umask command with the desired mode. In collaborative environments where all members of a group need read *and* write privileges, folders need the rwxrwxr-x mode or a umask of 002. The command for this is simply as follows:

```
umask 002
```

Setting the umask may not affect all running processes, and the result does not persist across reboots. To permanently set the umask in OS X 10.10.3 Yosemite and later, run this command and restart the computer:

```
sudo launchctl config user umask 002
```

For OS X 10.9.5 Mavericks and earlier, run this command and restart the computer:

```
sudo echo "umask 002" >> /private/etc/launchd-user.conf
```

POSIX permissions rely on the UNIX concepts of Owner, Group, and Everyone, but they are limited with regard to fine-grained permissions tuning. Some environments may need folder hierarchies where a group can read and modify contents, while multiple other groups can only read and maybe more groups can only add files (drop box). The better solution for managing permissions with both AFP and SMB, including access to resources on servers, is access control lists.

Access Control Lists

Access control lists for OS X offer granular control over resources, and they match Windows ACLs almost identically. In fact, the OS X NFSv4 ACL format is compatible with Windows ACLs. That means Windows Server administrators need do nothing different to support access to files from Mac clients.

ACLs free administrators and users from the constraints of the POSIX user/group/everyone paradigm and greatly simplify permissions management on Macs and network file shares. ACLs also define numerous different access levels and inheritance capabilities that allow especially effective permissions hierarchies. While files and folders might include both ACLs and POSIX permissions, ACLs take precedence. An access control entry (ACE), which is a single item within an access control *list*, may specify a group to have read and write permissions to a resource. If that group is not listed as the group for the POSIX permissions, users still gain read and write access.

To manage ACLs on an OS X file server, open the Server app and click the File Sharing service. Choose a shared folder and click the pencil button to edit its properties (Figure 4-47).

Figure 4-47. OS X Server file sharing and shared folders

To add an ACE, click the + button (plus) to begin entering a user or group name. Autocomplete assists to quickly enter names as you type more characters. Apple has greatly simplified adding and modifying ACEs for servers since it first introduced ACLs to OS X. An administrator can access only a select few permissions here:

- Read & Write
- Read
- Write

Continue adding ACEs until all users and groups needing access to the resource are listed and permissions assigned. What happens, though, if a user is a member of one group with Read & Write permissions and a member of another group with Write (no Read) permissions? ACL permissions are least restrictive unless a user or group containing the user is explicitly denied access to the resource. Therefore, if a user is a member of one group with modify access to a resource and a member of another group with write-only access, the user's effective permissions allow modify access. However, if the user or a group containing the user has Deny access applied, the user has no access.

The bottom three permissions entries are the POSIX permissions for the folder. They display permissions for Owner, Primary Group, and Everyone else. OS X will evaluate these last if a user requesting access to a resource does not fall into one of the ACEs at the top of the list. Note the POSIX permissions are

- Read & Write
- Read Only
- Write Only
- No Access

ACLs by default assume No Access if a user is not a member of a group in one of the ACEs (Figure 4-48). However, a user may gain access if POSIX permissions allow. This gets confusing quickly. Best practice is to use only ACLs for controlling access to resources and set POSIX Owner and Group to local server user accounts such as root and admin. Everyone should generally be set to No Access to avoid letting everyone access the resource.

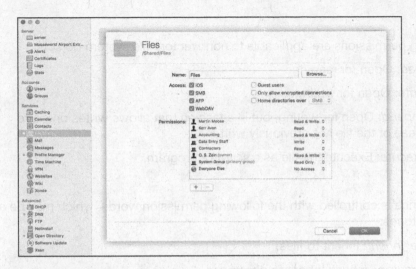

Figure 4-48. Adding ACEs to an ACL

For even more granular control of objects, the chmod command sets up to 21 unique permissions categorized into four areas of control.

All Objects

The following permissions are applicable to all file system objects:

- *delete*: Delete the item. Deletion may be granted by either this permission on an object or the delete_child right on the containing directory.

- *readattr*: Read an object's basic attributes. This is implicitly granted if the object can be looked up and not explicitly denied.

- *writeattr*: Write an object's basic attributes.

- *readextattr*: Read extended attributes.

- *writeextattr*: Write extended attributes.

- *readsecurity*: Read an object's extended security information (ACL).

- *writesecurity*: Write an object's security information (ownership, mode, ACL).

- *chown*: Change an object's ownership.

Directories

The following permissions are applicable to directories:

- *list*: List entries.

- *search*: Look up files by name.

- *add_file*: Add a file.

- *add_subdirectory*: Add a subdirectory.

- *delete_child*: Delete a contained object. See the file delete permission.

Files

The following permissions are applicable to nondirectory file system objects:

- *read*: Open for reading.
- *write*: Open for writing.
- *append*: Open for writing, but in a fashion that allows writes only into areas of the file not previously written.
- *execute*: Execute the file as a script or program.

Inheritance

ACL inheritance is controlled with the following permission words, which may be applied only to directories:

- *file_inherit*: Inherit to files.
- *directory_inherit*: Inherit to directories.
- *limit_inherit*: This flag is relevant only to entries inherited by subdirectories; it causes the `directory_inherit` flag to be cleared in the entry that is inherited, preventing further nested subdirectories from also inheriting the entry.
- *only_inherit*: The entry is inherited by created items but not considered when processing the ACL.

Managing Permissions

Use the `chown` command-line tool to change POSIX permissions and ACLs. Let's look at using chown for modifying POSIX permissions first. To change the owner, run the following command (If you are not the owner, run the command with sudo):

```
sudo chown mmoose /path/to/file
```

To change both the owner and the group for a folder and its contents, append the group to the owner name and use the -R option to recurse through the folder.

```
sudo chown -R mmoose:sales /path/to/folder
```

Or to change just the group, use the `chgrp` command.

```
sudo chgrp sales /path/to/file
```

The `chmod` command manages both POSIX and ACL permissions. Managing ACLs from the command line can get complex. Use OS X's GUI tools such as Finder's Get Info or Server's File Sharing area to set most permissions. Use chmod to set ACLs only if these tools are not enough.

To modify permissions to allow read and write access to a file but not execute, run the following command (if you are not the owner, run the command with sudo):

```
chmod 775 /path/to/file
```

To modify permissions to allow read-only access to a folder and apply these permissions to all subfolders and files, run the following command:

```
chmod -R 755 /path/to/folder
```

To create, modify, or remove an ACE using chmod, use the +a or –a option followed by a comma-separated list of permissions. For example, to grant full control of file test.txt to the user mmoose, run the following command (using sudo if not the owner):

```
chmod +a "mmoose allow read,write,execute,delete,append,readattr,writeattr,readextattr,
writeextattr,readsecurity,writesecurity,chown" test.txt
```

To view the ACLs on the same file after applying the changes, use the ls command with the –e option. (Note the 0 before the ACE. This is its index number, which is needed when removing or specifying an ACE.)

```
ls -el test.txt
-rw-r--r--+ 1 mmoose staff 12 Ot 9 13:00 test.txt
 0: user:mmoose allow read,write,execute,delete,append,readattr,writeattr,readextattr,
writeextattr,readsecurity,writesecurity,chown
```

Similarly, to grant full control for a directory named artwork, run the following command:

```
chmod +a "mmoose allow list,add_file,search,delete,add_subdirectory,delete_child,readattr,
writeattr,readextattr,writeextattr,readsecurity,writesecurity,chown,limit_inherit,
only_inherit" artwork
```

To remove an entire ACE, use the –a# flag followed by the ACE's index number.

```
chmod -a# 0 test.txt
```

To remove specific attributes, use the -a option with the user or group and then list the attributes.

```
chmod -a "mmoose allow delete" test.txt
```

ACLs are powerful tools for managing access to resources, but managing a large file system with numerous explicit permissions is difficult. Explicit permissions also override inherited permissions, which can produce unexpected results. Strive to keep ACLs simple and the groups you add to them clearly defined.

> **Tip**   Because of the way that the chmod utility parses the ACE, using the documented syntax
> for chmod does not work correctly when used with user or group names that contain spaces
> in the short name. This creates issues with many Active Directory groups. Fortunately,
> to get around this issue, you can use the colon as a delimiter. So, to assign an ACL for the group
> TALKINGMOOSE\Desktop Admins, use the following syntax (one line):
>
> ```
> chmod +a TALKINGMOOSE\Desktop Admins:allow:read,write,execute' /Artwork
> ```

Finally, you can also remove all ACLs with chmod's –N option. Combined with –R (recursive),
use chmod to recurse through subfolders to remove all ACLs.

```
chmod -RN /Artwork
```

Summary

In this chapter, we discussed the last five years of storage evolution for Macs. Media types
have boomed or become extinct in the Apple world, and with those changes, administrators
have a more difficult job securing data. But they also have more tools at their disposal, built
right in to OS X.

The chapter heavily focused on securing data at rest and in transit with regard to various
types of storage such as network, cloud, and local systems.

In the next chapter, we'll discuss various groupware options available to your OS X clients.
We'll cover topics such as integrating with Exchange as well as some Apple-hosted
products such as Calendar Server and Contacts Server. Where appropriate, we will also
discuss how to store back-end assets (if they are running on Mac OS X) on Xsan or other
clustered Mac OS X file storage offerings.

## Chapter 5

Messaging and Groupware

Groupware is one of the most important communication vehicles in the modern enterprise. Tracking what people are doing in shared calendars, and whom your organization does business with in shared contacts, and communicating with them all via e-mail are requirements today for any large organization. In fact, it goes a step further in that you need to extend the same functionality you have at the desktop onto mobile devices, including, of course, the iPad, iPhone, and iPod Touch.

For the purpose of this chapter, we will include messaging solutions as part of the overall groupware ecosystem. We do so because every conversation about shared contacts and calendars includes e-mail. Some even include instant messaging frameworks. Over the course of this chapter, we will cover the various solutions that have become common on the OS X platform, starting with Microsoft Exchange.

There are a number of groupware platforms, each with varying degrees of compatibility with the Mac. Microsoft Exchange is clearly the most prevalent, so we'll spend more time in this chapter covering Exchange than any other solution. However, Exchange isn't the only solution. Lotus Notes, GroupWise, and a few others have become fairly common in enterprise organizations, so these are included as well.

But what if you want to be in a purely OS X environment? Well, you can. We're not going to say that this will come with the same level of scalability, application functionality, cross-pollination among applications, and maturity that some of the other solutions (especially Microsoft Exchange) can provide, because it can't. The pure-Mac solution is just not there yet. However, OS X has some groupware features that certainly bring a first-party solution much closer to reality. Moreover, the Mac solution is worth exploring on a service-by-service basis, considering that licensing and complexity can cause many of the other solutions to come in at a much higher total cost of ownership for Mac clients than for their Windows counterparts.

Exchange Integration

OS X can communicate with Microsoft Exchange in a variety of ways; most notable is its support for Outlook Web Access (OWA) from a web browser. But if you use Microsoft Exchange 2012 or earlier, you need to consider Entourage, an e-mail client and personal information manager from Microsoft. You can use POP or IMAP mail accounts with other solutions, or you can use Mail, Calendar, and Contacts in an Exchange environment that you may already be leveraging. While not the only option, Outlook is a mature product for Exchange integration and the most widely adopted for such environments.

Exchange consists of a number of roles, each controlling the functionality that a server is able to offer to clients and to other Exchange servers. Most of the integration that will be done with Exchange will be done through the Client Access Server (CAS) role. For the most part, the technologies included in the CAS role existed in Exchange 2003 and earlier, but the idea of breaking Exchange into predefined roles, and the CAS role specifically, was new as of Exchange Server 2007. One component of Exchange that does not exist in versions prior to 2007 is the Exchange Web Services (EWS) API, which opens up a number of options, including using Entourage for Exchange EWS (an Exchange 2007/EWS-optimized Entourage app) or using Mail to interface with Exchange. However, as yet, adoption of Exchange has been relatively limited. In an Exchange 2003 environment, in many cases you will be able to leverage WebDAV, an extension to the HTTP protocol, when connecting from an OS X client.

Outlook

Microsoft Outlook is part of the Microsoft Office family of products that most environments have already deployed. Microsoft Outlook client licensing is not necessarily bundled with Exchange or Office 365. Exchange 2003 and earlier do provide a license for a stand-alone Microsoft Outlook client.

If licensing is not an issue (for example, you already own Microsoft Office for your Mac clients), then you should consider Outlook as an option for your clients to connect to Exchange. Outlook has a look and feel that is fairly similar to Microsoft Outlook for Windows, and it has many of the same features (although not all), so a user coming to a Mac from a PC will find it easy to use.

Paths

One of the first tasks to undertake when integrating OS X into Microsoft Exchange is to log into Outlook Web Access. If you can log into OWA without issue, you should also be able to set up Outlook integration or even configure an iPad, iPhone, or iPod Touch.

To authenticate into WebDAV, you should be able to access the server over HTTP or HTTPS. These are the same general paths (often dubbed *virtual paths*) you will use with Outlook. You can follow the paths with usernames in the form of fully qualified e-mail addresses if you're receiving errors that you can't authenticate when you haven't yet been prompted for a password. The following are paths you may need to use to access OWA. In this example, we are accessing an Exchange server at the address `exchange.krypted.com`:

These are the paths for mailbox access:

- `https://exchange.krypted.com/exchange/username@domain.com`
- `https://exchange.krypted.com/owa`
- `https://exchange.krypted.com/exchweb`
- `https://exchange.krypted.com`

These are the paths for public folder access:

- `https://exchange.krypted.com/public`
- `https://exchange.krypted.com/public/username@domain.com`

In Exchange 2007 and newer, there can be even more paths, because Exchange 2007 has a lot more features. This is not to say that the paths mentioned previously have been deprecated; in most cases, they have not. Exchange provides support for these using legacy virtual directories (made possible by `davex.dll`) that should be able to handle Exchange WebDAV requests. However, the following are the mailbox-access URLs you may run into:

- `https://exchange.krypted.com`
- `https://exchange.krypted.com/owa`
- `https://exchange.krypted.com/exchange`
- `https://exchange.krypted.com/exchweb`

Overall, WebDAV integration is a safe bet, but there is a newer and better way: EWS. EWS leverages Simple Object Access Protocol (SOAP) to exchange data through XML, allowing for more developers to interact with Exchange. EWS is faster and chews through less bandwidth, adding synchronization support for categories and tasks (not otherwise provided by WebDAV). If you will be using Entourage for EWS or Mail, you will instead want to check for EWS connectivity, which is different from the paths previously mentioned. The following are possible URLs that you will see:

- `https://exchange.krypted.com` (more than likely an administrator used a virtual directory to help shorten the path)
- `https://exchange.krypted.com/ews` (Exchange should throw a "Directory Listing Denied" error)
- `https://exchange.krypted.com/ews/Exchange.asmx` (the default setting)
- `https://exchange.krypted.com/ews/Serivces.wsdl` (a redirect to a blank page)

Once you have confirmed your paths, you can set up the client application.

> **Tip**   Paths may also be followed by a colon and then the port number that the service is running
> on if a custom port has been used (`https://exchange.krypted.com:8443/ews`).

Troubleshooting Exchange Virtual Directories

In a number of deployments, Entourage simply will not work, even though Outlook Web
Access will authenticate users. To resolve this, you can use a series of Windows PowerShell
commands. PowerShell is the command-line scripting language used for Windows Server
2008 and newer and Exchange Server 2007 and newer environments. To start, you can get
a list of all the virtual directories using the `Get-OwaVirtualDirectory` cmdlet without any
operators, as shown here:

```
Get-OwaVirtualDirectory
```

If you are having an issue with a specific virtual directory, you can delete it using this
command:

```
Remove-OwaVirtualDirectory "owa (Default Web Site)"
```

The preceding command uses the owa virtual directory, but it could have used `Exchange`,
`Public`, `Exchweb`, or `Exadmin` as well. To re-create the directory, use the following command
(again replacing owa in the quoted portion of the command with the specified virtual directory
you are re-creating):

```
New-OwaVirtualDirectory -OwaVersion "Exchange2007 -Name "owa (Default Web Site)"
```

Because a virtual directory is just that, virtual, you will not encounter any problems from
deleting it, except that while it is offline your clients who use it will not be able to connect to
the server. Note that when you re-create the virtual directory, you will need to go into IIS and
customize the permissions as defined by your organization's security policy before using the
virtual directory again. The ability to delete virtual directories (or, more importantly, to create
new ones) is a great help when troubleshooting connectivity issues. After you've created
a new virtual directory, before you customize permissions, test Entourage. Then, after you
customize the permissions, test Outlook again. Or, you may want to create an entirely new
virtual directory without deleting the existing one during testing.

Because `Exchange`, `Public`, `Exchweb`, and `Exadmin` are not native to Exchange 2007, you
would actually replace `Exchange2007` with `Exchange2003or2000` for those directories. So if you
wanted to re-create `Exadmin`, for example, you would use the following command:

```
New-OwaVirtualDirectory -OwaVersion "Exchange2003or2000"-Name "Exadmin (Default Web Site)"
```

Outlook Setup

First, install Outlook, and feel free to accept the default values during installation. Once the application has been fully installed, proceed to Updates, an option available through the Outlook Help menu, until the software is running the latest revision. If you will be automating the installation, read further for more information on doing so.

With the software installed, you can set up your first account. Though there is an account setup wizard that launches when you first open Entourage, we will walk you through configuring an account manually (without having Entourage "locate" the server). If you do run the Outlook wizard, you will have to provide your domain. Note that Outlook does not automatically supply all the different settings. Microsoft can attempt to autopopulate all the data it wants, but the fact is that in real-world environments, few DNS servers have the perfect records to do this. It's nothing that Microsoft has done wrong, just that some Active Directory environments have years of cruft hiding in their bowels. In some cases, you might see no other symptoms in your environment except that Outlook will not automatically complete setup (that is, until you go to prep your domain for the 2010 server).

To manually set up an account, click the Tools menu and select Accounts to bring up the Accounts window, shown in Figure 5-1. Now click Exchange or Office 365.

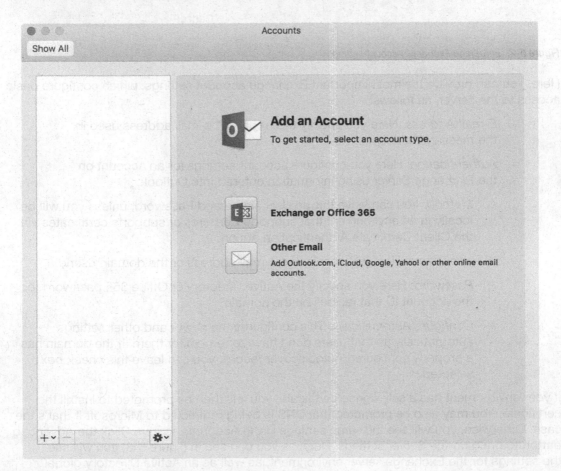

Figure 5-1. The Outlook Accounts pane

You will see the screen to provide your Exchange or Office 365 account information. If Autodiscover is set up correctly, you should need only an e-mail address and password; however, if you need to provide more information, you can uncheck the "Configure automatically" check box, shown in Figure 5-2. Instead, in this case, we will allow the automatic configuration process to authenticate the account and configure Outlook.

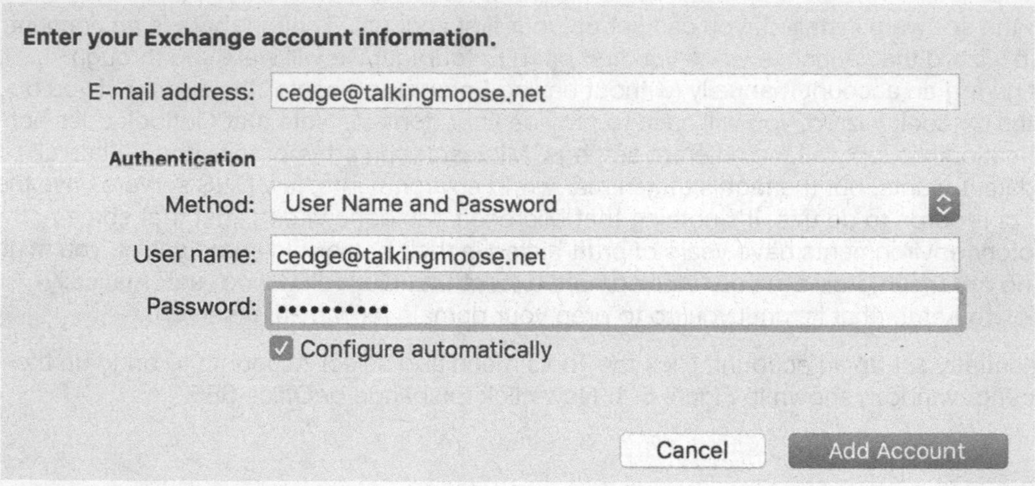

Enter your Exchange account information.

E-mail address: cedge@talkingmoose.net

Authentication

Method: User Name and Password

User name: cedge@talkingmoose.net

Password: ••••••••••

☑ Configure automatically

Cancel   Add Account

Figure 5-2. Entourage Exchange account settings

Here, you can provide the most important Exchange account settings, which configure basic access to the server, as follows:

- *E-mail Address*: Here you specify the "reply-to" e-mail address used in the message headers.

- *Authentication*: Here you configure account settings for an account on the Exchange Server using information entered into Outlook.

    - *Method:* You can leave this as User Name and Password, unless you will be locally in an environment that supports Kerberos or supports certificates via the Client Certificate Authentication option.

    - *User name*: Here you specify the e-mail address or the domain\userid.

    - *Password*: Here you specify the Active Directory or Office 365 password for the account ID that resides on the domain.

    - *Configure Automatically*: This configures the server and other settings automatically so that users don't have to remember them. If the domain has a properly configured Autodiscover record, you can leave this check box selected.

If your environment has a self-signed certificate, you will then be prompted to install the certificate. You may also be prompted that DNS is being redirected to Microsoft if that's the case. Otherwise, you will see the same settings in the Accounts screen. Click the Advanced button to bring up the Server settings. Here, as you can see in Figure 5-3, you will see the settings for the Exchange server environment, as well as an Active Directory global catalog server.

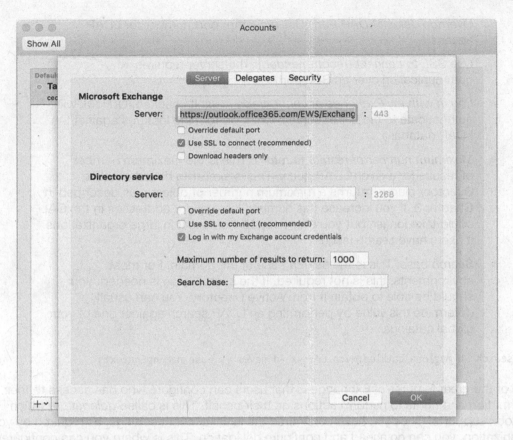

Figure 5-3. Outlook Exchange account settings

- *Server*: This is the URL to the server. This is usually more than just a server name but also includes the path to the EWS site from IIS.

  - *Override default port*: This setting allows you to configure another port, if needed, such as port 8080.

  - *Use SSL to connect (recommended)*: This connects using SSL, the default, but if you connect without a certificate, you can uncheck this box.

  - *Download headers only*: This downloads only message headers.

  You will also be able to configure Active Directory global catalog server settings in the "Directory service" section of the screen. Here, if needed, you can obtain the following information:

- *Server*: This is the IP address or host name of the server. LDAP is used for global address list (GAL) lookups. In some cases, you can use the Exchange server, although you may need to use a domain controller instead. If lookups are slow for branch offices, consider using a localized global catalog server for that office.

- *Override default LDAP Port*: Use a custom port number for LDAP access.

- *Use SSL to connect (recommended)*: The server requires communication over an SSL port.

- *Log in with my Exchange account credentials*: If checked, Outlook will authenticate to the LDAP servers when performing lookups against the LDAP database.

- *Maximum number of results to return*: This is the maximum number of results for a given LDAP query. This is similar to how the Active Directory plug-in returns a maximum number of objects, as described in Chapter 3. If you increase this number, lookups for addresses in the GAL could take longer, but you may need to increase it in large organizations if users have search issues.

- *Search base*: This is the search base of the domain. For most environments, this is not required. If the search base is needed, you should be able to obtain it from Active Directory. You can usually determine this value by performing an LDAP search against one of your global catalogs.

```
ldapsearch -h myglobalcatalog.myco.com -x -a never -s base namingContexts
```

One of the great features of Exchange is that users can configure who has access to their information and rights to perform actions on their behalf. This is called *delegation*, which Outlook supports. Once you have configured the initial account settings, as required by your organization, you can go ahead and configure delegation. This is where you can configure Outlook to allow you to send e-mail as another user of the organization or provide other users with access to send mail as the account being configured. To configure access, as shown in Figure 5-4, click the Add button and then select each user for whom access should be provided (or added to your "send as" options).

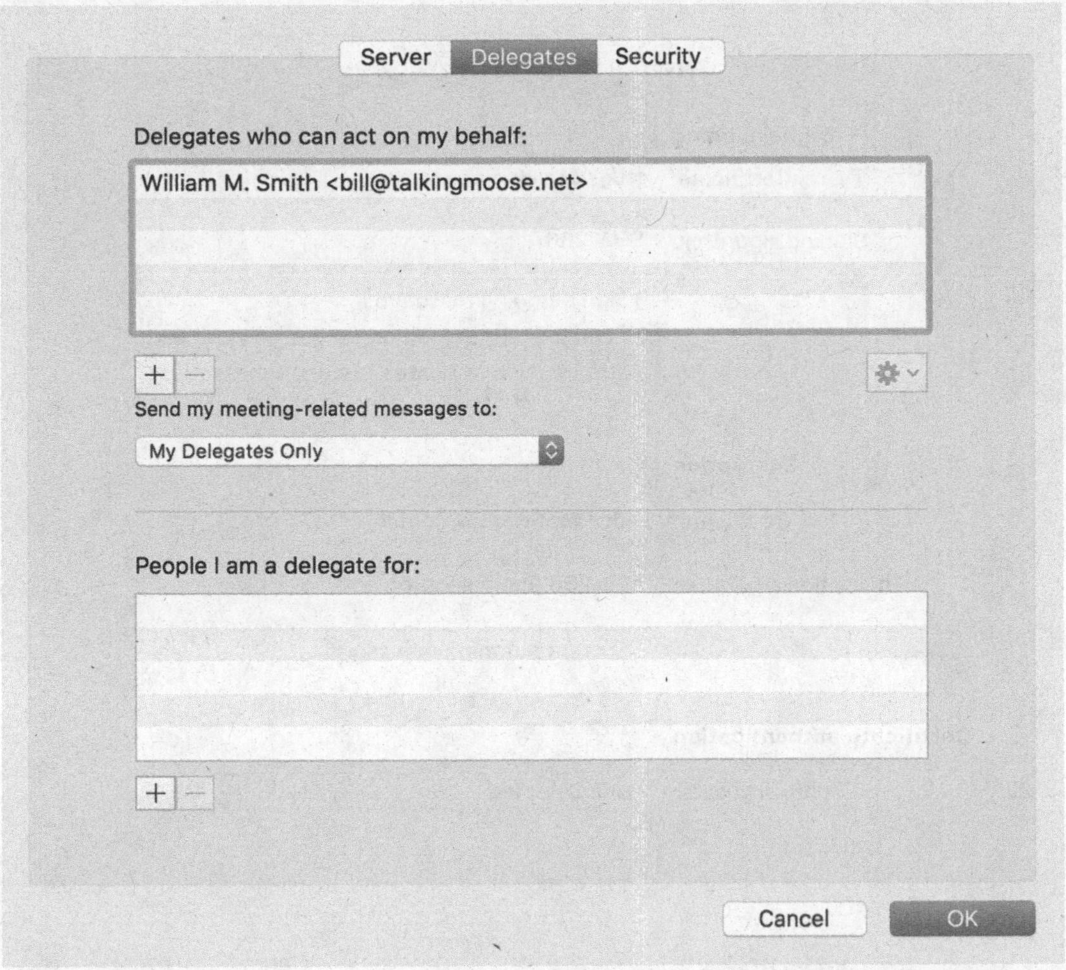

Figure 5-4. *Entourage account delegation user selection*

Finally, click the Security tab to configure the digital signing and encryption options of Outlook (see Figure 5-5). Be sure to have any digital signatures you need (whether supplied by a public certificate authority or by your own signing environment). Digitally signing objects allows for nonrepudiation (the objects definitely came from you because only you have your private key). Encryption lets you encrypt all mail, so users who receive your mail will need a predefined web of trust with your e-mail to be able to view the contents of the message.

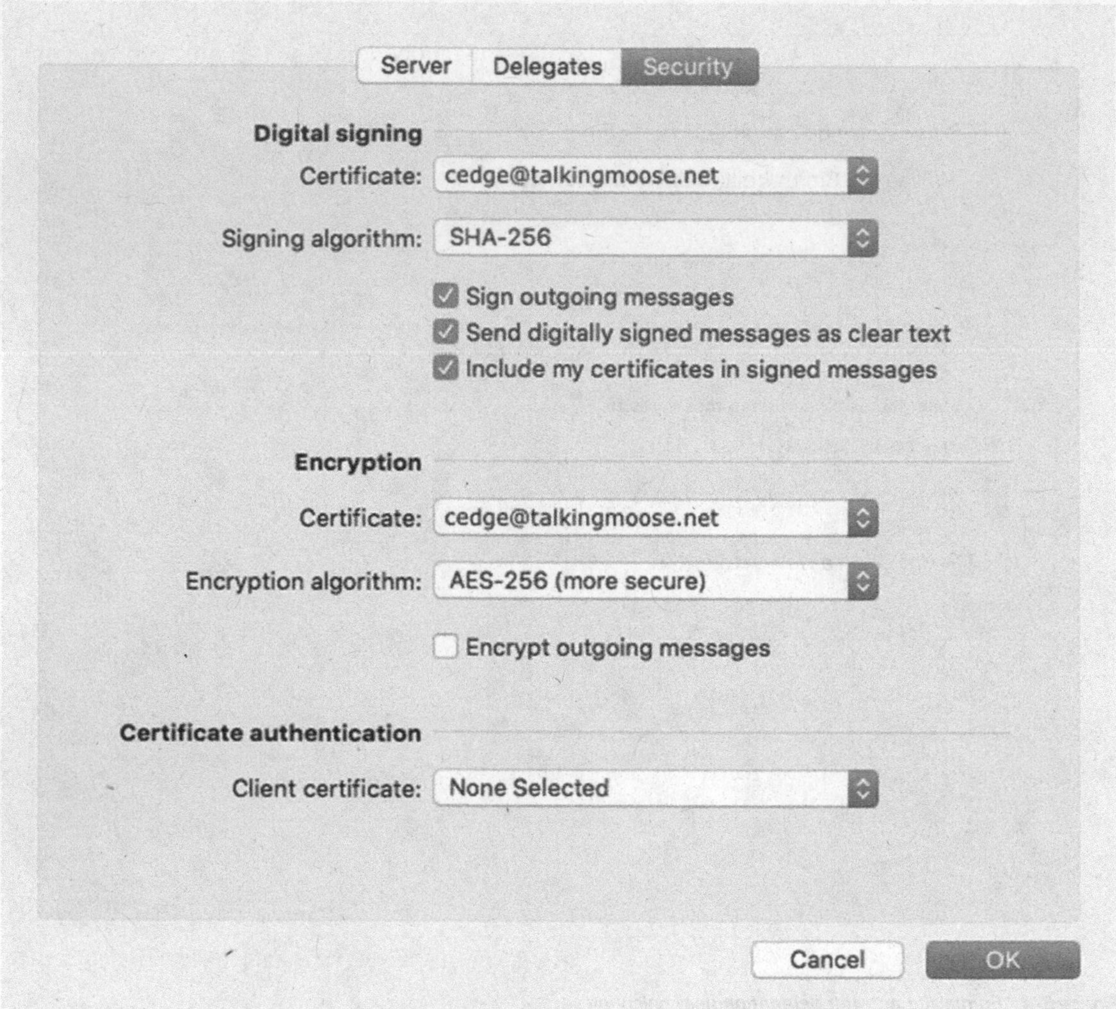

| | Server | Delegates | Security | |

Digital signing

Certificate: | cedge@talkingmoose.net | ⬍ |

Signing algorithm: | SHA-256 | ⬍ |

☑ Sign outgoing messages
☑ Send digitally signed messages as clear text
☑ Include my certificates in signed messages

Encryption

Certificate: | cedge@talkingmoose.net | ⬍ |

Encryption algorithm: | AES-256 (more secure) | ⬍ |

☐ Encrypt outgoing messages

Certificate authentication

Client certificate: | None Selected | ⬍ |

| Cancel | OK |

Figure 5-5. Outlook Exchange account security options

Automatic Client Configuration

In a large organization, you need to automate as much of the installation process as possible. Part of this automation might involve deploying the actual software, another part might be to customize the settings for the software, and finally you may want to automate the account configuration for a user. These three tasks need to be viewed as three separate automations.

Deploying the Package

Microsoft Office comes with a built-in package installer. The installer is a package that contains a number of other packages. All of these packages can be installed automatically using the following command (assuming that the package is stored in the hidden /private/tmp directory on your computer):

```
sudo installer -pkg "/private/tmp/Microsoft_Office_2016_Volume_Installer.pkg" -target /
```

Apple's installer tool supports using a choices XML file to omit or change parts of an installation. These are usually the options you see when double-clicking an installer and clicking the Customize button to select or deselect choices. For example, an administrator may choose to install the full Office 2016 for Mac suite without installing Microsoft OneNote or Microsoft AutoUpdate. Rather than dissecting the installer package and creating a new package without the applications, the -applyChoiceChangesXML option brings in an answer file. This file responds with which of the packages within the metapackage that you want to install or not install. To see the choices that you can use to make an answer file, use the -showChoicesXML option, along with the path to the package file (using the -pkg option), as follows:

```
installer -showChoicesXML -pkg "~/Desktop/ Microsoft_Office_2016_Volume_Installer.pkg"
```

If your environment doesn't use OneNote or AutoUpdate, then you could make the attributeSetting key false (or zero) for both and they would not be installed.

```xml
<?xml version="1.0" encoding="UTF-8"?>
<!DOCTYPE plist PUBLIC "-//Apple//DTD PLIST 1.0//EN" "http://www.apple.com/DTDs/
PropertyList-1.0.dtd">
<plist version="1.0">
<array>
    <dict>
        <key>attributeSetting</key>
        <integer>0</integer>
        <key>choiceAttribute</key>
        <string>selected</string>
        <key>choiceIdentifier</key>
        <string>com.microsoft.autoupdate</string>
    </dict>
    <dict>
        <key>attributeSetting</key>
        <integer>0</integer>
        <key>choiceAttribute</key>
        <string>selected</string>
        <key>choiceIdentifier</key>
        <string>com.microsoft.onenote</string>
    </dict>
</array>
</plist>
```

Save this file with a name such as `choices.plist` and deploy it along with the Office 2016 installer package. Then apply the choices XML plist file as part of the command.

```
sudo installer -pkg "/private/tmp/Microsoft_Office_2016_Volume_Installer.pkg" -target /
\-applyChoiceChangesXML "/private/tmp/choices.plist"
```

Once installed, open Office, and you will be prompted to activate Office using an Office 365 account, unless you're using a volume license key for your deployment.

Outlook Account Setup

You can also automate the setup of the actual Exchange account by leveraging AppleScript. To do so, you could have a launch agent that checks whether the AppleScript should run. However you choose to push out the AppleScript, it is worth noting that you can control Outlook to a large degree using AppleScript events. To get started, open the AppleScript editor of your preference and enter the following:

```
tell application "Microsoft Outlook"
        make new exchange account with properties {name:"My Exchange Account", user
name:"jdoe", full name:"John Doe", email address:"jdoe@myco.com", server:"mail.myco.com",
use ssl:true, port:443, ldap server:"ldap.myco.com", ldap needs authentication:true, ldap
use ssl:true, ldap max entries:1000, ldap search base:"dc=myco,dc=com"}
end tell
```

This AppleScript could be set up to launch when a user logs in and then to self-destruct. You can even add some code to pull data from the environment using the shell command `id -un` or continue with AppleScript using the following:

```
set userShortName to short user name of (system info)
set userFullName to long user name of (system info)
```

Using these values, you can then properly set the display name for the account, set the user's short name (used for authentication), and populate the user's Full Name record, which is used for displaying a friendly From name when sending e-mails (such as John Doe rather than `jdoe@myco.com`). Instead of a login item, you can also call the AppleScript using the `osascript` command. However, because this AppleScript is configuring a Userland application, it requires an active user session to run. Because of this, a launch agent item is generally the best avenue for this type of deployment.

Postflight Tasks

Assuming the serial number was deployed with the initial package, there should be only a few things remaining to complete your Office for Mac deployment and allow you to use Outlook effectively. The first is to suppress the Microsoft first-run dialog windows displayed when launching each application the first time (and usually causing a great number of calls to support teams unless suppressed).

To suppress them, you will need to add keys and values to the preferences plist for each application. Here, we'll provide a key of kSubUIAppCompletedFirstRunSetup1507 with a value of true, which indicates that the user has seen the first-run setup window. To do so, we'll use the defaults command and write the key information into the com.microsoft.application plists as follows:

```
defaults write com.microsoft.excel "kSubUIAppCompletedFirstRunSetup1507" -bool true
defaults write com.microsoft.outlook "kSubUIAppCompletedFirstRunSetup1507" -bool true
defaults write com.microsoft.powerpoint "kSubUIAppCompletedFirstRunSetup1507" -bool true
defaults write com.microsoft.word "kSubUIAppCompletedFirstRunSetup1507" -bool true
```

We could also have uploaded the plists into Apple's Profile Manager or other MDM to create a configuration profile. Once done, profiles can be pushed out to these property lists quickly and easily from the centralized management server. These plists are located in the Containers folder for sandboxed applications. For example, Microsoft Word's preferences plist is located in the user's home folder.

```
~/Library/Containers/com.microsoft.Word/Data/Library/Preferences/com.microsoft.Word.plist
```

AutoUpdate

Microsoft Office includes Microsoft AutoUpdate, which runs independently of Apple's Software Update. Many environments will control patch deployment to users to proactively keep help-desk calls from rolling in as patches are applied (user questions about why Office is asking for an update, plus potential support issues arising from a deployed update, can be lethal). Additionally, all Microsoft patches for Office for Mac are cumulative, which means an administrator needs to install only the latest update rather than all prior updates in a row.

If you have another vehicle to deploy the Microsoft patches (such as JAMF Software's Casper or Apple Remote Desktop), you can disable AutoUpdate using the defaults command to write the HowToCheck key into the com.microsoft.autoupdate.plist file as follows:

```
defaults write com.microsoft.autoupdate2 HowToCheck -string "Manual"
```

Similarly, you can push out the com.microsoft.autoupdate2 domain preferences using Profile Manager, Apple's built-in client management system (discussed in Chapter 7). Microsoft AutoUpdate is not sandboxed like the rest of the Office 2016 applications, so you'll find this preferences file in the user's home folder in the Preferences folder:

```
~/Library/Preferences/com.microsoft.autoupdate2.plist
```

Native Groupware Support

OS X traditionally has not had a strong first-party groupware presence. Traditionally groupware-inherent apps, such as Apple's earlier Address Book, iCal, and Mail, were largely consumer-oriented and, as such, did not participate well in groupware-oriented environments. This statement is a little less true for Apple's Mail app, which does support prominent e-mail protocols. Apple servers address groupware with Calendar server and Contact server.

Let's face it, though, when talking about groupware, the 800-pound gorilla in the room is Microsoft Exchange, and in OS X you might be using Outlook to address Exchange support. But Apple's native toolset is another great way to address Mac support for OS X. Native Exchange support in OS X includes full support for Exchange e-mail, calendaring, contact, and GAL access. Each respective function in OS X is provided via a dedicated app: Mail, Calendar, and Contacts. Each application leverages Exchange Web Service for integration, which provides excellent feature compatibility.

Manual Setup

The Mail app includes support for, well, e-mail and does the job adequately. There is also a Contacts app and a Calendar app, which provide access to contacts and calendars from Exchange, respectively. To configure the Mail app to connect to an Exchange server, start the app and open its preferences, found under the Mail menu. With the Preferences window open, select the Accounts tab and click the plus button in the bottom-left corner of the Internet Accounts preferences pane to create a new account, as shown in Figure 5-6.

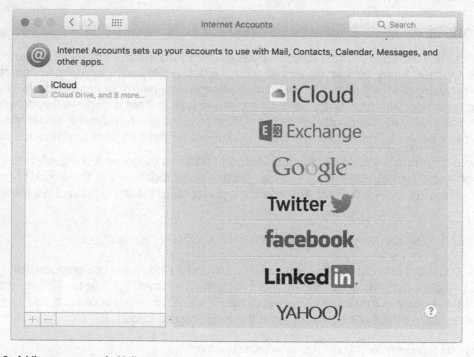

Figure 5-6. Adding an account in Mail.app

As shown in Figure 5-7, in the resulting window, enter the full name, e-mail address, and password for the desired account. Then click Sign In in the Exchange screen.

E邊 Exchange

To get started, fill out the following information:

Name: Charles Edge

Email Address: cedge@talkingmoose.net

Password: ●●●●●●●●●●

Cancel   Back   Sign In

Figure 5-7. Configuring Exchange in Mail.app

Provided that Autodiscover worked correctly, you will then be able to select which services will automatically be set up to work with Exchange, as you can see in Figure 5-8.

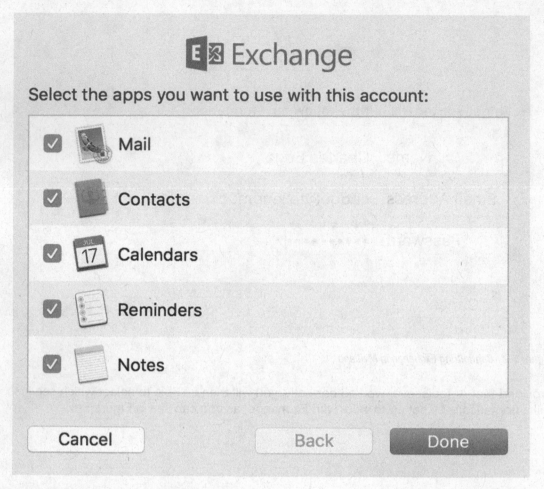

Figure 5-8. Select which apps you want to use

Once the account has been set up, it will be listed in the Internet Accounts list. From here, you can highlight the account and edit the same settings, as shown in Figure 5-9.

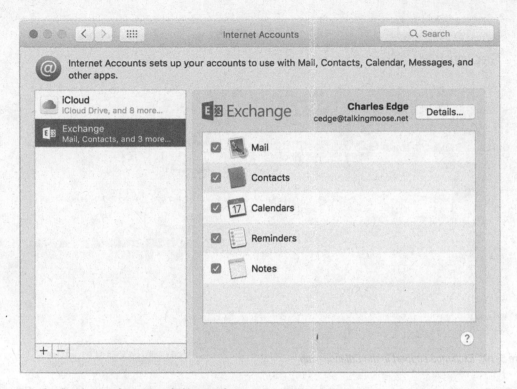

Figure 5-9. Configuring service access in Internet Accounts

> **Tip**   Though Exchange contacts and GAL access are provided via the Contacts app, Mail will search both when entering e-mail recipients.

Calendar support for Exchange is provided using the aptly named Calendar app (see Figure 5-10), which sports decent capabilities, including support for free/busy schedules, to-dos, invitations, file attachments, and delegation.

Figure 5-10. Exchange support in the Calendar app

The Contacts app provides support for Exchange contacts and allows users to search the Exchange GAL. When an Exchange account is configured in Address Book, the account will be listed in the left pane. Additionally, the configured account will have a new entry placed under the Directory group, which allows for searching of the GAL, as shown in Figure 5-11.

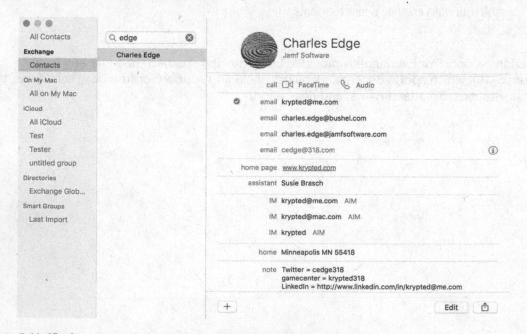

Figure 5-11. Viewing a contact in the GAL in the Contacts app

As mentioned, it is possible to configure Exchange accounts both in Calendar and in Contacts without configuring a mail account. To perform this operation in either program, open the preferences from the application's menu (the Calendar and Contacts menus, respectively) and select the Accounts tab. Here, you can deselect the Exchange account from within the app.

Deploy Exchange Accounts Using Profiles

Now that you've seen how to set up an Exchange account using Outlook and the native tools for OS X, let's look at automating the account setup in environments that have decided to leverage the native tools. To do so, you'll create a profile. Using that profile, you can automatically install the profile on systems to complete the Exchange account setup process on client Mac computers. We will cover doing so first through Profile Manager and then through Apple Configurator.

To set up your Exchange profile using Profile Manager, first set up Profile Manager, as described in Chapter 7. Once set up, open the web interface for Profile Manager and then click a group that you'd like to deploy settings for. Once selected, click the Settings tab and then click Edit. From the Settings screen, provide the settings for your Exchange environment. These include the following (Figure 5-12):

- *Account Name*: This is the name that will appear on a device when you open the account in Settings.

- *Connection Type*: This setting allows you to select EWS for Mac clients and ActiveSync for iOS clients.

- *User*: You can enter a user's short name, or you can leave this setting blank to prompt the user for a username when the profile is installed.

- *E-mail Address*: You can't leave this setting blank in Profile Manager.

- *Password*: You can leave this setting blank to prompt the user for the password on the device when the profile is installed.

- *Internal Exchange Host*: This is the name of the Exchange server when connecting over the LAN.

- *Internal Server Path*: This is the path within IIS when connecting to the Exchange server over the LAN.

- *Use SSL for Internal Exchange Host*: You can enable or disable the SSL connection.

- *External Exchange Host*: This is the name of the Exchange server when connecting over the WAN.

- *External Server Path*: This is the path within IIS when connecting to the Exchange server over the WAN.

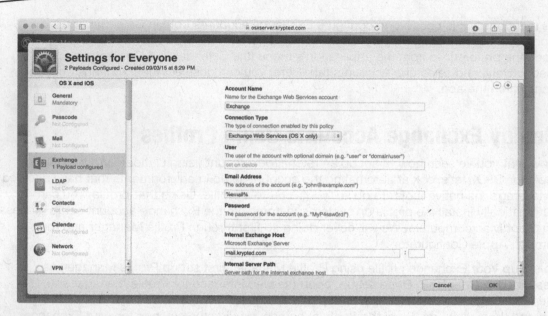

Figure 5-12. *Creating an Exchange profile using Profile Manager*

Now that you've looked at creating a profile using Profile Manager, let's look at doing so using Apple Configurator. To get started, first open Apple Configurator 2 and then click the File menu and select New Profile. At the new, untitled profile, provide a name and identifier in the General section of the profile (this is mandatory) and then click Exchange ActiveSync in the left sidebar of the screen.

As you can see in Figure 5-13, you'll see the same settings that were provided in Profile Manager. Here, you will provide a server, user, e-mail address, and password. You can optionally provide a few other settings, but for most environments where you were able to manually configure an account, you shouldn't need to do so.

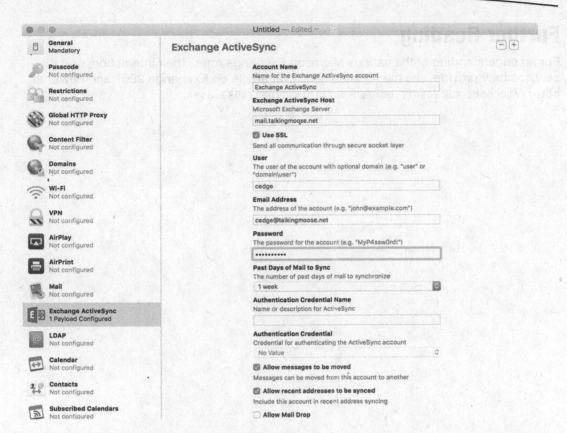

Figure 5-13. Creating an Exchange profile using Apple Configurator

Once you have provided all the necessary settings, close the screen, and you will be prompted to save the profile. Here, select where you'd like to save the profile to, and you will then be left with a `.mobileconfig` file at that location.

Once you have created your profile, you can install the profile using the Profiles preference pane or by double-clicking the profile. The account will then be set up in Internet Accounts. Profile management (installation, removal, and so on) is covered in much further detail in Chapter 7.

Summary

In this chapter, you learned how OS X clients can interact with various groupware solutions, most notably Microsoft Exchange. This provides access to the most common groupware platform on the planet. Connecting to many other services, such as Google Apps, is similar.

In the next chapter, we'll discuss the various technologies and tools involved with efficiently deploying software and operating systems en masse to your entire fleet.

Further Reading

For an understanding of the various Microsoft Exchange roles, their interaction, and the services they provide, see the Microsoft TechNet article on Exchange 2007 and newer at http://technet.microsoft.com/en-us/library/bb124937.aspx.

Chapter **6**

Mass Deployment

Chances are that if you deal with enterprise-level systems management, you'll need to deploy systems en masse from time to time. If you have a hardware refresh rate of, say, 25 percent per year and a total of 10,000 computers, you'll have to deploy 2,500 machines every year. The tasks involved in the process are usually repetitive, lending themselves to batch processing. As a result, you can—and should—put solutions in place that let you automate the deployment of systems on an ongoing basis. In some cases, this means imaging systems fully loaded with software, known as *monolithic imaging*. In other cases, this means imaging systems and automating the installation of software, known as *package-based imaging*. And in still other cases, this means imaging systems with just a daemon used to install items from a server, known as *thin imaging*.

If planned properly, you can extend the file sets and tools you develop, using them to provide everyday troubleshooting capabilities. For example, suppose a problem is resident on only one computer but the symptoms present themselves across multiple users. Many IT departments have a policy of simply reimaging such systems, on the assumption that the computer in question has somehow varied from an approved image. This may seem counterintuitive and an entry-level troubleshooting technique; however, while it may be technically satisfying to isolate an issue on a machine, doing so may take much more time than simply reimaging a system. In this way, the user has less downtime because you have cloned the same configuration onto all machines, so if an issue presents on only one, the chances of it being systemic are low. In most organizations, reimaging as part of a troubleshooting paradigm can sharply reduce the total cost of ownership (TCO) while simultaneously serving to keep the environment as homogenous as possible (which further reduces TCO).

To reduce the time spent reimaging, it's a good idea to keep user data in sync with, stored, or backed up on another host or segmented from the system in some fashion, such as a dedicated partition for user data or utilizing Apple's external account technology. In Microsoft Windows, this would commonly be accomplished using roaming profiles. In the Apple enterprise vernacular, there are two similarly common options for user data storage: portable home directories and network home folders. This helps save your support personnel from having to back up each user folder or computer prior to reimaging or replacing a system. One of the goals of implementing an imaging solution should be to reduce the amount of time spent fixing problems. Commoditizing computers will help you to achieve that goal. In Chapter 7, we'll cover portable and network home folders, although they are becoming less prevalent in Apple deployments.

Planning Your Mass Deployment

The first step in preparing to roll out a large number of systems (after you read this chapter, of course) is to sit down and make a checklist or matrix in the form of a spreadsheet. Include every task required to set up a new computer, listing each in the order your personnel must perform it. The items should be binding to the directory service, creating local administrative accounts, setting preferences, locking down permissions, installing software, installing updates, and doing whatever other specific procedures apply to your environment. Remember that mass deployment is sometimes one big hack and therefore needs to be documented for your predecessor and yourself six months from now.

Remember to solicit content for this deployment matrix from your end users. After all, your institution's primary purpose for having computers is to serve your end users and not your IT staff. This list should be ever growing and should be linked in some way to your trouble ticket's tracking system. If you consider imaging not to simply be a one-time process but to be an integral workflow in supporting machines, you can use it to track problems that can be circumvented or mitigated simply by adding preflight stages to your imaging process. For instance, if you see that 20 percent of your help-desk tickets relate to improper mail client configuration, perhaps your image should include one of the many automatic setup scripts available for common mail clients such as Microsoft Outlook.

The tasks that systems require may depend on factors, such as the department they're in and what they're used for. Next, you need to determine which tasks you'll carry out on which systems. If the steps are the same for all machines, then following these two steps will likely be the easiest approach. Initially, simply deploy a large, monolithic image to every system. A monolithic image is simply an image of an entire system, including applications, operating system, and other requirements. Follow that with other tasks (carried out by scripts, package installers, or both) that you couldn't include in the image—for example, Active Directory binding, which must run at first boot. While granularity is normally an IT person's best friend, keeping things as simple as possible can also be an important mantra with mass deployment. Much like lawyers are coached never to ask a question they don't know the answer to, never include an imaging step either pre- or post-flight that you cannot guarantee through testing will work with all the variables of your infrastructure. Imaging should serve to simplify your IT infrastructure, not complicate it. A good example of this was a deployment performed at a large institution. The onsite IT staff pushed out a nonuniversal copy of its antivirus software, which caused startup issues on older PowerPC machines. If the imaging testing would have been performed on both architectures, this would have been caught. The technician in charge of this deployment used a newer Intel machine for testing. Because of this, it's extremely important you have a cross section of hardware to test with that matches your organization's current computer inventory.

If procedures must differ for different parts of your organization, make sure to account for the specific differences in your matrix. Split your tasks (such as preferences to be set, bindings, and software to be installed) into two categories, as you can see in Table 6-1. The first should be the lowest-common-denominator tasks (and software, if required) that pertain to every single computer. Examples include operating-system installation, binding the OS into Active Directory (or other directory service), and other global tasks. This is sometimes best framed as a timeline, from start to finish. This timeline will separate the tasks that you will perform manually if you are asked to set up a new employee's workstation.

Tasks to put in the second category are those that involve taking the groups of computers and users in your checklist and making them correspond to constructed users and groups in your global directory service. Based on this checklist, you now have an object-oriented model for who gets what items in your environment. This will serve as the blueprint for your deployment system.

Table 6-1. Object-Oriented Tasks

Global Tasks	Packages
Enable FileVault master password.	Install Adobe Suite
Install Mac OS X.	Setup for VPN Access
Install Microsoft Office.	Fill Bookmarks for HR Dept.
Set up 802.1x.	Add Server Admin Tools
Add hidden local admin account.	Add Citrix Client
Bind to Active Directory.	Install iWork
Bind to Open Directory.	Set up Messages

If you are an ITIL-based IT shop, then you likely already have a repository of all "supported" applications in the form of a definitive software library (DSL). In this case, you will take the supported applications from your DSL and place them into one of the two columns.

Note   Once you know who gets what software, try to get volume-license keys` from every vendor. Sometimes the cost can be prohibitive, but you really want to try even if your automation choices become limited or if you have to install a unique key for even a single software package. Also, be aware that smaller software packages may still require activation even with volume license keys. Every vendor is different. Software that is not as widely deployed may have serious design considerations if the vendor does not officially support mass deployment. Always test your images and processes on at least two systems to see how your software will handle being moved between different machines and, if necessary in your environment, hardware platforms. Some software registration systems utilize machine-specific data, such as Mac address or other hardware information. In the event that software registration cannot be so easily baked into your image or package, you may need to utilize postflight scripting to accomplish your task.

Monolithic vs. Package-Based Imaging

OS X mass deployment is sometimes the subject of much debate. One of the leading topics in this debate is whether monolithic or package-based installations are the preferred methodology. We would like to put this to rest and say both are preferred in all environments with time permitting. The question then becomes more of a matter of workflow order rather than the headlining technology. Monolithic installations can simply be the end result of package-based installs, where package-based installs are just the steps of monolithic installs split up into different file sets. That said, the preferred methodology is typically to always start with packages and then build monolithic images from the resultant packages depending on their size. In this way, you can add and remove items as needed, without the same rebuild time that starting anew would require. If your end result is a large monolithic image, then larger datasets can be deployed as one stream of multicast data rather than independent package installs via unicast. An example would be a package installer in excess of 50GB, such as one of Apple's Pro Applications. While a single package installer would allow you to easily remove or update this in your image, including this much data in your "base" monolithic will impact deployments speeds for a number of reasons. If your network supports multicast, you would be able to push the image to an arbitrary number of computers via a single stream of data. If you have an image in excess of 50GB to be deployed to more than a dozen computers, this can mean big savings in network bandwidth and deployment speed. Multicast deployment of packages is not a capability available to any of the most popular deployment systems. In this regard, creating a large base image can result in a significant yet more efficient deployment, rather than have postflight installers run on each system independently. Each technique has its own merits, but when it comes right down to it, nearly every deployment will benefit from a mixture of the two.

While it can seem contradictory given the ease of creating an initial monolithic image, after a few years of imaging, it seems like everyone ends up learning that pushing out images monolithically is typically more time-consuming than breaking up that same image into parts. In package-based imaging, you put down a sparse "base" image, which could even be a bare-metal image containing nothing except for an OS X install that has never been booted (such as what is configured from the factory on a new machine) and then perform postflight tasks to add the rest of the software and do the configuration.

With the purely monolithic technique, each time you go to build a new image, you may have to start from a clean OS installation and then perform a certain series of tasks on the system before making the image of it. If you have multiple architectures in a deployment (such as PowerPC and Intel), you could find yourself carrying out the procedure once for every architecture. This redundant work compounds if you have different departments that receive different software, thus causing you to create more and more images. With each equipment refresh or major update to push to clients, you might need to create a new image. Additionally, because of what is typically a lack of documentation, if your original image builder leaves, you often have no idea which changes, scripts, and software applications were originally included in your image without backtracking forensics.

Why would anyone use a single large image? Well, for one, it's pretty easy to do. In fact, for most simple environments, it's far easier than breaking that image into parts in relation to preparation time. For example, if you want all the computers you deploy to have the same configuration, you can embed that into the computer from which you'll create an image.

For example, click a button that creates a preference, rather than create an installer that installs that preference. Then, when you push that image out, the setting is there. Later, if you want to change the setting, you can send a script to do so, either through Apple Remote Desktop (ARD) or as an imaging task for subsequent sets of imaged computers. At that point, however, you're going to have to figure out which files were created by that change or, better yet, how to do this programmatically (through a script) so you don't mess up other settings along the way.

As you get more granular with your packages and scripts, you may end up using an automation of some sort to alter each system preference pane, configuration file, application, serial number, and anything else you can think of that you do to each new machine. That automation may consist of a managed-preference procedure (discussed in Chapter 7), a script, or a package. It's not uncommon to have 100 tasks to perform on a system, post-imaging, but getting to that point can be time-consuming. In the long run, a truly package-based imaging system offers the most systems-management flexibility.

> **Note** While it may end up to be more work for some environments to build a number of scripts or packages to automate your deployment, it's a great learning experience if you have time and will aid in the ongoing imaging process as you have new machines and new operating systems (and builds) to redeploy under.

The monolithic image approach for an imaging environment as described in Table 6-1 would result in a solution similar to Figure 6-1, with packages deployed post-installation.

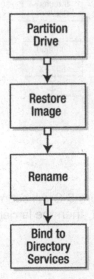

Figure 6-1. Workflow for monolithic imaging

Taking the imaging workflow to a more package-based approach would then result in a workflow more similar to Figure 6-2, where you take things into more of the object-oriented realm.

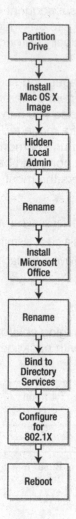

Figure 6-2. Package-based imaging

As we've indicated, on the outside, Figure 6-2 will seem like more work. However, when you introduce change into your environment, then the larger the environment, the less work this will inevitably be.

Automation

The more computers you deploy, the more you'll want to automate the setup process. If you have to bind 25 machines into Active Directory and each takes roughly 5 minutes, you'll dedicate about 2 hours—not too bad. But if you have 1,000 systems, we're talking about 83 hours. In that case, though writing a script to automate the process may consume 5 hours, you've saved 78 hours. On the other hand, for just 25 computers, writing a script wouldn't seem to make sense, since you'd spend an extra 3 hours. However, if those 25 systems ever need reimaging, the work you did to automate the process will have paid off. An often-overlooked component of this type of work is the massive number of scripts that are already currently available. Like many other IT professionals, we often publish our scripts online in publicly accessible forums. With this said, when estimating time to create a script such as one used for Active Directory binding, always research to see whether one is already available freely from some other source. This small amount of forethought may even mitigate all development time if the script does exactly what you need it to do, and if not, it may be easier to start with an example than from scratch.

Refer to your checklist to decide which tasks you'll automate. Generally, you perform automation one of two ways: using packages (thus the term package-based imaging) or using scripts. Packages are installers; scripts can also "install" items, but most often, you use them in the deployment process simply to augment or transform existing data. This line gets blurred a bit in the regard that packages can be "payload" free, meaning that they can be created with the express purpose of running scripts. Wrapping your final scripts in a package installer has huge advantages, as Apple's package installer infrastructure includes many different components, such as preinstall and postinstall scripts, sanity checks for memory, system version, and graphical installer bundles, which mean you can even put a basic user interface "on top" of your script to help with the uninitiated.

Take a good look at your checklist. Some software comes in the form of a package installer that you can use for deploying the software. If you do use existing package installers, budget a couple of hours for testing each. If you can't use an existing package, then you can either create a new one or write a script to place all the files, or even parts of files, in their appropriate locations.

> **Note** As experienced scripters (and managers of those who script), take our word for this. When you get a budget estimate for writing a particular script, just double it. This will save you a lot of grief down the road.

Image Delivery

Monolithic images can be pretty easy to deploy, especially on an ad hoc basis. The general outline of the process is this: reboot a target system (often referred to as an *imaging* or *base* system) into Target Disk Mode, connect it to a master-control computer, and then use Carbon Copy Cloner (http://bombich.com), Super Duper! (www.shirt-pocket.com/ SuperDuper/SuperDuperDescription.html), FileWave Lightning (https://www.filewave.com/ item/lightning), or Apple's Disk Utility (in /Applications/Utilities on OS X) to clone the master system to an attached system or an image file. You can also deploy images over a network using Apple Software Restore (ASR) or NetRestore (which is a graphical interface to ASR running on OS X Server), both available in the App Store; using NetInstall (a service that uses NetBoot for imaging); and using a variety of third-party products.

Most of the complexity of an imaging solution arises from the automation that you put in place, so whether to automate is an issue of economy of scale. As noted earlier, the more systems you have, the more you'll want to automate, starting with the delivery of an image, but then moving into renaming systems, binding to directory services, installing software, and making operating system or application configuration changes.

Through this section, we'll trace the emergence of an image-delivery environment from childhood toward maturity. We'll start with one of the simplest solutions—Disk Utility—to deliver an image directly to a computer, then move toward using the default solutions from Apple, and finally explore third-party solutions that can automate even the smallest of details.

If you actually try each of the options we lay out, you'll spend a number of hours simply waiting for images to be created—transferring what is typically a 5GB to 10GB file system into a file and reordering isn't exactly the fastest operation. So, feel free to follow along with the screens and commands, but don't feel you must wait for each step to complete unless you see a compelling reason to do so (for example, you're considering using that solution as a mass-deployment strategy).

Creating an Image

The ability to create a hard-drive image and copy it to another hard drive is a basic, longtime feature of OS X. We'll begin by illustrating the process using the tried-and-true Disk Utility, included with OS X. This tool can produce an image of the computer, which, by default, it does in the form of a disk image (DMG) file.

We'll start by building the base system that will act as the template. First, install OS X on a computer and go through the checklist of settings and procedures you normally follow. Don't, however, perform any trusted binding of the system into a directory service. (Creating this binding is the default with Active Directory, which we covered in Chapters 2 and 3, so don't do any Active Directory binding prior to making the image.)

Next, install the applications you normally run (using, one hopes, the volume licensing keys), populate them with your usual files, and reboot the system into Target Disk Mode. You can do so by selecting Target Disk Mode in the Startup Disk pane in System Preferences before you reboot or by holding down the T key at bootup. When the system has restarted, it will display a gray screen and a FireWire and Thunderbolt (if your hardware supports Thunderbolt) logo. At this point, connect the base system to the admin computer to create the image file on the latter.

One aside: If you don't have volume licensing for your software, you may be better off by *not* licensing the base-image applications, depending on how draconian the software's serial number mechanism is. On the other hand, there may be no such checks, and the maker may even bless using the same license on all machines as long as you've purchased it. Your mileage will vary heavily by application and vendor.

> **Note** An arbitrary version of OS X will usually support all hardware that was available at the time of its release. However, Apple will sometimes release a newer build of the operating system for a new hardware model that just shipped. This new build may have the same operating system version but may also contain additional components that were added for that specific hardware (i.e., new trackpad driver), which incremented the build identifier of the system. When presented with this scenario, you should typically make your base or monolithic image from that newest operating system build. However, the next OS point release should contain all additions in this "build train"–specific operating system (and more). You can determine a system's build number by running the terminal command sw_vers. If you must deploy your image before Apple releases its next point update, such as a lull between OS X 10.11, and your deployment date, be aware that "build train"–specific operating systems are not officially supported by Apple on anything other than the original hardware. While they often work, this is a consideration to be aware of if you phone in for support.

Next, as with Microsoft Windows, you'll want to remove those pesky unique cache files from that computer. If you don't, they may be re-created in the image file. The following are the files to delete:

- .DS_Store files (using the find /Volumes/volumename -name .DS_Store -exec rm {} \; command)
- .Trashes files (using the find /Volumes/volumename -name .Trash -exec rm {} \; command)
- /System/Library/Extensions.kextcache
- /System/Library/Extensions.mkext
- /Library/Preferences/SystemConfiguration/NetworkInterfaces.plist
- /var/db/BootCache.playlist
- /var/db/volinfo.database
- Contents of /var/vm/
- Contents of /Library/Caches/
- Contents of /System/Library/Caches/
- Contents of /Users/Shared/
- /var/log/secure.log
- /var/db/krb5kdc
- /var/db/volinfo.database
- /var/root/Library/Preferences/com.apple.recentitems.plist
- Contents of /var/root/Library/Preferences/ByHost/

> **Note** This step is similar in functionality to removing the files that are unique to a computer by using `Sysprep` in Windows environments, but the procedure does not carry out some other tasks that `Sysprep` does.

Once you've deleted the unique information, don't restart the clone. Instead, on the system connected to the target-disk-mode computer, open Disk Utility (Applications ➤ Utilities), which will produce the screen shown in Figure 6-3. Click Image in the application toolbar.

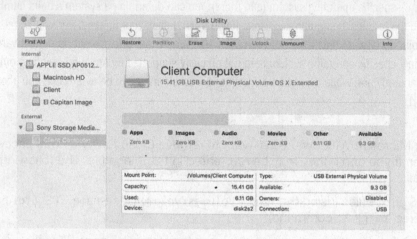

***Figure 6-3.** Apple's Disk Utility*

In the resulting window, click the target disk's volume name (listed along the left side of the screen), then select Image from the toolbar or choose File ➤ New Image ➤ Image from Folder. Either way, you'll get options you can apply to the new image, as you can see in Figure 6-4. Configure the Image Format setting to Read Only and verify that the Encryption option is set to "none." Click Save when you're done.

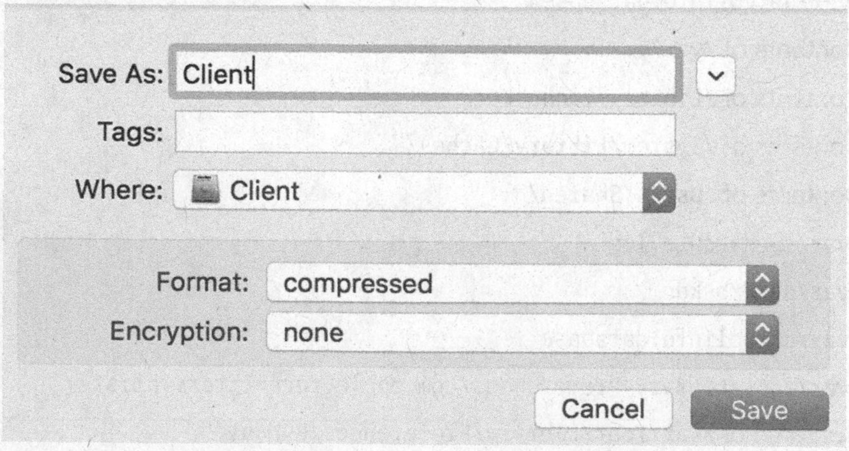

***Figure 6-4.** Choosing where to save the disk image*

Disk Utility will now image the drive. The process can take a while, so this is a great time to check out hdiutil by reading the next section, and maybe even using the section as a guide while you try the command.

> **Note** If you'd selected the actual drive device rather than the volume, the disk's partition and size information would have been embedded in the image. By choosing the volume itself, as shown in Figure 6-3, you prevent the utility from recording the size and makeup of the disk. This is extremely important, as it allows you to deploy the volume to other systems that have different capacities.

Creating an Image from the Command Line

OS X comes stocked with a number of tools to manage compressed files. Some, such as gunzip and tar, are standard tools found on most UNIX variants. But hdiutil is specific to the Mac and a pretty powerful implement for creating and managing disk images.

Use hdiutil to create an image, called MacBook.dmg, in your working directory by entering this at the command line:

```
hdiutil create MacBook.dmg -size 10g -fs HFS+ -type SPARSE
```

Note that, in this case, you don't need to include the file's path. But if you want the freedom to summon the file from wherever you've decided to put it, you can simply prepend the path.

The sample command, which leverages the create verb, simply tells hdiutil to produce a disk image, give it a maximum capacity of 10GB, and format it for the HFS+ file system. (But if you'd like, you can use the -fs option to specify an alternative format.) By default, the file's volume name will be the same as that of the file, minus the .dmg suffix. The command creates an imaged volume name of MacBook, but you can specify a different one using the -volname flag.

The -type SPARSE option causes the command to generate a file that takes up only as much room as the data it contains, rather than consuming the same amount of space as the entire disk. But with a sparse image, as you add data, the file can expand to accommodate the extra up to the limit you set—10GB, in this case. If that's too little capacity, you can change the maximum size of your DMGs, making MacBook.dmg bigger. To do so, use the resize verb with the size flag, as in the following code:

```
hdiutil resize -size 50g MacBook.dmg
```

If you want, instead of creating a new image from scratch, you can do so from an existing volume using hdiutil. The steps you performed earlier, graphically, were fairly straightforward, but you could have carried them out from the command line much more quickly. To do so, use the create verb along with an option to define the source folder (-srcfolder) of your imaging station. (This time, the example gives the path to the DMG file.)

```
hdiutil create -srcfolder /Volumes/MacHD /asr/MacBook.dmg
```

Notice that the command line specifies the -srcfolder option rather than -srcdevice. This is for the same reason that you select the volume, rather than the disk, in the graphical interface. At this point, you have a MacBook.dmg image file, so you can mount it. For that, you call on the attach verb and specify the DMG file you'd like to mount as follows:

```
hdiutil attach MacBook.dmg
```

> **Note** You could also have used the -attach flag with the create verb, which would have created the DMG file and mounted it in one command.

You can now copy data into and out of your DMG file as you would with a standard volume. This is useful for adding startup scripts, for example, binding to your directory service, and then running the sanitization process (removing files unique to the computer that created the image) defined in the "Creating an Image" section earlier in this chapter, just in case you forgot to do so before making the image. Once you're done, you can unmount the DMG using detach.

```
hdiutil detach MacBook.dmg
```

The detach verb has one useful flag, -force, which (obviously) you use only when you have to force a disk image to unmount.

The attach verb, on the other hand, has a variety of options. The -readonly flag will mount the volume strictly for viewing. The -nomount flag, as you might guess, doesn't actually mount the volume, which can be useful if, for example, you want to run disk utilities against it. If you want to mount the disk image at a path other than the default /Volumes directory, you can use the -mountroot flag followed by the directory path you prefer.

Another commonly used flag, -owners (followed by on or off), comes in handy. Set to off, this causes the drive to act much like one plugged into a system when you've checked the box to ignore permissions. We highly recommend that you always mount the disk image with ownership off; otherwise, it's easy to corrupt permissions—not good when you intend to duplicate this image to hundreds of computers in your fleet. Obviously, you'd prefer that the original permissions persist. There are other flags, but these are the ones we find ourselves using most often.

> **Caution** Whenever you work on a base-image volume or disk image, ensure that the volume is mounted with permissions enforced; otherwise, you may corrupt permissions on your base model. This means that if you make changes, you would need to do so with elevated privileges on your own system so as not to take ownership of files and then make sure to chmod based on the UID of the users on the target system rather than your own.

Next, let's say you want to burn that DMG file to optical media. Accomplishing the task is simple using the burn verb and referencing the image file, as you can see in the following:

```
hdiutil burn /asr/MacBook.dmg
```

The hdiutil command will prompt for a blank disk to burn.

Alternatively, you may want to convert the image file to a more compatible format, perhaps to facilitate mass duplication of the optical media on non-Macintosh systems. Because the ISO format provides a burnable, platform-agnostic image file, it's a commonly used choice for this type of task. To take the MacBook.dmg file from the current working directory and convert it into an ISO image, use the convert verb and specify the -format flag along with an output destination.

```
hdiutil convert MacBook.dmg -format UDTO -o MacBook.iso
```

You can also use convert to make the MacBook.dmg file read-only. Simply specify -format followed by the code for read-only and then the file name for the converted file, as shown in the following code:

```
hdiutil convert MacBook.dmg -format UDRO -o MacBook_ro.dmg
```

To make the mynew.dmg file read-write, save it as mynewreadwrite.dmg and then enter the following command:

```
hdiutil convert MacBook_ro.dmg -format UDRW -o MacBook_rw.dmg
```

The full listing of conversion options and what they produce (from the main page of hdiutil) is as follows:

- *UDRW:* UDIF read/write image
- *UDRO:* UDIF read-only image
- *UDCO:* UDIF ADC-compressed image
- *UDZO:* UDIF zlib-compressed image
- *UDBZ:* UDIF bzip2-compressed image (OS X 10.4+ only)
- *UFBI:* UDIF entire image with MD5 checksum
- *UDRo:* UDIF read-only (obsolete format)
- *UDCo:* UDIF compressed (obsolete format)
- *UDTO:* DVD/CD-R master for export
- *UDxx:* UDIF stub image
- *UDSP:* SPARSE (grows with content)
- *UDSB:* SPARSEBUNDLE (grows with content; bundle-backed)
- *RdWr:* NDIF read/write image (deprecated)

- *Rdxx:* NDIF read-only image (Disk Copy 6.3.3 format)
- *ROCo:* NDIF compressed image (deprecated)
- *Rken:* NDIF compressed (obsolete format)
- *DC42:* Disk Copy 4.2 image

With hdiutil you can also burn an ISO file as well as perform a checksum and segment an image file by using the verbs burn, verify, and segment, respectively. As you convert your disk image (if you do so), keep in mind that ultimately you'll need it to be in read-only format if you want it to be deployable via ASR or other methods.

Though hdiutil has a number of other great options (for example, the ability to use shadow files), we'll review just one more, encryption, because it's more relevant to our topic. When you execute hdiutil using the -encryption flag with create, the command asks you to supply a password. (And naturally, to mount the disk image, you'll have to enter whatever password you assigned.)

You can also pipe the password into hdiutil by using echo along with the flags -encryption and -stdinpass. But because this puts the password into your shell's history—which you don't want—you'll need a second command. The two look like the following:

```
echo -n "MyPassword" | hdiutil create -encryption -stdinpass -size 1g secret.dmg
clear history
```

The first line creates a 1GB disk image called secret.dmg that you can open using MyPassword. The second wipes out the history, including the saved password. This command pair can be useful for storing sensitive information created as part of preflight or postflight imaging or used for deploying sensitive information with a predefined password.

Operating System Packaging with Composer

Composer, a utility from JAMF software (www.jamfsoftware.com), creates package and image files. To make the latter, the drive you're cloning must be connected to your computer and can't be acting as a boot volume. With those conditions met, you can create an image quickly and easily. Open Composer and click the Build OS packages option when prompted with "Choose a method to create your package." Then check the boxes for Recovery HD and the name of the image for your operating system, as shown in Figure 6-5.

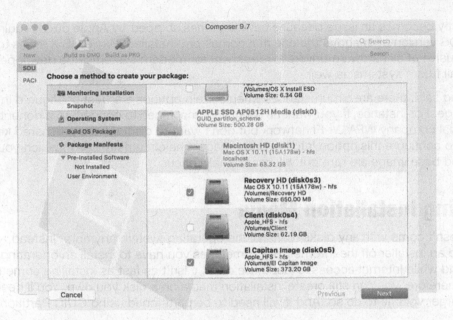

Figure 6-5. JAMF's Composer

Click the Next button until prompted for a place to store the image, and you've got two images, one for the recovery partition and one for the OS itself, that can then be used to deploy client systems. These images can be used in the Casper Suite but are also standard OS images and so can be used with other tools as well. Composer also handles the options of cleaning up all the machine-specific information discussed earlier in this chapter.

Bare-Metal Images

The steps we've just outlined are common when creating standard monolithic images. But there are a number of opinions about what constitutes a bare-metal image. Some consider it a base install of OS X. Others consider it to be the actual OS X installation media. Basically, though, for a solution that's more package-based than monolithic, the base image should have as little as possible in it—the more configuration that post-imaging packages and scripts handle, the more granular you can be with your imaging.

The difference between the two ways of creating a bare-metal image is this: when using the OS installation disk as your bare-metal image, once you've installed the base OS X disk image, you customize every single action as a task (*including* the operating system installation) at image-delivery time. As a result, you won't need to sanitize the system. When you use an installed system, you set up a base OS install, do nothing else to the system, and then create the image, so you need to sanitize out the unique information.

When should you employ one method of making a bare-metal image over the other? Create the image with the installation media when you're worried about having to sanitize or when you're concerned about incompatible hardware variations in machines you're deploying, and you'd rather just image a disk than install a new OS every time you need a new base image.

This mostly becomes an issue because new machines shipped by Apple often require a disk with an OS version at or above the one that comes pre-installed. While OS X tends to be fairly inclusive of all hardware drivers in retrospect for modern systems, the developers can't plan for all future systems as well.

That being said, there are circumstances when certain options are best configured in the base image. For instance, if you want all your client machines to connect to a nonenterprise but internal company WPA Wi-Fi network but don't want to disclose the preshared key, then it's best to configure this option into the base image. The circumstances in which you'll need a modified base image are rare but will occasionally occur.

Creating Installation Media

OS X doesn't come with any disks to install the operating system anymore. Instead, you download an installer off the Internet. But sometimes you have to install an operating system offline, and while Internet access is fast these days, it isn't as fast as installing something locally. Therefore, you can still create installation media on a disk you own. You'll need an 8GB or larger volume to do so. And it will need to be partitioned using GUID Partition Table.

To get started, first download Install OS X El Capitan.app from the Mac App Store. Once it's downloaded (by default, to /Applications), use the createinstallmedia command that Apple includes in the app bundle, located at Contents/Resources. In the following command, we'll use the --applicationpath option along with the --nointeraction options to make the installation go quicker because it won't prompt us for any information. We'll also use sudo because the command requires elevated privileges:

```
sudo /Applications/Install\ OS\ X\ El Capitan.app/Contents/Resources/createinstallmedia
--volume /Volumes/Client --applicationpath /Applications/Install\ OS\ X\ Mavericks.app
--nointeraction
```

Once the command is complete, you'll be able to boot the computer to the disk you just turned into an installer to start an installation. This disk can also be used in workflows with other imaging tools as part of an imaging workflow that installs the OS rather than copies the files that comprise the OS. You'll learn more about doing so later in this chapter.

Deploying Images

Deploying base images to hundreds of machines can be extremely hard on bandwidth and on the server hosting images. Multicasting can relieve the stress by offloading the heavy lifting to the switching infrastructure, and there are a number of solutions you can use for this type of image deployment, including DeployStudio and NetRestore (both use ASR as a back-end protocol). With multicasting, the server provides a single stream of imaging data to which client machines can subscribe and then read. In such a scenario, the server constantly streams the block data of the image over the network. On reaching the end of the image, the server starts re-streaming from the beginning. After subscribing to the stream, clients begin laying down data to their internal drives according to the current progress of the stream. A client will continue to write data until it has completed a full loop of the stream.

A multicast deployment becomes essential as deployment numbers scale; even a Gigabit Ethernet connection will become fully saturated after about 20 concurrent unicast restore streams. Solutions capable of multicast deployment in OS X include the Apple-provided ASR and NetInstall tools, two solutions that have been available for a long time. Over the past few years, a number of third-party solutions to help deal with imaging for OS X have also emerged. These range from free alternatives to proprietary solutions that come at a cost, such as the Casper Suite and LANRev. There are also a number of solutions that extend features of Windows- or Linux-based imaging solutions, such as Altiris and KACE.

Which is the best mass-deployment package? Whichever best automates the aspects of a deployment that your organization considers most important (and, as a result, provides the best return on investment by cutting hours involved in repetitious preflight and postflight imaging tasks). For example, Casper Suite is popular in environments implementing Information Technology Infrastructure Library (ITIL) because it takes into account a number of ITIL best practices, allowing for both deployment and long-term management of approved fixes and software. But many environments have less complex needs that an admin can satisfy simply by laying down an image, often opting to use cost-effective tools such as NetRestore, ASR, and DeployStudio when imaging over the network or to use tools such as Disk Utility or FileWave's Lightning when imaging over Thunderbolt or USB.

Most of these solutions support both unicast and multicast image deployment. While multicasting definitely is preferable in large environments, implementation isn't always possible because of increased network management complexity, particularly in larger, highly segmented networks. If this is an issue, either for technical or political reasons, unicast deployment may be the reality you face. In such cases, deploying site-, building-, or subnet-specific image servers may be desirable to more evenly distribute network load. Likewise, you'll want to perform deployments strictly during off-hours to prevent them from saturating your network backbone.

Restoring with Disk Utility

Earlier in this chapter, we described how to create an image. If you followed the instructions in the previous section, that was a monolithic image—likely one with no automation in it except for maybe a quick script to sanitize the system. Every computer that gets the image will have a unique computer name and should be named prior to being put into production. We'll be deploying the image over FireWire, which is a unicast method and limited to one computer at a time.

To roll out this image, you can again use Disk Utility, located in /Applications/Utilities. Simply click the destination volume for your image and then choose Restore under the Edit menu, as shown in Figure 6-6. Here you'll see one field, "Restore from." Use the Image button to select a volume or image file and then click the Restore button.

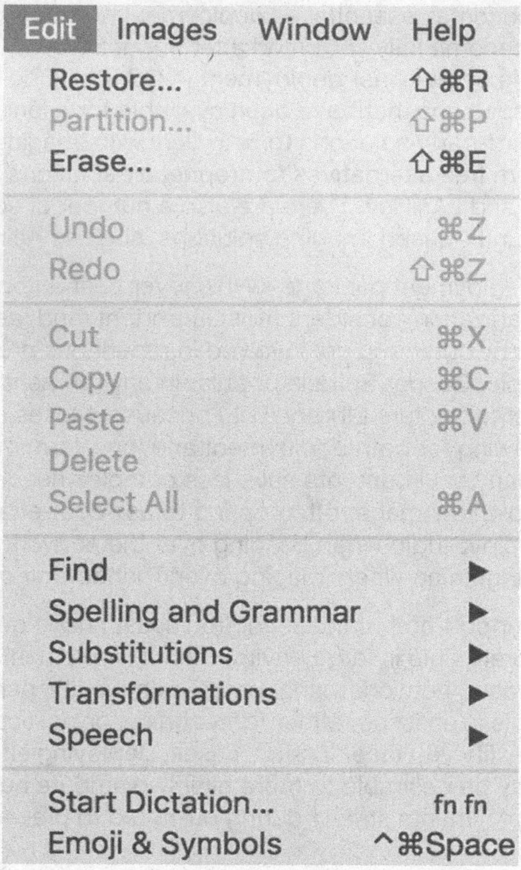

Edit	Images	Window	Help	
Restore...			⇧⌘R
Partition...			⇧⌘P
Erase...			⇧⌘E
Undo			⌘Z
Redo			⇧⌘Z
Cut			⌘X
Copy			⌘C
Paste			⌘V
Delete			
Select All			⌘A
Find			▶
Spelling and Grammar			▶
Substitutions			▶
Transformations			▶
Speech			▶
Start Dictation...			fn fn
Emoji & Symbols			^⌘Space

Figure 6-6. Restoring an image in Disk Utility

When the restore process completes, boot the computer with the destination drive and see whether everything is as it should be. This system should be identical to the source machine, with the exception that any settings unique to a computer (MAC address, and so forth) would have changed. Conveniently, Apple stores these settings together in the ByHost directory.

You can also perform the image restore from the command line using hdiutil, as we did to create the image in the first place. The more experienced you become with imaging, the more likely you are to use the command line—or even just a quick shell script—to do much of your imaging.

At this point, you've completed imaging in its most basic form. For some environments, this process will work; others will require a multicast deployment model or one that lets you simultaneously deploy to a large number of computers. Other environments might also require more granularity in the DMG as well as the preflight and postflight imaging tasks. In the next section, we'll review a few options for multicasting your image so you can go fishing, play some Halo, or do whatever you like while the systems configure themselves. Or better yet, learn about ASR in the next section so you image 50 (or 500) systems at a time and take a vacation instead.

Using Apple Software Restore

Every copy of OS X has included the command-line utility asr, so you can perform multicast imaging right out of the box without installing a thing. You can then use asr to perform a unicast or multicast restore (the command can be used to create images, restore images, and serve images). When the utility runs in multicast mode, it loops an image on the network as described earlier. The advantage of this is that whether you have 100 or 1,000 clients, they'll all image using the same stream of data without bogging down the imaging server by making disparate requests for different sections of the image.

The disadvantage is that if a client misses some data, which will happen eventually, that system will have to wait for the loop to come full circle to where the data was not properly delivered. With a unicast restore, in contrast, every client begins at byte 0 on the source image and requires its own dedicated stream of data from the server.

No matter which restore you use, you'll need to take an image and scan it first. To do so, you use the asr command along with imagescan to calculate checksums of the image file's contents and store it in the image. When you run imagescan on a disk image, the tool creates a number of checksums that are used to ensure successful restores. Additionally, the utility scans the image file and hints it for multicast restore, making sure the data arrangement on the image is optimized for block transfers. The command you issue will look like the following:

```
asr imagescan --source '/asr/MyImageName.dmg'
```

> **Note**   You can use the --filechecksum and --nostream options with the imagescan verb. The flags will, respectively, calculate checksums on a per-file basis and bypass reordering of the files for multicast. Versions 10.5 and later require images to be scanned to be restored using Disk Utility; however, asr can disable the check using the -noverify option from the command line. This is obviously never a best practice but will save time if you are testing.

To perform a unicast restore, run the asr command along with the restore verb from a host with access to both the DMG file from which you're restoring and the hard disk to which you're restoring. You can define the -source and --target as paths to files (tab autocomplete might just be your best friend if there as many spaces in your paths as in ours). You can also perform the erase and therefore have a proper restore, as shown in the following code:

```
asr restore --source "/Volumes/External HD/OS X 10.10.5 Image.dmg" --target /Volumes/
ClientMachineHD/ -erase
```

For a multicast restore, you must first create a property list for the ASR process, specifying the settings that the network service will use. For this example, we've created a folder called /asr and placed in it a plist called config.plist. To function, asr requires two settings: data rate and multicast address. The data rate is the maximum speed in bytes that asr can write data, which we'll set conservatively at 8000000 (8Mbps).

The multicast address is the address for the data stream. To write these settings into the file, use the defaults write command, the file path/name, the key you're writing into the file, a flag to indicate the type of key (if required), and the contents of the key. You then specify a multicast IP address where you announce your data stream.

The Internet Assigned Numbers Authority (IANA) defines multicast address ranges from 224.0.0.1 through 239.255.255.255, with 224.0.0.1 through 224.0.0.255 reserved for special purposes. Many common solutions, such as Norton Ghost, use addresses in the 224.77.0.0/16. Following this example, use the multicast address 224.77.2.2. It's important that you discuss the appropriate address to use for your specific network with your network administrators because multicast IP conflicts can arise if you do not. With that in mind, set the data rate and multicast address as follows:

```
defaults write ~/asr/config "Data Rate" -int 8000000
defaults write ~/asr/config "Multicast Address" 224.77.2.2
```

After you've written the data, read it and verify that it's correct using the defaults read command:

```
defaults read ~/asr/config.plist
{
    "Data Rate" = 8000000;
    "Multicast Address" = "224.77.2.2";
}
```

Now that you've scanned the image for restoration, load the ASR server. To do so, use the asr command with the server option.

```
asr server --source ~/asr/MacBook.dmg --config /asr/config.plist
```

> **Note**   When configuring the data rate, you must consider both your network connection speed and the speeds of your clients. The Data Rate value specifies not the speed of the actual network transmission but rather the speed at which your clients can write data to disk. This difference is particularly crucial in the case of compressed disk images. With these, data sent is compressed but will be uncompressed to disk. Modern-day hard drives can typically sustain much higher transfer rates than the older 2.5-inch drives we used to use, especially if they're flash drives. Decompression of data can also be a processor-intensive task. When deploying images to slower computers, using compressed images may actually result in longer restore times.

Once you've started the ASR server, you'll need to restore the ASR image onto a target computer. To do so, boot your clients to a system such as a NetBoot server or a boot disk that has network access to the ASR server and the asr command available to it. From there you can run the following command, which is similar to the previous restores but with asr://path to denote the multicast address of the ASR stream (in this example, the server will be 239.255.100.100):

```
asr restore -source asr:// 239.255.100.100-target "/Macintosh HD"
```

NetInstall

Every copy of Apple's $20 Server app includes NetBoot and its children NetRestore and NetInstall. As we showcase in the next sections, NetBoot can boot an OS X computer to an image created specifically for the purpose of booting off the NetBoot server (even in some high-security facilities without an internal drive present). A computer booted to a NetBoot image still provides a fully functional and interactive OS X experience, but any changes made to the system will revert to the standard configuration on reboot. (Network home directories, which are discussed in Chapter 7, can mitigate this behavior.) That makes NetBoot a fairly popular solution in lab environments and kiosks, where the operating system loaded on each system is fairly static. NetBoot requires your environment support DHCP-assigned IP addresses and either does not block or forward broadcast traffic between the network segments running NetBoot and the one with each client that connects to the NetBoot server.

NetInstall uses NetBoot, but rather than boot a fully configured system, it typically starts an Apple installer program. This pre-installation does not always include all the same components as normal operating system (such as the QuickTime framework or the Python and Ruby programming support files) so that it loads as quickly as possible. NetInstall is used to install OS X on a NetBooted computer. NetInstall boots a Mac using NetBoot. It then copies the operating system locally to the target computer, acting much like the stock installation media (and can use installation media to create images) but with the added benefits that it can be used to install multiple hosts concurrently over the network and that additional installation tasks can be configured. NetBoot and NetInstall are functionally the same, with the latter simply being a single-purpose NetBoot image created specifically for deploying the operating system software.

Both NetBoot and NetRestore can leverage HTTP, AFP, and NFS to copy your image across the network. Additionally, aside from a one-to-one "unicast" using NFS or HTTP, ASR can image client systems using one continuous stream of data, known as *multicast*. Whether you use NetInstall or NetRestore, the NetBoot server itself sees all the images are the same, but the client will interpret what to do with them differently based on the operating system stored inside the image. In the "NetRestore" section, we cover using NetRestore for deploying a fully populated image, and in this section we will look at deploying an image installation media because at this time NetInstall is to be used strictly to push out installers and provide preflight and postflight tasks.

The first step in using NetInstall is creating what Apple refers to as a *workflow,* using System Image Utility. System Image Utility is accessible in the Tools menu of the Server app or directly at /System/Library/CoreServices/Applications. The workflow is, at its most basic, simply a single task that images a computer. However, you can also use workflows for many other purposes, such as reformatting a hard drive or running preflight or postflight scripts and packages (which run, respectively, before or after delivering the package's payload, as you might guess). Later in the chapter, we'll discuss ordering packages appropriately in further detail.

To get started with your first workflow, first insert the operating system installation media into the system you will be running System Image Utility or download the Install OS X El Capitan. app installer from the Mac App Store. Then open System Image Utility using the Tools menu of the Server app. For this example, use the System Image Utility on the OS X Server computer that will run the NetInstall service (although for a savvy administrator doing so is not required).

When you open System Image Utility for the first time, you'll be given a list of options for which source to use to create the image. In this example, we'll use the Install OS X El Capitan entry, which is automatically loaded based on the presence of Install OS X El Capitan.app in the /Applications directory (Figure 6-7).

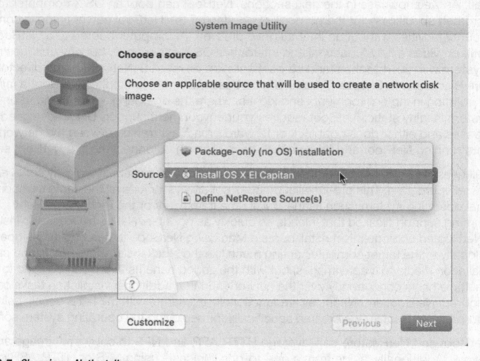

Figure 6-7. Choosing a NetInstall source

Provided that the installation media is installed, you'll see the Create a Network Disk Image screen, as shown in Figure 6-8. Here, you can select between a NetBoot, NetInstall, or NetRestore image, as we've discussed. Because we're using this to install a fresh operating system over the network, we'll select NetInstall (Figure 6-8) and then click Next.

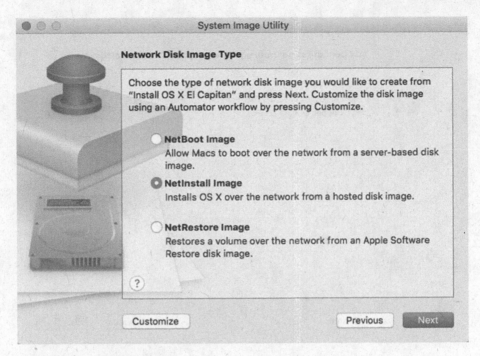

Figure 6-8. Creating an installer in NetInstall

You will then be prompted to provide the packages, configuration profiles, and scripts used during imaging. For example, here we chose to install Microsoft Office using a standard Office installation package and to add our computer to a management system using the provided packages, as you can see in Figure 6-9. If this is your first time with imaging a Mac, we recommend just building a test image to get used to the installation process. In that case, grab something like Google Chrome off the Internet to use in your testing. When you've added your packages and scripts, click Next.

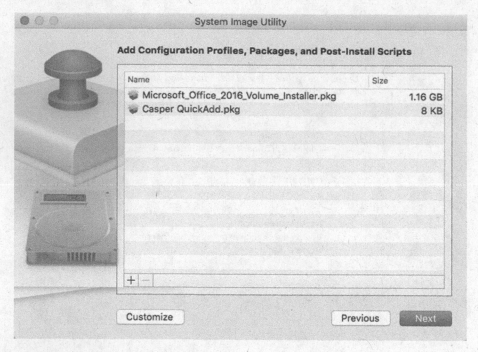

Figure 6-9. *Defining packages, profiles, and scripts*

Computers need unique names. Next, choose how the system will be named. Here, you can enter a name that will start the computer names in the Generate Names field or use a file to fill this information in for computers (Figure 6-10). Additionally, we recommend mostly checking the ByHost Preferences box to fix any issues caused with preferences files by imaging with a new computer name/MAC address (e.g., Bluetooth preferences).

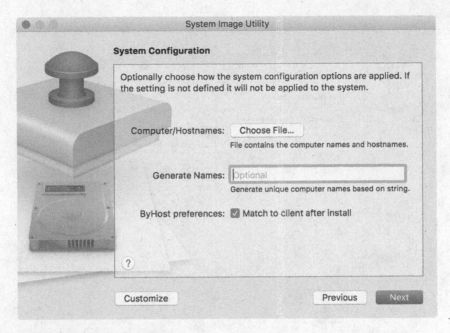

Figure 6-10. Naming freshly imaged computers

Many environments will have a directory service, such as Apple's Open Directory or Microsoft's Active Directory. Binding to that directory service is a core aspect of many an imaging workflow. At the next screen, choose your directory server and provide a username and password for an account that has privileges to perform an authenticated bind to that directory server. For more on directory services and binding to the two mentioned, see Chapters 1 through 3. If you know the required information to add a client to a directory server, provide the following, as shown in Figure 6-11:

■ *Server*: The name of the Active Directory domain or the Open Directory master hostname (or IP address)

■ *Identifier*: A MAC address (for most environments, leave this blank)

■ *User name*: The short name of an account with authenticated binding privileges

■ *Password*: The password of the account used in the User Name field

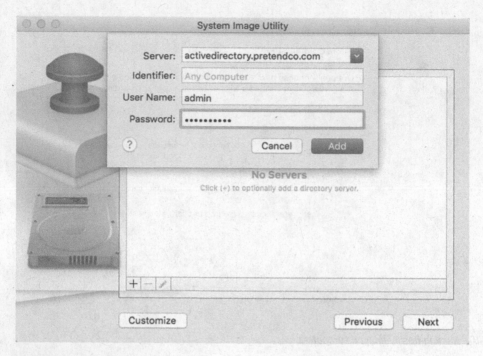

Figure 6-11. Binding to your directory service

As many environments can have multiple directory services that clients bind to (for example, one for policies and another for accounts and Kerberos), you can enter multiple directory services here. Click Next once you've entered all the services that will be bound to.

At the Automation Settings screen, you can eliminate a screen that the end user has to click when imaging the computer. If you have 5,000 client computers, you'll definitely want to use this because it will save you a boatload of time. But imaging to a specific volume name assumes that you know the name of the volume the image will be installed on, on every single computer you're setting up. If you have 10 computers, it's not such a big deal, and we wouldn't bother, but all those clicks add up on larger deployments. If you use this option, provide the name that the installer will expect the hard drive to have and then click Next. In Figure 6-12, we're assuming the drive will be called MacHD.

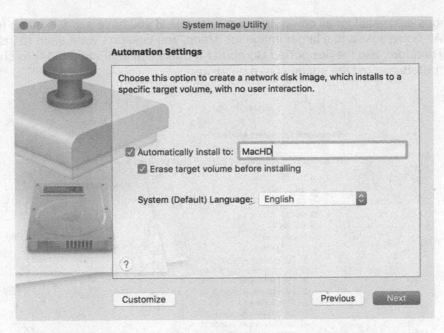

Figure 6-12. Automating the installer

At the Image Settings screen, provide a name for the network disk. This is something you choose that tells you what the image is. You can also add a description, which can include the various packages, settings, profiles, and so on. Each NetBoot image will get a unique index number. I recommend using the random image index option for most environments (as shown in Figure 6-13); however, if you will serve this image from multiple servers, assign one statically.

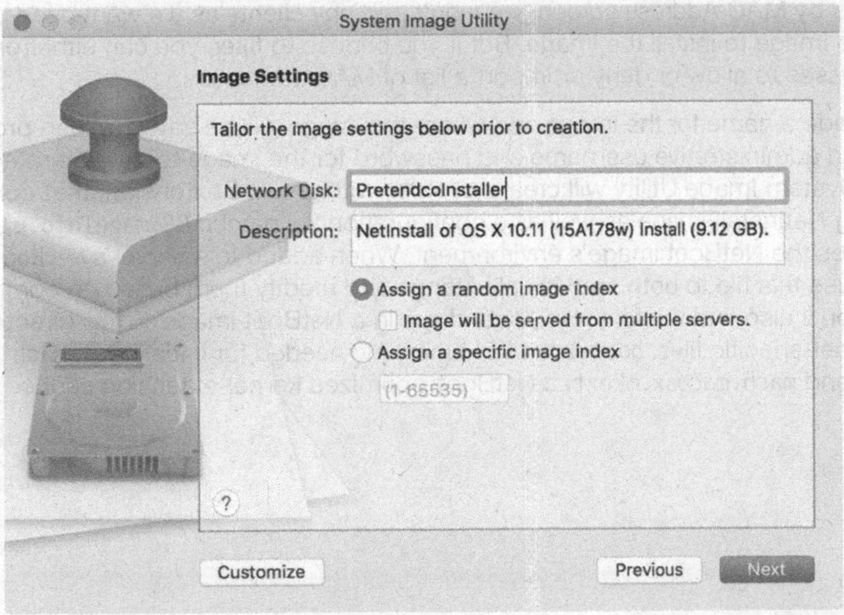

Figure 6-13. Naming your NetInstall image

Not all images are meant for all computers. For example, if you have a small image for MacBook Air notebooks and a larger image for iMacs, you wouldn't want each to install on the other. Therefore, use the Supported Computer Models screen (Figure 6-14) to choose which computers can get the image you're building.

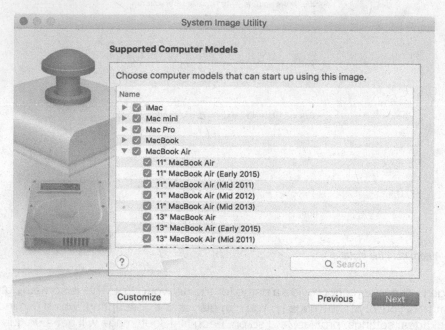

Figure 6-14. Choosing which computers the image will install on

You can also explicitly allow or deny specific MAC addresses that will get the image. At the Filter Clients by MAC Address screen, we won't add any clients as we want everyone who boots to the image to install the image. But if you choose to filter, you can either enter all the MAC Addresses to allow or deny or import a list of MAC addresses.

Finally, provide a name for the image and where the image will be saved. When prompted, also enter an administrative username and password for the image to be generated. At this point, System Image Utility will create a folder, with an .nbi extension, that contains the resulting NetInstall image as well as a configuration file named NBImageInfo.plist, which defines the NetBoot image's environment. When added to a server's NetBoot folder, Server will use this file to both read initial settings and modify them based on configuration changes. You'll also find the folders i386 and ppc in a NetBoot image's .nbi directory. These contain kernel-specific files: booter, an EFI binary file needed for initial boot; mach.macosx, the kernel; and mach.macosx.mkext, a NetBoot-optimized kernel-extension cache.

> **Note** By default, NetBoot will use the `/Library/NetBoot/NetBootSP0` folder as the first image to serve, so you can list the folder in the In field. You can also copy the image elsewhere and then share it manually through NetBoot later. OS X Server will recognize that image automatically; however, you may need to enable the image before it is visible on the network. Keep in mind that you may want to create your image on a model of your target host as it may have a newer build than what your server has currently installed.

Now that you've created your image, open the Server app from /Applications and locate NetInstall in the list of available services. Before you attempt to start the NetInstall service, you will need to verify that the server has an IP address that is reachable from client systems and that the IP address is running on a standard Ethernet interface. At the NetInstall service control screen, click the Choose Ports button to enable an Ethernet interface for your NetInstall service. Then, at the Network Interfaces screen, check the Enable box for the selected interfaces and click OK, as shown in Figure 6-15.

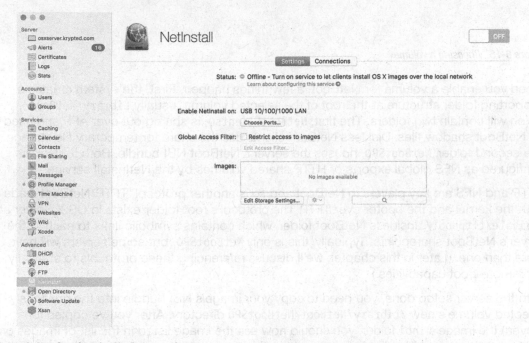

Figure 6-15. Starting the NetBoot service

Once you've enabled a network interface, you need to configure at least one volume to be able to store images. To do so, click the Edit Storage Settings button and choose Images & Client Data (Figure 6-16) for a volume that you'd like to use to store images (which are .nbi directories with a number of assets inside them, usually generated by System Image Utility).

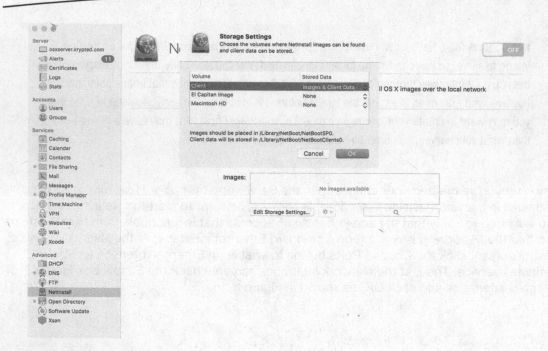

Figure 6-16. Choosing a volume

When you enable a volume for NetBoot, a few things happen. First, the system creates a supporting folder structure at the root of the selected volume, usually `Library/NetBoot/`, which will contain two folders. The first, `NetBootClients0`, is shared out over AFP and used for NetBoot shadow files. Diskless NetBoot clients use the share for temporary file storage. The second folder, `NetBootSP0`, houses the server's NetBoot NBI bundle. Both folders are configured as NFS global exports or HTTP shared volumes by the NetInstall service.

HTTP and NFS are key players in NetBoot and so is another protocol, TFTP. NetBoot loads both the kernel and the booter over TFTP. The protocol's root folder exists in OS X Server at `/private/tftpboot/`. Inside is NetBoot folder, which contains symbolic links to each of the server's NetBoot sharepoints. Typically, this is only `NetBootSP0`, but some servers will have more than one. (Later in this chapter, we'll discuss referencing these protocols to statically set remote-boot capabilities.)

With the server setup done, you need to copy your image's NBI bundle into the previously selected volume's new `/Library/NetBoot/NetBootSP0` directory. After you've copied (or moved) the image's `.nbi` folder, you should now see the image listed in the list of images on the NetInstall screen. The first image is automatically enabled, so click the start slider for the NetInstall service to bring up the actual service.

Once you've configured the service and have it running, you should be able to boot your client computers from it by pressing the N modifier key at boot, which instructs a client to attempt a network-based boot.

Boot Modifier Keys

OS X can boot from sources other than your default internal startup disk through the use of modifier keys. When you power a system on, using these keystrokes will send commands to the system to perform the following:

- *C:* Boot from optical media.

- *D (with restore disk in optical slot for some models):* Boot from hardware test mode.

- *Command-R:* Boot to OS X Recovery.

- *Command-Option-R:* Boot to OS X Recovery over the Internet.

- *Command-Option-O-F:* Boot from Open Firmware (if you have open firmware).

- *Command-Option-P-R:* Reset parameter RAM.

- *Command-Option-P-R (until you hear two tones:* Reset nonvolatile RAM.

- *Command-Option-N-V:* Reset nonvolatile RAM (similar to the previous according to hardware).

- *Command-Option-Shift Delete:* Bypass the default startup volume and look for another bootable volume.

- *Command-S:* Boot to single-user mode, a command-line-only environment where you need to mount disks manually.

- *Command-V:* Boot in verbose mode, which shows what's loading in a command-line-like environment as it loads. Boot test machines in this manner 100 percent of the time, using the nvram boot-args="-v" command.

- *Eject:* Eject media from the optical slot/tray.

- *F12:* Eject media from the optical slot/tray when there's no eject key.

- *Mouse button:* Eject media from the optical slot/tray.

- *N:* Boot from a NetBoot volume.

- *Option:* Boot from the startup manager, a list of available startup volumes that lets you select a startup volume.

- *Option-N:* Boot from a default boot image on a NetBoot volume.

- *Shift:* Boot into Safe Mode, which disables nonessential and third-party kernel extensions (drivers).

- *Shift (if held after submitting login credentials):* Disable user startup items, launch daemons, and launch agents.

- *Shift (left-Shift key at the OS progress menu):* Bypass automatic login.

- *T:* Boot into Target Disk Mode, turning a system into a glorified FireWire or Thunderbolt drive (including access to optical drives).

- *Trackpad button:* Eject media from the optical slot/tray.

Bless

You can use the `bless` command to define boot options in a more granular fashion programmatically. It can define where an OS X computer will boot from. The `-folder` option defines a directory to boot from, while you can use the `-file` option to choose a specific booter file (such as `bootx`).

To boot from a second volume, use the `-folder` option with the path to a volume's `/System/Library/CoreServices` directory.

```
bless -folder /Volumes/mySecondHD/System/Library/CoreServices -setBoot -nextonly
```

The command in this example calls `bless` with the `-setBoot` option, which tells EFI to use this device as its primary boot device. The `-nextonly` option is particularly helpful because it allows booting to a device just once, after which it resumes operation from the previous startup disk. This option has great utility: rebooting to maintenance partitions or NetBoot images, rebooting for complete reimaging, and rebooting into Boot Camp. Make this option your friend; take it out, wine it, and dine it. Your life will be dreary without it.

Speaking of Boot Camp, `bless` has dominion here too. To properly bless a Boot Camp partition, first figure out which partition, or *slice*, contains the foreign OS. Use Disk Utility or the `diskutil` command on the drive with the Boot Camp partition you want to boot from, as shown in the following code:

```
$diskutil list /
/dev/disk0
```

which will produce output similar to this:

```
#:              TYPE NAME                 SIZE         IDENTIFIER
0:              GUID_partition_scheme     *149.1 Gi    disk0
1:              EFI                        200.0 Mi    disk0s1
2:              Apple_HFS helyx            122.9 Gi    disk0s2
3:              Microsoft Basic Data        25.9 Gi    disk0s3
```

For Windows, specifically, look for the "Microsoft Basic Data" slice. From the previous output, you can see that you want to use disk0s3. To use Windows, you must specify the device and the `-legacy` option, which indicates BIOS support. Running the following command will tell your machine to reboot into Windows:

```
bless -device /dev/disk0s3 -setBoot -legacy -nextonly && shutdown -r now
```

The `bless` command also lets you specify a NetBoot location via the `-NetBoot` option. You define a specific server to boot from by using the `-server` option. For example, you'd tell the Mac OS X computer to boot from the NetBoot instance running on server 192.168.210.99 with the following command:

```
bless -NetBoot -server bsdp://192.168.210.99
```

By default, NetBoot doesn't function across subnets because the Boot Service Discovery Protocol (BSDP) is nonroutable. Specifying the -server option alone won't allow you to NetBoot across subnets. To boot an EFI-based Mac from a NetBoot server on a different subnet, you must also define the .nbi file, the mach.macosx file, and the .dmg file of the NetInstall file you created earlier. The following will perform the same command as earlier but assumes you're actually booting from a NetBoot image on a different subnet:

```
sudo bless -NetBoot -booter tftp://192.168.210.99.edu/NetBoot/NetBootSP0/NetInstall.nbi/
i386/booter kernel tftp://192.168.210.99/NetBoot/NetBootSP0/NetInstall.nbi/i386/mach.macosx
options "rp=nfs:192.168.210.99:/private/tftpboot/NetBoot/NetBootSP0:MacBook.nbi/NetBoot.dmg"
```

Using what we learned in the earlier command, the underlying technology of the NetBoot service might become a little clearer. The TFTP and NFS services do the heavy lifting, so it's entirely possible to provide NetBoot services, even if you don't have any OS X Server available. You can use the bless command for a wide variety of other common tasks. Issue the man bless command to check the man page for more information and features.

Apple's NetRestore

NetRestore is a graphical front end to the asr command-line tool, which we covered in the "Using Apple Software Restore" section of this chapter. Using System Image Utility on a Mac Server, it is possible to create a NetBoot disk image that automatically boots a client and runs the asr commands that we referenced earlier for both unicast and multicast (mASR) restores. Once a client is booted into the NetBoot environment, they can select a location (in the form of an image) to restore to their system and then start the restore using a standard-looking installer interface.

System Image Utility can also be used to create the image, providing another tool in the arsenal for image creation. To create an image for restoration using NetRestore, open System Image Utility from /System/Library/CoreServices/Applications with installation media inserted or with a volume mounted that will serve as the source for your NetRestore disk image. Provided that System Image Utility is able to read the media, the Define NetRestore Source(s) option will be available in the "Choose a source" screen, as you can see in Figure 6-17.

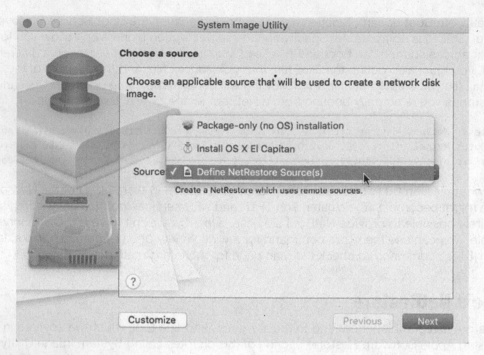

Figure 6-17. *Creating a network disk image*

Select NetRestore from the list of options. Then, at the Create User Account screen, provide the details for the account to create on each machine that the image is installed on. Here, you'll likely want to create at least an administrative account unless you already put one into your system image. These options, shown in Figure 6-18, are a subset of the options shown in the Users & Groups pane of System Preferences. Click Next once you've configured the necessary settings.

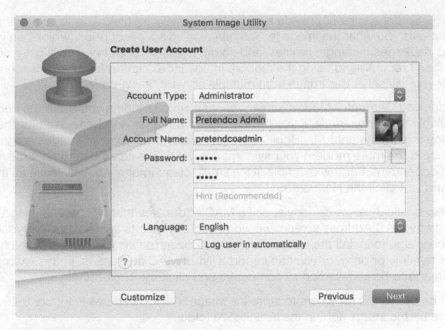

Figure 6-18. NetRestore image settings

At the Add Packages, Configuration Profiles, and Post-Install Scripts screen, as you were able to do when defining the workflow for NetInstall, you can automate the installation of software and the configuration of settings. For this example, we'll assume that everything we need is built into our system image, so click Next.

As was done previously, at the System Configuration screen, choose how to rename systems. The options here are to choose a file to augment the names of computers, automatically generate new file names based on a pattern you provide (the Generate Names field), and whether to reset ByHost preferences, which are preferences that are specific to each MAC address on a system. These settings are all optional. Having a bunch of computers with the same names can cause problems in deployments. For example, you might have no clue which computer you're looking at when trying to transfer files between systems. If you don't change anything here, the name used on your system image will also be used on all clients, and so you'll need some kind of automation to change that. For this example, we'll use Pretendco Mac in the Generation Names field and click Next.

As in the section on NetInstall, choose a configuration for the directory servers and click Next. This is where you would, for example, bind systems at first boot to Active Directory.

At the Automation Settings screen, choose whether to automatically install the image when it's selected. If you choose this option, then you won't be prompted. However, you will need to provide the name of the hard drive you are installing the operating system on. This is also where you'd choose a language. In this example, we'll choose not to automatically install the image and just click Next.

At the Image Settings screen, provide a name for the network disk. This is something you choose that tells you what the image is. You can also add a description, which can include the various packages, settings, profiles, and so on. Each NetBoot image will get a unique index number. I recommend using the random image index option for most environments; however, if you will serve this image from multiple servers, assign one statically.

At the Supported Computer Models screen, choose which models you'd like the image made available to. For example, if you have an iMac with a large volume used for the image, don't deploy that image onto MacBook Air notebooks. Model-specific images are much less of concern the more modern your systems are, as Apple continues to become less build-train dependent. For this example, it's a small, clean image, so we'll leave all the boxes checked and just click the Next button.

You can also explicitly allow or deny specific MAC addresses that will get the image. At the Filter Clients by MAC Address screen, we won't add any clients as we want everyone who boots to the image to install the image. But if you choose to filter, you can enter all the MAC Addresses to allow or deny, or you can import a list of MAC addresses. In this example, we'll allow the image to be installed on all computers and click the Next button.

You'll then be prompted for where to store the image. As you can see in Figure 6-19, we're going to create the image right in the NetBootSP0 folder.

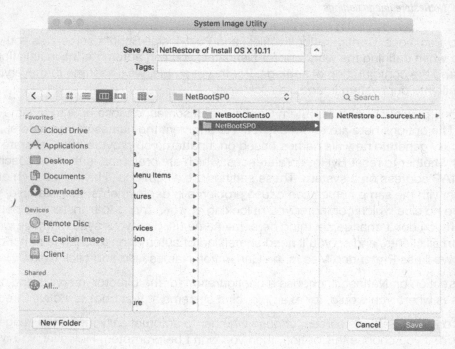

Figure 6-19. Saving the image

In this example, we're using an image of a cleanly installed Mac. While waiting, ponder the fact that in addition to installing an operating system, you could have installed a number of software titles, configured settings as you would like them to be, and then booted that system into Target Disk Mode and made a NetRestore set from the populated system. This would in effect have the same result as running the image and then any subsequent postflight actions. However, as your environment moves into a more mature imaging framework, it would inevitably become too cumbersome.

Once the image has been created, you'll then want to use the steps described in the "Using ASR" section earlier in this chapter to configure an ASR stream. Alternatively, you can place the resultant image onto a sharepoint or even on an HTTP server. Document the path that you'll then use for accessing the image, and now it's time to set up that NetBoot image so that you can provide access to restore the disk image.

To create the NetBoot image, open System Image Utility again. Then click the Customize button in the lower-left corner of the screen to create a new Automator workflow. Remove each of the prepopulated workflow actions by clicking the X in the upper-right corner of each item. Here you can drag actions from the Automator Library to the workflow. First, drag Define NetRestore Source and then drag Create Image, as you can see in Figure 6-20.

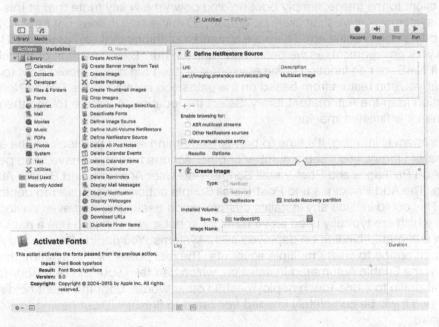

Figure 6-20. Creating a NetRestore workflow

Once you have populated the actions that comprise the workflow, you can move on to configuring the settings for each task. For the Define NetRestore Source settings, first click the plus sign and then provide the path to the location that you have hosted the image. If you are creating the path for multicast ASR, then check the box for ASR Multicast Streams. If you would like to list other disk images that can be restored, check the box Other

NetRestore Sources, and if you would like for the user to be able to type in a path to restore, click the box Allow Manual Source Entry. (This final option is useful for new environments where you are testing to check the path and potentially type in other paths if needed.)

For the Create Image action, select a type of image that you will be creating, which should be NetRestore. Then provide a name for the image in the Image Name field and finally a location to save the image to, which if NetBoot has previously been used will default to the /Library/NetBoot/NetBootSP0 directory that the NetBoot service looks to by default for which images to host. From Server you can now use the enable check box for your NetBoot service for the newly generated image and test booting a client to the image.

Now, while we're creating a simple image to operate as a NetBoot instance that can help you install an image (in this example, elcap.dmg sitting on http://imaging.pretendco.com), you can click the Customize button from any screen in the previous workflows and get a massively awesome list of Automator actions to perform on any of your images. Being able to string together a lot of options makes the capabilities of System Image Utility pretty limitless. So if you have some cool custom things that you didn't see going through the previous example, go ahead and check here before you start writing elaborate shell scripts to do tasks as part of your imaging framework.

To boot a client to the image, simply boot holding down the N key (note that at this point that client system will more than likely be erased, so make sure it does not have data that you need on it prior to doing so). There are a number of things that can cause NetBoot not to work in your environment, as we described earlier in the "Bless" section of this chapter. However, if NetBoot can function in the environment, then the client should boot to a list of images that you can restore from based on the paths you entered in the Define NetRestore Source action from the Automator Library. Select the location to restore to and then test the system when it is finished imaging.

While the system is imaging, it's time to ponder something else. If you look on the server in the Automator Library, you'll see a number of other actions that could have been performed, including Add Packages and Post-Install Scripts, Add User Account, and Enable Automated Installation. The Add Packages and Post-Install Scripts action can be used to deploy a package. This could include any installer, custom-made packages, and even payload free packages, which are typically used as vehicles for scripts; you can also use a package to perform automated binding on deployed client systems. You could also use the Add User Account option to create multiple accounts. The real power of this system, though, comes from the Enable Automated Installation, which can take your three- or four-touch deployment down to a one-touch deployment. In other words, boot the client holding down the N key, and it will be completely imaged from start to finish, without having to "touch" the system again.

DeployStudio

DeployStudio is similar to NetRestore but is in many ways a much simpler interface once you get used to using it. DeployStudio, like all modern imaging tools for OS X, automates the setup of ASR and a number of other technologies described previously. It uses a series of automations, called *workflows* (similar to those in System Image Utility but without the raw Automator-style interface), to set up an automation routine. Example workflows include partitioning a disk, deploying a master image, installing numerous post-imaging packages, and perhaps, to end the process, performing a Directory Service Binding script interface. DeployStudio presents all this functionality via a simple, easy-to-understand graphical interface that is constantly being improved. Best of all, it's free. So, why didn't we lead off with this tool? Because whether you use the graphical tool or the command line, it's vital you understand both as they all use the same basic set of technologies for all the tools we cover.

You can also use DeployStudio to roll out Windows for Apple Boot Camp environments using Winclone. This isn't to say that it's going to Sysprep the OS, but it will format the drive appropriately and lay the OS down on it, which itself may then contain a Sysprep file ready for the mouse trap to spring. Further automation is up to you (see Chapter 9).

To get started with DeployStudio, download the latest stable installer at www.deploystudio.com, extract the installation files, and start the actual install, which means clicking the DeployStudioServer installer package. In the Welcome to the DeployStudio Server Installer screen, click Continue and then click Continue again at the Important Information page, reading each along the way. Next, read the software license agreement, clicking Continue if you're OK with having no major strings on your free software. Then click the Agree button. Now you'll see the Standard Install portion. Select where on your hard drive you want to install DeployStudio (by default it's placed in the /Applications/Utilities directory). You can also select the applications you want to install. Note that the setup program will install DeployStudio's Admin, Server, Runtime, and Assistant components as well as a tool called Startup Disk, which provides access to the Startup Disk control panel. Available options include the following:

- *DeployStudio Admin:* Used to configure workflows in an interface similar to the one used by NetInstall.

- *DeployStudio Assistant:* Setup tool for performing initial configuration, creating NetBoot sets and USB2/FireWire/Thunderbolt disk images for booting clients.

- *DeployStudio Runtime:* Used to manually run DeployStudio workflows from machines not booted to the DeployStudio disks (NetBoot, FireWire, USB2, or Thunderbolt). The runtime is pretty useful in seeing both what the environment for a station being imaged looks like and creating masters (or images).

Once you're satisfied with your selections, click Install and wait for the setup to complete; then click the Close button, go to /Applications/Utilities (or wherever you placed your application bundles), and verify that you see them. Next, open the DeployStudio Assistant, which will guide you through the configuration of DeployStudio.

> **Note**   DeployStudio runtimes can now be run on live volumes. Therefore, you can now run the DeployStudio runtime as a package installer and release packages to users or groups as a means of a self-installation solution, allowing for a more zero-tier support mechanism with regard to package installers.

When you first open the DeployStudio Assistant, you'll be prompted to start the services. For the purpose of this walk-through, start the service immediately, and, if prompted, choose to allow the service to accept incoming connections. At the first Assistant screen, choose one of the following:

- *Set up a DeployStudio Server:* Configures the DeployStudio Server and the DeployStudio repository (all the following options will require a DeployStudio Server to be set up in your organization)

- *Set up DeployStudio PC on this computer:* Sets up server to accept PXE booted clients and image hosts based on information from the DeployStudio Server

- *Create a DeployStudio NetBoot set:* Similar to the previous choice for NetInstall option but pulls the automations from a DeployStudio Server

- *Create a DeployStudio bootable external drive (USB & Firewire):* Similar to the previous option for unicast deployment over FireWire but pulls the image from a server (http) running DeployStudio

> **Note**   As you toggle through the DeployStudio options, you'll notice that the choices on the left side of the screen will change, providing you with a general idea of which tasks remain to be completed in your specific configuration.

Assuming this is the first DeployStudio server, select the Set up a DeployStudio Server option and click Continue. At the Welcome screen, read the instructions and then click the Continue button to bring up the "Server connection" screen. As requested in this window, enter the server address, username, and password. For the address, fill in the IP or DNS information for the server, prepended with http:// and followed with the port number :60080. In the next field, enter the username of the local system, and in the last text box, type in the password of the local system, as you can see in Figure 6-21.

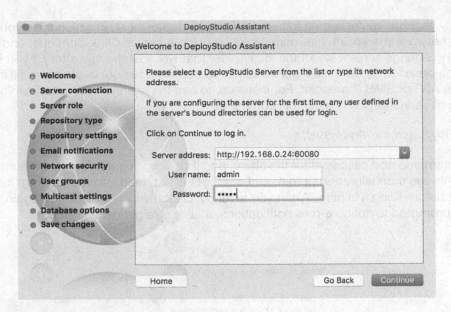

Figure 6-21. NetRestore server connection

If you're accessing the server from the host on which you initially installed DeployStudio, you should be able to click the drop-down list for the "Server address" field to populate it with the information for the address itself. If you're running Assistant directly from the DeployStudio Server and you don't see the server populated in the drop-down list, more than likely you chose to not start the services earlier. You can do so now using launchctl, as illustrated in the following code:

```
sudo launchctl load -w /Library/LaunchDaemons/com.deploystudio.server.plist
```

> **Note**   If you start the services and then later decide that you don't want to use DeployStudio, it has a removal tool included in its installation disk image. You can also stop and unload the daemon services to temporarily free up the typically minor amount of resources its database components use. The command to disable is as follows:
>
> ```
> sudo launchctl unload -w /Library/LaunchDaemons/com.deploystudio.server.plist
> ```

When you've completed the server-connection information, click the Continue button. At the "Server role" screen, choose "a master," assuming this is the only DeployStudio server, and then click Continue.

At the Repository Type screen, enter the repository location you'll use. The repository contains the DeployStudio database, software packages, master images, scripts, and logs. It can become pretty big, so plan accordingly. If you'll be deploying systems using a USB, Thunderbolt, or FireWire drive, you can choose to have a local repository.

Most likely, though, you're setting this up to do mass deployment, in which case you want to specify a network sharepoint, assuming you'll be using a server. Click Continue, and at the Repository Settings screen, select the local folder that will host the repository if you chose local in the previous screen (see Figure 6-22). If you chose a remote destination, fill in the URL to an AFP or SMB sharepoint. For instance, to use the sharepoint DeployStudio on the deployment server deploy1, issue this command:

```
afp://deploy1.myco.com/DeployStudio
```

Enter a username and password for the share, and if desired, a subfolder and mount options. Always manually attempt to mount a remote client, read information from it, and write to It before filling it in here. When you're ready, click the Continue button again, and you'll be prompted to set up e-mail notifications, a fairly straightforward step.

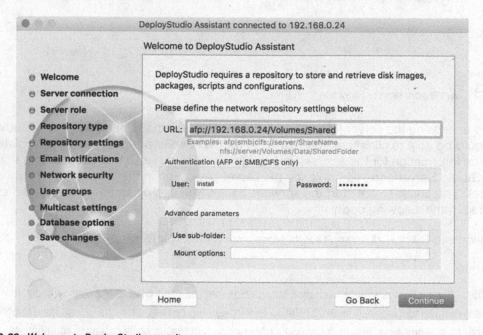

Figure 6-22. Welcome to DeployStudio repository

By default, these alerts go out to an administrator only when an error occurs. You can, however, change this so that a notice will go out when the imaging process completes. (Reminders are nice, aren't they?) Optionally, you can check the box to include the log file in the mail body to see a granular report of the imaging options you've applied. When you're satisfied with your e-mail settings, click the Continue button to move on to the Network Security screen (see Figure 6-23).

Here you can choose whether to use HTTPS during your imaging. If you choose HTTP, the default port will be 60080. With HTTPS, it will be 60443. You can also customize the TCP/IP port that DeployStudio will use by typing a different integer into the Port field. When you've finished this, click Continue to move to the next step.

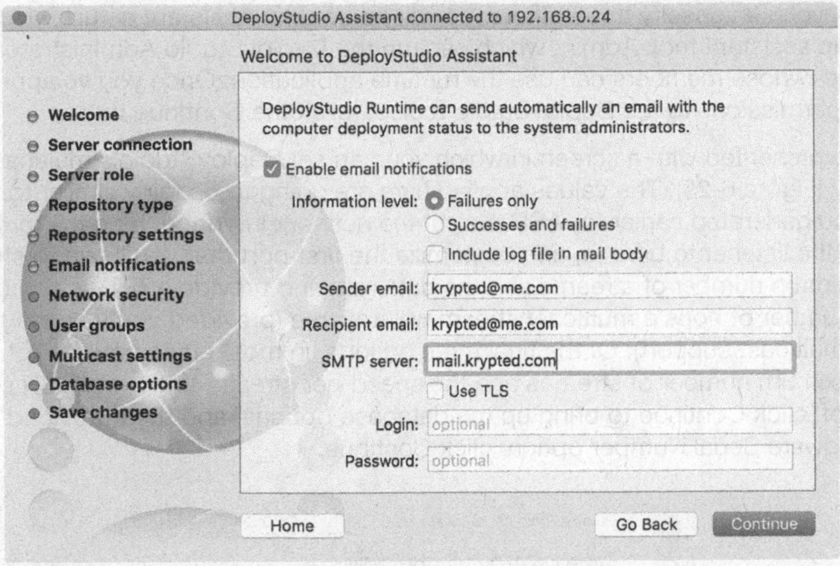

Figure 6-23. DeployStudio Assistant: e-mail notifications

Now you've arrived at the User Groups screen (Figure 6-24). Here, you can define who can perform various tasks on the server and which groups have access to which features. The groups can exist either in the local directory or in remote directories such as Open Directory or Active Directory. Create a local group on your DeployStudio using the Users & Groups pane in System Preferences for dsasst, dsadmin, and dsruntime. That makes adding members with local accounts pretty simple. In larger environments, you may want to use only directory groups.

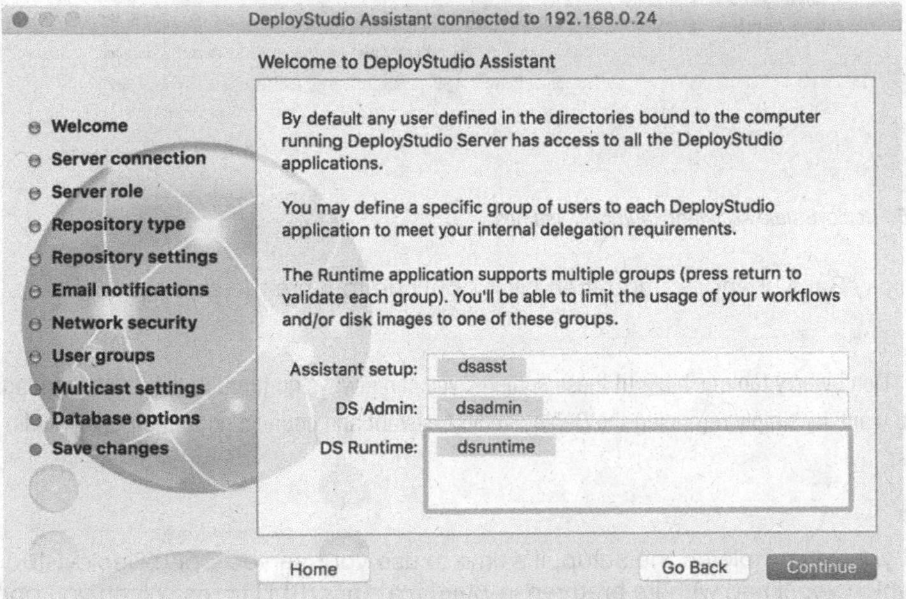

Figure 6-24. DeployStudio Assistant: user groups

In any case, you can specify three different privilege groups: Assistant setup, which can run the setup assistant tool; Admin, which can run the DeployStudio Administrator tool; and Runtime, whose members can use the runtime application. Once you've appropriately configured permissions to the DeployStudio toolset, click the Continue button.

Next, you're presented with a screen in which you can set DeployStudio's multicast functionality (Figure 6-25). The values applied here are going to be fairly similar to those in the file you generated earlier for ASR. Select the network interface, type the multicast address for the listener to bind to, and customize the first port that you'll use to stream. Now set the maximum number of streams and the data rate and provide a TTL, which defines the maximum number of hops a multicast stream will traverse (provided you've configured your routers for multicast support). Of the final three options, In most environments you customize only the maximum number of streams and the speed per stream. With your ASR settings taken care of, click Continue to bring up the database options, and then provided you can use the Hardware Serial Number option, click Continue.

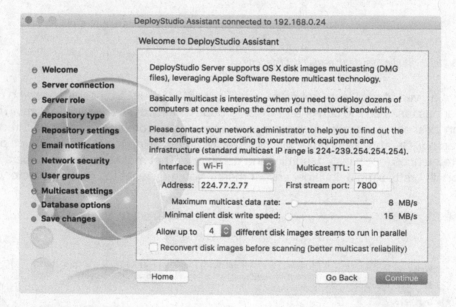

Figure 6-25. DeployStudio Assistant: multicast settings

Finally, click "Save changes," and then click Continue to write the settings to disk.

> **Tip**   Don't worry too much about these settings; you can always go through and enter them again, if you want, by simply rerunning the DeployStudio Assistant and connecting to the DeployStudio server.

Now that you've completed the setup, it's time to use your server. Open DeployStudio Admin, which you'll find with its brethren in /Applications/Utilities. When you open the admin tool, it prompts you for a valid server, username, and password. Log in as one of the users in the DSadmin group and enter the address, followed by the port number just specified in the DeployStudio Assistant. By default, the connection information should be available in the drop-down menu. Once you've connected, along the left side of the screen (Figure 6-26), you'll see the five options described here:

- *Activity:* Allows you to view events.

- *Computers:* Lists the computers, by serial number, that you will be imaging (or have imaged). You can import information into Computers using ARD or CSV files.

- *Workflows:* Similar to the Automator-style interface of NetInstall, allows you to configure the steps for an installation.

- *Masters:* Lists all images located in the repository. To populate the Masters list (the base or bare-metal images you will use in your workflows), you will need to use the DeployStudio runtime.

- *Packages:* Lists packages that can be installed.

- *Scripts:* Central repository for scripts to be run as part of workflows on computers specified (the existing scripts are mostly for Mac OS X 10.4 and should not be used to image computers with later versions of the OS). You can pull most scripts from your NetRestore deployment and use them on a DeployStudio deployment. You'll also find other scripts, located in subfolders of the DeployStudio root directory defined during installation.

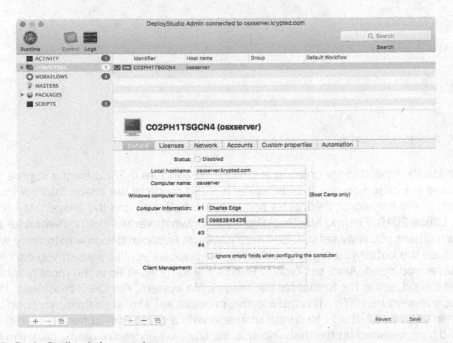

Figure 6-26. DeployStudio admin computers

> **Note**   If you're migrating to DeployStudio from NetRestore, you'll be happy to learn that both store data in the same format. The format of the CSV file should be as follows:
>
> ```
> Serial number,computername,hostname
> ```

You use the DeployStudio runtime to play workflows, including those for capturing an image or putting one onto your desktops, which you'd typically want to do for mass deployment. You can run DeployStudio Runtime manually from OS X as well, so you can test your workflows by playing images onto a local FireWire, Thunderbolt, or USB drive. We'll use the runtime to create a master (base image) from a source volume. Open DeployStudio Runtime and authenticate to the server you set up earlier in this section; then select "Create a master from a volume" and click the Play button, as shown in Figure 6-27.

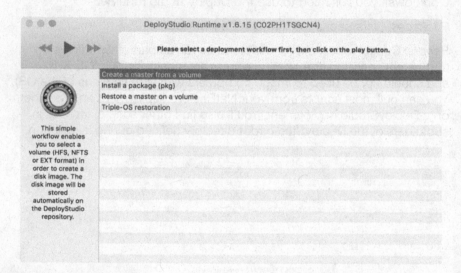

Figure 6-27. DeployStudio Runtime

Next, provide the specifics for creating the image (see Figure 6-28). Select a source hard drive to base the image on and then enter the desired name of the image into the Image Name field. In the Keywords field, enter some text to help you find the image later (for example, Office 2016, Firefox, MacBookPro June, or whatever will help differentiate this image from others you may set up). Software package lists can become extremely well-populated, so the better you tag your software, the happier you'll be when you can easily find whatever you need. Also, set Type to Read Only for now—this is the most reliable, albeit the slowest. Next, enter the format for the image's file system. For OS X machines, this will pretty much always be HFS+. The tasks in this process are similar to those you performed earlier when you used `hdiutil` to create an image with a given format from a specified source and then cleaned up the machine-specific files. When you're ready, click the Play icon (near the upper-right corner of the window) to begin building an image of the hard drive.

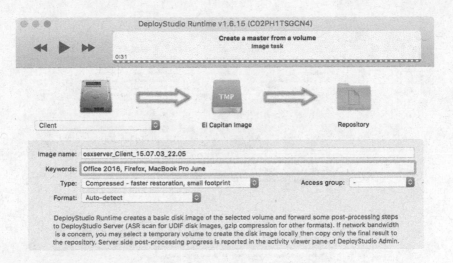

Figure 6-28. Creating a master

You should be able to see your initial master (image) now that it's in the repository (if you were patient enough to let the imaging process complete). Click Masters from the DeployStudio Admin program, and you should see it listed. Next, upload any packages you've built into the Packages directory in the DeployStudio root folder. Once you've added them, you can install them using a workflow. To create one, click Workflows (see Figure 6-29) and then click the plus sign at the bottom of the screen. Give your new workflow a name, such as Marketing Dept MacBook Deploy, which we used in our example.

Next, click the plus sign on the gray bar in the center of the screen, and you'll see a slider appear with a number of task options. For our workflow, we'll choose Partition Disk, followed by Restore a Disk Image. And, finally, we'll install any custom packages and scripts pertinent to our build. You may not want to install all the packages in your system, but you certainly could. The fact that you're performing imaging in an almost object-oriented fashion means you can pull any supported applications from your entire library with a package and copy the package to the repository. (If you need to embed serial numbers and the like, you may want to wait until we cover packages in more detail in a few pages.) You can also use scripts to implement the various settings and configurations each client needs. The workflow concept will be a recurring theme through just about any imaging application.

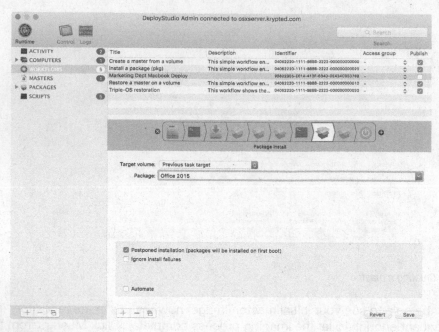

Figure 6-29. *Configuring workflows*

Once you have a functional workflow you'd like to test, you can use DeployStudio Assistant to create a DeployStudio-bootable external Thunderbolt, USB, or FireWire drive. For instance, you can make a USB jump drive that you use to boot a machine and load the runtime to image over a network. To set this up, select the appropriate option from the DeployStudio Assistant screen and click through the various dialog boxes until you get to the Available Volumes field. Select the drive to use as an external boot drive or the option to make the drive into a single partition if you'd like to erase multiple partitions on it currently. In the next pane, specify the remote server connection that the new volume's Runtime application will connect to.

Next, enter a username and password to allow communication between DeployStudio Runtime and the DeployStudio server, and optionally, type in a Virtual Network Computing (VNC) password, which lets you control hosts booted from the runtime through VNC (see Figure 6-30). The remaining options let you specify whether to display the log window by default, when to put the host display to sleep (to save energy while it's imaging), and how long the runtime will remain open yet inactive (for example, if imaging were to finish or fail to complete). When you're ready, click Continue.

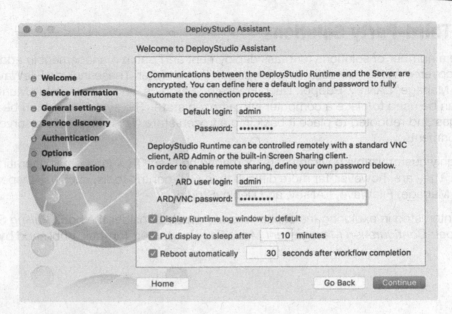

Figure 6-30. Creating a DeployStudio NetBoot set

You can also configure a NetBoot set that will achieve much the same goals of the USB drive, but rather than booting to removable media, you boot to a NetBoot server. The resulting NetBoot system is a small installation capable of running only the runtime and giving you VNC access to control the host. The steps are similar to those described earlier, except that rather than erase the target drive, you create a NetBoot set, which you can copy into your /Library/NetBoot/NetBootSP0 directory and enable in Server Admin. After this, you can boot clients by holding down the N key (if it's the default image) or by selecting the volume in Startup Disk.

If you use your DeployStudio Server for other tasks, you may want to turn DeployStudio off to avoid consuming resources. To do so, open the DeployStudio pane in System Preferences and then click on/off or use the launchctl command-line method covered previously in this chapter.

> **Tip** You can upgrade DeployStudio by installing the package for the most recent version, which simply updates the application bundles and leaves the database itself untouched. While generally updates have been fairly stable, consider backing up the Deploy Studio repository folder prior to any major upgrades.

Other Third-Party Solutions

There are a number of solutions for mass deployment and patch management in addition to those covered from a technical point of view in this chapter. These include FileWave, Absolute Manage, LANrev, Puppet, Deep Freeze by Faronics, and most notably Munki. Deep Freeze can be used to place a computer into a frozen state. The system can then be thawed for changes and rebooted to place it back into a frozen state. This is typically reserved for lab environments.

All are highly customizable environments for managing Mac OS X (and other operating systems). They are, however, far more difficult than GUI-centric tools, such as Casper Suite, Absolute Manage, FileWave, LANrev, and DeployStudio.

If you're interested in exploring the capabilities of Puppet, consider the book *Pulling Strings with Puppet: Configuration Management Made Easy* by James Turnbull, published by Apress.

Munki

The most popular open source management system for Macs is munki. Its fundamental purpose is to manage software deployments, which include not only packages but other items such as scripts and configuration profiles. Administrators often pair munki for software management with DeployStudio for imaging. And munki's server component is based on web services, which means it runs on most any server operating system. Network administrators are unlikely to block its HTTP traffic, which is a common protocol.

For a more thorough discussion of munki, related open source projects, and detailed instructions for creating a munki environment, see Chapter 10, which reviews free and open source tools for Mac admins.

Casper Suite

Earlier, we looked at using Composer to create monolithic images. Though you can purchase the product by itself, it's actually part of Casper Suite, which includes tools for OS X mass deployment—and the rest of the bundle is pretty darn useful. Its server-side component, JSS (for JAMF Server Software), integrates with Active Directory, Open Directory, and eDirectory. The JSS component determines which computers and groups receive which packages in an object-oriented fashion. Casper Admin manages the process of installing items during imaging, but the JSS component can also do so.

Policies put packages, scripts, and other maintenance tasks into groups configured to run at certain times. A highly customizable scheduler lets you activate policies during specific time windows. You can have policies apply to computers based on a number of criteria, such as IP subnet, computer group membership, or even membership in *smart groups*. The last are similar to iTunes smart playlists in that they're dynamically generated based on prespecified criteria.

For instance, you could create such a group for all computers running OS X versions prior to 10.10. You might then design a policy that's active from 7 p.m. to 7 a.m. and add the 10.10 to 10.11 update package. Thus, every night, any machines not running 10.11 would execute the update. Policies are dynamic and powerful tools for managing software deployments across a large number of systems.

Casper Suite also comes with a self-servicing solution that allows users to install their own packages. Letting users select from a list of acceptable tools—installing and removing them without contacting system administrators—can greatly reduce support requirements. Casper Suite can do a lot for you, including asset tracking, network reconnaissance, and more, but using the JSS component, Casper Admin, and Composer together provides the biggest productivity boost.

Automation

Once you've built your base image for deployment, it's time to consider the other tasks from the checklist you created at the beginning of this chapter. These chores may include items such as creating an admin user, customizing the user template, binding to Open Directory, binding to Active Directory, or installing third-party software such as Microsoft Office or Adobe Acrobat. Chances are that nearly everyone reading this chapter will want to perform at least one of these tasks, so let's step through an example.

Types of Automations

Preflight automations run before imaging, and postflight automations (whether packages, scripts, or image copies) run after. Thus, you can apply automations in the order that will most logically supply the necessary software or configurations to a desktop. You can also nest automations by including one script in another or by using different scripts as functions within larger scripts. Generally, though, the more granularity you have, the better, and so it's often best to leave each as a stand-alone script unless you need to transfer data from one automation to another. If you do so, you can then set your certain automations to execute either before or after others.

Packages, images, and scripts are the major elements of deployment automations in OS X. The easiest of these to create and use is probably the package, which houses files that you can copy (or drop) into the file system of a computer as a postflight task. Scripts are useful primarily when you have an extremely small but focused payload—one, for example, that simply enables a service or performs a regex operation on a configuration file. Deployment scripts generally are AppleScripts or shell scripts; the former are useful mostly for configuring GUI apps that generally have no command-line interaction. Packages can be the most complicated deployment elements but also the most powerful.

Delivering file system payloads is the primary purpose of packages, but you can also use them to fire scripts prior to and after performing an installation. You can also create packages that, rather than containing a file system payload, exist solely for the purpose of running pre- or postaction scripts. For this reason, packages represent the most feature-rich option. Using tools such as Composer, you can build your own packages, but the easiest implementation method is likely to be reusing the one distributed with the original software installer.

At first, determining which type of automation to use for each task can be daunting. But as a rule of thumb, if you just need to put some files into a location, you're best off using an image or a package. If you need to run a command to rename a computer or perhaps to perform a trusted bind to a directory service, you'll likely want to use a script (though you might use a package to actually deploy that script). Additionally, the software you use can play a big part in determining whether to use packages, scripts, or images—and in what order.

When people are getting started with automating tasks for images, they typically use snapshots to capture changes and create packages. Over time, though, you'll realize that a snapshot replaces the entire file, which may not be appropriate for preferences files, given that they often store information for a number of different functions. Most experienced imaging aficionados move away from snapshots and use shell scripts to automate the setting of preferences on imaged computers.

> **Tip**   You can also create a DMG file based on the contents of, say, a scripts directory—useful if you'd like to keep a directory with a number of scripts in a folder called `Scripts` on the root of your hard drive. To do so, you'd use `hdiutil` with the `create` verb, followed by the name of the DMG file and finally the `-srcfolder` flag, which requires the actual source directory. As an example, if you wanted to turn this folder into a DMG called `myscripts.dmg`, you could use this command:
>
> ```
> hdiutil create myscripts.dmg -srcfolder /Scripts
> ```

User Templates

New users on Mac computers have a certain set of default settings that are copied into their user profiles the first time they log in. If a home directory for a user doesn't exist when that person first logs in, the system will create a new one using the contents of the directory `/System/Library/User Template/English.lproj` as a template (for English users). You can modify the contents of this directory, copying new files or editing existing ones. When someone creates a new account, the system will copy these files into it. This customizes the look and feel, default documents, fonts, and other aspects of user accounts without you having to do so each time you create a new user or whenever someone logs in for the first time. (In OS X 10.11 El Capitan, the `User Template` folder is exempt from Apple's new System Integrity Protection feature, which disallows modifying certain system folders such as `System`.)

This can be incredibly useful when you're not using network or mobile accounts, when you have a number of different people logging into computers, or when you want to provide specific settings or files. It goes without saying that you could set many policies more easily using configuration profiles, but this won't always cover the settings you want, and modifying the `User Template` folder can be easier in many circumstances.

For example, let's say you want to provide all users with a default set of stock fonts. By simply copying fonts into the /System/Library/User Template/English.lproj/Library/ Fonts directory, you'll provide the fonts to users when they log in. You could just install the fonts in /Library/Fonts and be done with it, but a user who has the fonts in the home directory can remove them, if needed, rather than being stuck with them. The same would be true for any items stored in the home directory, including Microsoft Office preferences, many of which you can't manage via profiles.

You can also employ the User Template folder to perform scripts the first time a new employee logs in. For example, if you have a Microsoft Exchange environment, you can have Outlook automatically set up a user account on the person's initial login by having a self-destructing launch agent in the user's home folder (~/Library/LaunchAgents). This would put the LaunchAgents folder, a script, and the agent itself in the User Template folder, but if you have a large number of users, it would save a lot of time in setup.

Of course, if you're using Open Directory, Active Directory, or some other directory service, there are better ways to accomplish much of what you can do with the User Template folder. Still, templates are great tools to keep in your tool belt.

Migrating from Monolithic Images

A number of organizations currently use monolithic images. Moving to a package-based solution may seem like a time-consuming and complicated task, but you can take small steps toward accomplishing it. Composer gives you one of the quickest and easiest ways to get to a package-based imaging solution. And the product has a great feature that will scan your hard drive for installed packages, letting you create one package per installed software product. This allows you to, for example, take a monolithic image, generate a package for individual pieces of software installed on the image, and then create a package for each. You can download Composer from www.jamfsoftware.com.

After the installation, when you first open the software, you'll see a screen asking you to choose a method for creating your package (see Figure 6-31). Select Pre-Installed Software on the left side of the screen, and you'll see a listing of each software package installed on the computer. Select the appropriate title and click the Next button.

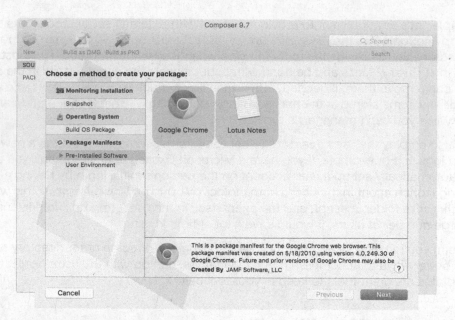

Figure 6-31. Creating a new package with Composer

Composer will begin generating the package, and it will use the original software you installed as the source. Once Composer has finished, you'll also add your custom bindings and then create any scripts and other automations to complete the items on your checklist. But even if you don't do that, Composer can perform a number of the tasks for your migration.

Custom Packages with Composer

You can also use Composer to generate other types of packages. One of the product's powerful features is its tool for taking system-state snapshots. To put the feature to use, build an original file-system state list (by performing a software installation or configuration change) and have Composer record it. Then build another and record that. Comparing the before and after snapshots lets you create a list of modified files, which (for the most part) will be representative of the software you installed.

To start the process, from the main screen of Composer, click the New button in the toolbar. In the left pane of the dialog that appears (Figure 6-32), choose the Snapshot option. In the main part of the window, you should see three options: Normal Snapshot, New & Modified Snapshot, and Monitor File System Changes. For the sake of speed, pick the last.

This option does its monitoring using FSEvents, which is the primary system behind Spotlight and Time Machine and provides the ability for Composer to track file system changes. You could use Composer's Normal Snapshot, which creates before and after picture but records only enough data to detect new (rather than modified) files. Unfortunately, this method, though faster (creating a snapshot is a fairly slow process), will miss any file modifications.

That, potentially, is a large problem, and it's the reason for the New & Modified option—which, sadly, takes even longer than Normal Snapshot. However, it has benefits. One of the main advantages to using snapshots instead of FSEvents is that change-tracking persists through reboots and is generally more stable when there are large numbers of data changes.

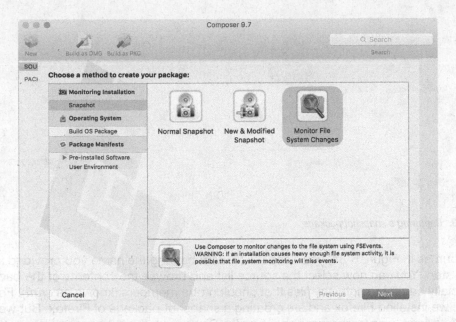

Figure 6-32. Making snapshot packages with Composer

Once you've chosen Monitor File System Changes, at the resulting screen, type a name for the software package and then click the Begin button to initiate file system activity monitoring. Now, just install the software as you would normally. You can minimize Composer if needed, but make sure to leave the application running. When you complete the software installation and configuration, come back to the Composer window and click the Create Package Source button (Figure 6-33).

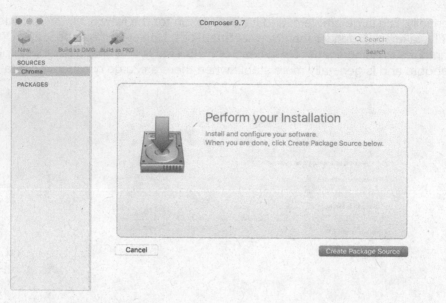

Figure 6-33. Capturing a snapshot package

Under Sources in Figure 6-34, you'll see a new item bearing the name you provided in the previous step. You can now select the source list and browse the contents of the package. Be especially careful to note any files that shouldn't be members (known as *cruft*). For example, we installed Firefox and are creating a snapshot package of Firefox. But we ended up with data from /var/servermgrd and /var/vm. To remove the extraneous files, you click / var in the package and then click the Delete button in the Composer 9.7 toolbar.

When first building packages from snapshots or monitoring, including unnecessary and potentially harmful files is a common mistake. So again, take extra care to check thoroughly for unwanted items. You should be especially vigilant about getting rid of unnecessary items in /System, /Library, /private, /var, and /etc.

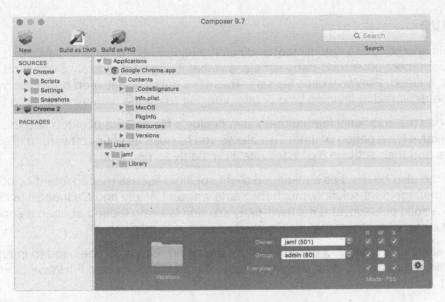

Figure 6-34. Browsing package contents and assigning permissions with Composer

Once you've whittled down the contents appropriately, click Build as PKG. When prompted, choose a location to save the package and then click the Save button to create a standard Apple package installer.

If, instead, you click Build as DMG, the same data that would otherwise be in the package will go into your DMG file. But as mentioned previously, packages give you the ability to deploy scripts and ensure version control, making them the preferred choice in general. So, choose Build as PKG, select a valid location for saving your package (you'll get a prompt to do so), and finally, test the package.

But once you've gone to the trouble of creating a package and have been using it for a while, expect to encounter one of the more annoying aspects of being on a deployment team. Vendors continue to update their offerings (sometimes before you get the initial deployment complete).

> **Tip** Snapshots are incredibly useful when you just want to figure out what data changed—for example, if you need to determine which property-list file to deploy a setting to. If there's only one setting in a property list, then you can make a package out of it. But if a preference file has a number of items, you may be better off simply creating a script to augment the file. That way you don't risk changing other settings by accident—or worse yet, rendering systems unbootable because you change a file in a way that's inconsistent with what the operating system demands.

FileWave

FileWave is another mass deployment and patch management solution. FileWave is different from most other third-party solutions in that it does not natively create and leverage packages. Instead, FileWave uses file sets. These are portable between operating systems and can be deployed at imaging time or after imaging using the native installers to FileWave.

FileWave has the additional feature that it can deploy a file set to a desktop and then leave it there inactive for a period of time. This allows you to push all your software to client computers and then activate it or inactivate it on the fly as needed.

FileWave can also be used as a managed client solution, license management solution, and inventory management solution, much the same way as LANrev and Casper Suite can be used. It is a solid solution, and if a third-party solution is being looked at, then it should be on the list along with others that are covered more thoroughly.

FileWave also has a great tool called FileWave Lightning, which can be used to image systems directly attached to an imaging station. As the name implies, FileWave Lightning is really fast!

Making Packages

Composer is one way to make package installers. You can also use `pkgbuild` and `productbuild`, which are Apple command-line tools that while completely functional aren't the easiest tools to get started with. Another tool that has become pretty popular is called Packages. Packages is available at `http://s.sudre.free.fr/Software/Packages/about.html`.

As with Composer, you can use packages to create packages from snapshots. But packages let you define a lot more information for a package, including information that gives more granular control over scripts. Composer can add scripts to a package but can't provide as much control over how they're handled.

Once you've installed packages, you can find the Packages app in the `Applications` folder.

When you run packages for the first time, you'll be prompted for the package template to use for your project. For this example, you'll learn how to create a distribution package, so click Distribution and click Next.

When prompted, enter a name for the project. This can be something like Chrome or Firefox, which indicates what is being installed. You'll also need to provide a directory for the project, which will contain all the files that make up the project. Click Finish after you've told packages what you're making and where it will go.

Now that you've built the package-project directory structure, you can save the untitled package-maker project on the same level as the faux root (`Chrome`) and the `Resources` folders, but take care not to save the project in one of the two subfolders. The name of the packages project can differ from the final package name. This example uses the same name as the faux root folder (`Chrome`) for consistency.

Now that you've saved the Packages project file in the `package-project` directory, you can associate the project file with the faux root directory. The easy way to do this is to drag the faux root directory and drop it into the Contents section of the Payload tab while the package is highlighted. You'll then be prompted for the permissions. For this example, you want the files deployed in the package to have the same permissions as the source files, so check the box "Keep owner and group." You can also configure how the path is referenced. This one should be absolute because you want it to go into the same place you're placing it (Applications), as shown in Figure 6-35.

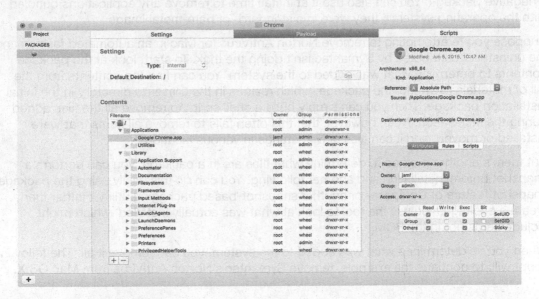

Figure 6-35. Dragging items into packages

You'll need to repeat this operation for any other files and folders you want to create on the target systems. Scripts can augment the file system in ways other than just placing files on the volume. For example, you can unload and reload a launch daemon, delete temporary files, or kill a PID. If any of these assets are scripts, then you'll need to configure when those scripts will run. To do so, click the Scripts tab in Packages. From the Scripts tab, drag any preflight scripts into the Pre-Installation section of the screen and any postflight scripts into the Post-installation section of the screen. You can then save the package and use the Build entry in the Build menu to create your package.

Next, run the package to test that it did everything you told it to do. Keep in mind that when testing, you always want to mimic your final installation environment as closely as possible. This may require that instead of actively installing with Apple Remote Desktop, you run the package installer on a volume other than the current startup disk so you can mimic how a network installer would passively install files. Or using Casper, Munki, FileWave, Absolute Manage, or LANrev to install your package, you can check that positional parameters are as expected, and so on.

> **Note** Pick the right tool for each job. Composer is easy to learn, making it well worth the minimal investment to purchase it. However, when you reach the limits of what it can do, chances are good you'll look to extremely customized package creation tools as a next step.

Negative Packages

Negative packages are those you use to remove (rather than add) applications. The easiest way to remove an application is with an uninstaller that the application vendor provides. If you don't have that (or if it doesn't work, which happens), more than likely you'll want to use a negative package. You can also use it at install time to remove any applications bundled with the operating system if they were in a standard- or bare-metal image.

Suppose you're attempting to remove Norton AntiVirus for Mac in an automated fashion and the uninstaller distributed by Symantec isn't doing the trick. To start, look at the package contents to determine what was added to the system. You can find the contents from the bill of materials (BOM) for the package, which resides in the Contents directory in the initial installation package. Then you can simply build a shell script to remove all the files added during the installation. Note, however, that this often fails to remove all items that were installed or moved, and it can also leave settings in various locations.

But there's another method to determine what files are in a package: you can perform a snapshot before installation and another following. You can do this easily using the package-snapshot feature of Composer or another snapshot-based packaging utility. Rather than create a package, you use the tool to look at what was actually installed, which might include items not in the BOM.

When you've determined what was added to the system, you can remove it all. The following script will, to continue the example, remove Symantec's Norton AntiVirus from Mac OS X.

```
#! /bin/bash
launchctl stop $( launchctl list | grep com.symantec.SymSecondaryLaunch | awk '{print $3}' )
launchctl stop $( launchctl list | grep com.symantec.scanNotification | awk '{print $3}' )
launchctl stop $( launchctl list | grep com.symantec.diskMountNotify | awk '{print $3}' )
launchctl stop $( launchctl list | grep com.symantec.quickmenu | awk '{print $3}' )
kextunload -b com.Symantec.SymEvent.kext
kextunload -b com.Symantec.SymOSXKernelUtilities.kext
kextunload -b com.Symantec.kext.KTUM
rm /etc/liveupdate.conf
rm /etc/Symantec.conf
rm /usr/bin/symsched
rm /usr/bin/navx
rm ~/Library/Preferences/com.Symantec.Scheduler.plist
rm /Users/Shared/snorosx
rm -rf /Library/Contextual\ Menu\ Items/NAVCMPlugin.plugin
rm -rf /Applications/Symantec\ Solutions
rm -rf /Applications/Norton\ AntiVirus
rm -rf /Library/Receipts/NAVContextualMenu.pkg
rm -rf /Library/Receipts/NAVEngine.pkg
rm -rf /Library/Receipts/Norton\ AntiVirus.pkg
rm -rf /Library/Receipts/SymEvent.pkg
rm -rf /Library/Receipts/SymOSXKernelUtilities.pkg
rm -rf /Library/Receipts/NortonQuickMenu.pkg
rm -rf /Library/Receipts/SymSharedFrameworks.pkg
rm -rf /Library/Receipts/Norton\ AutoProtect.pkg
rm -rf /Library/Receipts/Symantec\ Scheduled\ Scans.pkg
```

```
rm -rf /Library/Receipts/Symantec\ Scheduled\ Scans. Pkg
rm -rf /Library/Receipts/Symantec\ Scheduled\ Scans.pkg
rm -rf /Library/Receipts/navx.pkg
rm -rf /Library/Receipts/LiveUpdate.pkg
rm -rf /Library/Receipts/Symantec\ Scheduler.pkg
rm -rf /Library/Receipts/Stuffit.pkg
rm -rf /Library/Receipts/SymInstallExtras.pkg
rm -rf /Library/Receipts/SymHelpScripts.pkg
rm -rf /Library/Receipts/SymantecUninstaller.pkg
rm -rf /Library/Receipts/Symantec\ Alerts.pkg
rm -rf /Library/Application\ Support/Norton\ Solutions\ Support
rm /Library/Application\ Support/NAV.history
rm -rf /Library/Application\ Support/Symantec
rm -rf /Library/PreferencePanes/SymantecQuickMenu.prefPane
rm -rf /Library/PreferencePanes/APPrefPane.prefPane
rm -rf /Library/PrivateFrameworks/SymAppKitAdditions.framework
rm -rf /Library/PrivateFrameworks/SymBase.framework
rm -rf /Library/PrivateFrameworks/SymNetworking.framework
rm -rf /Library/PrivateFrameworks/SymSystem.framework
rm -rf /Library/PrivateFrameworks/SymScheduler.framework
rm -rf /Library/StartupItems/NortonAutoProtect
rm -rf /Library/StartupItems/NortonMissedTasks
rm -rf /Library/Documentation/Help/Norton\ Help\ Scripts
rm -rf /Library/Widgets/Symantec\ Alerts.wdgt
rm -rf /System/Library/Extensions/SymEvent.kext
rm -rf /System/Library/Extensions/SymOSXKernelUtilities.kext
rm -rf /System/Library/Extensions/KTUM.kext
rm /System/Library/Extensions.mkext.NxdE
```

A package with just that script in it and no files to place into the file system is a payload-free (given the lack of files) negative package and would remove data rather than add it.

Installing a Package

You can install a package by double-clicking it and following the prompts until the process completes. You can also use the `installer` command to install a package.

The installer command also has an option, -applyChoiceChangesXML, which allows you to build an answer file for any options that can come up during a package. The answer file is used to toggle options in a package on or off in XML format. The most notable use of the –applyChoiceChangesXML option is to choose which component of Microsoft Office is deployed during installation, which was explored in Chapter 5.

Package Scripts

As mentioned previously, a package file can contain a number of scripts that execute at various points in the installation process. There are a number of choices of predefined script designations that you might find in a package's resources folder. We've listed their names here, along with their functions:

- *InstallationCheck:* Runs at the beginning of the installation process, prior to authentication. This is typically used for basic sanity checks.

- *VolumeCheck:* Fires when a user is given the option to choose a destination. This runs against each attached volume to determine eligibility.

- *preflight:* Runs prior to installation.

- *preinstall:* Executes prior to installation but requires that the current package has never been installed on this machine.

- *preupgrade:* Identical to preinstall but is triggered only in upgrade situations when it finds a receipt, in /Library/Receipts, with a previous version.

- *postinstall:* Activates after the successful first installation of a software package.

- *postupgrade:* Fires after a successful upgrade installation.

- *postflight:* Runs at the end of an installation, regardless of the success of the installation.

Each script typically gets three variables as arguments—Package Path, Target Location, and Target Volume. The exception here is VolumeCheck, which receives only the path to a volume. In every case, an exit code of 0 signifies success, and you should make sure your scripts exit cleanly. A script failure reports to end users as an installation failure.

Customizing OS X Preferences

Often, in the course of a mass deployment system, you'll want to customize OS X system or application preference files on a machine-specific basis. With the advent of OS X, the standardized format for many of these files is that of the property list (plist). These files contain serialized data organized in a key-value format capable of storing common data types: strings, numbers, dates, Booleans, arrays, dictionaries, and raw binary data. Using these data elements, applications can store complex data structures for a wide variety of uses.

The plist format isn't the most efficient for large data sets, though, so the information stored rarely exceeds a few hundred kilobytes. Still, that's ideal for application-preference storage.

While XML files are convenient for human perusal and hand editing, they're not the most efficient for runtime processing. So, in an effort to optimize performance, Apple introduced the plist binary format for more efficient access by running processes.

You can edit plist files in numerous ways. With those in XML, you can use the text editor of your choice. But generally, when a running process accesses the file, the OS converts the format into the more efficient binary, after which your favorite text editor is all but useless. Thus, before opening the file, you may want to verify the format using the `file` command-line tool.

```
$ file /Library/Preferences/com.apple.AppleFileServer.plist
/Library/Preferences/com.apple.AppleFileServer.plist: Apple binary property list
```

> **Note** In OS X, plist files typically use a naming convention known as *reverse-domain notation*. Basically, this notation is similar to that used for DNS but with the hierarchy reversed. So long as developers follow this naming convention, they don't need to worry about another application creating a preference file with the same name.

In this instance, the preference file `com.apple.AppleFileServer.plist` is in binary format, and were you to attempt to open it in a text editor, you'd be greeted with a nice display of gobbledygook. All is not lost, though. If you want to explore the raw XML, you can use the `plutil` command-line tool, which can convert between XML and binary formats as well as run syntax checks on the file. To convert the previous example into hand-editable format, you can call `plutil` with the -convert argument with a statement like this:

```
$ plutil -convert xml1 /Library/Preferences/com.apple.AppleFileServer.plist
```

Now, you can run `file` against the plist again to verify that the conversion worked properly.

```
$ file /Library/Preferences/com.apple.AppleFileServer.plist
/Library/Preferences/com.apple.AppleFileServer.plist: XML 1.0 document text
```

Sure enough, the plist file is now in XML format, and you can view it with any text-capable editor. To convert it to binary format, run `plutil` again, substituting `binary1` for `xml1` (though, as noted, the OS will usually handle the conversion for you).

Converting a plist file to XML is all well and good, but hand-editing files is of limited value in a mass-deployment scenario. Certainly you can use command-line tools such as `perl`, `sed`, or `awk` in combination with extended regular expressions to modify an XML plist, but that's a fairly ugly endeavor and not for the inexperienced. Luckily, a number of tools exist to help edit plist files programmatically; most notable are `defaults` and `PlistBuddy`, described in the next few sections of this chapter.

The defaults Command

When you need to deal with the contents of a property-list file, you can call on the `defaults` command, which lets you read, write, and delete data in the plist format. You can also use `defaults` to list the contents of a preference domain. In OS X, each application has its own preference, often referred to as *defaults*. To prevent configuration collisions, each application must belong to a different domain, which is structured based on a dictionary of keys and values that can be strings, numbers, or even another dictionary or array.

Each key in a preference domain represents the configuration of a particular setting or a behavior within the application that the domain represents. For example, the command `defaults read com.apple.mail` will read all preferences used by Apple's Mail application. On the file-system level, each domain has a `.plist` file to store these settings.

All applications and services built into OS X have their own domains. There is also the `NSGlobal` domain, which contains CoreServices preference items. Most third-party programs will also leverage the property list format to store their own preference files, considering that Apple has made it clear in developer documentation that this is the preferred method to store preference settings. At first, the `defaults` framework within OS X may seem fairly complicated. If you're familiar with the Microsoft Windows registry, using that as an analog might help. The registry has a number of keys, each specifying a number of settings available from either the operating system or third-party applications (whether available through the GUI or not). The OS X `defaults` system is a feature-rich and easily integrated method of changing application and operating systems settings.

Showing hidden files in the Finder provides another example of using `defaults`. To see the contents of a property list, you can use `defaults` along with the `read` verb. To look at the contents of the `com.apple.finder` domain, which controls the Finder, you simply type the following command:

```
defaults read com.apple.finder
```

Though this will display the contents of `com.apple.finder` by default, the contents include no key for showing hidden files or for hiding files. With a little research, however, you'll discover that you can use the `AppleShowAllFiles` key, which is Boolean value. So, to see hidden files, enter the following command:

```
defaults write com.apple.finder AppleShowAllFiles -boolean true
killall Finder
```

But there's a problem with viewing hidden files. You may see a lot of stuff you really don't want to see. To return to a state where you don't have to view all the invisible files, just delete the `AppleShowAllFiles` attribute.

```
defaults delete com.apple.finder AppleShowAllFiles
killall Finder
```

Alternatively, you could simply set the opposite value.

```
defaults write com.apple.finder AppleShowAllFiles -boolean false
```

In addition to working with the `defaults` command to edit standard string and Boolean values in a key, you can also bring information in from other sources using a script. For example, here's a script that pulls a URL from a random list of servers:

```
#!/bin/bash

Sus="http://swupd.krypted.com:8088
http://sus.krypted.com:8088
http://sus1.krypted.com:8088
```

```
http://sus2.krypted.com:8088
http://sus3.krypted.com:8088
http://sus4.krypted.com:8088
http://sus5.krypted.com:8088
http://sus6.krypted.com:8088
http://sus7.krypted.com:8088
http://sus8.krypted.com:8088
http://sus9.krypted.com:8088
http://sus10.krypted.com:8088"
sus=($Sus)
num_sus=${#sus[*]}
echo -n ${sus[$((RANDOM%num_sus))]}
exit 0
```

This simply creates an array of the supplied software update servers (the items that start with http:// and located between the quote marks) and then chooses a random item from the list, writing the output to the screen of the chosen item. In this case, the array has been called sus, and the randomization is performed using the $RANDOM function. If you have a number of software update servers, you could replace the servers in this array with your own, and the script would simply write the server chosen from the array to the screen. Then to have it actually specify the server, remove the line that begins with echo -n and substitute the following:

```
defaults write /Library/Preferences/com.apple.SoftwareUpdate CatalogURL
${sus[$((RANDOM%num_sus))]}
```

For deployment, we've handled updates two different ways. With the first, we run this script at startup as a login hook (it's really quick since it doesn't do much) and let the OS run software updates based on whatever schedule we've employed. The second method sets execution of software updates to occur strictly manually but adds a line at the end of the script to run the updates, allowing you to schedule the task using launchd or to run it manually over ARD. To configure software updates to run manually, issue this command on the target system one time (it will persist):

```
softwareupdate --schedule off
```

Now, after it randomly chooses a software update server, the script will encounter an instruction telling it that each time it runs, it should install all available software updates from that server. Here's that instruction, which we put at the end of the script:

```
softwareupdate -i -a
```

You could build a lot more logic into this process, but this shows you the basics of assigning a random software update server using a shell script, highlighting the defaults command in, for example, a non-MCX-managed environment. (We'll discuss more about MCX and software-update scripts in Chapter 7.)

When Not to Use defaults

OS X comes with a variety of commands for managing settings without having to edit a configuration file or, in some cases, making it so you actually don't want to edit a plist file. For example, you can get and set the computer name far more easily than with defaults by using scutil. This command returns the computer name:

```
scutil -get ComputerName
```

If you want to change the name, you use -set. So, to make the computer name kryptedmacbook, you use the following command:

```
scutil -set ComputerName kryptedmacbook
```

Now, let's say you're writing a shell script and you want to put the computer name in a variable called computernm. At the command line, type the following:

```
computernm=$( scutil -get ComputerName )
```

Network settings are another aspect of client and server configuration that you can deal with more easily using a tool other than defaults. (You'll look at that more in network setup in Chapter 8.)

Modifying Property Lists

OS X comes with a number of ways to augment property lists. We discussed defaults, which edits default domains and, therefore, the underlying property lists. OS X also comes with a tool called plutil, at /usr/bin. The plutil command-line tool can also convert property lists from binary format, which can't be edited normally, to XML, which can be edited. You can also use a tool called PlistBuddy, located at /usr/libexec.

In many ways, the functionality of the defaults command and PlistBuddy overlap. But PlistBuddy is better suited for more complex structures. The defaults command is great for modifying simple data types, such as numbers, strings, dates, and, to an extent, arrays. Once you start dealing with more complex structures, though, such as nested dictionaries, you can quickly find yourself in a headache-inducing maze of nested braces. For these complex files, PlistBuddy can help.

You'll find the tool in the /usr/libexec directory, and you can invoke it either interactively or noninteractively. For the purposes of deployment, we'll focus on the latter. PlistBuddy has many options, but for most scenarios you'll use the following arguments:

- *Print key:* Prints the value of the specified key or the entire file if none is provided.
- *Set key value:* Sets the value at entry.
- *Add key type value:* Adds a key with the specified type and value. Types include string, array, dict, bool, real, integer, date, and data.
- *Delete key:* Deletes the specified key from the plist.

These four options can handle the majority of your interactions, and you can learn about handling others by examining the PlistBuddy man page (type man PlistBuddy).

As mentioned, while the defaults command is useful for basic plist interaction, PlistBuddy is absolutely essential for more complex interactions. An excellent example of this involves modifying an OS X machine's SystemConfiguration preferences file. The file, which resides in /Library/Preferences/SystemConfiguration/preferences.plist, contains extensive data about a computer's configuration including the ComputerName value, as noted in the previous section where we discussed defaults. In that context, we recommended that you not use defaults, opting to use the scutil instead. But scutil can modify ComputerName only for an active running system. What if you want to change the computer name on a nonrunning system, as in a mass-deployment imaging situation?

While most such systems we discuss in this chapter contain some sort of automated naming systems, if you decide to roll your own using ASR, you may want to modify the system configuration on a nonactive system after deploying an image. For this scenario, PlistBuddy is the perfect utility. First, though, you need a database of computer names to poll. The easiest structure to use for the data set is a flat-file CSV arrangement. For instance, consider the following data in a file:

```
00:1f:f3:d1:d5:c7,Macbook-1234
00:1f:f3:d1:55:77,Macbook-1234
```

Here we have a basic comma-delimited list consisting of computer MAC addresses and computer names. This CSV file could be stored on a remote server and provided via web services. By using curl to fetch this remote CSV file and then PlistBuddy to modify the preferences .plist file on the newly imaged system, you can create a fairly basic postimaging script that can dynamically rename a machine.

Say the data is stored in the file machinedata.csv on the web server NetBoot.myco.com and you've just finished laying down an image to your volume mounted at /Volumes/MacbookHD. Here's a script to update this newly imaged system with the appropriate computer name automatically:

```
#!/bin/bash

## setup a variable for our offline system's system configuration file
preferencesfile="/Volumes/MacBookHD/Library/Preferences/SystemConfiguration/
preferences.plist"

## fetch the csv file
curl http://NetBoot.pretendco.com/machinedata.csv -o /tmp/machinedata.csv

## get our primary ethernet MAC address
## this assumes we are booted off our target computer as opposed to imaging
## an external system over firewire
ethernetAddress=$( ifconfig en0 | awk '/ether/ {print $2}' )

## search our machinedata.csv file for the appropriate ComputerName
computername=$(grep "$ethernetAddress" /tmp/machinedata.csv | awk -F, '{print$2}')
```

```
## make sure we have a computername value, if not, use the ethernet address
if [ -z "$computername" ]; then
    computername="Mac-$ethernetAddress"
fi

## set the computer name on our offline volume's system configuration
/usr/libexec/PlistBuddy -c "Set:System:System:ComputerName $computername" "$preferencesfile"

## also update the bonjour name
/usr/libexec/PlistBuddy -c "Set:System:Network:HostNames:LocalHostName $computername"
"$preferencesfile"
```

This is an optimal scenario for PlistBuddy, and its advantages become immediately apparent if you attempt to replicate this functionality using defaults. (Hint: it's not worth your time.) The PlistBuddy commands are actually referencing multiple nested dictionaries, specified by the hierarchy System:System:ComputerName or System:Network:HostNames:Local HostName. Here, each colon-separated item up to the final key represents a nested dictionary. In each instance, the last key, ComputerName and LocalHostName, is a string element containing the respective values.

You can use PlistBuddy to read these values by simply substituting Print for Set.

```
/usr/libexec/PlistBuddy -c "Print:System:Network:HostNames:LocalHostName" "$preferencesfile"
```

When Not to Use PlistBuddy

While PlistBuddy is a great utility for dealing with more-complex plist data structures, it's important to note that the utility is simply modifying the contents of a file. But you should avoid modifying the preference files of an actively running process—doing so can cause problems with the running state of the process. In less-extreme cases, the process could simply overwrite your changes with active runtime values. Also, newer versions of OS X employ a new process named cfprefsd, which caches application changes to plist files before writing them to the plist. Apple designed the defaults command to work with cfprefsd, but it didn't design PlistBuddy to work with it. That means using PlistBuddy to alter plist files may work, but the cfprefsd process may overwrite your changes with cached data.

Image Regression Testing

When you're creating a large number of images, testing each one can be critical to verifying a successful deployment. Here are the types of testing you might undertake.

The most straightforward form of image testing is going through the process manually and seeing what happens when you try to do a number of predefined tasks. Doing so requires having a testing system that you can re-image as needed. But manually testing images may give only a fraction of what can be done in the same amount of time if the process is automated. If you have a well-regimented image and software deployment environment, the results of testing against specific known configurations typically provide an early warning sign of problems in the image or a specific build of a package.

There are a few different solutions for OS X that can be used for regression testing. Eggplant is primarily used to test software applications during development but can also be used for this purpose. Regression testing is mostly useful in larger environments, with a large number of builds. Not only can it be used to qualify images, but regression testing can also be leveraged to qualify updates. By automating various testing tasks, you can often quickly reduce the change and release management times for new software and operating systems. Eggplant is a tool that can be obtained from Redstone Software at `www.testplant.com`. You can also use a tool like Sikuli, which is a free alternative to Eggplant. Sikuli is available at `http://sikuli.org`.

Eggplant uses VNC to run checks on the remote systems and then recognizes events based on known, predefined patterns. If the pattern is a match, then the test is a pass; if not, it is a fail. Because Eggplant uses VNC, it comes with the VINE server, although you can use ARD as well if you've enabled VNC in your ARD configuration. Eggplant is pretty straightforward once you get started, allowing you to define visual patterns in the form of screenshots and letting Eggplant click those for an expected result.

Sikuli can do the same but doesn't require VNC. Sikuli uses jython (a mix of Java and Python) to provide a pretty rich framework for scripting regression testing. For example, you can have Sikuli or Eggplant open Word and check to see whether specific fonts are in the list of available fonts. This checks to verify that the fonts load. And you can run these tests without touching a system, allowing you to define test cases and then perform quality assurance (QA) on your image prior to deploying that image to client computers en masse.

Summary

Imaging environments often reflect the maturity level of your infrastructure. In the beginning, you may be creating a large image with all your software and automations included in the image. Over time you'll likely create an image and then move into more of a package-based deployment to supplement the image, perhaps going so far as to move to a bare-metal image with full package management layered on top.

In this chapter, you looked at creating and deploying images and then creating and deploying packages. We covered the Apple solutions, and we also covered a number of third-party solutions. The amount of page space provided to each solution is not worthy of any single solution, but if your interest was piqued by any solution, get an evaluation or an engineer from the vendor onsite to your organization to fill in the gaps. Additionally, some solutions from developers such as Apple, JAMF Software, and FileWave have dedicated training courses with substantially more information than is possible to include in this chapter.

## Chapter 7

Client Management

Put simply, no environment is too small to preclude evaluating your client management strategy. Whether you have two desktops or 100,000, there are tools and practices that can make both your life and your users' lives easier. A properly managed environment can save endless administration hours and in many cases thousands of phone calls to an organization's support center. Long gone are the days of shuffling from computer to computer meticulously duplicating settings. Numerous tools now abound to save you from this monotonous nightmare—tools that provide you with the ability to affect tens, hundreds, or thousands of computers from a central point quickly and effectively. These tools empower you to effectively manage a computing environment with minimal staff.

What exactly is entailed in a good client management system? The answer will certainly vary depending on who you ask. If you ask a Windows system administrator, you're likely to hear talk of proper Active Directory organizational unit (OU) structure and elaborate Group Policy object (GPO) inheritance trees, or you might hear of third-party solutions and deploying .msi installers for settings. From a help-desk perspective, the focus will largely be on finding, connecting to, and controlling client desktops (both the screen and the policies). Policy enforcement to ensure consistent environments across a multitude of desktops is also an invaluable way to ease the burden of remote support.

Mass deployment and imaging, along with patch management systems, are often lumped into the client management category because they intertwine. However, there is a distinction to be made. The latter is utilized to ensure a consistent, specially tailored software environment that is preconfigured to utilize your management systems. It is primarily focused on the deployment of a particular system's software environment. In contrast, controlling the user desktop experience is one of the main focal points of client management, providing facilities for automated setup of supported userland applications. These include Dock, desktop, and Finder customization; login items; network mounts; application preferences; media access; and any application that writes data into the user's home folder, such as Microsoft Outlook. For the purposes of this book, client management picks up right where mass deployment ends—once the systems are deployed, client management can be used to push default settings out and then lock certain features of the system down.

This chapter provides insight into the important considerations that are needed to ensure that your post-deployment environment is planned in a manner that will not only ensure its initial success but will also be easily adaptable as technical needs or policies change. A successfully planned and managed client implementation is predicated by numerous metrics.

- There is a tiered management hierarchy, structured appropriately for the environment to ensure granularity and scalability.

- The chosen policy implementation properly addresses the technical needs of the managed node's workflow, as well as the managed user's workflow.

- The chosen policy implementation adheres to global MIS policies.

- Management restrictions are as unobtrusive to end users as possible.

- Policy implementation is performed centrally, is dynamic, and can be easily changed across both small and large scopes of machines or users.

After reading this chapter, you will become familiar with numerous management principles to achieve these goals: building configuration profiles to remotely install software on clients, managing Open Directory's managed preferences system, user data planning, implementation and management, software update management, account and password policy management, and, last but not least, live interactive management of your computer fleet using Apple Remote Desktop.

Profiles

The preferred way to manage client preferences is by using configuration profiles. A profile is an XML file that contains a number of keys. Each key is used to manage a setting in OS X. When you configure settings with profiles, you're configuring a key or some keys that push a setting (or a digest of settings) into the appropriate location in a property list (such as a file in /Library/Preferences or ~/Library/Preferences). You can then install these profile files on devices directly (e.g., using the profiles command or double-clicking the profile to install the profile) or leverage a Mobile Device Management (MDM) solution that installs profiles on systems in a dynamic fashion.

There are also a number of tools that can help an administrator create and configure profiles en masse. These tools help to automate the creation of profiles, and then a patch management solution such as the Casper Suite, Munki, Absolute Manage, and others can be used to manage which computers get which profiles.

Create Profiles

Each profile has a number of keys. Since these keys aren't necessarily human-readable, administrators will need to use a tool to create a profile. There are a few different tools used to create profiles.

- *Apple Configurator*: This is Apple's tool for creating profiles and managing iOS devices. Profiles can then be exported and used on a variety of operating systems.

- *Profile Manager*: This is Apple's Mobile Device Management tool, easily enabled in OS X Server.

- *Third-party MDM tools*: Most of the third-party MDM solutions on the market can be used to export profiles once groups are configured and security settings are added.

In this section of the chapter, you'll look at creating a profile using Apple Configurator 2. The reason we'll use this tool in this chapter is because most environments that leverage an MDM solution will use one of about 25 tools. Most of those tools have a look and feel that is similar to that used in Configurator.

Installing Configurator

To get started with Configurator, first install the tool, which is free from the Mac App Store, by opening the App Store, searching for *Apple Configurator 2*, and then clicking Install or Get (according to whether you have used the tool previously with the Apple ID you're logged in as). Once Configurator is installed, open it and click New Profile from the File menu.

At the new profile screen, you will need to provide a name (in this case Passcode Policy) for the profile, as well as a unique identifier (in this case, com.krypted.passcodepolicy), as you can see in Figure 7-1. In the sidebar, you will see a list of options called *payloads* that can be configured.

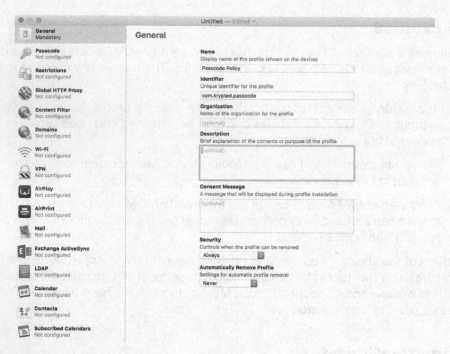

Figure 7-1. *The General options for a profile*

These payloads include the following (as shown in Figure 7-2):

> *General*: Specifies the name of the policy as well as how the policy can be removed
>
> *Passcode*: Specifies what passcodes are allowed, for example, whether you are required to use special characters and how long the passcode is
>
> *Restrictions*: Disables certain features of the operating system, such as the iTunes Store
>
> *Global HTTP Proxy*: Forces devices to use a proxy server for HTTP traffic
>
> *Content Filter*: Allows you to whitelist and blacklist Internet traffic
>
> *Wi-Fi*: Configures Wi-Fi settings on devices, including 802.1x if you use a secured network
>
> *VPN*: Sets up connections to a VPN server
>
> *AirPrint*: Installs printers automatically
>
> *Mail*: Automates the setup of IMAP and POP e-mail accounts
>
> *Exchange ActiveSync*: Automates the setup of Exchange, Kerio, and Google Apps accounts

Calendar: Automates the configuration of CalDAV calendars from a server

Contacts: Automates the configuration of CardDAV contacts from a server

Web Clips: Puts links to web sites into LaunchPad or as icons on an iOS device

Fonts: Installs font files automatically

Certificates: Embeds certificates in the profile (useful for 802.1x and self-signed certificates to talk to OS X and other types of web servers or e-mail certificates)

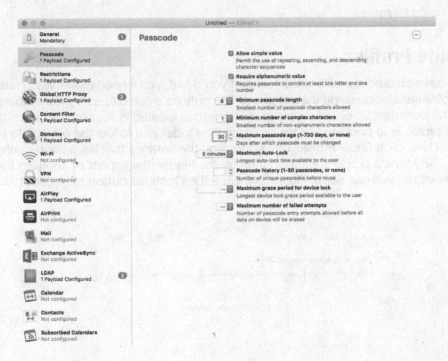

Figure 7-2. *Creat the profile*

As you can tell from the types of profile settings, you can automate the configuration of lots of options in OS X. Here, you'll look at the Passcode Policy discussed earlier. The example will configure a passcode of at least eight characters, with at least one number, one letter, and one special character. The passcode will need to be changed every 30 days, and the computer will automatically require the passcode after five minutes of inactivity.

Once you have created the profile, choose Save from the File menu. This will bring up a dialog (Figure 7-3) that allows you to place the profile wherever you'd like for distribution on clients.

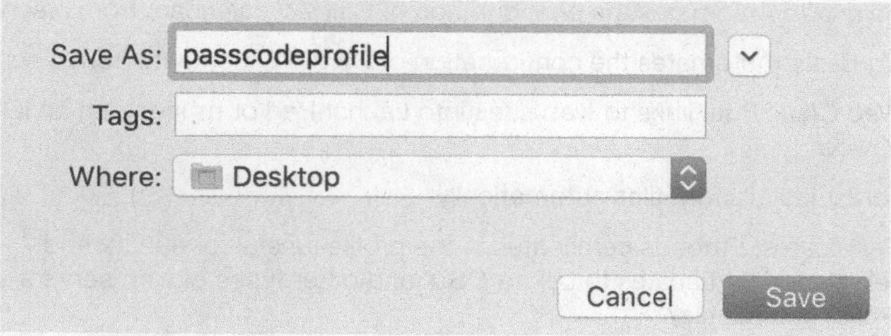

Figure 7-3. Placing the profile

Distribute Profiles

Once you have created a profile in the tool that you'd like, you'll need to install it. Here, you'll look at profile installation using the command-line options available, easily remembered because the command is called simply `profiles` and is located in `/usr/bin`. The simplest way to install a profile is to double-click the profile in the Finder and follow the options to install the profile. Here, click Show Profile. This shows you the settings that have been configured in this profile. Any time a profile is installed through the Finder, the impact of applying the profile can be viewed, as you can see in Figure 7-4. Click the Continue button to get started.

Figure 7-4. Installing a profile using the Finder

You can sign a profile before you save it, using the Sign Profile option under the File menu of Apple Configurator. Without signing, you'll see at the next screen a warning while installing the profile. If you click the Show Details button, you will see that the profile is not signed.

You won't want end users to see this error, and so you should typically sign your profiles before you distribute them. This protects them from being altered before being applied. As shown in Figure 7-5, click Install to install the unsigned profile.

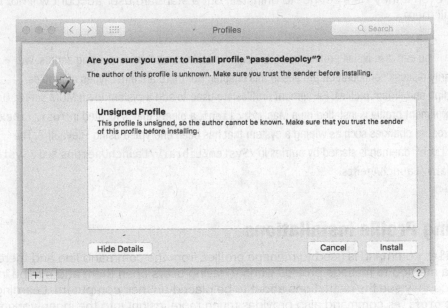

Figure 7-5. Accepting an unsigned profile

If prompted, enter your administrative credentials to complete installing the profile. As you can see in Figure 7-6, once the profile is installed, you can view it in the Profiles pane of System Preferences, which wasn't available before you actually installed a profile.

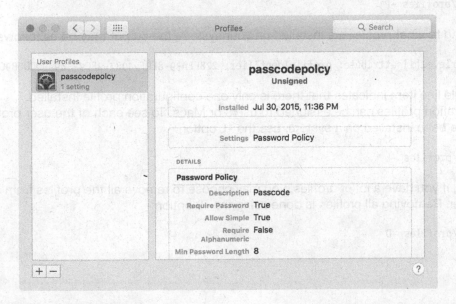

Figure 7-6. Viewing an installed profile

You can also click the minus button at the bottom left of the Profiles pane (Figure 7-6) to remove a profile that has been installed. Provided that the Always option was selected in the Security setting of the profile, the profile can then be uninstalled. Profiles can still be removed, even if they were set not to uninstall, but a standard user account will not be able to uninstall them.

Note   You can also install profiles using the command line and, therefore, using scripts. We primarily discuss configuration profiles in this chapter. But there are other types of profiles, including enrollment profiles. Enrollment profiles are used to add a system to an MDM server. Once an enrollment profile is installed on a Mac, `mdmclient`, a binary that is located in `/usr/libexec` will process changes such as wiping a system that has been encrypted using FileVault 2. The `mdmclient` daemon is started by entries in `/System/Library/LaunchDaemons` and `/System/Library/LaunchAgents`.

Scripting Profile Installations

The `profiles` command is used to manage profiles from the command line and therefore provides a method to manage profiles without having users open them and maybe install the profile once they see the restrictions about to be placed on their computers. Learning how to use the `profiles` command also provides much more insight into the inner workings of a profile.

With the most basic form of the `profiles` command, you can view configuration profile contents (`.mobileconfig`). To see what's installed by a given profile, use the `profiles` command with the `-P` option.

```
/usr/bin/profiles -P
```

According to what profiles are installed on your system, the output may be as follows:

```
_computerlevel[1] attribute: profileIdentifier: 228FFA39-8EDF-4987-28C9-549990CD0B9C
```

The single line item indicates that there is only one configuration profile installed. Configuration profiles can be assigned to users or Macs. To see each of the user profiles that have been installed on a system, use the `-L` option.

```
/usr/bin/profiles -L
```

At times, if you have a lot of profiles, you may choose to remove all the profiles from a computer. Removing all profiles is done using the -D option.

```
/usr/bin/profiles -D
```

The -R option removes an individual profile. Here, use the -p option to indicate that the profile is from a server or use the -F option to indicate the source of a profile is a file. For example, to remove a profile called apress.mobileconfig from /tmp/apress.mobileconfig, use the following command:

```
/usr/bin/profiles -R -F /tmp/apress.mobileconfig
```

To remove a profile that came from a server, where the profile is called com.apress.server, use the following:

```
/usr/bin/profiles -R -p apress.server
```

Use the -I option to install a profile using the command line. -F indicates that the profile being installed is a file, followed by the name of the file. Given this, use the following command to install apress.mobileconfig from the /tmp directory:

```
/usr/bin/profiles -I -F /tmp/apress.mobileconfig
```

Profiles can also be installed at the first boot, using what we call *startup profiles*. If you use the -s option to indicate you will use a startup profile, that profile installs at the next reboot, or attempts to do so until successfully installed. For example, the following will install apress.mobileconfig at first boot (we also used the -f option to confirm we structured the command correctly):

```
profiles -s -F /Profiles/SuperAwesome.mobileconfig -f -v
```

The dscl command, which we'll cover in further detail later in this chapter, has extensions that manage profiles. These include the following MCX profile extensions:

```
-profileimport -profiledelete -profilelist [optArgs] -profileexport -profilehelp
```

To list all profiles from a user in Open Directory, use -profilelist option. Here, run the dscl command with -u option to specify a user. We are also using the -P option to specify a password for the user defined with the -u option as well as the name or IP address of the Open Directory server. Follow this with the profilelist verb and then the relative path. In the following command, we're putting all that together, using a username of diradmin for the directory, a password of emerald, and charles as the user.

```
dscl -u diradmin -P emerald 192.168.100.2 profilelist /LDAPv3/127.0.0.1/Users/charles
```

To delete that information for the user you listed profiles for in the previous command, use the profiledelete option instead of the profilelist option.

```
dscl -u diradmin -P emerald 192.168.100.2 profiledelete /LDAPv3/127.0.0.1/Users/charles
```

Finally, export all profile information to a directory called ProfileExports on your desktop.

```
dscl -u diradmin -P emerald 192.168.100.2 profileexport. all -o ~/Desktop/ProfileExports
```

Two other options that are useful when scripting solutions that leverage profiles are the -H option, which shows whether a profile is installed, and the -z option, which is used to define a password that is required to uninstall a profile.

> **Note** To remove individual configuration profiles that are deployed by an MDM solution, unenroll the computer to automatically remove those configuration profiles.

Profiles can also be added into images using System Image Utility, covered earlier in Chapter 6, as well as a number of other popular Imaging solutions. Most of these tools use the profiles command but do not require you to master it unless you want to script more complicated changes than what are available natively in those tools.

Manage Profiles Using Open Source Tools

The options available in Profile Manager and Apple Configurator 2 are only a few of the options that are available to profiles. For example, the profiles created in the graphical interfaces provided will create profiles that keep the managed settings enabled all of the time. This means that when you install a configuration profile, a user cannot change the settings that you have enabled. But profiles support other options that allow you to manage a setting at first and then allow users to change their settings. This makes some profiles incredibly useful for initially configuring computers but puts the power of settings in the hands of the users, which in Apple's world is pretty much where they belong.

Additionally, you will find scenarios where you can set up a lot of keys to manage settings at the same time. Or you will find property lists that manage settings that might not otherwise be available. To put this in perspective, let's look at disabling the shadows on a screenshot. The setting that controls this is in com.apple.screencapture.plist. You can manually disable screen captures using the following command, which sends a disable-shadow key into ~/Library/Preferences/com.apple.screencapture.plist:

```
defaults write com.apple.screencapture disable-shadow -bool true
```

Once the command is run, a new com.apple.screencapture.plist file will appear in the ~/Library/Preferences directory. Next, manually download a tool called mcxToProfile from https://github.com/timsutton/mcxToProfile. Next, run this Python script to convert the .plist file to a .mobileconfig file. Here, you'll invoke this command using the -plist option, identifying the property list that operates as the input for the command. You'll also need to provide an --identifier value, which is used to identify the creator:

```
./mcxToProfile.py --plist ~/Library/Preferences/com.apple.screencapture.plist --identifier
com.krypted.screencapture
```

This command creates a `mobileconfig` file called `com.krypted.screencapture.mobileconfig` in the current working directory. If you view the contents of the file, you'll notice that there is a `disable-shadow` key in the file and that the key is set to `true`.

```
<key>disable-shadow</key>
<true/>
```

You can swap the `true` out for a `false` to then turn shadows back on when this profile is installed. You can also import most any property list from `/Library/Preferences` or `~/Library/Preferences` to manually control their settings in this same fashion.

Managed Preferences

Managed preferences in OS X provide administrators with a valuable tool set for managing many aspects of the OS X computing environment. Their capabilities run a wide berth, providing many functions, such as managing individual userland application settings, applying user restrictions to inserted or removable media, controlling application access, and deploying network proxy settings. And they can also provide for managing computer hardware energy saver settings, including the ability to centrally deploy computer shutdown and reboot schedules.

Managed preferences in OS X are based on Apple's MCX system, so the terms are often used interchangeably. Short for Managed Client for OS X, MCX is a piece of Apple's solution to the user and computer management equation. MCX settings utilize LDAP for their application. This is typically Apple's Open Directory, but it is certainly possible to extend the schema of alternative LDAP servers to provide full functionality (such as Active Directory or eDirectory).

You can download Workgroup Manager 10.9 from `https://support.apple.com/kb/dl1698?locale=en_US`. Once it's downloaded, you cannot install Workgroup Manager, as it can be installed only up to 10.9. Therefore, you will need to use a tool called Pacifist to extract the items from the package. Once extracted, the Workgroup Manager application can be opened and run.

> **Note** The fact that you have to go through such lengths means that Workgroup Manager is no longer officially supported. Another good indication of this is that Workgroup Manager is really, really slow, but it works.

Managed preferences are configured through the Preferences interface of the Workgroup Manager application, as shown in Figure 7-7. On a macro level, preference management can be applied at four different levels, each represented by a tab in the top-left region of Workgroup Manager. These levels include individual users, groups, individual computers, and groups of computers. Standard groups, once managed, are referred to as *workgroups*. The other levels are simply referred to as *managed users*, *managed computers*, and *managed computer groups*.

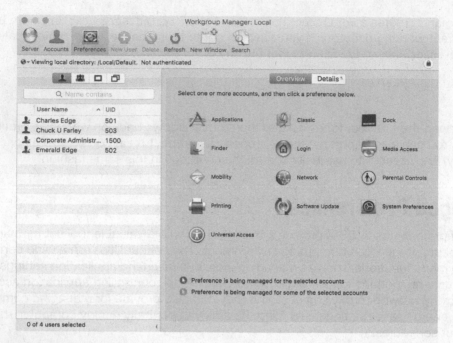

Figure 7-7. Managed preferences overview

Adding all computers to your Open Directory can be done via authenticated binds. However, many an organization will prefer to simply add computers to Open Directory and have some policies apply globally to computers. For this reason, there is a Guest computer that can be created in Open Directory. The Guest computer is found on the Computers tab of Workgroup Manager, but it is not available until explicitly created. To do so, there is a nifty Create Guest Computer menu item under the Server menu in Workgroup Manager.

Certain management settings are not available at the user and workgroup levels. These management levels apply to active user sessions, so settings outside of this purview, such as login scripts, energy saver settings, and login window preferences, are managed only on the computer and computer group levels. Time Machine settings are another noteworthy management capability applicable only on the computer level. On the flip side, the computer-oriented management levels do not share the same deficit—they have access to the entire purview of applicable management. Because of this, having a well-structured and populated managed preferences paradigm that includes users, groups, and computers is highly recommended.

Preference Interactions

One key feature of MCX behavior to understand is the way that managed preferences are determined when managed on multiple levels. Apple defines three different managed preference behaviors, referred to as *preference interactions*, which determine the resultant policy from multiple levels of management. *Overriding* preference interactions refers to scenarios where two different levels manage the same domain, each explicitly providing conflicting settings. In these cases, OS X prioritizes management levels, as shown in Figure 7-8 (managed users, workgroup, managed computers, and managed computer groups).

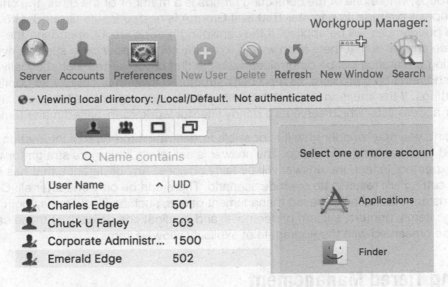

Figure 7-8. *Account types election in Workgroup Manager*

This works out well for the most part, although there are a few ramifications to discuss. Most important, managed preferences applied at the user level will be the dominant preference, persisting for that user in any environment that they log in to, despite any computer or computer list managed preferences that are applied. After this, you have computer and computer groups taking precedence over workgroups. This proves to be beneficial in lab or kiosk environments where the nodes are typically special usage and may need specific configurations. Workgroups, though the lowest on the totem pole, will be your primary application point. The granularity of user-based management is both a blessing and a curse. While it's great to ensure VIP status for certain users and implement further managed preferences for high-touch users, it becomes a management nightmare in medium-to-large environments where a number of policies overlap on a given object because of a combination of users, groups, computers, and computer groups.

Another form of interaction is referred to as *combined interactions*. Some examples of these include printers, login items, and Dock items. In a combined interaction scenario, preferences from all the different levels are aggregate. Therefore, if you have a login item deployed for a specific user and a login item deployed for a group the user is in, then both login items will take effect when the user logs in.

Inherited interactions are the third type of preference interaction and simply refer to a managed preference that is managed only at a single level.

For the most part, standard preference interactions apply when combining workgroup management. However, an obvious conflict presents itself: When an overriding preference interaction occurs between two groups, how is precedence determined? In the case of nested groups, where one of the conflicting groups is a member of the other, the child-most group will override its parents. That is, if GroupA is nested inside GroupB, GroupB's managed preferences will be applied. If the conflicting groups are independent, the unfortunate answer is that there is no way to explicitly set precedence in such an event—the resulting preference will be determined from the first group sorted alphabetically. This typically shouldn't be a problem, as a properly structured system should avoid conflicting group settings. If the situation is absolutely unavoidable, one option available is to utilize computer access lists, which serve as a handy filter for workgroup-based management.

At this point, you may wonder how it is possible to determine the type of interaction that will be applied to a managed preference. The answer is actually a little more straightforward than may be expected. In fact, the answer will be fairly obvious. Any preference that has a single definitive setting will result in an override scenario. There can be only one after all. Combined interactions are utilized in list-based management panes, such as Dock items, login items, home sync items, printers, system preferences, and applications. In each of these cases, the user will be presented with the aggregate of explicitly allowed items.

Utilizing Tiered Management

Once mastered, the system provides for flexible and granular management. To truly utilize the system to its potential, you must first have a good understanding of the environment where it is being deployed. This is typically best accomplished by tailoring the system to the organizational structure of the business that it serves. Take note of the various delineations in your workforce, and consider categories such as tenure, job roles and duties, departments, and locations, if applicable. Perhaps some of these categories transcend others, but the goal is to tailor the specific groups that you would want to target for management; the more specific, the more adaptable the system will be for your needs.

Picture a fairly large media organization, like Mediaco. Mediaco has two different campuses, each with fully staffed departments. Mediaco has numerous editors at both locations that need access to the global company media repository. Each campus also has a file server hosting data for multiple departments. Figure 7-9 outlines a flexible group management structure.

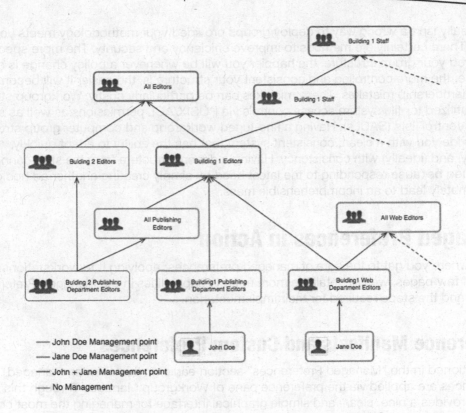

Figure 7-9. *Tiered management*

In this example, you have created numerous groups to represent your structure. The user, John Doe, has been added to the group, Building1 Publishing Department Editors. This group is in turn members of both the All Publishing Editors group but the Building1 Editors group, which is once again nested into multiple groups. In this example, even though the user is only a direct member of one group, you can still apply management at six different workgroup tiers. Through the root All Editors group, you may add a login item for the company media repository file share. You can then specify your departmental file server login item on the group Building1 Publishing Department Editors. Now, when John Doe logs in, he has both his department's sharepoint and the global sharepoint mounted and ready for access.

Computer groups can be similarly tiered, though there is a strong case to be made for the ability to provide logistical-based management. For instance, Mediaco wants to turn off desktop computers at night to save energy costs. Immediately, the need to distinguish between laptop and desktop machines is apparent. Further delineation may be advisable in your organization to account for backup/maintenance schedules, usage patterns, and so forth.

There really isn't a wrong way to deploy groups provided your methodology meets your needs. There certainly are methods to improve efficiency and security. The more specific and tiered your group structure, the happier you will be whenever a policy change is needed. Likewise, the more controlled and consistent your structure is, the easier it will become to avoid membership mistakes. These mistakes can be particularly costly. Workgroup structure is also utilized for file system access controls via POSIX/ACL permissions as well as service access control lists (SACLs). Having a fine-tuned workgroup and computer group structure will provide you with a clean, consistent system that has the ability to adapt quickly, securely, and (ideally) with consistency. Having a decent structure from the start cannot be overstated because responding to the latest need by simply creating another ad hoc group will ultimately lead to an incomprehensible mess.

Managed Preferences in Action

Here's where you get to the core of managed preferences: applying it to workstations. Over the next few pages, we will detail the more notable capabilities in the Managed Preferences system and the steps required for their implementation.

Preference Manifests and Custom Preferences

As mentioned in the "Managed Preferences" section earlier in this chapter, managed preferences are applied via the preference pane of Workgroup Manager. Through this tool, Apple provides a nice, clean, and simple graphical interface for managing the most common applications. However, this is not a definitive list of what can and cannot be managed through MCX. After all, third-party programs can be constructed in such a way to fully support MCX management. Preference manifests allow a third-party application to provide an interface that can be utilized by system administrators to apply management settings to the application. In Workgroup Manager, you access preference manifest support via the Details tab of the managed preference interface. In this interface, you can click the plus button and navigate to the application on the file system that you want to manage. Upon selecting the desired app, the interface presents the option to import the current settings (see Figure 7-10).

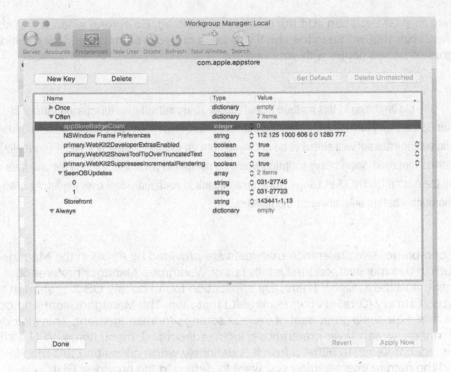

Figure 7-10. Preference manifest keys

To determine whether an application supports preference manifests, uncheck this option. If the application has no manifest, you will immediately be presented with an error stating this. Once a manifest has been added to Workgroup Manager, it will be presented permanently for that user. Each manifest is stored in the directory at ~/Library/Preferences/com.apple. mcx.manifests and in the file ~/Library/Preferences/com.apple.mcx.plist. If desired, you can clear them out by deleting these files.

If the application does have preference manifest support, then upon importing the application into the system (without importing your personal settings), the details pane in Workgroup Manager will have an entry for the applications preference domain, such as com.myco.myapp. The new management functionality isn't apparent until you try to add a new key under the Once, Often, or Always section in that domain. When you create a new key, you will be presented with a menu selection of supported attributes. Each attribute will often have associated applicable values presented via a selection menu. However, often custom values can be entered and properly utilized. It all depends upon the application.

If an application does not support manifests, you're not completely out of luck. If this is the case, you must resort to the second method that Apple provides to manage an app: you can push out just about any defaults-based setting to an app (that is, any application that properly utilizes Apple's provided preference system and results in preferences being stored in a file found at ~/Library/Preferences/com.myco.myapp.plist). By selecting the option to import settings, regardless of manifest support, it will copy settings for the application in question from your current operating environment and apply them to the managed machines.

Alternatively, in WGM you can add the preference file itself. Be careful when doing so as there is often cruft that will be in the file. If you push out your starting window position, other users might not be too happy with your choice.

Note   One big limitation to this method is that the %@ string substitution (discussed further in Chapter 8) used for preference manifests is not supported. This means that preferences with user-specific settings are not well suited to be deployed from an existing preference file. If you really must cross that road, some heavy scripting would be needed to parse the settings file and then deploy the customized MCXSettings attribute additions to each individual user object. As always, test thoroughly before unleashing on the masses.

The most comprehensive preference manifests are provided by Apple in the ManagedClient MCX. To utilize this manifest, on the Details tab of Workgroup Manager preference management, add the ManagedClient.app application found on any OS X system at the path /System/Library/CoreServices/ManagedClient.app. The ManagedClient app contains a manifest that exposes a great deal of various settings for management. This includes the ability to manage screen saver preferences, login redirections, menu items, VPN settings, and Finder sidebar items, to name a few. It is definitely worth consulting this manifest if you cannot find the management setting you want to deploy in the provided GUI.

Automated Client Setup

This section covers various MCX configurations that can be deployed to assist with configuring the user environment: managing application preferences and configuration, network proxy configuration, and printer deployment.

Mail

MCX has the ability to automatically configure a mail account for your users. It is fairly basic in nature and provides the ability to populate a single e-mail account. Unfortunately, preference interactions for mail result in an override, so it is not possible at this time to deploy both a personal mail account at one tier and a departmental or group account at a different tier. The single account that you do deploy can be either a POP account or an IMAP account.

To deploy mail accounts, first get com.apple.mail.managed or com.apple.mail into your Details screen following the steps covered in the "Preference Manifests and Custom Preferences" section earlier in this chapter. Once you've added this to Workgroup Manager, you can automatically deploy e-mail accounts for clients using the com.apple.mail domain (the com.apple.mail.managed domain is for 10.5 and older clients). There are a number of keys that allow you to manage client settings for Mail, as shown in Figure 7-11.

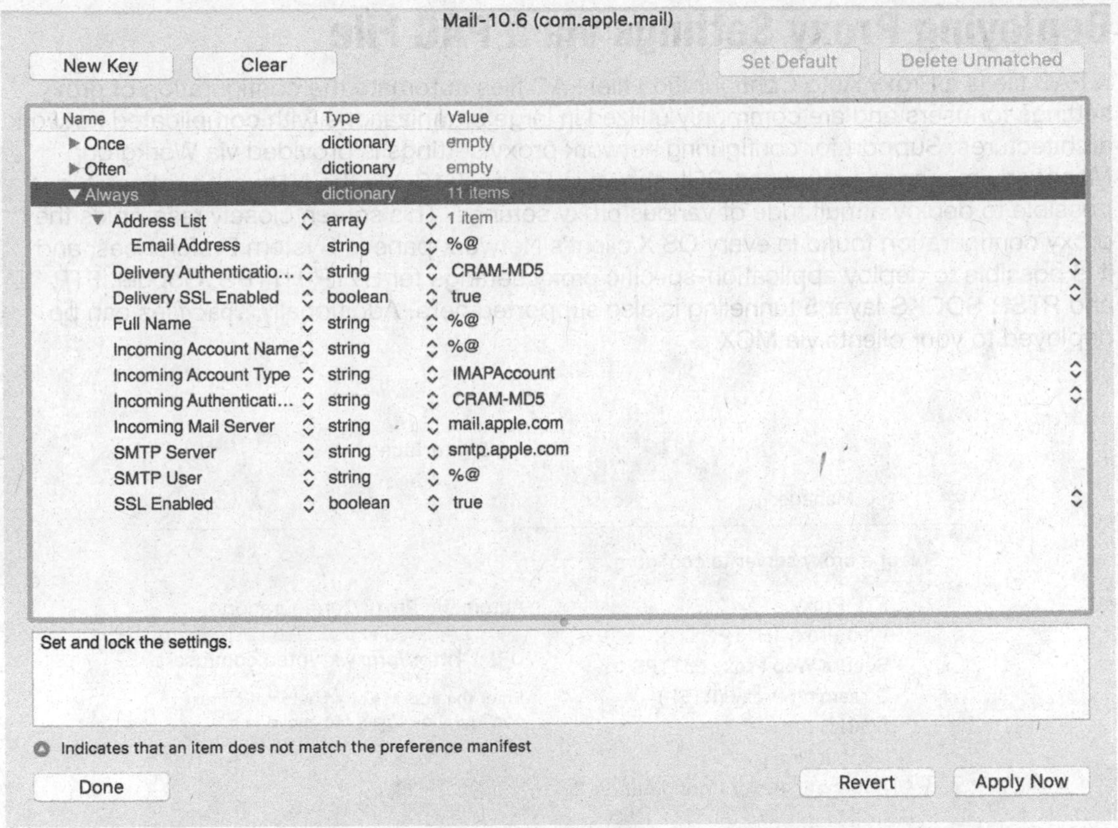

Figure 7-11. *Deploying managed preferences for Mail*

Figure 7-11 represents a recommended configuration for a mail account (mileage may vary according to the setup of each organization). Notice the variable substitution being used here as well: the string %@ is a variable for the user's short name.

> **Note**   In Mac OS X 10.5 and older, the com.apple.mail.managed manifest would be used rather than com.apple.mail, which is for Mac OS X 10.6 through 10.11. The com.apple.mail.managed domain only provides Mac OS X 10.5 and doesn't have as much functionality as the 10.6 and up implementation. For instance, com.apple.mail.managed also does not support deploying SSL settings.

In this example, you are setting up an IMAP account with CRAM-MD5 authentication. To deploy a POP account, you specify an Incoming Account Type setting of POPAccount.

Deploying Proxy Settings via a PAC File

A PAC file is a Proxy Auto Configuration file. PAC files automate the configuration of proxy settings for users and are commonly utilized in large organizations with complicated network architectures. Support for configuring network proxy settings is provided via Workgroup Manager's managed preference GUI, shown in Figure 7-12. Via the Network section, it is possible to deploy a multitude of various proxy settings. This screen closely resembles the proxy configuration found in every OS X client's Network pane in System Preferences, and it is possible to deploy application-specific proxy settings for HTTP, HTTPS, Gopher, FTP, and RTSP. SOCKS layer 5 tunneling is also supported here. Additionally, .pac files can be deployed to your clients via MCX.

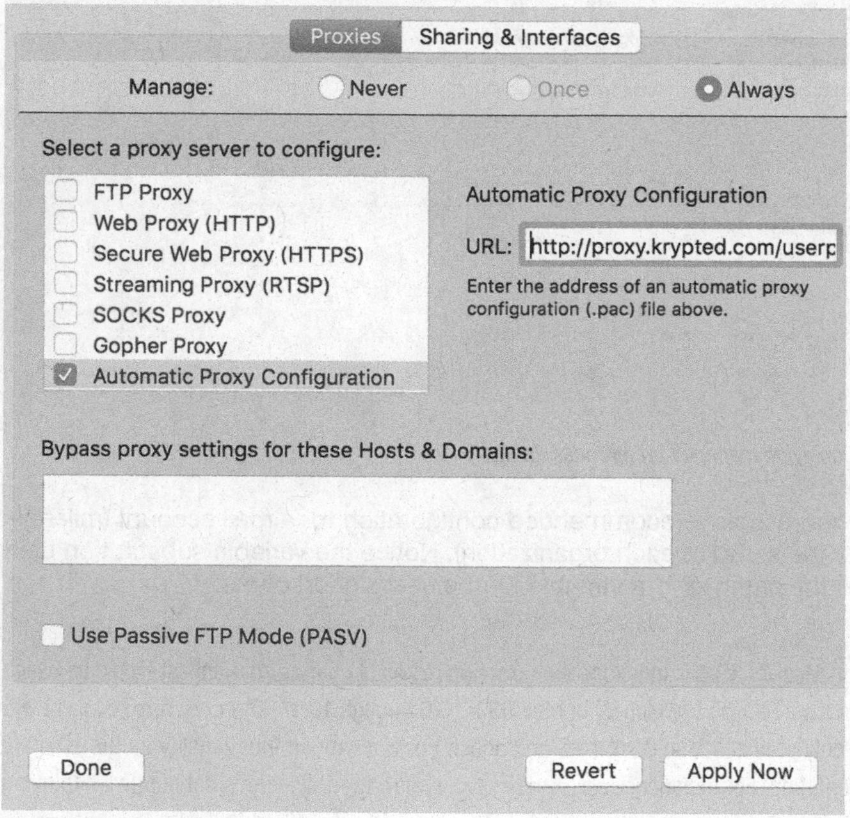

Figure 7-12. *Proxy managed preferences configuration*

Proxy configuration is available at all MCX levels. However, it is important to note that not all applications will utilize these settings. Firefox is by far the most notorious offender here. It has its own internal proxy configuration and ignores the global system setting. Indeed, Firefox generally snuffs Apple's defaults system and is immune to the reach of MCX. Likewise, command-line apps will often require their own internal proxy configuration or will require the configuration of environmental variables for this purpose. The exact configuration will vary from application to application, but if needed, environmental variables can be deployed via MCX as well.

To configure the proxy auto config option, open Workgroup Manager and then click Preferences. Click the computer or computer list to manage, click Network, and then click the Proxies tab. Figure 7-12 represents the deployment of a .pac proxy configuration file located at http://proxy.krypted.com/userproxy.pac. You can also use the Bypass proxy settings for these Hosts and Domains fields on a per-domain basis.

Network Printing

The ability to easily deploy printers to your user base can be a huge time-saver—managing printers across multiple locations and hundreds of users by hand would take enormous amounts of time. The good news is that MCX works well for managing which network printers are available to users, allowing an administrator to remotely assign printers at all of the typical MCX management layers. From an end user's perspective, they will simply see all of their deployed printers from the available printer list in any printer dialog box. Beyond this, MCX provides numerous facilities: setting default printers (useful for deploying at the computer and computer group levels); forcing a footer on the printout that includes the user's name, date, and optionally the printing computer's MAC address; and restricting access to a printer by requiring administrative access.

To deploy a network printer via MCX, you must first configure the printer on your administrative computer. Once it's configured and tested, open Workgroup Manager, select the object that you want to manage, and then select the Printing preferences pane, as shown in Figure 7-13. There is no right answer here for deploying printers. In some cases, it may make sense to deploy an occasional printer to an individual user. In lab or kiosk environments, it makes more sense to deploy at the computer group and set a default printer. This way, when a user logs into that computer, their default printer will be the closest one to the computer.

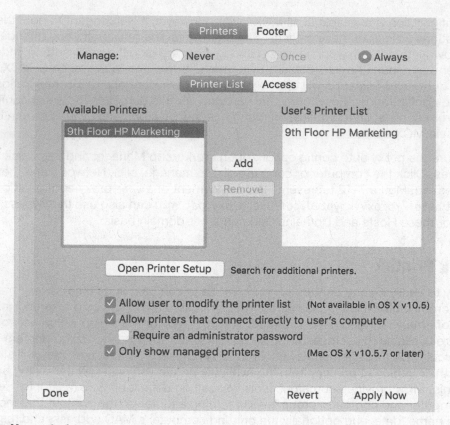

Figure 7-13. Managed printers

In large environments, it may even be desirable to create and utilize groups specifically for printer management to provide better visibility and scalability.

The one major "gotcha" to MCX printer management is that it has somewhat limited support. Its support lies primarily in network printers, which support the PostScript protocol and PostScript printer description (PPD) files. Printers, which require specialized binary drivers, are not going to function properly with this system. If you desperately need to support such a printer through MCX, your best bet is to deploy the binary prior to adding the printer. To do so, first deploy the package that installs the print server on the client computers. Then you can deploy the printer via MCX.

You can use MCX to display only managed printers. This is a handy option to ensure that only the printers that are managed are displayed in the list. This is also a handy feature to ensure that any other printers that had been set up at one point or another will no longer be accessible. This option is hidden a bit; to access the functionality, first deploy the desired printer preferences to your desired target. Next, select the Details tab of managed preferences, and edit the preference domain com.apple.mcxprinting. Under the Always domain, add a new key named ShowOnlyManagedPrinters. Set the value type to boolean, and specify a value of true, as shown in Figure 7-14. From here on, the printers you specify in MCX will be the only printers listed in a user's print dialog box.

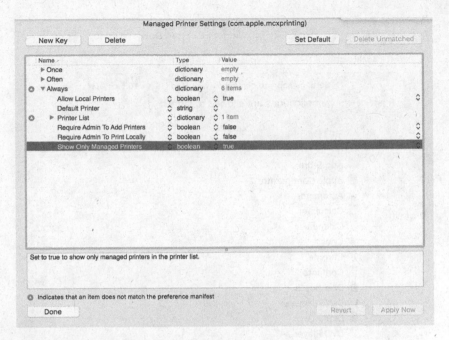

Figure 7-14. com.apple.mcxprinting managed preference manifest

Managed printers deployed across multiple groups will result in a combined MCX interaction. That is, a user will have access to all printers deployed from all applicable workgroups, computer groups, and so on. Other settings such as custom presets and the default printer will result in an override, following the standard MCX pecking order.

> **Tip** There is an option available that allows users to add their own printers. We recommend using it so your service desk does not get inundated with hundreds of calls from users who simply want to add a printer at home.

Restricting Applications

Restricting applications with MCX is done on an explicit allow basis. That is, once you choose to restrict applications for a user, an implicit deny will be applied to all applications that are not in the allowed applications list. Because of this, it is important to have a good understanding of the applications that will be utilized in the managed environment prior to embarking on this endeavor. If it's not properly planned, you will be flooded with support requests from users claiming that they can't access their applications. However, when implemented using application signing, the system proves to be extremely resilient to various hacks that might be used to subvert it.

When restricting applications with MCX, you have two primary options, both accessible from the Applications pane of Workgroup Managers preference interface, as shown in Figure 7-15.

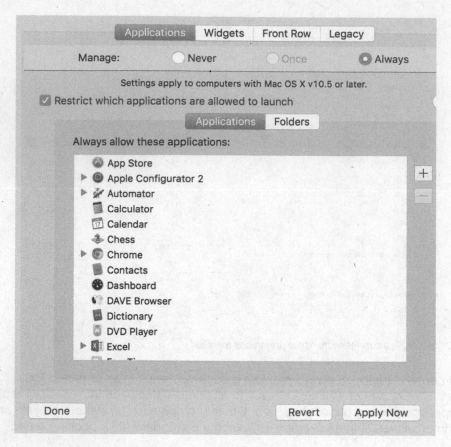

Figure 7-15. Configuring application whitelisting

> **Note** When you add unsigned applications to the list, you will be prompted to sign the applications. Go ahead and sign the applications. There's really no reason not to.

Using this interface, you can allow a specific application, or you can specify a whitelisted folder wherein any application resides is always trusted. The latter, if set up improperly, can be easily exploited. However, if you ensure that you specify only directories, which are not writeable by the user, then it can be an acceptable measure. However, local file system permissions can be easily bypassed through single-user mode, so it may be desirable to configure a firmware password to prevent this easy avenue.

There are a few general whitelist folders, which will make life a bit easier. Specifically, enabling all applications located in the folder /System/Library/CoreServices will allow numerous support applications to run. Whitelisting the /Library/QuickTime folder is needed to prevent numerous QuickTime plug-ins from malfunctioning, and whitelisting /Library/ Printers is necessary for certain printer drivers. Each of these folders is immutable to non-admin users, so they are generally fine for whitelist exclusions. /Library/Application Support is another directory that can contain binary support files needed by various applications.

For the most part, though, you will want to allow specific applications. This allows for fine-grained targeting without the need to worry whether file system restrictions have been bypassed. Combined with application signing, the system is a secure way to ensure that the only applications that launch are the intended applications. Application signing is a feature introduced with Mac OS X 10.5 Leopard and allows for an application to be signed by a trusted certificate, similar to a standard SSL environment. The Mach-O binary format is a bit notorious for being an easy target for code injection, exposing a potential avenue for viral infection. By signing an application, you can ensure that the code present in the executable is in the state shipped by the manufacturer. If it is modified, it will no longer match your signature and will thereby be treated as a foreign entity. This shouldn't cause much concern because it's an easy fix.

Application signing is heavily utilized by iOS, the operating system used on the iPad, iPhone, and iPod Touch as well as in Mac OS X 10.5 and later. All Apple apps are signed. MCX and the application firewall use signing as a means of adding and removing access to opening an application and the network stack of OS X, respectively.

> **Note** When adding an application to an allowed applications list, you must first specify the application from the client machine running Workgroup Manager. If the application that you want to allow is not resident on this computer, you will not be able to select it from the list and will not be able to provision access to the app.

Likewise, when you add an unsigned application to the allowed applications list, you will be greeted with an option to sign the application or add it to the list without signing it. If you choose the latter, the application will be allowed to launch, but it will be possible to utilize this inclusion for exploitative purposes. Because the application is not signed, it is possible to alter any arbitrary application to impersonate the application and thereby bypass any restrictions that would otherwise be applied. As such, if any allowed application is unsigned, it represents the ability for the user to launch any application, provided they have the skills to do so. When an allowed application is not signed, it will appear with a yellow triangle next to its entry, as shown for DeployStudio in Figure 7-16.

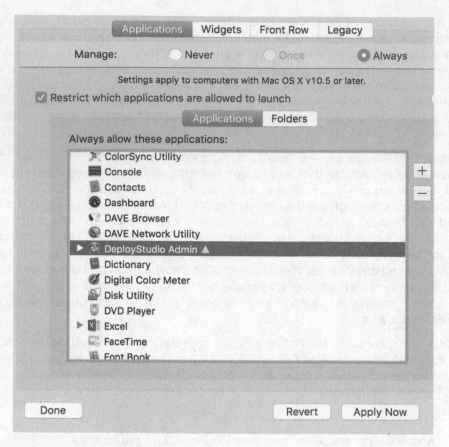

Figure 7-16. Adding an unsigned application

There are some ramifications for signing an application when adding it via Workgroup Manager. Most notably, when you sign the application with Workgroup Manager, you are signing only the local copy of that application. As such, all those hundreds of copies of that application in the field remain unsigned and therefore restricted from launching. To fulfill a securely restricted environment, it will be necessary to deploy the signed applications to all of your clients. Alternatively, Apple has provided the command-line utility codesign, which allows for the signing of applications from the command line. The syntax to sign an application is as follows:

```
codesign -s identity /Path/to/Application.app
```

For most environments, the identity in the previous command will be the name of the certificate as you see it listed in the keychain in which it is stored. Whereas the identity is determined by searching the keychain search path for a certificate whose subject matches the provided string, by using this utility and a self-signed certificate, you can sign any applications on the client side through automation. As long as you have deployed your root CA to all of your clients as outlined in Chapter 2, then you can ensure proper validation of your applications.

> **Note**   You cannot use an invalid certificate to sign applications. If you see a red "x" on the certificate in Keychain Access, this will have to be resolved prior to using the certificate to accomplish a successful codesign operation.

Using the codesign command, you can sign the RecBoot application for resetting iOS devices using a certificate in the keychain. For this example, you will call the certificate mycert. Simply use the following command:

```
codesign -s mycert /Applications/RecBoot.app
```

Deployed applications result in an additive process. If a user's management surface has application restrictions applied at any level, those application restrictions will be applied everywhere. This is particularly noticeable when application restrictions are applied at the computer level. When this occurs, all managed users on that computer will have application restrictions. If an administrator opts to not disable management globally, the admin will also inherit the computer's application restrictions. While the application preference pane does indeed allow an option to uncheck "Restrict which applications are allowed to launch," this setting will be overridden based upon standard MCX search policy. Thus, if you apply management to an admin group and deploy this setting unchecked, it will be overridden because of the MCX search policy. Computer and computer groups take precedence over user groups, meaning that you need to deploy this option at the user object to override your computer settings. Unfortunately, this becomes a pretty big hassle and isn't even possible in some environments, such as an Active Directory/Open Directory dual directory, where user objects are stored in Active Directory and outside the purview of MCX.

Thus, deploying application restrictions at the computer and computer group demands a decent amount of consideration and testing. In many cases, it makes more sense to create separate user groups for computer-specific application classes and then use computer access filters to grant access to that specific application-based group.

Computer Access Filters

In larger environments, the likelihood of having groups, which have conflicting settings, is increased. In many cases, it may be desirable to filter out which group settings are applied to specific levels. Alternatively, it may be desirable to control which users actually have access to log in to a particular computer. Both of these features are provided in Workgroup Manager preferences management, on the Access tab of the login managed preference pane (see Figure 7-17). Because computer access is a computer-specific task, the Access tab is accessible only in the computer and computer group sections.

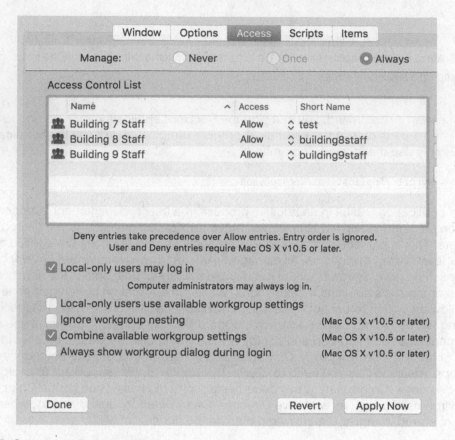

Figure 7-17. Computer access control lists

This interface allows you to control which groups have access to log in to specific computers. This has the additional effect of filtering out which groups apply MCX. As with application management, once you define access restrictions, an implicit deny is applied to any user or group not in the list.

For example, consider a scenario where a user is a member of two groups, Mobile Home Users and Network Home Users. Perhaps the former group has mobility configured for the user, such that a mobile account is created for the user of this group on login. It may be desirable to suppress this behavior on certain computers; therefore, you would simply create an allow rule on these computers for the group Network Home Users. When the user logs in, they will not inherit any of the management settings defined for Mobile Home Users because of the implicit deny nature of login restrictions. This in turn becomes a handy tool for you to filter the group MCX application. The downside of this is that you must now explicitly allow all groups, including the entire nested hierarchy, if you want all of these tiers' management settings applied. You have then allowed entries for numerous groups, including some potentially very broad groups (such as All Staff).

To use a tiered management hierarchy along with actual computer access restrictions, you have a rather large conundrum. On one hand, you want to apply the management settings applied to the All Staff group, but the unintended consequence is that you now have granted login window access to all members of the All Staff group. From here, you must use explicit denies to deny access to the desired users and groups. Using explicit denies isn't a bad idea, but this means your computer access list may easily reach 20 to 30 entries in larger environments. These challenges are some of the reasons that Apple developed profiles, which have an added bonus of not requiring you to bind computers to a directory service and therefore allowing you to use a patch management system as a means of deploying configuration settings more easily.

> **Note** Implementing an explicit deny entry on a group will always take precedent over any explicit allow entries. An explicit deny on a group will prevent all members of that group access, regardless of whether they have membership to a different group that is allowed access. This means that deny entries should be utilized only where login access to all members of a group must be unconditionally prohibited.

Common Tasks

There are many other common managed preferences management tasks worth mentioning. Notably, one of the most common managed preferences to apply is automated login items, which specify applications, documents, or sharepoints that launch when a user logs into a computer. Login items are handy for initiating user environments, such as by firing up support applications or by automounting a network share.

To add a login item, simply add it to the list on the Items tab in the Login Workgroup Manager preferences pane. This item can be an application, a document, or a network share. For the former two, the added asset will need to be accessible at the same path on the target client as on the system running Workgroup Manager. To deploy a network share login item, simply connect to the sharepoint from your admin station. Once the sharepoint is mounted on the desktop, simply drag it into the login items list. With the network share highlighted, make sure to check the box "Authenticate selected share point with user's name and password," shown in Figure 7-18. This will ensure that proper access to the share is provided to the user.

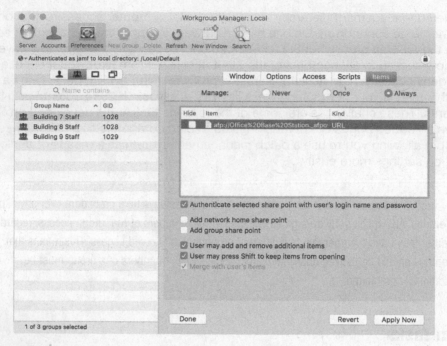

Figure 7-18. Adding login items

This list is additive, so login items across all of a user's managed groups will be applied. It is worth noting the options for users to be able to add their own items. This can be handy if you want a few things to launch but you want the user to be able to customize their own environment as well.

At some point, you may also want to modify a user's Dock, perhaps adding a reference to a company sharepoint or a business application (to some end users, after all, an application does not exist unless it's in the Dock). Apple has a nifty GUI both for adding items to the dock and for organizing the order in which they appear. Like login items, managed Dock items are additive across management groups. The option "Merge with user's items" allows users to modify the Dock, outside of the management preferences that you want. This is probably preferable in nonkiosk environments because the Dock is a powerful, important part of the OS X experience.

To add a network sharepoint, first mount it on your administrative workstation and then drag it into the Documents and Folders list. This will create an .afploc file with the information used to mount the sharepoint initially. Alternatively, you can construct your own .afploc file and drag that in. This is definitely useful if you do not want to, or simply can't, connect to the sharepoint at the time of management. Constructing your own .afploc file can be done only from the command line.

```
## defaults requires absolute paths to the file!
defaults write /Users/myuser/Desktop/myhost URL "afp://myhost.myco.com/MyCoShare"
mv ~/Desktop/myhost.plist ~/Desktop/MyCoShare.afploc
```

The contents of the .afploc are as follows:

```
<?xml version="1.0" encoding="UTF-8"?>
<!DOCTYPE plist PUBLIC "-//Apple//DTD PLIST 1.0//EN"
"http://www.apple.com/DTDs/PropertyList-1.0.dtd">
<plist version="1.0">
<dict>
        <key>URL</key>
        <string>afp://192.168.210.2</string>
</dict>
</plist>
```

You can replace the URL information (in this case, afp://192.168.210.2) with the FQDN for your server, allowing you to create new .afploc property lists on the fly. From here, you can simply drag the location file into the Documents and Folders section. These files can also be utilized by the Login Items pane, and they can be double-clicked from the Finder. When the files are added to the Dock, the resulting Dock item will utilize the file name for the mouse-over display text.

Another option in the Dock preference management pane lets you add a My Applications folder to the Dock, which is a dynamically generated list of allowed apps for a user to use. This is a handy folder in heavily managed environments. If you plan to deploy these apps, make sure to test the feature thoroughly because you may be presenting applications to the user that you weren't aware you granted them privileges to. In addition, you can add links to the user's Documents folder or to mount their network home. (This is useful if you configure users with local home directories but want them to have easily accessible personal storage space on a server.)

> **Note** Apple utilizes another popular location file, the .webloc file, for numerous other purposes. For instance, you can embed vnc://, smb://, cifs://, and http:// protocols in a .webloc file utilizing the same procedure specified here.

Another common MCX management setting involves deploying a software update server. Configuration for this is provided via a basic Software Update pane in Workgroup Manager preferences, which allows you to specify a software update server to query.

Many other management settings are available through the GUI, preference manifests, and custom .plist files. Worthy of another mention are the Apple-provided manifests provided in /System/Library/CoreServices/ManagedClient.app, which exposes a great deal of various settings for management. This includes the ability to manage screen saver preferences, home directory redirections (discussed later in the section "User Home Folders"), menu bar items, VPN settings, and Finder sidebar items. It is definitely worth your time to add in this manifest and peruse its offerings.

Troubleshooting and Testing

In elaborate environments, it can become difficult to track all the different groups and tiers where specific preferences are managed. On top of that, accurately predicting how all the various preference interactions will unfold obviously becomes more difficult as more elements are included. Luckily, Apple provides several tools with the ability to review the resultant policy in a particular environment. The first method to determine the final applied management settings for an environment is to take a look at System Information from the managed desktop. Under the Managed Client heading of the Software section of System Information.app, you can find a breakdown of each active managed preference by domain, including the source of each applied setting. Alternatively, you can use the command-line equivalent by querying the data type: SPManagedClientDataType.

```
system_profiler SPManagedClientDataType
```

The primary limitation to both of these tools is that they must be run from the actual environment. That environment may even have application restrictions to prevent the running of these tools, which naturally makes troubleshooting a challenging endeavor. In this case, there are a few options. One option is to temporarily enable access to System Information.app so that you can open it and review and tweak managed client settings. This is a bit of a pain, and you have to be careful to ensure the restrictions are put in place when done. Another option is to invoke the system_profiler command-line binary remotely via an Apple Remote Desktop (ARD) admin station. This works fine, but the main limitation here is that the output can be a bit difficult to parse.

Apple provides another command-line tool, mcxquery, which can be used to query the resulting MCX settings from arbitrarily passed data. It is possible to specify a user, a group, and a computer and view the resulting MCX data. For instance, to query the MCX for the user johndoe, logging into computer johndoe-macbook, you can use the following syntax:

```
mcxquery -user johndoe -computer 'johndoe-macbook$'
```

Note the $ at the end of the computer name. This character will be suffixed to the names of computers when they perform a trusted bind to Open Directory. In the previous example, johndoe-macbook$ should be the corresponding name for the computer when viewed in Workgroup Manager. Because the character $ is a bash special character, you must wrap the computer name in single quotes. Alternatively, you can specify a MAC address:

```
mcxquery -user johndoe -computer 00:1f:f3:d1:d5:c7
```

or the guest computer:

```
mcxquery -user johndoe -computer guest
```

This command becomes handy for testing new policy changes, but it of course has caveats. The most important mcxquery limitation is that the tool does not do automatic user membership lookups. That is, if you don't explicitly specify a group with the -group option, then *no* workgroup management settings will be output, regardless of the group membership of the specified user. This limitation becomes a larger issue when logging into a computer involves combining several workgroup settings. Outside of nested groups, determining combined workgroup settings isn't possible with this tool at this time. Oddly, computer group resolution is fully supported. When specifying a computer, you will see all the applicable computer group settings that are in play.

Compared to this, the second caveat is really more of a quibble. Output isn't the cleanest. There isn't a great way to query specific preference domains, so you just have to sort through all the settings until you find what you're looking for. The tool supports outputting to XML, but that isn't really pleasant to read either. Luckily, you can take advantage of the powerful tools available to OS X to make your life easier. One key tool is Apple's Xcode, which contains the old Property List Editor. With Xcode installed, you can pretty easily send it output from mcxquery, giving you a pretty decent way of traversing through the MCX domain. You can do this with the following syntax:

```
mcxquery -user johndoe -group editors -computer \
'johndoe-macbook$' | open -f -a /Applications/Xcode.app
```

Once this command is run, Xcode will open and display the mcxquery data in a presentable fashion. For frequent testing, you may want to create an alias for this command.

To accomplish this in the bash shell, open your ~/.bash_profile file and add the following text, all on a single line:

```
function gmcxquery() { /usr/bin/mcxquery -format xml $@ | open -f -a /Applications/Xcode.app ;}
```

If you use the tcsh shell, then edit ~/.tcshrc and add the following text as a single line:

```
alias gmcxquery='/usr/bin/mcxquery -format xml \!:* | open -f -a /Applications/Xcode.app'
```

After completing the edits, save the file and reload your shell (most easily accomplished by quitting Terminal and reopening it). Now, type the following command:

```
gmcxquery –user johndoe –group editors –computer guest
```

If all went well, the output will be nicely displayed in Xcode. With identical syntax to the original mcxquery executable, you now have an easy way to test managed preferences on a machine without actually logging into the machine. This can be a significant time-saver.

At some point after changing an application's managed preferences via the GUI, you may find remnants of management settings. This symptom most often occurs when you switch management settings from Once or Always to Never. Every once in a while, MCX gremlins can rear their ugly little heads and have you pulling your hair out. Never fret. Use gmcxquery to determine the source of the errant management setting, and then follow it up with a dscl mcxdelete command. For instance, an administrator decided to remove application restrictions from a lab for the summer, but despite the GUI claiming the application restrictions were set to Never, users still could not open supposedly allowed applications. Using gmcxquery, this is an easy problem to solve. After a quick untrusted bind of the machine to the domain, he ran:

```
mcxquery -user myUser -group lab -computer 'lab2-par145$'
```

From here, he looked for the application of com.apple.applicationaccess.new, which he was quickly able to spot. However, he also easily spotted some legacy settings in the com.apple.application domain, which is used for legacy 10.3 and 10.4 support. In each case, the source of the settings was the lab computer group. Resolving the issue was easy enough, harnessing the power of dscl's MCX capabilities.

```
dscl -u cedge /LDAPv3/mydirserv mcxdelete /Groups/lab com.apple.applicationaccess
dscl -u cedge /LDAPv3/mydirserv mcxdelete /Groups/lab com.apple.applicationaccess.new
```

Upon the next login, users proceeded to successfully open previously restricted applications. Between System Information, its command-line equivalent system_profiler, and mcxquery, you have some decent tools to troubleshoot an MCX environment. Each tool has its own benefits: mcxquery is highly accessible and can be utilized to test basic policy application changes but will not always give the whole picture because of its failure to perform group lookups on specified users. System Information, on the other hand, displays the final absolute settings but must be run from within the managed environment, limiting its usefulness outside of a troubleshooting environment.

User Home Folders

In a standard desktop computing environment, for a user to be able to do anything useful and have the merits of their work persist, they must have a nonvolatile place to store that work. Most modern-day multiuser operating systems provision a specific directory, typically called a *home folder*, on the file system for this purpose.

In OS X, there are two different types of home directory storage. A *local* home folder is the most common type and simply means that a user's home folder resides on a local disk of the machine the user is using. A *network* home folder, on the other hand, resides directly on remote storage accessed via a network file system, while data appears to reside on the local disk. In actuality, all activity results in file system activity on a remote server.

The following sections will explain the differences between these different storage types, explain how to determine which scheme is right for your users, and provide you with the necessary information to implement an efficient, effective home directory strategy.

Local Home Folders

In OS X the default store location for user home directories is on the root volume at the path /Users. Every user created using the Users & Groups pane of System Preferences will be automatically provisioned a folder in this directory, named after the user's short name. For instance, if you were to create a user and specify a short name of bob, that user would be provisioned a local home folder at path /Users/bob. If you were to inspect this folder, you would see a default OS X user directory containing the following folders:

- *Desktop*: This folder serves as the user's desktop folder. Any item residing in this folder will be displayed on the user's desktop.

- *Documents*: This folder is used primarily for user-generated documents. Occasionally, applications will store support files in this folder, but this is considered poor form.

- *Downloads*: This folder is used for content downloaded via Safari, iChat, or other supporting Cocoa-based apps. This folder typically contains only transitory or low-priority items. Users should be encouraged to properly move items from this folder into more appropriate folders in their home directory.

- *Library*: Hidden by default, the user's Library folder is a user-specific version similar to the /Library folder at the root of the drive. This is where the behind-the-scenes data resides that can be edited by applications. Data in this folder is typically not fit for direct user interaction or presentation. Its uses include, but are not limited to, application databases, preferences, plug-ins, fonts, and cache files.

- *Movies*: This folder is pretty self-explanatory and is intended for storing videos. This folder in an average user's home directory is typically pretty barren. This folder isn't heavily utilized by applications. The most notable app to make use of this folder is iMovie.

- *Music*: Like Movies, this folder doesn't leave much ambiguity. The most notable app to make heavy use of this directory is iTunes, which stores all its music, movies, podcasts, and iPhone/iPod Touch applications. It is not uncommon for users to sneak in 10GB to 15GB or more of data into this folder.

- *Pictures*: This folder is utilized for picture storage. Photos maintains its database in this folder, as do other third-party photo organizers.

- *Public*: This folder serves as a public store for other users. This folder is readable by all users on the machine and serves as a place for a user to save work and allow other users' access to it. This folder also contains a Drop Box, where other users can leave work to be viewed only by the home folder's owner.

A user's home folder is their own private repository, meaning there are access restrictions in place to prevent other users from violating this privacy. However, there are a few limitations to these restrictions that are important to know about, both as a user and as an administrator. The most notable characteristic is that the root of the user's home directory is world-readable. That is, every user on the computer can read and open any item placed in this directory. This is primarily notable in that many users have absolutely no qualms saving items in the top level of their home directory, unwillingly exposing these items to any user on the system. You do not want your users to fall into this habit, especially if you are dealing with sensitive data. It is important that you train your users to properly utilize the folder structure in place. If you have a user base that is particularly unwilling to learn, in some cases it may be desirable to simply restrict users from saving directly into this folder, forcing them to save to an existing subdirectory. Refer to the "User Templates" section to learn how to do this.

Another notable characteristic of the default restrictions in a user's home folder is the use of access control lists (ACLs) to maintain the in-place folder structure. Specifically, all the default folders contain an "everyone deny delete" ACL to prevent their removal.

```
[helyx:/Users/cedge] cedge$ ls -el
total 0
drwx------+  9 cedge  staff    306 Jan  9 12:37 Desktop
 0: group:everyone deny delete
drwx------+  4 cedge  staff    136 Jan  9 00:46 Documents
 0: group:everyone deny delete
drwx------+  4 cedge  staff    136 Jan  9 01:24 Downloads
 0: group:everyone deny delete
drwx------+ 30 cedge  staff   1020 Jan  9 12:18 Library
 0: group:everyone deny delete
drwx------+  3 cedge  staff    102 Jan  9 00:46 Movies
 0: group:everyone deny delete
drwx------+  3 cedge  staff    102 Jan  9 00:46 Music
 0: group:everyone deny delete
drwx------+  4 cedge  staff    136 Jan  9 00:46 Pictures
 0: group:everyone deny delete
drwxr-xr-x+  6 cedge  staff    204 Jan  9 01:23 Public
 0: group:everyone deny delete
drwxr-xr-x+  5 cedge  staff    170 Jan  9 00:46 Sites
 0: group:everyone deny delete
```

These ACLs ensure that a default baseline is maintained across all user directories on the system.

The standard home folder also provides a means for users to privately exchange files with other users. This is implemented through the Public and Sites directories. As can be seen the previous output, these folders are the only folders inside a default home folder that are world-readable. The Public folder is meant for file exchange. A user can place an item inside their public folder, and it will then be accessible to all users, but only with read access. They will not be able to make changes to any files. However, they do have the ability to upload new files. Inside every user's Public folder, there is a directory named Drop Box (not to be confused with the application Dropbox). This Drop Box folder is world-writeable but not world-readable. This means that users can place items into this folder, but they cannot see any of the items inside (including their own). The Drop Box folder is, of course, accessible to the home folder's owner, so only they can see items left for them in this directory. Though everyone has write access to this folder, a user will not be able to overwrite an existing file with the same name created by a different user, only their own.

The Sites directory is a unique directory and requires that the Apache web service be enabled via command line for it to be utilized as intended. When web services are available, users can place items in this directory, and they will be accessible for public consumption via a standard web browser. For instance, a user could place a PDF file, like presentation.pdf, into their Sites folder. Other users would then be able to download and review this document in a web browser through the URL http://computer_ip_or_dnsname/~username/ presentation.pdf.

In large environments, the functionality of the Public and Sites folders can be less attractive when used with local home folders, and in such environments these folders are typically barren. Each workstation must have file and/or web services enabled, each with their own data stores. Other users must remember both the node to connect to and the user's short name. In small workgroups, Bonjour discovery largely combats this problem, so all workstations on the same subnet with file sharing enabled will be automatically listed under the Shared group in the Finder sidebar. Conversely, Safari's Bonjour network discovery feature makes it easy to discover local machines running HTTP services. In a Windows environment, an OS X workstation with SMB sharing services enabled will behave much like a native Windows machine.

In environments such as heavy media where workstation performance is paramount, behind-the-scenes file server activity may be an unwelcome resource drain. Network home folders are better suited for use here. Data is centralized and can be served from fewer points (if not a single point), so resource utilization can be better tracked, managed, and scaled. From an end user's perspective, a user only need remember the server's address and their co-worker's short name to find the resource that they want.

Local home folders have their advantages and disadvantages. Their primary advantage lies in their minimal reliance on infrastructure. You need not have super robust network or storage systems to maintain a good user experience. All user resources are stored locally on a user's desktop internal storage, which is storage that will typically provide the fastest, lowest-latency access to data. For this reason, local home folders are often desirable whenever performance and user experience are paramount.

The disadvantage in local home folders lies in the decentralization of data that is inherent in such a model. All data maintenance routines become more complex because you now have to deal with each individual node to gain access to data. This is particularly true for the deployment of file-system security auditing and policy enforcement. For instance, if data retention requirements stipulate that all user data be backed up, then support requirements to manage and maintain the backup system to provide coverage for all your nodes will increase. This isn't a big deal for a few dozen nodes, but scalability is definitely a consideration that needs to be made. Luckily, there are tools available to aid in this type of management, such as Apple Remote Desktop.

Local Home Folder Configuration

The process of configuring a user with a local home directory depends mainly on the directory services model you are working with.

No Directory Services

If you have forgone the option of a centralized directory service, then your primary interface will be the Users & Groups pane of System Preferences. You can access System Preferences in the Apple menu, in the Dock (by default), or in the Applications folder. As mentioned previously, any account created using this tool will receive a home directory in the default directory of /Users. However, you have the ability to specify an alternate directory as well as make additional modifications. You can find this interface by right-clicking (or Control-clicking) any account listed and selecting Advanced Options. As shown in Figure 7-19, you have the ability to change numerous attributes including the user ID, group ID, short name, shell, and home directory. Additionally, you can change the user's GUID or assign aliases to the account.

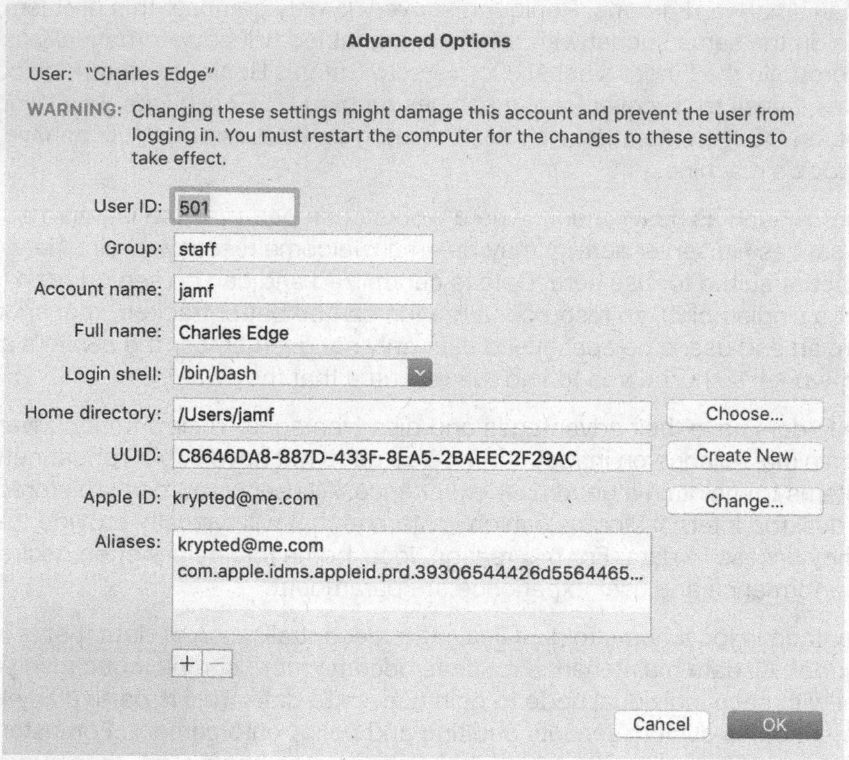

Advanced Options

User: "Charles Edge"

WARNING: Changing these settings might damage this account and prevent the user from logging in. You must restart the computer for the changes to these settings to take effect.

User ID:	501
Group:	staff
Account name:	jamf
Full name:	Charles Edge
Login shell:	/bin/bash
Home directory:	/Users/jamf
UUID:	C8646DA8-887D-433F-8EA5-2BAEEC2F29AC
Apple ID:	krypted@me.com
Aliases:	krypted@me.com
	com.apple.idms.appleid.prd.39306544426d5564465...

Choose...
Create New
Change...

+ −

Cancel   OK

Figure 7-19. Changing a user's GUID in System Preferences

Open Directory

If you are utilizing Open Directory for your directory system, you'll define your home directory for your users by utilizing the Workgroup Manager application, described earlier in this chapter.

Once installed, open the application and connect to your server. To assign a user a local home directory, go to the Home tab with the appropriate user selected. Listed in this tab will be any predefined home directory paths as well as any configured automounts. As shown in Figure 7-20, /Users is the default home directory location and will typically be a predefined option. If this is not the case, you can manually specify the path. Once a path has been defined for any user, it will be listed as a predefined option. To manually specify a new local path, first note the user's short name, found on the Basic tab, and then click the plus button. In the Full Path field, enter the local path for that user. For instance, if I wanted to utilize the standard /Users directory for the user with the short name bob, then I would enter the value /Users/bob. From then on, the /Users path will be listed as an option in the list. You can also mass select users and assign them the home directory path with a few clicks.

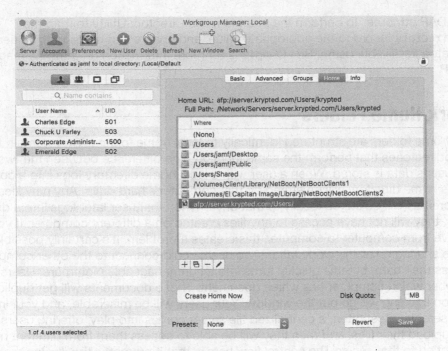

Figure 7-20. Selecting a home directory in Workgroup Manager

Active Directory

You can configure Active Directory users to utilize local home directories in a few different ways. If all Active Directory users on the machine are going to have local home directories, then the most straightforward way to do this is by utilizing the Force Local Home on Startup Disk option in the Active Directory plug-in. Alternatively, the "Create mobile account at login" option will provide the same effect, with a few differences. When used, the latter option will create a mobile account, caching all user information locally for any user who logs in. For more information on Active Directory, see Chapter 3.

Third-Party LDAP Directory

You can configure LDAP users to utilize local home directories in a few ways, depending on your user implementation. If your LDAP schema already contains the homeDirectory attribute, it is typically utilized for this purpose. You just need to map the NFSHomeDirectory attribute in Directory Utility. Each user will need the value of this attribute set to /Users/ shortname in your LDAP database. Upon login, they will be assigned a home directory in the /Users folder. If your LDAP schema does not support this attribute, you have a few options. The cleanest way to implement this without altering your schema is by mapping the record type NFSHomeDirectory to value #/Users/uid, where uid is the attribute that is utilized for the user's short name. This sets all users' home directories to the path /Users/shortname. The big limitation here is that all users on this machine will have their home directory in /Users, which may not always be desirable. To maintain granularity, you would have to extend your schema to support the homeDirectory attribute, or you could utilize an existing, unused LDAP attribute. To perform the mapping, use Directory Utility to map the `NFSHomeDirectory` record to the appropriate value, and ensure that home path values are prepopulated for all your users. See Chapter 2 for more information on attribute mapping with LDAP.

Network Home Folders

Network home folders are structured identically to local home folders. They contain the same subdirectories that perform the same function. The difference between the two is where a user's data is stored. When a user with a local home directory logs into a computer, that user's home directory will be stored on that computer's hard drive. Any new files that the user creates will be stored locally to that drive. When that user later logs into a different computer, they will not have access to any files created on a different computer. If your users move from computer to computer, this creates a problem. It's certainly possible to enable file sharing on all the workstations, so users could connect to the other computer and access their data, but this quickly turns into an unmanageable nightmare. Users need to remember which computer has which document. Those documents will get duplicated, and version tracking will go out the window. Your users will be miserable, and you, in turn, will be miserable. Most often, a centralized file server comes into play, offering users the ability to upload their files, and then they will be able to access them from different nodes by connecting to that server. The central flaw here is that it promotes the *illusion* that data is centralized. Oftentimes in these scenarios, desktop-resident data is completely forgotten. If it's not on the server, it doesn't exist and doesn't require protection. This mind-set can lead to expensive mistakes because your data is only as protected as your users are regimented.

Enter network home folders. Network home folders store data on a network file server. (It's not just a clever name.) When a user logs into a computer, the user's home directory is never stored on that local machine but rather directly referenced from a remote network file server. When a user creates or edits documents, those documents are actually updated on a remote server. This all happens transparently, unbeknownst to the user. The main benefit provided by this is mobility. By freeing user data from the embrace of each individual workstation, users are capable of freely moving from node to node, with their entire computing experience traveling with them. If your organization does not use assigned workstations, with network home directories, your users will enjoy a single experience wherever they log in. The benefits of this experience are reaped by IT as well. The advantage of having all user data centralized on the home directory server(s) is not small. Indeed, the ability to mass deploy software, settings, and files; audit security; and provide data protection are all greatly increased when data is consolidated.

OS X currently supports home directories over a handful of network file protocols, such as AFP and SMB, as well as NFS. AFP is your native protocol and will typically be your first choice when available. SMB support has greatly improved in OS X over the years and can be utilized for an acceptable experience as well, though it will typically be relegated to environments with Windows-based file servers.

The network home folder model is not without its flaws. The largest barrier to entry is the necessary server-side resources needed to provide an acceptable computing experience, let alone approach the performance provided by fast local storage used by local homes. Robust server, network, and storage infrastructure are needed. Gigabit Ethernet to the desktop will help and to the server is also highly recommended. A dedicated server with fast external RAID storage and gigabit Ethernet can acceptably host 40 to 50 simultaneous light to moderate users when implemented properly. This is not a hard limit or a guarantee because the qualification for "acceptable performance" will vary greatly from workflow to workflow and from user to user. If performance is paramount in your environment or if you are unfortunate enough to host particularly feisty users, then the decision to migrate to network home folders should not be taken lightly.

Special consideration must be paid to your user's workflow to identify data usage patterns, which can be detrimental to a file server. Economies of scale play a large role here. If all your users run applications that are I/O heavy, then all those transactions hit the wire, and your server will begin to lag. Likewise, if your users are in the habit of dealing with large data sets, then even a gigabit pipe on a server can be easily saturated. Luckily, OS X supports 802.3ad link aggregation, also referred to as *NIC bonding*. This is the process of taking two network interface controllers on a server and presenting them to the network as a single unified connection. This provides benefits both in redundancy and in throughput.

Redirection

As previously mentioned, network home directories are both a blessing and a curse. On one hand, they provide a valuable service to any environment where users do not have pre-assigned computers and may move about from node to node at will. However, if you take into account all the various activities that can occur inside a user's home directory, it quickly becomes apparent that the overhead necessary for deploying the storage infrastructure to handle the burden imposed by such activities is not insignificant. An IMAP account of even a moderately sized user mailbox can easily contain tens of thousands of files. A user logging into a computer results in a flurry of activity as numerous components load their support files. There is the occasional application in which file system needs are particularly burdensome on a file server. Photos and other media management applications involve not only high levels of I/O requests, but they can also be throughput intensive when used with higher-quality or uncompressed media. Another class of horrible offenders are video editors because they require a consistent, uninterrupted data stream. While most high-end applications of this variety rarely use the home directory for media storage, the nearly ubiquitous iMovie does. Even at its lowest quality, DV media played in iMovie requires a 5MBps stream, and things get worse with HD formats. The main thing to understand is that if your user's standard usage patterns involve high I/O or high-bandwidth activities, the viability of network-based storage deteriorates. However, their exclusion shouldn't be a forgone conclusion.

Redirection is the process of utilizing symbolic links in a network home directory to redirect traffic to a local disk. For instance, if your users utilize IMAP mail (you're not using POP, right?), then there's no reason to let that traffic burden your server. Through redirection, you establish a symbolic link at ~/Library/Mail, which redirects traffic to a local path of your choosing, say /Users/theUser/Library/Mail. This way, whenever you start up mail, all your data will be accessed from your local disk. When a user migrates to another machine and opens up mail, it will need to re-download any messages, but this will be of minor consequence compared to the alternative. The typical candidate for redirection is ~/Library/Caches, which contains a decent amount of application cache data that has no business burdening your server. If your users have large numbers of fonts, redirection of the

~/Library/Fonts folder can help to reduce login times. However, this can often present its own management problems. For this reason, it is encouraged to install fonts at the machine level in /Library/Fonts or to utilize font management software, such as Extensis Universal Type Server.

Implementation of redirection can be deployed with two distinct methods. The first method is new to 10.5 and involves the use of MCX and the preference manifest provided by /System/Library/CoreServices/ManagedClient.app. Specifically, you will be editing the preference manifest for domain com.apple.MCXRedirector. When you create a new key, the Always target provides three different keys to choose from.

- *Login redirections*: These are redirections that are fired upon login.

- *Logout redirections*: These are redirections that are fired upon logout.

- *Other redirections*: These are fired periodically whenever policies are set. After a network change, login, logout, or reboot.

The former two are primarily the ones you're interested in. You can have a login hook that creates your symbolic links at login but then destroys them at logout.

Once you have created your MCXRedirector key under the Always target, you want to set the key Login Redirections. With the new Login Redirections key highlighted, you create yet another key, which is used to define your redirect actions and paths. The redirection system provides you with four actions to choose from:

- *deleteAndCreateSymLink*: This action deletes the network folder and creates a symbolic link to the specified local path.

- *renameAndCreateSymLink*: This action renames the existing network folder, prepending *Network* to the name of the directory. After renaming, it creates a symbolic link to the specified local path. Unfortunately, because of the lack of consistent logout cleanup, avoid this option and instead utilize a login hook, which gives you much more flexibility. However, this option can be used instead of deleteAndCreateSymLink to ensure that you avoid deleting user data.

- *deletePath*: This action simply deletes any item at the specified path.

- *deleteSymLinkAndRestore*: This action is the counterpart to renameAndCreateSymLink. Essentially, it will delete the existing symbolic link and restore the previously renamed directory. Unfortunately, this option does not function reliably. For this type of functionality, implement a login hook instead.

For these purposes, you are going to choose the second option. This allows you to maintain a network version of the redirected folder, but promotes local storage for the primary folder itself. Thus, if you were to perform redirection of the Movies folder because your users utilize iMovie, then they will have the ability to access their network movies folder at ~/Movies (Network). This provides your users with the ability to manually copy files to the network folder to facilitate migration to a different machine. At the same time, it relieves the burden of iMovie's heavy data usage from your server. While a user's movie media may not seamlessly transfer with them like the rest of their home folder, it is an acceptable compromise in many environments.

To finish the policy creation, you will specify your Folder Path value, which is ~/Library/ Movies. You also want to specify the Destination Folder Path key, which signifies the local path that will house your data. For this, you enter a value of /Users/%@/Movies. As discussed in Chapter 8, %@ is a variable for your user's short name. Thus, when bob logs in, his home directory's Movies folder actually references /Users/bob/Movies.

To ensure a clean environment, you might also want to deploy a logout redirection, which deletes all the redirections that you created at login. To do this, you will create a new Logout Redirections key under your Always target and create a new deletePath action key. The key Destination Folder Path is ignored by this action and can be removed. The path specified by Folder Path is used to determine the alias to remove. If you specify the value ~/Movies, the action will delete the symbolic link at ~/Movies but will leave the data on the local disk untouched. It will also rename your Movies (network) folder back to just Movies so that order is restored to the universe (see Figure 7-21).

Figure 7-21. Setting MCX login and logout redirects in Workgroup Manager

Basic redirections deployed through MCX are quick and easy, and they work. However, there are a few implications that will determine their usefulness in your environment. The MCXRedirector can be deployed at any level, user, group, computer, or computer group. For reasons previously discussed, I discourage the use of user-level management, though it's important to recognize that the granularity that they provide can be useful. If you have only a couple of network home users, this may be a good option, but utilizing a group for this still scales better. It is also recommended to avoid deploying these at the computer or computer group level.

The main reason for this is that these redirections are user agnostic. That is, when they're deployed at the computer level, they will redirect the folders of all users who log in, even those with local homes. This isn't a terribly big deal, but it's unnecessary and unsightly. If you use /Users/%@/… as your redirection store or if you utilize portable home directories (discussed in the section "Home Directory Syncing" later in this chapter), then you will definitely have problems. Therefore, this really leaves you to deploying at the group level. This works for the most part, but what if certain users have network homes on some computers (wired nodes) but should also have local homes on others (laptops)? If you deploy redirects at the group level, then you get your redirects on your local homes. This example illustrates the main problem with MCX-based redirections. There is no way to introduce them with logic.

This leads you to the other method of redirection: login hooks. Because of the unparalleled freedom that you have, redirecting folders is just a few lines of code away. Login hook scripts, when done properly, require a decent amount of logic. A basic login script is pretty easy to assemble.

```
#!/bin/sh
PATH="/bin:/usr/bin:/usr/sbin"

# simple login redirection script

# get our user
theUser=$1

# get our home
eval theHome=~$1

# if we are a local user, exit
if [ -x "/usr/bin/nicl" ]; then
# 10.3 & 10.4 test
[ $(nicl . -read /users/"$theUser" &> /dev/null) == 0 ] &&
echo "User is a local user, aborting! " && exit 1
elif [ -x "/usr/bin/dscl" ]; then
#  10.5 and higher test
[ $(dscl . -read /users/"$theUser" &> /dev/null) == 0 ] &&
echo "User is a local user, aborting! " && exit 1
else
        echo "DS Tool not found. " && exit 1
fi

# specify our redirect folder, make sure it exists,
# set ownership and permissions
redirectDir=/Users/Local/"$theUser"
mkdir -p "$redirectDir" &> /dev/null
chown "$theUser" "$redirectDir"
chmod 700 "$redirectDir"

# redirect ~/Library/Caches. For 10.3 compatibility,
```

```
# operations on the home directory must be performed as
# the user. root does have write access to AFP shares.
mkdir -p "$redirectDir"/Library/Caches
sudo -u "$theUser" rm -rf "$theHome"/Library/Caches
sudo -u "$theUser" ln -s "$redirectDir"/Library/Caches \
"$theHome"/Library/Caches
chown "$theUser" "$redirectDir/Library/Caches"
echo "Redirected $theHome/Library/Caches to \
$redirectDir/Library/Caches"

exit 0
```

Here is the requisite logout hook (don't blink):

```
#!/bin/sh
PATH="/bin"

# simple logout redirection script

# get our user
theUser=$1

# get our home
eval theHome=~$1

# if there's a symlink, break it down
[ -L "$theHome"/Library/Caches ] &&
rm "$theHome"/Library/Caches &&
echo "Removing symlink at $theHome/Library/Caches"

exit 0
```

For the logout hook, you don't need to test for a local user. If the users are local, they won't have a symlink to begin with. If they do, it shouldn't be there, so you may as well delete it.

This is a pretty bare-bones login redirection script, and it doesn't have a ton of sanity checks. What if the destructive redirect destroys valuable data and you need to move it rather than delete it? What if a user is logged in to two sessions at once? When one instance is logged out, the other's symbolic links will be torn down, leading to an unstable environment. Therein lies the strength in login hook-based redirections; you can pretty much add any functionality that you're willing to invest time into scripting. Unfortunately, in reality, network home directories just aren't well suited for certain uses. Make sure to take care to thoroughly test your productivity apps before deploying network home directories on a wide scale.

Network Home Folder Configuration

Depending on your directory service model, you will utilize configuration profiles, Workgroup Manager, or Directory Utility to configure network home directories. While it is possible to implement network home directories in environments without centralized directory services, their presence is highly recommended.

Open Directory

To assign a user a network home directory in an Open Directory environment, you must first configure the home directory called Shared and automount, specifying the automount as your user's home directory. When logging in as a network home user, the bound client will utilize values stored in the user's record as well as the configured automount information in order to properly mount the user's home.

To configure the sharepoint and automount, use the Server application, located in /Applications. Once open, click the File Sharing section and then open the share that will contain home directories. Check the "Home directories over" box to enable automount and select the protocol that home folders will use. We selected AFP, as shown in Figure 7-22.

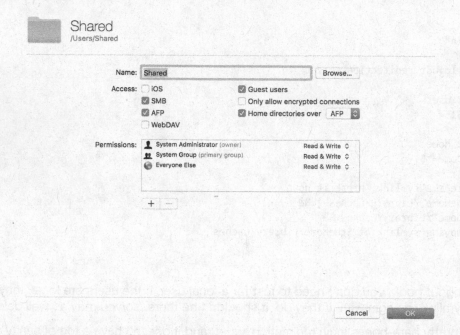

Figure 7-22. Server Admin: sharepoint automount options

You can verify this by observing your Open Directory Mounts container with Workgroup Manager's Inspector or with dscl.

```
/LDAPv3/127.0.0.1/Mounts > read osxserver.krypted.com:\/Users\/Shared/
dsAttrTypeNative:objectClass: mount top
AppleMetaNodeLocation: /LDAPv3/127.0.0.1
AppleMetaRecordName: cn=osxserver.krypted.com:/Users/Shared,cn=mounts,dc=osxserver,
dc=krypted,dc=com
RecordName: osxserver.krypted.com:/Users/Shared
RecordType: dsRecTypeStandard:Mounts
VFSLinkDir: /Network/Servers
VFSOpts: net url==afp://;AUTH=NO%20USER%20AUTHENT@osxserver.krypted.com/Shared
VFSType: url
```

An automount record contains four essential attributes in your directory. The `RecordName` attribute indicates the server's IP or DNS name, a colon, and then the path to the share. In this case, it will be the full file system path of the share from the root of your server's file system. Therefore, if your `Users` sharepoint resides on a secondary volume (as it always should), then your mount `RecordName` might be `myserver.com:/Volumes/dataVolume/networkHomes`. The path portion of the value is utilized on the client side as the file system mount point for the automount. The `VFSLinkDir` attribute specifies the base path, which is prepended to the path provided by `RecordName`. In the previous scenario, a client machine would mount the user's home directory at `/Network/Servers/hax.lbc/dataVolume/networkUsers`.

One important limitation to know about here is that there is a character limit to an automount path name when used specifically with network homes—the entire path, including /Network/ Servers, cannot contain more than 89 characters. This leaves 72 total characters at your disposal, which is ample for most environments, but if you find yourself running against this limitation, you do have a couple of options.

The first option is the cleanest, and it cuts out a decent amount of fat depending on your environment. The basic concept is that you map the top level of your share's path to the root of your file system. To understand this, consider the previous example, where the automount mount point for the `Users` sharepoint was at `/Network/Servers/myserver.com/Volumes/dataVolume/networkHomes`. This path contains more than 19 characters that apply to only a single machine, the server itself. Your remote clients know only about the server name (`myserver.com`) and sharepoint (`Users`). Why can't you cut out all this excess, like `/Volumes/dataVolume/networkHomes`? In fact, you can confidently bypass this once you realize a few things about automount behavior. First, every OS X machine has a symbolic link at `/Network/Servers/fqdn`. On my server, the command `ls -l /Network/Servers/myserver.com/networkHomes` yields the same results as `ls -l /networkHomes`.

Thus, by placing a symbolic link of the sharepath to its base name on the root of the file system, you can simulate this on the server.

```
$ln -s /Volumes/dataVolume/networkHomes /networkHomes
```

Once run, `/Network/Servers/myserver.com/networkHomes` is a fully functional path to your data. All that's left to do is modify the automount data, replacing the old path with your modified version.

The `VFSOpts` attribute specifies that this is a dynamic AFP automount. The `;AUTH=NO%20 USER%20AUTHENT` string specifies that the machine will first attempt to mount the automount as guest. Once a user logs in, it will reconnect to the sharepoint with the user's access levels. However, there is an important ramification here. If you have a limited-license server, each connected home directory user will utilize two connections. This value can be changed to `;AUTH=Client%20Krb%20v2` to utilize Kerberos authentication on the automount. Alternatively, an authentication string can be dropped altogether. `Loginwindow` will dynamically authenticate and mount the share.

```
VFSOpts: net url==afp://;AUTH=Client%20Krb%20v2/server.krypted.com/networkHomes
```

Home Directory Syncing

Also referred to as *portable home directories*, home directory syncing allows a user to use a local home directory but also periodically synchronize files with a network home directory. This type of setup is great for users who utilize both a personal laptop and a wired desktop machine. In such cases, the wired desktop machine could utilize either network home directories, or it could be configured to utilize a local home and then sync the content with a network home directory as well. In either case, you can configure settings that manage these preferences, specifying specific folders to include in the sync, and the interface also provides a capable filtering system to easily ignore cache files and other machine-specific files.

Home directory syncing is broken up into two different sync types: login/logout syncs and background syncs. As the name suggests, login and logout synchronizations fire upon the beginning and end of a user session. The best utilization of login/logout syncing is probably best described by the setting's preference keys: `syncedPrefsFolders`. That is, this option is best used for application preference files or any file that during a user session is constantly in use and therefore not a good candidate for background syncing. By default, Apple specifies two folders to sync at login/logout: `~/Library` and `~/Documents/Microsoft User Data`. The Former option includes application preference and support files, Safari and Firefox bookmarks, and user fonts. The latter folder contains many Microsoft Office settings, most notably the Outlook 2011 database. (Outlook 2016 for Mac's mail data is stored in the user's hidden `Library` folder.)

Background synchronization, as its name implies, synchronizes files and folders in the background during an active user session, by default every 20 minutes. As mentioned, not all files are good candidates for this. For the most part, background synchronization should be configured for user-generated content, such as the `Desktop` and `Documents` folders.

One thing to consider is that login and logout syncing can cause significant delays in the login and logout process as the user must wait for the synchronization to finish before they can begin to use the computer or close the laptop's lid for the day. Because of this, users may be prone to simply hitting the Cancel button. Essentially, if you do not build a specific login item sync list, then the entire login syncing process will likely be compromised because of user intervention. Most users will not find a 30-minute login time to be acceptable. So, keep this list slim. If you need to synchronize Firefox bookmarks, explicitly specify the folder `~/Library/Application Support/ Firefox`. Use `~/Library/Safari` for Safari, but use `~/Library/Preferences` for all user application preferences. Avoid directories with deeply nested hierarchies because these will cause syncing delays as the system scans through everything. For the brunt of the work, background syncing is your go-to player.

One other noteworthy aspect of login/logout synchronizing is that the system has detection routines to determine whether another computer has synchronized changes. If, upon logging in, the `FileSyncAgent`, which is responsible for synchronization, detects that the user has had an active session on another machine, it will present the user with a dialog stating that another login session was detected. The dialog will ask the user if they would like to delay syncing. Upon the next sync, the system will require the user to choose a default conflict resolution source, presenting the option of local files versus network files. This setting is then applied to all items for that synchronization. This differs significantly from conflict resolution on background synchronizations, which allows you to specify the preferred source of each conflict individually.

If you have sync settings applied to a user account, upon first creation of the account, a complete sync of both login items and background items is required in order for the login process to complete. If the initial synchronization is cancelled, then the login will fail, and the user will be returned to the login window. Make sure that if your users have large home directories that you set this expectation when you deploy the change. Subsequent login syncs will attempt to perform a synchronization of background items as well, but they can be cancelled without detriment to the login; the sync will simply pick up where it left off during the next scheduled scan.

To configure a user to utilize a portable home directory, you can use a process that is a bit of a hybrid between a network home directory user and a mobile user with a local home directory, often referred to as a *portable home directory*. In Workgroup Manager, the desired user must have their home directory specified to a configured automount sharepoint, exactly as you would configure a user with a network home directory. Once this is configured, you must specify mobility management for the user, such as you would do when setting up a user with a local home directory. Once you have done this, you must use managed preferences to define the user as a mobile user. For the purposes of this exercise, you are going to utilize a computer group named Mobile.

First, open Workgroup Manager and connect to the Open Directory master. Next, find the desired management object to apply the managed settings to. Once selected, open the Mobility pane in the Preference Management section. On the default Account Creation tab, under the Creation section, select the option to create a mobile account at login, but do not require confirmation, as shown in Figure 7-23. Click Apply.

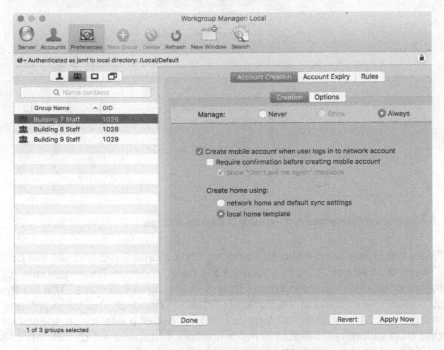

Figure 7-23. Forcing mobile account creation on login using Workgroup Manager

After this change, when the user logs into a computer that is a member of this group, a mobile account will be created—a copy of the user Open Directory record is copied into the local directory services store. This record contains the user's password and enables the machine to permit a user to log in to the computer even when the machine cannot contact the Open Directory server. Creating mobile accounts is an absolute must on laptops that will routinely leave the company campus and thereby lose access to company internal servers. In fact, in many wired-desktop environments, it may be desirable to force mobile accounts for users. This creates a more robust desktop setup that will more gracefully deal with any Open Directory outages. There are not many benefits management-wise to not create a mobile account for any user who will utilize a local home directory.

Now that you have configured mobility, you must also configure the actual synchronization settings. First, you'll define the preferences that are to be synchronized, using the "Merge with user's settings" option to reduce the number of conflicts in the synchronization process (see Figure 7-24).

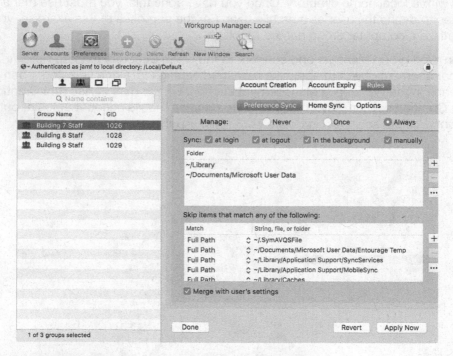

Figure 7-24. Configuring login/preference syncing using Workgroup Manager

Next, configure the Home Sync options. To do so, click Home Sync and set the option to Always. Then, choose which times you want the sync to occur. The "manually" option will synchronize only when a user indicates they'd like to sync their data. The "in the background" option syncs data in the background when needed. The "at login" and "at logout" options sync when a user first logs in and logs out of a session, respectively. Only synchronizing data at login and logout is not an option, but these are usually necessary. These days, it's best to leave all the options checked.

Next, define what synchronizes. In this instance, synchronize the user's Desktop and Documents folders. You are not concerned about other media content, such as Pictures, Movies, and Music. Users can certainly connect to their home folder manually (or you can mount it for them using MCX), and they can upload any media files that they deem important (perhaps only the server-side home directories are backed up). In this case, you want to make sure you exclude some potentially sync-busters, such as the Entourage database at ~/Documents/Microsoft User Data, or potential virtual machines at ~/Documents/Virtual Machines (or ~/Documents/Parallels if you are using parallels instead of VMware), as shown in Figure 7-25.

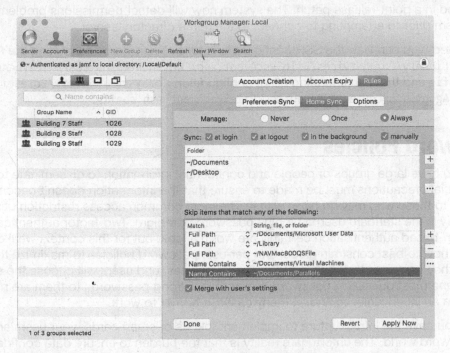

Figure 7-25. Configuring background/home syncing using Workgroup Manager

Click Apply Now to save your changes and test your home folder synchronization.

Troubleshooting Syncing Issues

Troubleshooting home directory syncing issues is something that you will inevitably have to deal with when you deploy them at a large scale. The following few paragraphs summarize the players involved to help you to determine the possible origin of different issues.

When syncing issues arrive, the first thing to determine is the breadth of the issue. Is the problem occurring only with a single user or is it affecting all users with the applied management settings? One of the most common causes of syncing problems is because of conflicting sync settings. Your ~/Library/Preferences folder isn't going to sync if you exclude the ~/Library folder. Use the system_profiler and mcxquery functions discussed earlier to verify applied settings.

After this, consult the log files at ~/Library/Logs/FileSyncAgent.log and ~/Library/Logs/ FileSyncAgent-verbose.log. Between these two log files, there will typically be evidence as to the nature of your problem.

If server-side tracking is enabled, then the client uses public key authentication to contact the server over port 2336. For this authentication, preshared keys are stored at ~/Library/ FileSync/FileSyncAgent_key_dir. In this directory, there contains a public key and a private key used to authenticate to the server. In earlier versions of 10.5, if permissions of this folder were such that the user was not the owner and did not have exclusive access to the keys, then authentication would fail. This would result in a complete sync failure. This issue was addressed in a point-release patch. The system now will detect permissions problems and repair them prior to attempting to connect to the home directory server.

If interested, you can view the SSH configurations for this service by consulting the files /System/Library/CoreServices/FileSyncAgent.app/Contents/Resources/FileSyncAgent_ sshd_config and the corresponding client configuration at /System/Library/CoreServices/ FileSyncAgent.app/Contents/Resources/FileSyncAgent_ssh_config.

Password Policies

When you have large groups of people and confidential information to disseminate to them, then special precautions must be made to ensure that the information doesn't become available to those who may do harm with it. The most common access restriction utilized in IT today is the standard username plus password paradigm. Two-factor authentication and token-based authentication certainly are worth a look, but for this context we'll discuss primarily how to best constrain global and per-user password policies to maximize the security they can provide. When left to their own devices, end users will choose the shortest, easiest, and most guessable password as possible. Strong passwords to them are nothing more than an inconvenience and, in many cases, a barrier to work.

Unless you have the infrastructure to implement tokens or smart cards, your users are stuck in a password world. The unfortunate reality is that the burden to ensure data confidentiality ultimately falls on you, the system administrator. Luckily, OS X Server includes a set of tools for implementing password strength requirements and implementing required, scheduled rotations. These tools are presented to you via the familiar Server application. Additionally, in typical fashion, Apple provides a command-line tool, pwpolicy, for more advanced uses.

To access global password policy settings, first open the Server application in / Applications and click the Users option in the sidebar. Choose Edit Password Policy using the cog wheel icon. Figure 7-26 demonstrates the user's password tab, providing options to force password strength, such as minimum length, numeric digit, special character, and uppercase character requirements, and it even allows for preventing users from reusing previous passwords. On this tab, you can also force global rotation requirements, designating an arbitrary timeframe between password changes.

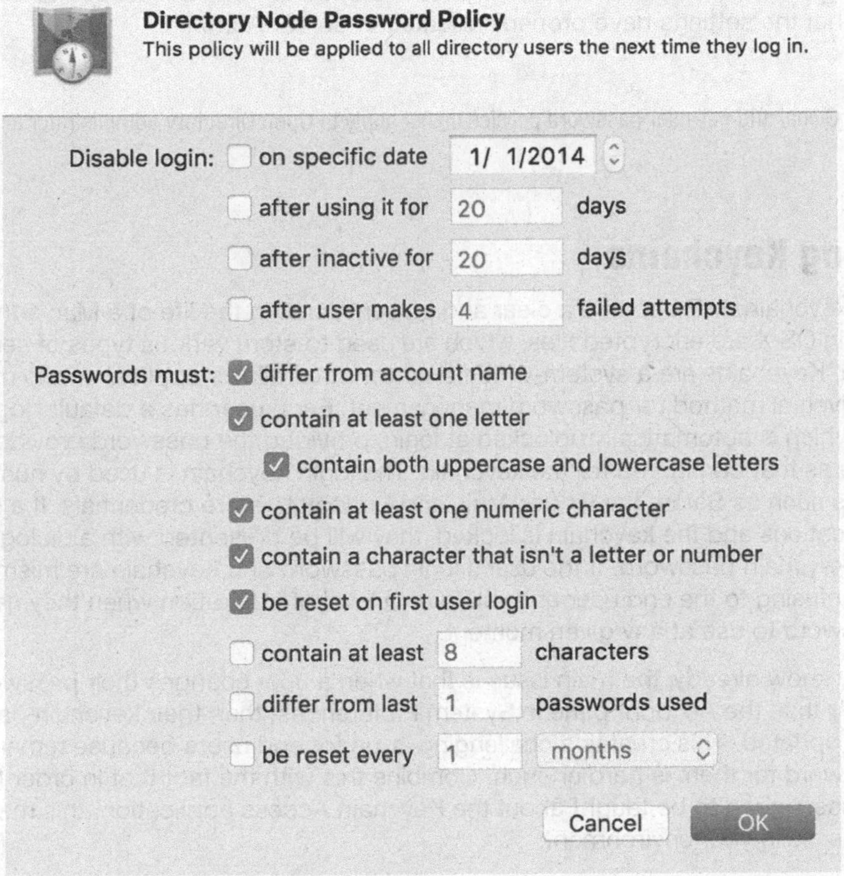

Directory Node Password Policy
This policy will be applied to all directory users the next time they log in.

Disable login: ☐ on specific date   1/ 1/2014 ⌃⌄

☐ after using it for   20   days

☐ after inactive for   20   days

☐ after user makes   4   failed attempts

Passwords must: ☑ differ from account name

☑ contain at least one letter

☑ contain both uppercase and lowercase letters

☑ contain at least one numeric character

☑ contain a character that isn't a letter or number

☑ be reset on first user login

☐ contain at least   8   characters

☐ differ from last   1   passwords used

☐ be reset every   1   months ⌃⌄

Cancel   OK

Figure 7-26. Configuring global password policies in Server

The command-line equivalent to these settings is found using the pwpolicy command, specifically, the -getglobalpolicy and -setglobalpolicy flags. To require a minimum of eight characters, you should use an alphanumeric password with at least one special character for all users. The following is the syntax:

```
sudo pwpolicy -a cedge -setglobalpolicy "requiresNumeric=1 minChars=8 requiresAlpha=1
requiresSymbol=1"
```

In this example, you specify an Open Directory administrator username with the -a flag and then use -setglobalpolicy to set your specific items. To both ensure your settings took and to get a list of possible settings, you rerun the command with the -getglobalpolicy flag.

```
sudo pwpolicy -a cedge -getglobalpolicy
Password:
usingHistory=0 canModifyPasswordforSelf=1 usingExpirationDate=0 usingHardExpirationDate=0
requiresAlpha=1 requiresNumeric=1 expirationDateGMT=12/31/69 hardExpireDateGMT=12/31/69
maxMinutesUntilChangePassword=0 maxMinutesUntilDisabled=0 maxMinutesOfNonUse=0
maxFailedLoginAttempts=0 minChars=8 maxChars=0 passwordCannotBeName=1 requiresMixedCase=0
requiresSymbol=1 newPasswordRequired=0 minutesUntilFailedLoginReset=0 notGuessablePattern=0
```

After reading this output, you can definitely see the options that you just set. Likewise, you can verify that the settings have properly updated in Server Admin.

> **Note**   Global and per-user password policies do not apply to Open Directory administrator accounts.

Managing Keychains

Managing keychains will become a clear and present issue in the life of a Mac administrator. Keychains in OS X are encrypted files, which are used to store various types of sensitive information. Keychains are a system-wide framework that allows applications to utilize a single universal method for password management. Each user has a default "login" keychain, which is automatically unlocked at login, provided the password provided at login is the same as that configured for the keychain. The login keychain is used by numerous applications such as Safari, the Finder, Mail, and Outlook to store credentials. If a user opens these applications and the keychain is locked, they will be presented with a dialog box to enter their keychain password. If the user's login password and keychain are mismatched, it will be confusing to the end user and will force a level of frustration when they never know which password to use at any given moment.

As you may know already, the main issue is that when a user changes their password via any means other than the Account pane in System Preferences, then their keychain password will not get updated. This creates a challenging issue for end users because remembering a single password for them is hard enough. Combine this with the fact that in order to address the issue, users need to be taught about the Keychain Access application, this may or may not be plausible in your environment.

Apple Remote Desktop

Apple Remote Desktop (ARD) is a desktop management tool sold as a separate product in the Mac App Store. The client for this application is installed by default on every OS X machine. Prior to management availability, a client machine must have the service turned on and access levels configured for users. This can be done by visiting the Remote Management service in the Sharing pane of System Preferences. In the Remote Management service UI, you will find options to configure the service for all users or for specific users. From here, you can add individual users or groups and configure levels of remote access, though typically, the only local users that would need remote access would be administrative users. They will typically have full access to the machine and may or may not present visible queues to the end user when they are being observed or controlled. You can also configure this application via the command line and the `kickstart` command, found at /System/Library/CoreServices/RemoteManagement/ARDAgent.app/Contents/Resources/ kickstart. For example, to configure access to your machine for all users with a local account, use this:

```
/System/Library/CoreServices/RemoteManagement/ARDAgent.app/Contents/Resources/ kickstart
-configure -allowAccessFor -allUsers -privs -all
```

From here on out, the machine will accept login connections for users, regardless of whether you enabled the service in the Sharing pane or from kickstart.

Scanning Networks with ARD

Apple Remote Desktop possesses a network scanner that can detect machines via Bonjour, by a specific IP address or by a range of IP addresses. Multiple scanners can be set up, making it easy to rediscover DHCP machines on remote subnets.

To create a network scanner, simply select New Scanner from the File menu. Name the scanner appropriately, and in the right pane, configure the scanner's settings. Options are Bonjour, Local Network, Network Range, Network Address, File Import, Task Server, and Directory Server. These are mostly self-explanatory. Local Network searches subnets local to all interfaces on the machine. Network Range allows you to specify starting and ending IP addresses, which is handy for scanning remote subnets. File Import allows you to import a file that has newline-delimited subnet ranges. This is handy if you have rather intricate subnet configurations and want to capture multiple ranges in a single scan.

```
10.0.1.2-10.0.2.50
10.0.3.100-10.0.3.102
```

> **Tip**   To list or to scan? ARD has both static lists and dynamic scanners. If you find yourself coming and going from a network a lot, you will be much happier with a scan. If you are managing static IP addresses only or have only a single subnet for all machines, then lists are probably better suited. Lists are also better suited if you need to repeatedly target specific machines.

Controlling Machines

Controlling machines is pretty straightforward. First, you must add client machines to your local database. To do so, use a scanner that you previously configured. The scanner will display found machines with a blue icon. Simply drag them to the All Computers container on the left. Once you have performed this action, computers listed in the scanner will have a blue icon next to them, as shown in Figure 7-27.

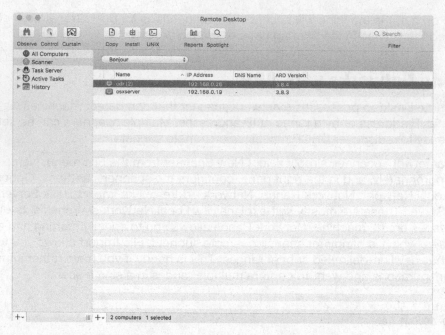

Figure 7-27. Discovering machines with the scanner in Apple Remote Desktop

Once added, you can control a machine by selecting it in the list and clicking the Control button. Now you will have remote control of the remote client's console session, assuming (or sharing) control of its keyboard and mouse. ARD sessions and loginwindow sessions do not need to share the same console. Select one or more Macs in a list and choose File ➤ Get Info. On the Control & Observe tab, the default behavior is "Share the display." However, choose "Connect to a virtual display" to log in as a second user on the remote computer. Neither you nor the current console user will see the other's session. An administrator can use this second session to run a GUI application installer without interrupting the console user or access other GUI applications accessible only via the Finder.

Sending Commands, Packages, and Scripts

One extremely powerful feature of ARD lies in its ability to distribute package installers, send remote UNIX shell commands, and even copy files to machines. When copying files, ARD will attempt to utilize multicast for distribution, making distribution of files and packages to machines on the same subnet extremely efficient. To push installation of a package to multiple machines, simply select them in your scanner or list and click the Install button. Here, you can install standard package-based applications. You can deploy multiple packages at one time, and they will execute in the order that they appear in the list. This makes it especially useful for pushing software installs and then subsequent updates all in one swoop. Figure 7-28 shows the GUI for remotely executing UNIX shell scripts via ARD's Send UNIX Command option.

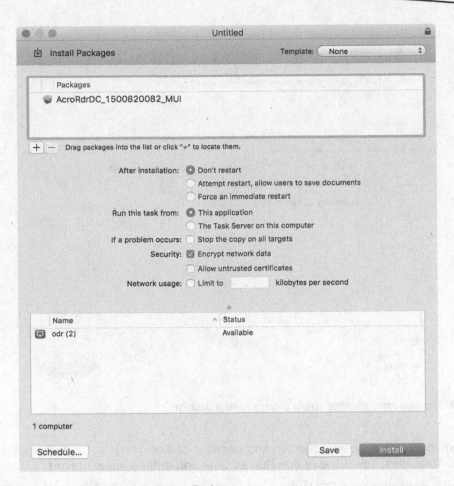

Figure 7-28. Deploying packages in Apple Remote Desktop

UNIX shell commands are an equally invaluable utility for remote machines. For example, you may need to temporarily enable SSH access on a group of machines for remote management. Using ARD, you can easily push out the command to do this. First, select the desired target computers from a scanner or list and select the Send UNIX Command option from the Manage menu. Alternatively, you can click the UNIX button in the toolbar. Regardless of your choice, you will be presented with the window shown in Figure 7-29. In the top field of the window, enter the following command:

```
launchctl load -w /System/Library/LaunchDaemons/ssh.plist
```

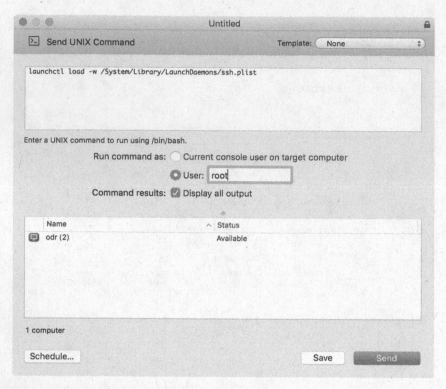

Figure 7-29. Remotely executing shell scripts in Apple Remote Desktop

This command loads a system daemon and because of that needs to run with root privileges. To do this, select the option Run as User and enter a value of **root**.

When you're done with your SSH work, you can disable it by simply redeploying the command with the `unload` parameter.

Login Hooks

As discussed earlier, login and logout hooks provide the means to run scripts prior to and after a user's login session. Here, the term *hook* is synonymous with *script*. The term *hook* is used simply as a colloquialism referring to the manner in which the script is caught by the login or logout process. Login and logout hooks are functionally identical, so you we use the term *login hook* going forward. Unless otherwise indicated, information is similarly applicable to logout hooks.

Login hooks are executed under UID 0. That is, they run with root privileges. To properly identify the user environment in which they are running, the system passes the logging-in user's short name as the first argument to a login script. Login hooks can be utilized to perform custom folder redirections, custom mounts, and file system modifications. The real beauty of login hooks is that you have access to the same tools that you would have in an OS X shell environment. You can use it to deploy Perl, Python, and bash scripts, which can pretty much do your bidding.

Login hooks in OS X are deployable only at the computer and computer group levels. However, out of the box, OS X clients are not configured to trust login hook settings deployed from a directory server. To enable this trust, you must modify loginwindow's root domain preference to enable login scripts.

```
defaults write /var/root/Library/preferences/com.apple.loginwindow EnableMCXLoginScripts
-bool true
```

Next, you have to establish your acceptable trust level, represented by your MCXScriptTrust attribute. The following are a number of trust levels (ordered from most to least strict):

- *FullTrust*: The client will only trust login scripts specified by Directory Servers to which the client has performed a trusted bind to. A FullTrust relationship also requires that the options to block man-in-the-middle attacks and digitally sign every packet are checked.

- *Authenticated*: The client will trust a server only if it has successfully authenticated via a trusted bind.

- *PartialTrust:* Like a full trust, a partial trust requires a trusted bind. Packets here must also be digitally signed. Active Directory bindings typically occur at this level.

- *Encryption*: The client will trust only servers supporting ldaps:// connections and for which the rootCA file is defined in /etc/openldap/ldap.conf. (See Chapter 1 for more details on SSL and directory services.)

- *DHCP*: The client will trust only servers specified in Option 95 of their active DHCP packet, as discussed in Chapter 1.

- *Anonymous*: The client will trust login scripts configured in any configured directory server.

If you are unsure of which option to set, you can run a query from a client to determine the possible levels.

```
dscl localhost read /LDAPv3/dirserv.myco.com dsAttrTypeStandard:TrustInformation
TrustInformation: Authenticated Encryption
```

You can now use this information to configure your client. When setting your MCXScriptTrust value, the value that you set will determine the trust level such that if your client trust connection is at least as secure as the value specified, then the login script will be trusted. For the preceding example, you could set either Authenticated or Encrypted. If you are confident that all other Macs in your fleet will have a similar trust level, then you can pick the strongest of the values—in this case, Authenticated. To establish this MCXScriptTrust, you run the following command (as root on every client):

```
defaults write /var/root/Library/preferences/com.apple.loginwindow MCXScriptTrust -string
Authenticated
```

At this point, you have now laid the groundwork for deploying login scripts. Obviously, life will be much easier if you build the previous measures into your standard configuration at imaging time. Now, it's time to actually deploy your login hook script. To deploy a script, a little prework needs to be done. First, the script needs to have a shebang statement (#!/bin/bash) as its first line. Second, it cannot have a file extension. Lastly, the script must be marked as executable on the file system. To make a script executable, use chmod.

```
chmod +x /path/to/scriptfile
```

With this prework done, all you need to do is deploy the actual login hook managed preference. To do this, open Workgroup Manager and log in to the Open Directory master as a directory administrator. Once connected, find and select the computer(s) or computer group(s) where you want to deploy the login hook. With the desired object(s) selected, navigate to the Login preference pane. In this pane, shown in Figure 7-30, on the Scripts tab you will find the ability to specify login scripts. Additionally, you can specify whether login hooks configured in the machine's local loginwindow.plist file will be allowed to run. Be careful if you have any client management systems, such as JAMF Software's Casper, because disabling this option can interfere with its function.

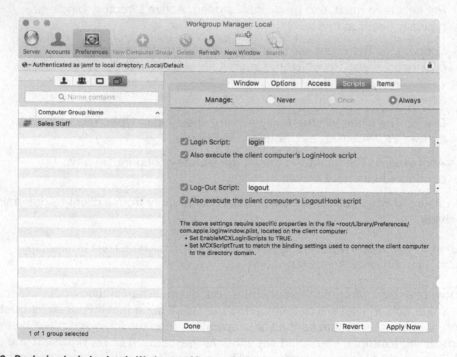

Figure 7-30. Deploying login hooks via Workgroup Manager

To set local login hooks, run the following command as root on the local client:

```
sudo defaults write com.apple.loginwindow LoginHook /path/to/loginhook
```

Software Update Server

With OS X server, Apple provides the Software Update service, which allows you to host your own local software update repository. Referred to as swupd and built on top of the Apache web server, this service can provide updates to all client computers on your local LAN. Not only does this save potential gigabytes of data from hitting your WAN connection, but it also allows you to funnel updates to your clients, releasing them only after your IT organization has had the ability to vet their compatibility with business-critical applications.

To configure Software Update, use the Server application to start the service and enable the appropriate updates. You have a few options in regard to how the service handles new updates. For instance, you can choose to automatically copy all updates or only new updates from Apple's centralized server. By choosing to copy but not automatically enable the updates, you ensure that the updates are local to your LAN and available for immediate deployment when you are ready to enable. If you choose not to automatically enable updates, then you must manually specify which updates will be enabled for deployment. The process swupd_sync is responsible for syncing enabled updates from Apple and presenting any new updates in the interface.

> **Tip**   Enabling the Software Update or Caching service on a server can result in a significant amount of data to the folder /usr/share/swupd. Make sure the system has adequate space on its disk drive prior to enabling either service. If necessary, you can move the software update store by moving the directory to a separate volume and then setting up a symlink. The second option is to modify the apache.conf file utilized by swupd, located at /etc/swupd/swupd.conf.

To configure software update services on the client side, you can do so locally on each by running defaults.

```
sudo defaults write /Library/Preferences/com.apple.SoftwareUpdate CatalogURL
http://myserver.myco.com:8088/
```

Alternatively, you will probably prefer to deploy these settings via MCX or a profile. To do so via managed preferences, Workgroup Manager provides a managed preference pane (called Software Update). This preference can be deployed at all tiers of management.

In addition to the graphical Software Update service, it is possible to run software updates in the background, without the user's knowledge. To do so, you will want to utilize the software update binary, located at /usr/sbin. This command has a few common uses. If you run your own update, you'll probably want to automate the following command with launchd or cron:

```
softwareupdate -i -a; shutdown -r now
```

With this syntax, the command will install any available updates and then restart.

8

Automating Administrative Tasks

One of the greatest strengths of OS X is the abundance of scripting languages supported out of the box. Many of these languages are interpreted by a host program rather than run directly as lower-level machine code, and thus they are text files with human-readable syntax. Because such languages are translated into machine code at run time, interpreted programs are sometimes much slower than their compiled equivalents. However, because you can edit these programs and then run them immediately, they are common tools used by system administrators to automate tasks.

Some interpreters are specifically made to run code such as Python, Perl, or Ruby, while others are more interactive and are meant for day-to-day use, facilitating most of the command-line administration tasks covered in this book. Typically, this interactive interpreter component is referred to as a *shell*. The primary purpose of a shell is to translate commands typed at a terminal into some kind of system action. In other words, the shell is a program through which other programs are invoked.

There are several different UNIX shells, including the C shell (csh), the Bourne shell (sh), and their more modern equivalents, tcsh and Bash. In the most recent versions of OS X, new users are assigned the Bash shell as the default shell. In early versions of Mac OS X, the default user shell was tcsh, perhaps because of the presence of Wilfredo Sanchez on Apple's team. The former lead engineer for Mac OS X was also a developer of the tcsh shell. However, Bash has proliferated through the various Linux distributions and has become one of the most prominent shell programs in use today. Perhaps recognizing this, Apple switched the default shell to Bash in Mac OS X 10.3 Panther, and it remains as such today in OS X 10.11 El Capitan.

While the choice of a shell and its resultant scripting language can sometimes be difficult, we recommend you learn at least the basics of the Bash shell before moving onto any other shell and language that may be better suited to your higher-level tasks. This is because, unlike with languages such as Python or Perl that are more strictly used for scripting, you will typically use the Bash shell every time you open a terminal to run any command. The more comfortable you become with Bash scripting, the more you may find yourself writing one-line scripts that allow you to automate even basic operations. For instance, every principle discussed in the "Scripting the Bash Shell" section of this chapter applies to the interactive environment presented when you fire up Terminal.

In this chapter, we present some basic building blocks you need to build your own complex automations. In the process, we attempt to show you some real-world syntax examples of scripting in action. By the end of this chapter, you'll be armed with enough knowledge to tackle the problems you face in your environment. We'd like to make a strong point at the outset: while you do not have to use the command line to be a good system administrator, most good system administrators do. This is because a simple operation, such as creating a series of folders, can be done using basic scripts, and in using these scripts you will find your administration becomes not only more efficient but also (and importantly in large environments) more consistent.

This chapter is not intended to provide in-depth coverage of all shells; that could be a book unto itself. This chapter will introduce you to scripting with Bash and then supply some information on Perl for those who begin to outgrow the Bash environment. We will walk you through the basic constructs and control statements, providing a decent foundation for you to build on. Because of its default support in the latter iterations of OS X, we will focus primarily on the Bash shell syntax.

The Basics

Every shell has some built-in functions that it performs directly, but most commands you enter cause the shell to execute programs that are external to the shell. This sets the shell apart from other command interpreters, as its primary mechanism for invoking functionality is largely dependent upon other programs. That's not to say that shells don't have built-in capabilities. They do. They can read, create, and append files; manipulate data through globbing and variable mangling; and utilize looping constructs. However, the ability to parse and extend that data will more often than not require external calls. This chapter seeks to arm you with the ability to fully utilize the Bash shell's internal functions, as well as introduce pertinent external functions that will help you to fully employ the power of the command line.

The first step toward learning the shell is actually firing it up and getting your feet wet, preferably on a nonproduction box. In OS X, this is done simply by opening the Terminal application on your system. When the application opens, provided your user account has the default shell assigned, you will be presented with a Bash prompt, something like this:

```
krypted:~ cedge$
```

The default prompt consists of the following template:

```
computername:current directory username$
```

In this example, the current directory is ~. The tilde represents a user's home directory. Thus, for any respective user, ~ expands to /Users/username. The tilde can be used when specifying paths for commands. You can always reference your own home directory via ~, and you can even reference other users' home directories.

```
krypted:~ cedge$ cd ~emerald
krypted:emerald cedge$ pwd
/Users/emerald
```

In this text, we are issuing the cd command to change directories and passing ~emerald as an argument. You can see at the shell prompt that the new directory is emerald. You can then issue the pwd command, which outputs the current path. In this case, it's emerald's home directory at /Users/emerald.

Note   Path names can be passed to commands in two different forms. An *absolute* path contains every folder and element relative to the root (/) of the drive. A *relative* path contains items relative to the current directory. For instance, if you run the command cd /Users, you have provided cd with an absolute path to the Users directory. Next you run the command ls emerald, providing a path emerald, relative to the current directory, /Users. Alternatively, you can run the command using an absolute path, as in ls /Users/emerald, and net the same results regardless of the current directory.

You'll want to become familiar with the basic commands that are normally used for administration. Here's a list of some of the most common ones:

- cd: Changes the directory. This command takes a single argument—a path to a directory. You can use cd .. to change to the parent directory.

- pwd: Lists the current directory. Pwd accepts no arguments.

- ls: Lists the contents of the current directory. Ls has numerous options. A common set of arguments, -hal, will show all items in list form (by default, any file beginning with a period is invisible) with human-readable file sizes. Optionally, a directory or file can be provided, and ls will output either the file's information or a directory list. For instance, ls -hal /Users will output a detailed list of files and folders present in the directory /Users.

- cat: Displays the contents of a file or concatenates files.

- more: Displays the contents of a file page by page and allows you to scroll down to see the rest. This is useful with large files, when cat shows too much information to see on the screen.

- tail: Displays the end of a file. This is useful when used with the -f option, as you can watch the end of a log file and view on the screen new lines as they're written to the file.

- rm: Deletes a file or directory. rm offers several options. It can be passed a file or directory for deletion. If a directory is passed, the -r flag must be used to recursively delete all contents. For instance, the command rm -r /Users would delete the entire /Users folder (probably best to avoid that one).

- pico: Allows you to edit files from the command line. Pico (nano) uses emacs-style keyboard shortcuts, supports arrow keys for navigation, and is pretty basic. It accepts a path to a file as an argument. When you're finished editing, press Ctrl+O to save and Ctrl+x to exit the document. (Another common text editor is vi, but that utility, though rewarding, is much more difficult to learn.)

- sudo: Executes a command with root privileges. By default, this command can be run only by administrators. It has numerous options, but in its most basic form, it can simply be prefixed to any command to execute that command with root privileges. For instance, to edit a system configuration file, such as Software Update server settings, run the following, which invokes the defaults process with root privileges:

```
sudo defaults write /Library/Preferences/com.apple.SoftwareUpdate
CatalogURL http://swupdate.krypted.com
```

- history: Shows the last commands completed from a command line. The history command requires no other parameters or options.

- whatis: Searches the whatis database, handy for determining the appropriate command to run. For instance, by using the command whatis "change owner", you can determine that the chown command may be what you're looking for. You can then use the man command, discussed next, to determine the capabilities of the chown command.

- man: Used to access manual pages for the hundreds of command-line programs that come with your computer, so it may well be the most important command to know. For instance, you can type man hier to see information on OS X's directory structure, while man chown brings up the manual page for the chown command, giving you the syntax and functionality of that command. man even has its own manual. Explore how to use it: man man.

- find: Lets you search for a file or directory by name. find is a fairly complex command and has a lot of utility. In its most basic form, it can be used for a simple directory search. For example, if you were trying to hunt down .DS_Store files on a network share mounted at /Volumes/MyCoolNetworkFolder, you could run the command find /Volumes/MyCoolNetworkFolder -name ".DS_Store". Pretty nifty. Even better, find lets you take the output and act on it. Say you want to delete all .DS_Store files. To do this, run the command find /Volumes/MyCoolNetworkFolder -name ".DS_Store" -delete.

- echo: Used to output text to the stdout data stream (discussed later in the section "Standard Streams and Pipes"). When writing scripts, the echo command is a great way to ensure that your script gives proper feedback to the user.

- grep: Used in combination with piping to filter a command's output (piping is discussed later in the section "Standard Streams and Pipelines"). For instance, the command ls /Users | grep -i admin would filter the output of ls /Users, outputting only user home folders that match the admin criteria, using a substring match so that user home admin would match, as would mycoadmin. The -i flag means that grep will ignore capitalization. In another form, grep can be used to search files for strings. The command sudo grep -r http://www2.krypted.com /etc/apache2 would search the directory /etc/apache2 and output the file names containing the string http://www2.krypted.com. The -r flag tells grep to recursively search through a directory. You can omit the -r flag and search across a single file if necessary. You can prefix the sudo command to ensure that the grep search has access to all necessary files.

- ps: Lists running processes. This command has numerous arguments. One common iteration is ps auxww. The flags auxww result in the output of all running processes across all users on the system. You can use piping to filter this list: the command ps auxww | grep httpd will determine whether the Apache daemon (httpd) is running. If httpd is found, the command will display the process's running ID (the PID column), as well as CPU and memory utilization.

- chmod, chown: Can be used respectively to change permissions and ownership on a file or group of files. Both commands utilize the -R flag to recurse across all children of a directory. In the following example, chown changes the owner of the folder /Users/cedge to cedge and changes the group to admin. You can then utilize chmod to ensure that the owner (o) has both read and write (rw) access.

```
chown -R cedge:admin /Users/cedge
chmod -R o+rw /Users/cedge
```

- kill: Terminates a running process. This command has a few optional arguments, but in its most basic form, it is simply given the process ID of a running process to terminate. A process's ID can be determined through the ps output, as discussed earlier. The kill command must be run with root privileges via sudo to terminate a process running as root. Other common flags include -HUP, which can be used to restart a process. Alternatively, the infamous -9 argument, equivalent to -KILL, can be used to forcibly terminate a process without prejudice regardless of state or any pending activity.

These are merely a selection of the available commands. If you know a few commands that, when executed, will complete a larger overall task, you can then combine them to make a program, which we'll call a *script*. This is how most people start to learn shell scripting.

> **Note** The Bash shell has the ability to search back through your history file. Press Ctrl+r to do a "reverse" search through the history file by typing some or all of the original command or its arguments. Continue to press Ctrl+r to cycle through previous incarnations.

To switch between shells, you need only type the name of the shell you desire to use. As you alternate between shells, you'll notice that the appearance of the screen and the area where you input text appears slightly different.

Scripting the Bash Shell

The makings of a typical script includes a shebang line (#!/bin/bash), variable declarations ("declare FOO=BAR") , and optionally command variable declarations. This is all you need to create a static script. We will cover these terms more in-depth in the following section, as well as explore the logical constructs that make a script such a powerful wrapper for the command-line tools OS X provides.

The Bash shell is based on the Bourne shell (sh) and is syntactically backward-compatible. In fact, the *b* and *a* in *Bash* stand for Bourne Again, a tribute to sh and its author Stephen Bourne. The Bash shell is capable and has support for numerous control statements. This includes support for standard control statements: if/elif/else constructs, case statements, and for, while, and until loop statements.

A control statement in a programming or scripting environment provides ways for a coder to control the execution of code. These statements provide the means to perform basic tests on data, which will then define the flow of execution, all based upon the criteria you design. Through the use of if/else and case control statements, you can control whether code gets executed at all. These functions are referred to as *branching* statements because they control specific paths of code execution. Looping statements, such as for, while, and until, are control statements that allow for reuse of code through iteration. Bash provides looping statements in the form of for, until, and while loops. Each of these looping statements provides capabilities to help you manage highly repetitive tasks. Control statements serve as the fundamental tools for logical execution of your code.

The Bash shell also includes some internal data manipulation routines, provided via globbing and variable mangling; however, for any advanced parsing, such as regular expressions, you'll be much better off with an external program that is suited for the purpose. That being said, we'll walk you through some of the commonly used Bash constructs, which will bestow upon you the building blocks toward implementing your own automations.

> **Note**   On many systems, /bin/sh is linked to the Bash installation. However, be aware that with Bash built upon the basic sh constructs, language like declare will not work when called from an sh script. We will show you how to set the shebang to specify that your script runs in Bash; you can add [-z "$BASH"] && exit 1 at the top of your script to check for this as well.

Declaring Variables

Variables are the single most important concept of scripting in relation to automating administrative tasks. While other languages have relative benefits, most admins typically end up using Bash for basic day-to-day administration, where many tasks can be accomplished by simple scripts or even a single line of chained commands (*one liners*). A one-line script could look something like this:

```
systemsetup –setnetworktimeserver my.pretendco.com
```

This code is straight to the point, but perhaps you are in a Windows Active Directory environment and the server you use for time is also your authentication server. Your script may have my.server.com listed 10 to 20 times by the time you are finished. Now imagine you need to change that code later. You could cut and paste all 20 lines, but if you use variables, you can declare the server once and then retrieve this value over and over again in your script. You can even then use it to echo output. Even for your one-liner scripts, using variables will allow them to grow over time and cut down on the number of typos because you have just one line rather than 20 to check when you have a problem.

```
declare TIME_SERVER="my.pretendco.com"
systemsetup –setnetworktimeserver "$TIME_SERVER"
echo "Time Server: $TIME_SERVER has been set"
```

> **Note**   When a variable is used in a script, the script "expands" the variable to its respective value (in this case $TIME_SERVER becomes my.pretendco.com). However, a variable may not always contain string data, which is why you can have a dynamic error message using the simple echo command. Because of this, it is important to always double quote variables. Expansion works within double quotation marks, not single quotes. Double quotes also help when working with file system paths that have spaces, often the cause of issues with novice users. When in doubt, quote. If you want to see variable expansion as it occurs (often helpful for debugging a script), add -x to the shebang, like this: #!/bin/bash -x.

Each variable has a name that uniquely identifies it within scope. Variable names need to begin with an alphabetic character and cannot contain a period. In other words, if you work for a company called 318, you'd often need to declare variables called, for example, THREE18 to avoid starting with a number. Variables can't be longer than 255 characters.

In traditional programming languages, you must declare a variable and the kind of information that will go into it before using the variable (in other words, you tell the script what's going into a variable before you actually "put" something in it). In modern scripting languages, this is usually considered good practice (and great for readability), but it's not required. In the Bash shell, the command to declare a variable is declare. When you declare a variable, you can then call it multiple times, adding and removing data from it, augmenting it, or just reading it for reference.

For example, in Bash, the two following statements will both work:

```
#!/bin/bash
declare -i CUSTOM_PORT=8088

echo "My software update server is running on port $CUSTOM_PORT."

# Example script 2
CUSTOM_PORT="8088"

echo "My software update server is running on port $CUSTOM_PORT."
```

In the first example, you are explicitly defining the variable CUSTOM_PORT as an integer and setting it to 8088. In the second, typecasting in Bash automatically determines the type of data that a variable contains. Typecasting occurs when a variable is set to a certain type (such as an integer) and then used to store a different data type (say the string "Hello World"). In this case, there is a type conversion from integer to string. While both of the preceding examples work, relying on automatic typecasting can present problems in certain circumstances; if your script logic is expecting a numeric (integer) value and is passed a string instead, your script will die with a fatal error. The following script shows how this works:

```
#!/bin/bash
# A simple script that checks if a console user is active
# We will cover the "who | grep 'console' -c" portion later
# for now just know that this test will return "1" if a user
# is logged in and nothing if no one is logged in

declare -i CONSOLE_USERS="`who | grep 'console' -c`"

# The command above returns nothing if no users are logged in.
# However, when declared as an integer, if this variable is
# set to a null / nothing string, it will convert that to the
# number zero; that way the result of the command doesn't matter.
# We can always rely of the result being a numerical value,
# which we can then numerically test against, using the greater
# than or equal to syntax -ge. This type of test expects
# CONSOLE_USERS to expand to a numerical value
# If we did not use -i, then any numeric tests on $CONSOLE_USERS
# would fail if there were no users logged in. The script would
# expand CONSOLE_USERS to nothing instead of 0
```

```
# You can test this by changing the declare line above to
# declare CONSOLE_USERS=
# which will simulate the command returning nothing
# and without the use of the -i, it will stay just that: nothing
# which will cause the test below to fail with the error:
# "line 17: [: -ge: unary operator expected"

if [ $CONSOLE_USERS -ge 1 ] ; then
        echo "Console user logged in, exiting…"
        exit 1

else
        echo "No console users, we can go to town…"
        # Your code goes here
fi
```

This script uses comments to explain the flow of the script; these are covered later in this chapter. For now, be aware that any line that starts with a # (except for line 1) is a comment, and the script will not "run" that text. This is a best practice, and you should always comment all your code, adding notes to explain your script's logic and activity. The more complicated a script gets, the more important that commenting becomes. If you do not comment the script effectively, you will not be able to trace your own steps at some point, much less have anyone else be able to take over your work when you, say, get a promotion to Senior Deity of Computer Operations for integrating 10,000 Macs into your enterprise in a week.

Variable Mangling

The Bash shell has several facilities for internally altering data in variables. This is referred to as *variable mangling*, and Bash allows for numerous string operators to be applied to a variable that will filter its value. Mangling in Bash uses curly brackets ({}) that enclose the variable name prepended to a number of possible special operator characters.

One common use of variable mangling is to perform pattern matching on a variable, both left to right (specified by the hash [#] character) and right to left (specified by the percent [%] character):

```
MY_VAR="the value of a variable"
echo ${MY_VAR#the}
        returns:  "value of a variable"
echo ${MY_VAR%a *}
        returns: "the value of"
```

This can be handy for grabbing filenames or extensions explicitly.

```
MY_FILE=songname.mp3
echo "Filename: ${MY_FILE%.*} extension: ${MY_FILE##*.}"

returns: Filename: songname extension: mp3
```

Notice the use of the greedy string operator (##); this ensures that even if the file has additional periods in its name, the only one you consider the extension (and thereby exclude from your filter) is everything past the last dot. The ability to remove file extensions this way is handy. For instance, the Apple defaults command used to require you pass in the file name without the .plist extension (no longer the case today). In the following script, we utilized this method to isolate the file extension when needed, allowing us to perform our operations. The commands here are not as important as the concept—now that you can use the same variable for both operations and have the extension automatically removed for commands that require it.

```
#!/bin/bash

declare -i TIME_OUT=5
# This sets the timeout of the AD plug-in in 10.5+

declare PLIST_FILE=\
"/Library/Preferences/DirectoryService/ActiveDirectory.plist"

# The path of the plist \ is used to continue the command on the next line
# Note that the path has a .plist extension, which normally would cause
# The defaults command to fail. However, with variable mangling we can
# remove the .plist extension of the PLIST_FILE value when we use it
# with defaults and then call it normally when we use a command that
# requires a more standard path with file extensions like plutil.

if [ -w "$PLIST_FILE" ] ; then

        defaults write "${PLIST_FILE%.plist}" 'LDAP Connection Timeout' $TIME_OUT

        plutil -convert xml1 "$PLIST_FILE"

else

        echo "File is not writable try sudo $0"
fi
```

> **Note** We used a variable that is automatically set by the shell, $0, here. This is the full path to the script, and it's good for making dynamic usage error messages match your script path and name automatically.

Another form of variable mangling provided by Bash is substitution, which uses four operators: :-, :=, :+, and :?. Suppose you use the command echo ${MY_VAR:-hello}. If the variable MY_VAR exists and isn't null, the command will output its value. If MY_VAR doesn't exist or has a null value, the string "hello" will not print out. The := operator is similar. The main distinction is that when := is used, it will set the variable $MY_VAR to the value specified, in this case "hello." The :+ operator is essentially the inverse of the :- operator. In the command echo ${MY_VAR:+hello}, if $MY_VAR exists and is not null, then it returns "hello." If it doesn't exist or is null, it will return a blank value. Lastly, the :? operator can be used to perform sanity checks. For instance, when used with the syntax echo ${MY_VAR:?my error}, if the variable $MY_VAR is not set, the script will immediately terminate, printing the error message "my error." If no error is specified, a generic "parameter null or not set" error is output, along with the variable name. Using the :? operator is a great way to ensure that critical variables are set.

> **Note** Scripts can be damaging if certain operations are called with malformed data, so be extra diligent in using these string operators to verify that appropriate values are set.

The Bash shell also provides further capabilities for data substitution via the / and // operators. For instance, if MY_VAR has a value of Hello World, the command echo ${MY_VAR//Hello/Hi} would output the text "Hi World." The use of // vs. / simply denotes how greedy the matching is: echo #{MY_VAR/o/a} would output "Hella World," while the command echo #{MY_VAR//o/a} would output "Hella Warld." A real-world example of this follows. Excuse the rather "hacky" use of AppleScript via osascript to get this MAC address value, but it's a simple way to get only your MAC address returned.

```
#!/bin/bash
declare MAC_ADDRESS=`osascript -e 'primary Ethernet address of (system info)'`
echo "Address with colons: $MAC_ADDRESS"
echo "Address without colons: ${MAC_ADDRESS//:/}"
```

Standard Streams and Pipelines

In any *nix terminal environment, numerous information channels exist that control the flow of information between a process and its console session. The three primary data channels from a scripting perspective are standard input (stdin), standard output (stdout), and standard error (stderr). These data streams can be captured, evaluated, and redirected through scripting.

- Standard input, or stdin, represents data resulting from a read operation. This can be text input via keyboard or text that has been programmatically redirected.

- Standard output, or stdout, represents any data output by a program. The output will typically go to the current console session but can also be redirected to other programs or files.

- Standard error, or stderr, is a data channel that represents textual error information. For instance, if a program detects an error in one of its subroutines, it will typically spit the details of this error out to stderr. Understanding the use of these channels by any program you intend to script will help you to more efficiently write your code.

As mentioned, you can use pipelines or redirects to control the flow of data between separate programs. The most common use of pipelines is the practice of piping stdout from one script to stdin of another. For example, you can call the following command:

```
ps auxww | grep -v "grep" | grep -c "Finder"
```

If you were to look up the man page for grep (man grep), you would find that the program takes optional flags and two arguments, a string pattern, and a path to a file. However, in this context, you are simply calling grep with only one argument. How does that work? Well, the answer is that because of the implementation of command pipes: |. As mentioned, the pipe is used explicitly for passing data between programs. In this case, you are passing data from the ps command out to grep. The grep command recognizes that it is being passed data over stdin and utilizes this data as its second argument. After filtering this data and removing any occurrences of the term grep, it outputs the modified data to stdout, which is piped to yet another instance of grep. This program is responsible for outputting a numeric count for the number of times the term *Finder* appeared in data passed to it through stdout. In a command pipeline, the resulting text output will be that parsed by the final command in the chain.

In many cases, you may want to redirect the flow of data to a file. To do this, you use data stream redirectors. In Bash, the most common implementation of redirectors is through the >> and > operators.

```
ps auxww > ~/process_list.txt
```

In this example, you are redirecting stdout of the ps program to the file located at ~/process_list.txt. The use of the > operator means it will overwrite any data that previously existed with the file. Thus, every time the previous command is run, the file will contain data only from the most recent operation. The >> operator in contrast is an append operation; any data previously will simply have the latest data added to it. This is a less destructive redirect and is desirable in many scenarios.

It is also possible to redirect the data streams themselves. For instance, perhaps you want to set a variable to the output of the ls command.

```
lsTxt=$(ls /Applications)
```

This syntax will capture the output of the ls program's stdout as a single string. However, if ls is passed a nonexistent path, it will output its text to stderr, which will never be passed to the lsTxt variable. To address this issue, you can use data stream redirects once again. To pull this off, you want to redirect the stderr channel (in *nix systems channel 2) to stdout channel, channel 1:

```
lsTxt=$(ls /Applications 2>&1)
```

This way, lsTxt will contain either the file listing or any subsequent errors. With Bash, it is also possible to perform two redirects.

```
ls /Applications >> /lsLog.txt 2>&1
```

In this context, youare redirecting stdout to append your file found at /lsLog.txt. However, you are also redirecting stderr to stdout. This command will output the results of both data streams into the file. This becomes a handy way to log all activity reported by a process, rather than just merely relying on stdout.

if and case Statements

if/else and case statements in Bash serve primarily as traffic routers. Both of these facilities are specifically referred to as *branching statements*; their purpose is to directly affect the flow of code. For instance, perhaps there is a VIP user on the network who needs VIP treatment. If this particular user logs into a computer, you need to ensure he has a Deep Thoughts folder on his desktop, and then perhaps you need to prune this folder for old files, sweeping them away into a Stale Thoughts folder. In the end, the specific task doesn't really matter; it is only important that you recognize that all this activity represents a "branch" of code: a full path of activity initiated by the evaluation of an initial if statement. That if statement represents a test—is this user my VIP? If he is, the next step is a flurry of activity. Otherwise (else), skip the code and proceed as usual.

> **Note**   When coding or scripting in any language, the general rule of thumb when implementing branching statements is to organize your code so that the most commonly executed branch is in the first block.

For basic string comparison, both if/else and case statements are pretty similar, though lengthy case statements tend to be easier to read than lengthy if/else statements. Here is the syntax to implement each in Bash (note that the USER variable is set automatically by the Bash shell and expands to the username of the user running the script):

```
# Check to see if our user is "jdoe"
if [ "$USER" = "jdoe" ]; then
      echo "My name is John"
      exit 0
elif [ "$USER" = "janedoe" ]; then
      echo "My name is Jane"
      exit 1
elif [ "$USER" = "jsmith" ] ; then
      echo "My name is jsmith"
      exit 1

else
      echo "Failed over to catch all..."
      exit 192
fi

# While the above works, it's rather ugly, so a case statement normally is much more readable
```

```
## case statement
case $USER in
r"jdoe")
            echo "My name is John";
            exit 0;;

    "jsmith" )
            echo "My name is jsmith" ;
            exit 1;;

    "janedoe")
            echo "My name is Jane";
            exit 1;;
     *)
    echo "Failed over to catch all…";
    exit 192 ;;
esac
```

> **Note**   When you are using case, you will specify each entry with a ;; following the line, and then when all possible matches have been specified, you will use esac (end of case) to close out the case statement.

We have introduced a few new concepts here. First, you will see the test brackets: [ ]. The use of brackets represents a conditional expression, which will ultimately evaluate to true or false. In Bash, test brackets are used with conditional operators to form tests. One example of this is the previous example's if statement.

```
if [ $CONSOLE_USERS -eq 1 ] ; then
\
```

This logic in English would translate as, "If the string variable $USER is equal to the string jdoe, execute the following code." In this case, "is equal to" is syntactically denoted by a string comparison operator, =, which compares two arguments (referred to as a binary operator) and returns true if they have equal string values. Its antithesis, !=, will return true if the two given arguments are not the same. In the case statement, the variable $USER is tested in a similar fashion (=) against each of the possible matches, each denoted by the values specified prior to the closing parenthesis. When a match occurs, the respective code block is executed until it reaches the break specifier, ;;. In the case statement, the last line, *), represents a wildcard and is the equivalent to an else block in an if statement; its execution is dependent on all prior matches failing.

> **Caution**   Not all languages, such as PHP and Python, regard the symbol = as a comparison operator and will actually interpret it as a value assignment. In many cases, it is best to use the == operator to do string comparison to prevent altering your variable's value. The == comparison operator is fully supported by Bash.

In addition to these two binary operators (= and !=), Bash provides several arithmetic-based binary operators.

> -eq: arg1 equals arg2.
>
> -ne: arg1 does not equal arg2.
>
> -lt: arg1 is less than arg2.
>
> -le: arg1 is less than or equal to arg2.
>
> -gt: arg1 is greater than arg2.
>
> -ge: arg1 is greater than or equal to arg2.

Beside binary operators, the test facility provides you with many valuable unary operators (to test against a single argument). Unary operators more often than not are used to perform tests against filesystem objects. Two of the most common unary operators are -f and -d, which respectively test for the presence of a file or directory.

```
if [ -d /System/Library/CoreServices/Finder.app ]; then
        echo 'Finder was Found!'
fi
```

This code will print the text "Finder was found!" if a directory exists at the path /System/Library/CoreServices/Finder.app (which is true in any OS X system because the application bundle "Finder" is in fact a directory like almost all modern apps). There are numerous unary operators, most easily found by consulting the man page for test, using man test. Here are some that are notable:

> -f string: True if string is the path to a regular file
>
> -d string: True if string is the path to a directory
>
> -r/-w/-x string: True if string is a file that is readable, writeable, or executable (respectively)
>
> -L string: True if string is a path to a symbolic link
>
> -z/-n string: True if string is zero or nonzero length (respectively)

Note You can also run these checks directly using the test command (although you might have to wrap the test condition in quotes or double parentheses depending on exactly what you're attempting to test), like so:

```
test -d /Users/ && echo "directory exists"
```

```
#!/bin/bash
if ( [ "$USER" == "janedoe" ] || [ "$USER" ="jsmith" ] ); then
echo "User is jane or john"
else
        echo "User is not jane or john"
fi
```

In the if/elif example, we are also demonstrating the use of the logical OR operator, ||.

```
if ( [ "$USER" ="janedoe" ] || [ "$USER" ="jsmith" ] ); then
```

The logical OR operator and its partner the logical AND operator (&&), often referred to as Boolean operators, are used to test against multiple expressions. In the previous implementation, you are using the logical OR operator to test against two possible usernames, janedoe and jsmith. You want to know if a user is *either* of these usernames, so you need to be able to run both tests. In this example, if you used && instead of ||, the end result would always evaluate to false, as the $USER variable will never be equal to both values. When using logical operators && and || to combine expressions, execution of the control statement will terminate immediately after it evaluates to false or true, respectively. Thus, in the previous example, if the username is janedoe, the test will never be executed against jsmith. In similar spirit, if you used && in that statement, the test against jsmith will only ever get tested if the first expression is true (the username is janedoe). Understanding this becomes important when writing clean, effective code. Recognizing this, you can take previous example:

```
if [ -d /System/Library/CoreServices/Finder.app ]; then
        echo 'Finder Found!'
fi
```

and then slim it down to a single "one-liner":

```
[ -d /System/Library/CoreServices/Finder.app ] && echo 'Finder found!'
```

As you learned earlier, if the expression returns false (in this case because the directory could not be found), then the test will abort, and the printf statement will never fire. In this iteration, you are also omitting the if control statement because the branching code (printf "Finder found!\n") can easily fit onto a single line.

In the previous example, the case statement, as you may have deduced, also uses a logical OR operator, implemented by supplying multiple matches in a single test block.

```
case "$USER" in
"janedoe")
        echo "My name is Jane Doe";;
"jsmith")
        echo "My name is John Smith";;
*)
        echo "Remember Sammy Jenkins…";;
esac
```

In this example, by placing both janedoe and jsmith together, you are implying a logical OR between the two values. A case statement will then perform a string comparison of $USER to the string janedoe and, if no match is found, will test against jsmith, and so on. Once a match is found, it will execute any preceding lines of code until it runs against the break specifier (;;). In the case of janedoe or jsmith, a match would result solely in the execution of the code: echo My name is Jane Doe. Unlike if/else statements, case statements do not have access to the more advanced unary or binary operators provided by Bash. They are pretty much limited to string comparisons and thus provide only limited (but important) functionality.

for, while, and until Statements

So, at this point, you have learned how to define the flow of a program through the use of branching statements, expressions, and conditional operators. Automation, however, is rarely about performing an operation once; the benefits of automation lie in the ability to scale production as needed with minimal investment. Automation is particularly well-suited for boring, repetitive tasks that will result in hundreds, thousands, or even millions of iterations. To harness the ability of repetition and iteration, Bash provides three looping statements: for, while, and until. The for loop is utilized for iterating over items.

```
declare plistbuddy="/usr/libexec/PlistBuddy"
declare python="/usr/bin/python"

REQUIRED_COMMANDS="$plistbuddy $python"
for COMMAND in $REQUIRED_COMMANDS; do
        if [ -x $COMMAND ] ; then
                echo "Command: $COMMAND is installed"
        else
                echo "Command: $COMMAND is missing"
        fi
done
```

Every element of this script is native to Bash and would output the following text:

```
Command: /usr/libexec/PlistBuddy is installed
Command: /usr/bin/python is installed
```

> **Note** To determine whether a command will result in the execution of an external program, use type followed by the name of the function. If the process is external to the shell, it will specify the absolute path to the binary (as found in $PATH). For example, type echo returns echo is a shell builtin, meaning that Bash will use its internal echo ability rather than the external command /bin/echo when the echo command is called in a script.

The while and until statements are used for building more customized looping structures. The -ge operator allows you to loop while certain criteria are met.

```
while [ $( ps aux | grep -v "grep" | grep -c "Finder" ) -ge 1 ];
do
        echo "Finder is still running"
        sleep 15
done
```

In this example, there are a few new concepts. First, whenever you use expressions, they are primarily expecting string arguments. If you want to call an external program inside an expression, you must designate that the text not be treated as a string but rather as an external process. To do this, you wrap the entire command pipeline inside $(). This wrapper tells the shell to evaluate the contents of the entire pipeline in a subshell. This same behavior applies if you want to assign the output of a command to a variable. The following syntax is used to set the value of variable $psTxt to the output of the ps command chain (this time you will use grep with pipes to accomplish the same count):

```
psTxt=$( ps aux | grep -v "grep" | grep -c "Finder" )
```

Examining this command chain, you see that you are utilizing the external programs ps and grep. The ps command lists running processes, and grep is a basic filtering tool. Because grep is a program, it will sometimes be found in the ps process list, so you must first filter out the own grep line, using the -v flag. Then you do a search for the string "Finder." The -c flag specifies that you will output the number of matches. If you find one or more processes, you proceed through the loop. Next you output a simple text line stating that the program is running, and then you sleep for 15 seconds. At this point, the end of the loop has been reached, and you will once again test for the criteria. If the criteria match, you proceed through the loop again, indefinitely, until the criteria fail to match.

The until loop represents a different utility. In Bash it does not represent true trailing logic (as it does in C) but rather serves as an inverse of the while loop. Because of this, it is of rather limited use. For example, you can pretty easily replicate the logic of the previous example's while loop, simply inversing the conditional logic.

```
until [ $(ps aux | grep -v "grep" | grep -c "Finder" ) -lt 1 ];
do
        printf "Finder is Running\n"
        sleep 15
done
```

Note   Bash, like most languages, provides control statements for managing individual loop iterations. For instance, the control statement continue will instruct a loop to terminate the execution for that particular instance, at which point it will return to its evaluation statement (or the next iterated item in the case of a for loop) and continue through the loop. The break statement will instruct a loop to terminate completely.

Arrays

An array, sometimes known as a *vector*, is one of the simplest data structures. Arrays hold a collection of values, generally of the same data type. Each element uses a consecutive range of numbers (integers) to retrieve and store the values. Bash has basic support for one-dimensional arrays. Creating a basic array in Bash is pretty simple.

```
## set the variable MY_APPS to an array populated with a directory listing of /Applications
declare -a MY_APPS=(/Applications/*.app)
```

You can then iterate through these items with a for loop.

```
for APP in "${MY_APPS[@]}"; do
      echo "Application: $APP"
done
```

There are a few things to note in this code. In the for statement, you quote the array string ${MY_APPS[@]} to ensure that individual items with spaces or tabs in the data are escaped. When accessing a specific index in an array, the curly braces are always needed with the index number specified inside them. For instance, here's how to access the first item list in the applications:

```
${MY_APPS[1]}.
```

You can also assign arrays using numeric methodology.

```
declare -a USER_NAME[501]=charles
declare -i USER_UID=501

echo ${USER_NAME[501]}
        returns: "charles"
echo ${USER_NAME[$USER_UID]}
        returns  "charles"
```

Arrays are handy for collating and organizing data. However, their support in Bash is a bit limited compared to more robust programming environments. Also, be aware that one of the major limitations of an array is that their scope is downward only, meaning you can't export an array between scripts or functions of a script. Basically, arrays are going to work only in your main body of code and not in subprocesses you launch. In practice, this is a major limitation to consider before trying to use Bash arrays in a complicated fashion.

Exit Codes

Command-line applications, when implemented properly, will provide what is called an *exit code* or *return code* after execution. This exit code is internally defined in the program and is used to signal proper execution, or perhaps a specific error code. When a UNIX command-line utility executes successfully, it should return an integer value of 0, which indicates successful operation. Any nonzero value will represent an error condition in the code, which this is a handy way to determine whether a program properly executed. Exit codes vary from application to application and are often referenced in a command's documentation (192 is also a common error status). To check the exit code of a process, you can test against the special variable $? immediately after the command has executed:

```
rsync -avu /Folder1/ /Folder2/
if [ $? = 0 ]; then
      echo "The Rsync finished without an error!"
else
      echo "The rsync had problems!!"
fi
```

Alternatively, you can do the same thing on one line.

```
rsync -avu /Folder1/ /Folder2/ && ( echo "Rsync Finished" || echo "Rsync had problems" )
```

When writing your own scripts, it is important that you follow good practice and properly report the script's status. You do this by utilizing the exit statement in your code, followed by an integer value defining the proper state; remember to exit 0 on proper execution and use an arbitrary value of 1 or greater on error. If your script is primarily a wrapper for a different program, it may not be a bad idea to mirror its exit code by referencing the $? variable immediately following the execution of your command. Because $? will change with each process that is run, you will want to save the $? value into a separate variable for later reference in the script, allowing your script to exit with the same value of the original command that you are wrapping your logic around (such as an if or for statement).

```
rsync -avu /Folder1/ /Folder2/
declare -i RSYNC_CODE=$?
if [ $RSYNC_CODE =0 ]; then
      echo "The Rsync finished without an error!"
else
      echo "The rsync had problems!!"
fi
exit $RSYNC_CODE
```

Constructing a Shell Script

To be properly processed by a shell, a UNIX executable script must specify which interpreter the shell should use to parse and execute its contained shell code. This information is provided via a shebang or hash-bang (#!) specifier, which should always be at line 1 of the script and should precede the absolute path to the file's interpreter. For instance, in this chapter you are primarily utilizing Bash scripts. To specify the Bash interpreter, you use the following shebang specifier at the start of the script:

```
#!/bin/bash
```

> **Note** You can add an -x to the interpreter line of Bash scripts to assist with debugging. This will echo the expanded variables and actual runtime code in addition to the more common output vectors such as the echo command. Here's an example: #!/bin/Bash -x.

Using this syntax, you can also specify atypical shell interpreters, such as Perl (#!/usr/bin/perl), Python (#!/usr/bin/python), or Ruby (#!/usr/bin/ruby); the list goes on. For the most part, OS X and most *nix variants all utilize the same directory to store interactive user shells in: the /bin/ folder. This folder is defined by BSD as housing: "User utilities fundamental to both single-user and multi-user environments." This folder is common among the *nix variants and can usually be trusted to contain at least the Bourne shell (sh) and, on most modern systems, the Bash shell. However, nonshell interpreters, such as Python, Perl, or Ruby, are going to vary greatly from OS to OS. Because of this, if you want your shell to be portable (which these languages provide), then providing a static path is not going to provide much utility on nonconforming systems. If portability is your goal (and certainly it's never a bad one), you may want to forgo specifying an absolute path and instead let the parent shell dynamically determine its location. To do this, utilize the following shebang specifier:

```
#!/usr/bin/env python
```

The key thing to know here is that /usr/bin/env is a commonly supported binary and will cause the shell to search through its $PATH to locate the Python executable. If that's found in your path, this executable will be used as the interpreter for the script. The $PATH variable is an environmental variable used by nearly all shells and specifies a number of directories that should be consulted when searching for a binary. This variable contains a colon-delimited string of directories and will search through them in order of preference from left to right. For instance, if you run the command echo $PATH, you will see all the directories in your path.

```
echo $PATH
/usr/bin:/bin:/usr/sbin:/sbin
```

Thus, if you were to run the command `ifconfig`, your shell would first look for the binary `ifconfig` in the `/usr/bin` folder, then in `/bin`, `/usr/sbin`, and so on, until it ultimately finds the command (in this case, in the `/sbin` directory). If the command is not found after searching the entire path, the shell will terminate execution of the script with an error. On top of this, the PATH variable becomes a good way for a user to inject his own versions of a binary in place of a system binary. For instance, Mr. Joebob Poweruser always likes to have the latest, greatest version of Perl on his system, dutifully installed at `/usr/local/bin/perl`. However, with a default PATH variable, when Joebob runs the command `perl`, he will be treated to your localization's binary stored at `/usr/bin/perl`. To change this, Joebob will want to modify his `~/.profile` file, adding the following line:

```
export PATH="/usr/local/bin:$PATH"
```

After doing this, when Joebob starts a shell, the path `/usr/local/bin` will be the first folder searched in his path. Knowing all of this, it is easy to see how utilizing `/usr/bin/env` in your shebang line can provide benefits if your script will have a wide audience.

> **Note**   With all the variants of Linux and UNIX systems, it certainly can be a mental exercise to remember each one's folder hierarchy. For this purpose, many such systems provide documentation as to their particular folder eccentricities. On such systems, you can access this documentation via the `hier` man page by running the command `man hier` at your Terminal prompt.

With the shebang out of the way, you can now start writing your script. Typically at this point in the script, you will do what is referred to as *initialization*. That is, you will define the variables to be utilized by the script. Initializing all your variables at the beginning of the script provides many benefits. Primarily, it serves as a blueprint for your script. Assuming you adopt good naming conventions for your variables, the general utility and configurability of a script can often be deduced by scanning the variables, at least to an extent. To assign a variable in Bash, you simply specify the variable name, followed by an equal sign and then the value. Here's an example:

```
USER_NAME="charles"
```

With this line, you are assigning the global variable USER_NAME the value of charles. Variables in Bash can be uppercase, can contain underscores such as PLIST_FILE, and can even be camel case, as in `plistFileNumberThree`. The choice is up to you—just be consistent. Notice that during assignment, you do not prepend the variable name with a $ specifier, unlike Perl. However, utilizing the global scope in Bash will ultimately make your code less extensible. For instance, if you were to refactor the code into a function, you could have issues with scope conflict. To address this, you can utilize the `declare` statement, which will initialize the variable only in the local context.

```
declare USER_NAME="charles"
# Charles is available only to the local context

declare -x USER_NAME="bill"
# Bill is only available to the local and sub shells

export USER_NAME="emerald"
# Emerald is available to the local sub shells and parent shells
# (but no type assignment such as array "-a" or "-i" integer)
```

Any local declares will not export to subprocesses or script functions but will stay within the current scope of code running. If you use declare in a function, once the function is complete, the variable will no longer be active. This may be advantageous if, for instance, you have a function that contains a password as a variable. If you want to keep a function's variable around after the function is complete, you can use export, as shown in this example:

```
#!/bin/bash

# This is a basic function
littleFunction(){
        declare LITTLE_VAR="local"
        export BIG_VAR="global"

        echo "$FUNCNAME: LITTLE_VAR: $LITTLE_VAR"
        echo "$FUNCNAME: BIG_VAR: $BIG_VAR"
}

littleFunction # This is how we run a function

echo "$0: BIG_VAR: $BIG_VAR"
echo "$0: LITTLE_VAR: ${LITTLE_VAR:?}" # This should error out

$ ./bigscript

littleFunction: LITTLE_VAR: local
littleFunction: BIG_VAR: global
./bigscript: BIG_VAR: global
./ bigscript: line 16: LITTLE_VAR: parameter null or not set
```

While not always necessary, it is a good idea to get in the habit of using declare statements with Bash. It will definitely save you time and headaches down the road as you find yourself needing to repurpose code.

One mistake rookie coders make is that they rely heavily on utilizing PATH resolution in shell scripts. That is, instead of typing the following command:

```
/usr/sbin/networksetup -getdnsservers "Airport"
```

they actually type the command as follows:

```
networksetup -getdnsservers "Airport"
```

This won't necessarily prove to be an issue because `networksetup` resides in the default path at `/usr/sbin`. The main problem with this methodology is that PATH variables can be manipulated rather easily. If this script were ever to get called with the `sudo` command, which escalates privileges to `uid 0`, then you could potentially compromise a machine simply by injecting your own path variable into the user environment. This way, instead of the system calling `networksetup`, someone could call your own program identically named `networksetup`, which might install goodies all over the machine. Modifying a user's PATH is rather trivial to do once a user account has been compromised and can then be used for local privilege escalation and to ultimately control the box. Several OS X escalation vulnerabilities have been found because of failure to sanitize PATH exploits.

To combat this issue, you have a few options. The first option is to manually specify the PATH variable in your script. This way, you can utilize the dynamic lookup capabilities of scripts and still provide your own known-good paths. To do this, you simply declare PATH in the global scope of the script.

```
#!/bin/bash
PATH="/usr/local/bin:/usr/bin:/bin:/usr/sbin:/sbin
```

By specifying the PATH variable, you are in essence designating trusted paths. Because you are doing this, it is important that you ensure proper restrictions are applied to these paths. You want to make sure that all specified paths are locked down from modification, restricted only to admin users. For instance, the Bash `/usr/local/bin` does not exist by default, so it could theoretically be possible for a user to create this directory, inject his own executables, and then interject those executables into your script. To prevent this, you utilize filesystem permissions. In the case of `/usr/local/bin`, a user would first have to create the `local/bin` branch. Thus, that user would need to be able to modify the directory at `/usr`. Luckily, filesystem privileges are locked down such that a user would need root access to alter any of the specified directories. If they have the ability to alter these system paths, youhave bigger issues to worry about.

Specifying a PATH for the shell script doesn't solve all issues. For instance, what if the user installs a copy of a command, which is syntactically incompatible with the options specified in your script? Perhaps only part of what you utilize the utility for in the script actually works with the user's app. In such case, your script would certainly execute abnormally, at best merely failing to execute, but in a worse-case scenario, the side effects could certainly prove to be damaging. For this reason, you may want to allow a specific binary to be utilized only for the context of your script. The standard methodology to implement this is to declare full commands as variables and then call that variable instead of the command. Also, you can use the `-x` test to see whether the command is executable.

```
#!/bin/bash

declare networksetup =" /usr/sbin/networksetup "

if [ -x $networksetup ] ; then
     $networksetup -setv6off "Airport"
else
     echo "$networksetup is missing, is this Tiger(10.4)?"
fi
```

This practice certainly has its benefits. First, you ensure that all binary paths are hard-coded to the system defaults. Of course, ensuring that the system's default software has not been altered is outside of your control. You could certainly calculate md5 sums or check binary version output, but the risk/effort rewards really aren't there; it is perfectly sensible for your script to assume a stock software package, particularly in the context of this chapter.

The second benefit to declaring your commands is that you now have a nice list of all external commands utilized by the script, which is great way to show your users what you are using to make your script work.

Passing Arguments to Shell Scripts

When a script is called, it can have options, much like the options present in commands you run in OS X. These commands are programmatically stored in a predefined variable called a *positional parameter*. The positional parameters are easily identified because they are $1, $2, $3, and so on, with each position the area between a space and the next input. For example, to send a command called foo a variable called bar, you would use the command foo bar, which would result in being able to use the variable $1 in the script. In the following script, you declare a number of variables and even put the target of the script and the information to change within the script as follows. This is an example postflight script in a package installer. Apple's installer will pass these parameters to a script automatically, but you can simulate them with the following command:

```
sudo /path/to/this_script 1 2 /Volumes/Macintosh\ HD  /Volumes/Macintosh\ HD

sudo /path/to/this_script 1 2 /Volumes/ /
```

> **Note** We are putting the placeholders 1 and 2 here to stand in for what would really be passed during an install. In this case, because we don't use $1 or $2, any value here would do just to make sure the count was right. This is a common way of testing scripts that are destined for Apple package installers.

```bash
#!/bin/bash
# This script removes the time machine prompt from newly created users
# $1 and $2 are not used in this script
declare -x DSTROOT="$3" .              # Installation Volume of mount point.
declare -x SYSROOT="$4"                # The root directory for the system.
declare -x USER_TEMPLATE="/System/Library/User Template/English.lproj"
declare -x PLIST=\
"${DSTROOT:?}/${USER_TEMPLATE:?}/Library/Preferences/com.apple.TimeMachine.plist"

declare defaults="/usr/bin/defaults"
"$defaults" write "$PLIST" 'DoNotOfferNewDisksForBackup' -bool 'YES' &&
echo "$PLIST updated successfully"
exit 0
```

Scheduling Automations

There will be times when you will need to schedule your scripts to perform various tasks. Maybe you want to periodically run a backup, check and repair permissions, run system maintenance, run updates, or perform whatever it is that you want your machines to do in the wee hours of the morn. No matter, OS X has a scheduler that will fit your need. OS X's scheduling capabilities are rooted both in the past and in the present; its BSD heritage has provided it with traditional *nix schedulers in cron and at. A more modern scheduler is provided with launchd, which brings with it a number of advantages and a prerequisite to reconsider how schedules are run.

launchd

launchd is a fairly complex beast and much more than "just" a scheduler. It provides a job-watching capability, allowing your scripts to loop and even crash and be restarted. It can also watch a folder path or individual file for changes, a common way of triggering an action. Moreover, launchd allows for items to be created and run by root but also by ordinary users. As we will show, you can even include scripts right in launchd items, making the whole thing self-contained. It also presents an interesting solution to the scheduling problem and as such becomes a handy tool for scheduling automations. To schedule an automation, you must first construct a launchd.plist file. This plist file contains a number of keys that tell launchd how to treat your program. Each launchd.plist file contains a unique label, a series of program arguments, and a schedule defined for that program. When loaded by launchd, the superdaemon will fire your program and specified arguments.

A launch daemon is a plist file that can be deployed in two different domains, which ultimately control the resources that the respective process will have. Launch daemons, installed at /Library/LaunchDaemons and /System/Library/LaunchDaemons, are considered system domains, though the latter should not be touched outside of Apple-provided files. The plist file should be named using reverse-domain notation, similar to other preference files in OS X. As the name *launch daemon* implies, most standard UNIX daemons are now handled through launch daemons. For instance, ntpd, OS X's time synchronization service, can be found at /System/Library/LaunchDaemons/org.ntp.ntpd.plist.

A launch agent, on the other hand, is a `launchd.plist` file that specifies a process that will run in the context of the user's environment. For this reason, agents are extremely useful for deploying user-based automations but a poor choice for system-level automations. If your process has dependencies on a windowserver process, such as an AppleScript/osascript, launch agents afford you access to that resource. Outside of these differences, all information provided over the next few pages describing `launchd.plists` are true of both launch daemons and agents, unless specifically stated otherwise.

From a scheduling perspective, `launchd` allows for two different types of schedules: recurring intervals and specified schedules. The `StartInterval` key can be used to specify a sleep interval in seconds that will take place between executions of a program. In contrast, the `StartCalendarInterval` key consists of a dictionary, which can be used to specify regularly scheduled maintenance. This dictionary consists of keys for `Hour`, `Minute`, `Weekday`, and `Day` (1-31). In both cases, `launchd` will monitor the processes that it launches and ensure that there are never any overlapping instances.

To create a `launchd plist` from scratch, luckily you can use the familiar `defaults` command (assuming a `com.krypted.syncdata` defaults domain).

```
sudo defaults write /Library/LaunchDaemons/com.krypted.syncdata Label com.krypted.syncdata
sudo defaults write /Library/LaunchDaemons/com.krypted.syncdata ProgramArguments -array
"/usr/bin/rsync" "-avu" "/Folder1/" "/Folder2/"
sudo defaults write /Library/LaunchDaemons/com.krypted.syncdata StartInterval -int 3600
sudo plutil -convert xml1 /Library/LaunchDaemons/com.krypted.syncdata.plist
```

This will create a `launchd plist` file that performs the following command, every hour (3,600 seconds):

```
/usr/bin/rsync -avu /Folder1/ /Folder2/
```

and has the following structure:

```
<?xml version="1.0" encoding="UTF-8"?>
<!DOCTYPE plist PUBLIC "-//Apple//DTD PLIST 1.0//EN" "http://www.apple.com/DTDs/
PropertyList-1.0.dtd">
<plist version="1.0">
<dict>
        <key>Label</key>
        <string>com.krypted.syncdata</string>
        <key>ProgramArguments</key>
        <array>
                <string>/usr/bin/rsync</string>
                <string>-avu</string>
                <string>/Folder1/</string>
                <string>/Folder2/</string>
        </array>
        <key>StartInterval</key>
        <integer>3600</integer>
</dict>
</plist>
```

> **Tip**   For human-readable text, convert the plist file to xml1 format (from binary) prior to viewing or editing. Do so using the following syntax:
>
> ```
> plutil -convert xml1 /Library/LaunchDaemons/<file>.plist
> ```

As you can see, a program and its arguments are specified in the plist as individual items in an array. Each item will be passed to the command as individual (escaped) strings.

To use a calendar interval, you can specify a `StartCalendarInterval` dict. First, though, you will delete the `StartInterval` key. While both `StartInterval` and `StartCalendarInterval` entries will be honored, it's not an elegant way to do automations (though perhaps useful in some circumstances).

```
sudo defaults delete \
/Library/LaunchDaemons/com.krypted.syncdata StartInterval
sudo defaults write \
/Library/LaunchDaemons/com.krypted.syncdata StartCalendarInterval -dict Hour -int 3 Minute
-int 0 Weekday -int 0
sudo plutil -convert xml1 /Library/LaunchDaemons/com.krypted.syncdata.plist
```

This will change the automation to fire every Sunday at 3 a.m. All these values are strict integer values, and no logic is allowed. If you are looking for more flexibility in scheduling, cron might be a good solution.

If you are looking for an easier way to generate launchd plist files, consider the popular GUI tools Lingon, available at `https://www.peterborgapps.com/lingon/`, or LaunchControl, available at `www.soma-zone.com/LaunchControl/`.

cron

Although deprecated by Apple in favor of launchd, cron still exists to some degree in OS X. The cron daemon itself is fired via `launchd`. Its `plist` is found at `/System/Library/LaunchDaemons/com.vix.cron.plist`. However, this has no impact on the actual operation of cron as you would find on a different system. Individual users can configure their own crontab, stored in `/var/at/tabs/username`, which is symlinked in later versions of OS X from `/usr/lib/cron`. Naturally, each user's `crontab` runs in the context of that user but does not necessarily need the user to be logged in (unless a window server connection is needed by the called process). You can edit a user's `crontab` by running the terminal command `crontab -e` while logged in. When run, the command will drop you into a `vi` editor and will open the user's crontab. A crontab is a file that lists a process and its scheduling information on a single line of text. The schedule is the first part of the line and includes five tab-separated values, shown here, that precede the actual cron entry:

```
##Minute Hour  MonthDay(1-31) Month (1-12) Weekday (0-7)    Command
*    *    *    *    *                      /usr/local/bin/myscript.sh
```

> **Note** You can change the default editor from vi to pico by running export EDITOR=pico
> before you run crontab -e. However, we suggest you give vi a chance because it's a lifesaver
> when it comes to toolkits.

This code is a valid cron entry. The * designates it will match any condition. Therefore, the previous script will fire once per minute forever. cron also supports ranges and logic.

```
##Minute Hour MonthDay(1-31) Month (1-12) Weekday (0-7) Command
*/15     */2  *              *            1,3,5         /usr/local/bin/myscript.sh
```

In the previous entry, the script will run every 15 minutes, every other (even) hour, on Monday, Wednesday, and Friday. While this particular schedule may seem a little silly, it is meant mainly to illustrate the flexibility of the cron scheduling engine. Certain workflows have particular schedules, and the ability to shape your automations around such schedules is great to have at your fingertips.

Aside from editing individual user crontabs, a global "root" crontab exists, now also found at /var/at/tabs/root rather than at /etc/crontab with earlier versions of OS X. This file is similar to other crontabs, but it introduces yet another element, the username under which the process will be executed.

```
##Minute Hour MonthDay(1-31) Month (1-12) Weekday (0-7) User Command
*/15     */2  *              *            1,3,5         root /usr/local/bin/myscript.sh
```

OS X also has support for the at scheduling engine, though it is disabled by default. For the most part, launchd and cron should be able to meet your needs, but if you must have at, it is there for you. To use it, all you have to do is load its launchd plist file.

```
sudo launchctl load -w /System/Library/LaunchDaemons/com.apple.atrun.plist
```

Now you can use at for scheduling.

```
at now + 1 minute
echo "hello" > /test.txt
job 4 at Tue Jun 9 01:16:00 2009

atq
4       Tue Jun 9 01:16:00 2009
```

Daily, Weekly, and Monthly Scripts

OS X ships with a number of scripts that run on a timed interval, including those that run on a daily, weekly, or monthly schedule. These scripts are invoked by entries in the /System/Library/LaunchDaemons directory: com.apple.periodic-daily.plist, com.apple.periodic.weekly.plist, and com.apple.periodic.month.plist, respectively. The periodic scripts are located in /etc/periodic and include the following:

- /etc/periodic/daily/110.clean-tmps
- /etc/periodic/daily/130.clean-msgs
- /etc/periodic/daily/140-clean-rwho
- /etc/periodic/daily/199.clean-fax
- /etc/periodic/daily/310.accounting
- /etc/periodic/daily/400.status-disks
- /etc/periodic/daily/420.status-network
- /etc/periodic/daily/430.status-rwho
- /etc/periodic/daily/999.local
- /etc/periodic/monthly/199.rotate-fax
- /etc/periodic/monthly200.accounting
- /etc/periodic/monthly/999.local
- /etc/periodic/weekly/320.whatis
- /etc/periodic/weekly/999.local

Triggered Automations

Scheduled automations are nice, but wouldn't it be great to fire certain automations just when you want to? The answer is yes, and the solution is triggers. A *trigger* is a generic term for any event that can affect, or "trigger," the operation of a process. In OS X, there are a number of different triggers that can fire automations. Discussed fairly extensively in Chapter 7, login hooks are a popular form of triggers. Similarly, launch agents can be instructed to run at login. To do this, set the key RunAtLoad to true, using the command that follows:

```
sudo defaults write /Library/LaunchAgents/com.krypted.syncdata RunAtLoad -bool true
```

In addition to this, OS X has a few facilities you can use to trigger your automations. The most common use of triggers in OS X are filesystem watchers, which fire based on certain filesystem activity. These types of automations in OS X are provided through launchd. Specifically, launchd provides three functions for monitoring filesystem activity.

- *WatchPaths*: An array of file paths that, when modified, will trigger a script
- *QueueDirectories*: An array of directory paths that will trigger whenever a file is added or removed
- *StartOnMount*: A bool value that, if set to true, means the script will fire whenever a new filesystem (disk) is mounted

For instance, you could utilize this behavior to sync a directory to a volume whenever it is mounted. To perform this task, you will first write your basic script, as shown here:

```
#!/bin/bash

## check for the presence of our volume
if [ "$(df -lh | grep "MyVolumeName" )" ]; then
        rsync -av /Folder1/ /MyVolumeName/Folder1_backup/
fi
```

and then create and edit the plist at /Library/LaunchDaemons/com.krypted.MyVolumeSync.

```
<?xml version="1.0" encoding="UTF-8"?>
<!DOCTYPE plist PUBLIC "-//Apple//DTD PLIST 1.0//EN" "http://www.apple.com/DTDs/
PropertyList-1.0.dtd">
<plist version="1.0">
<dict>
        <key>Label</key>
        <string>com.krypted.myvolumesync</string>
        <key>ProgramArguments</key>
        <array>
                <string>/usr/local/bin/myVolumeSync.sh</string>
        </array>
        <key>RunAtLoad</key>
        <false/>
        <key>StartOnMount</key>
        <true/>
</dict>
</plist>
```

Now, whenever MyVolume is plugged in, the script will fire, pass its test, and perform the sync. Alternatively, you may want to fire a script whenever a network configuration changes. Network configuration changes occur whenever an interface is taken off or brought online and therefore can be a good way to trigger a script when a machine first joins your network. This can be handy for initiating client-side backups on laptops that are rarely in the office. By configuring a backup to fire at network change, you can ensure these mostly absent machines don't waste any time in initiating their backup upon returning to the network.

Self-destructing Scripts

In some cases, you may want your script to run only once and then remove all traces that it ever existed on a system. In such cases, you can actually have the script delete itself. Because the entire script is loaded into memory, this won't affect the operation of the script's code; the file will just disappear after execution. This can be handy if you have sensitive data in the script. For instance, a bind script will likely contain a password, and it would be undesirable to leave that sitting around on every machine in the fleet, even if the credentials have extremely limited access. To remove a script when it is complete, you can just put the following line at the end of the script:

```
srm "$0"
```

The srm command is an Apple-provided equivalent of the rm command but will perform a "secure erase" by writing new, random data over the file's previous data to limit its recoverability.

The same logic can be applied to launchd items. If you want to deploy a one-time login action, you can make the launchd item itself self-destructing. For example, the following launchagent will enable Apple Remote Desktop (ARD), but when it's done, it will remove itself. This is done by chaining multiple commands together via a single ProgramArgument string.

```
<plist version="1.0">
<dict>
        <key>Disabled</key>
        <false/>
        <key>Label</key>
        <string>com.krypted.enableard</string>
        <key>OnDemand</key>
        <false/>
        <key>ProgramArguments</key>
        <array>
                <string>bash</string>
                <string>-c</string>
                <string>/System/Library/CoreServices/RemoteManagement/↩
ARDAgent.app/Contents/Resources/kickstart -configure -access -on -privs↩
 -all -users adm_mako ;
/System/Library/CoreServices/RemoteManagement/ARDAgent.app/Contents/Resources/↩
kickstart -configure -clientopts -setdirlogins -dirlogins yes -setdirgroups↩
 -dirgroups ardadmin ; /System/Library/CoreServices/RemoteManagement/↩
ARDAgent.app/Contents/Resources/kickstart -activate ;
/System/Library/CoreServices/RemoteManagement/ARDAgent.app/Contents/Resources/↩
kickstart -configure -allowAccessFor -specifiedUsers -setreqperm yes;
/usr/bin/srm /Library/LaunchDaemons/net.walledcity.enableard.plist;
/bin/launchctl remove /Library/LaunchDaemons/net.walledcity.enableard.plist
exit 0</string>
        </array>
</dict>
</plist>
```

> **Note** In most UNIX shells, the semicolon (;) can be used to separate individual commands on a single line. When separating commands via a semicolon, once the first command finishes running, regardless of its exit state, the next program will fire.

Automating User Creation from a Third-Party Database

In some cases, you may need to integrate an OS X directory system with a third-party information system, such as an employee database. In an education environment, for example, tens or hundreds of thousands of student records exist, with new records being added every day. All of this user information exists largely in third-party databases, and you may need to ensure that records added to one system can easily be added to Open Directory.

To successfully import the data, you must get it into an acceptable format. Importing data into Open Directory can be performed from the Server app, which supports importing data. This makes it a flexible tool for importing from third-party databases because most of these systems can import into a delimited format of some sort, most commonly .csv (comma-separated values). Once you have a .csv file in hand, you can import the file into the system. Consider a .csv file with the following data structure:

```
shortname,fname,lname,pass
jdoe,John,Doe,JD09876
jsmith,Jane,Smith,JD09876
```

This is about as clean as .csv data gets. To import the file, you can open the Server app from your Open Directory master, click Users in the sidebar, and then click the cogwheel icon under the list of users. Here, select Import Users and click the Options button to see where you'll be importing users to.

Apple has a page dedicated to importing users and groups. It was written for OS X 10.9 but is still pretty unchanged from how it's been for a long time. You can find this page at https://support.apple.com/kb/PH15663?locale=en_US; it outlines the exact values that should be in an import file and how they're processed.

This data consists of a number of values. In this code, the first value, 0x0A, denotes the record delimiter (a UNIX newline \n). The second value, 0x5C, specifies the escape character (a standard backslash: \), which is used for escaping the attribute delimiter should its value actually be required for a field. For instance, importing computer data involves importing MAC addresses, which contain a colon. If your attribute delimiter is a colon, you must escape it with the character specified, so 00:50:56:c0:00:08 must be represented as 00\:50\:56\:c0\:00\:08.

The next value in the header, 0x2C, is the attribute/field delimiter (in this case, a comma: ,). 0x3A then specifies the attribute value delimiter, used if a particular field/attribute contains more than one value. The next value, dsRecTypeStandard:Users, specifies the record type for import. You can use this tool to import users, groups, computers, computer groups, or computer lists (using the values Users, Groups, Computers, ComputerGroups, or ComputerLists).

Next, you specify the number of columns in your import file (4) and the header for each column. The headers consist of dsAttributeStandard entries, which are records abstracted for use by the Directory Services API. These attributes do not correspond to LDAP attributes directly but rather the abstracted field name. In this example, you are specifying four headers: RecordName (shortname), FirstName, LastName, and Password. A header of IGNORE can be set here to ignore the column of data. Once you specify headers, the rest of the file should consist of record and attribute data conforming to the specified delimiters.

If you have programmatic control over your information system or if its export options are decently featured, you may be able to craft your own dsimport file. If not, you'll need to process your exports so that they can conform for import.

So, to import a dsimport file into an Open Directory system, use the following command:

```
dsimport ~/Documents/users_dsimport.txt /LDAPv3/odserver.krypted.com M --userpreset
"Staff Member" --username diradmin --password 'mydiradmin password'
```

In this example, you are importing a user file into your LDAP directory using a merge. Here, you specify the -userpreset flag, which allows you to set up a preset in Workgroup Manager to establish group memberships, home directory settings, and mail and print settings. (You can create presets using Workgroup Manager.) In this command, you also supply your diradmin credentials to provide access for the import itself, presenting one of the biggest barriers to full automation for this process: any automated processes will need to have a directory administrator's credentials embedded.

However, embedding administrator credentials in a script to automate import from a CSV is not the only issue with a fully automated user-generation process. For instance, say you set up a launchdaemon with a QueueDirectory entry, which watches a directory for any new files from your information system, passes them to csvtoServer, and then uses the resulting file for import via dsimport. Such a script might look something like this:

```
#!/bin/bash

PATH=/bin;/usr/bin;/usr/local/bin

## set our variables
declare -x watchFolder="/Library/dsimportwatchdir"
declare -x dirNode="/LDAPv3/odserver.krypted.com"

## create our folder
mkdir -p "$watchFolder" &> /dev/null

## loop through all of the csv files in our watch folder, format them,
## import them, delete the formatted versions, and copy the original
## into an archive directory.
for file in $(ls -1 "$watchFolder" | grep ".csv"); do
        declare -x tempFile=$(mktemp /tmp/dsimport_XXXXX)
        cat "$watchFolder/$file" | csvtoServer -o "$tempFile"
        csvtoServerResultCode=$?
```

```
        if [ $csvtoServerResultCode == 0 ]; then
             dsimport "$tempFile" "$dirNode" M -username importadmin -password
             'importpassword'
             rm "$tempFile"
             mkdir "$watchFolder/archive/" &> /dev/null
             mv "$watchFolder/$file" "$watchFolder/archive/"
        else

             echo "Error generating import file! error num: $csvtoServerResultCode"
             exit $csvtoServerResultCode
        fi
done
```

This code would get the job done, but it does present numerous concerns. First, you are trusting the security of your user base to the contents of this folder. By using a merge import, it would certainly be possible for a file to be dropped into your watch folder that completely trashes your directory, potentially overriding data for admin accounts or simply generating accounts for itself.

Because of concerns such as these, the exact level of desired automation and, more importantly, sanity checking within your scripts will greatly vary from environment to environment and will depend on the sensitivity of the data housed by the system and the security requirements set forth by the organization. *A fully automated import process such as this is not advisable in any environment where security is a concern.* However, even if the final dsimport is a manual step, simply by generating dsimport-style import files, you are greatly reducing the possibility for human error, streamlining the import process, and ensuring more consistent results.

Note A common automation would be to tailor this same script to create computers based on imaging events on a live system. For example, an imaged computer can write a text file or copy its computer information into a centralized database to aid in managed preferences. Additionally, the imaged system could automatically connect to the patch management framework you are utilizing. Finally, for larger installations where users are actually created in out-of-band solutions (e.g., Oracle-based Student Management System or SAP-based ERP solution), you can automatically generate user accounts based on events from those databases.

Logging

If your script does anything more than a basic task, it is a good idea to log your output. Logging output can be useful to ensure that any automations are working as they should be and to catch any errors that are discovered during the operation of your scripts. Likewise, log files can prove extremely handy for the historic evaluation of performance and operation.

Depending on your script, you may want to log to ~/Library/Logs, /Library/Logs, or /private/var/log. So, how do you know which to log to? ~/Library/Logs can be used whenever a script is initiated by a user, such as through a LaunchAgent or a user-specific `crontab`. For the majority of scripts, though, which likely run with root privileges, Apple's addition of a global `/Library/Logs` is ideal for administrative script logs affecting the entire computer instead of just a user.

Logging to an output file can be achieved in a couple of ways. First, you can simply use the echo command and redirect its output to your log file. For instance:

```
logFile="/private/var/log/myprogram.log"
echo "My Program: starting rsync!" >> "$logFile"
```

This works great for sending updates to a log file, and you can use the same type of technique with any command-line program.

```
rsync -avu /folder1/ /folder1_copy/ &>> "$logFile"
```

Here, you utilize the redirect operator `&>>`, which redirects both stdout and stderr streams to `/private/var/log/myprogram.log`, appending to the end of the file. In this instance, you use this redirection if `rsync` outputs any errors; you want the errors to be written to your log.

Alternatively, you can redirect all output streams of a script to a certain file in one line. This provides a quick and easy way to ensure logging of all your script's events. To implement global redirects to your script, add the following line after your shebang and prior to the implementation of any commands or log statements:

```
logFile="/private/var/log/myprogram.log"
exec &>> "$logFile"
##From here on, all of our output will be redirected to our log file.
```

It may also be desirable to send log messages to `syslog`. This provides the added benefit of time-stamping output and provides you with the ability to integrate your script logging with a more complex `syslog` system, should your organization employ one. To send messages to syslog, use the `logger` command.

```
logger -t "$0" -p user.notice -s "hello"
```

The `-p` flag tells `logger` to log using `user.notice` priority, which `syslog` will output to the system log, `/private/var/log/system.log`.

```
Sep 7 21:23:31 helyx /usr/local/bin/myprogram.sh[1461]: hello
```

The priority `user.notice` is the default priority, and in this case, the entire `-p user.notice` flag can be omitted; it is added mainly to illustrate how to define custom logging priorities should you want to integrate with a more complex `syslog` system. The string "hello" is also output to the console because of running `logger` with the `-s` flag. This makes it extremely handy for scripts that might be run by hand. By using `logger` instead of `echo` and global redirects, you can ensure that users receive feedback from your program directly in the terminal. In addition, by utilizing `syslog`, your scripts will be more adaptable, should you adopt a more capable logging system.

Working with Date and Time

There are many instances where it can be beneficial to work with dates in your script. At a terminal prompt, it is really straightforward to grab the date—simply use the date command with no arguments, and you will get something similar to the following, including the day, date, time (with seconds), time zone, and year:

```
Wed Oct 28 22:11:45 CDT 2015
```

In a shell script, this output can be fairly challenging to parse, especially in cases where you need to do calculations based upon the time. Here you're going to grab the current system date from ESX, OS X, or Linux (or any OS really) and then use a variable, currentdate, to put that date into a pretty standard format, YYYYMMDD:

```
declare -x currentdate="$(date "+%Y%m%d")"
```

This will set the value of current date to the following:

```
20151028
```

Now, in the shell script, you can create files, add lines to files, and so forth, with the shortened date stamp. Some of you will be using log analyzers that depend, for example, on UNIX epoch time. To grab the date formatted as such, use the following command:

```
currentdate="$(date +"%s")"
```

UNIX epoch time is a numerical value representing the number of seconds since January 1, 1970, UTC. It is extremely useful if you want to perform basic math on time because this value can be used in base 10 arithmetic. For instance, you can use it in your script to track the amount of time a process takes and then output as you please.

```
#!/bin/bash
starttime="$(date +"%s")"

## redirect all output to my logfile
exec &>> /var/log/myscript.log

ditto /folder1/ /folder2/

## do our time calculations
endtime=$(date +'%s')
totaltime=$(expr $endtime - $starttime)

## format time values in human readable format
if [ $totaltime -ge 7200 ]; then
    hours=$(expr $totaltime / 3600)
    adjtime=$(expr $totaltime % 3600)
    hourmsg="$hours hours"
else
    adjtime=$totaltime
fi
```

```
min=$(expr $adjtime / 60)
secs=$(expr $adjtime % 60)
timemsg="$min minutes $secs seconds"
if [ "$status" = 0 ]; then
        echo "$instance Finished with no errors! Duration: $hourmsg $timemsg"
else
        echo "$instance Encountered error code: $status Duration: $hourmsg $timemsg"
fi
```

The date command isn't used as much to set time anymore since most systems rely on a Network Time Protocol (NTP) server to supply date and time information. However, it is worth noting that the date command can also be used to set the time on a computer.

Configuring Local Administrative Permissions

One thing you may notice after working with Open Directory is that there is no good way to define local administrator access to desktops via an Open Directory group. You can add users to the Open Directory Admin group, but because of the way that the DS search path is traversed (explained in Chapter 2), OS X desktops will search the local admin group for many administrative checks. Unlike the Active Directory plug-in, the LDAPv3 plug-in does not provide the ability to specify a local administrative group mapping. So, you, the administrator, are left to your own devices to accomplish this task. Luckily, you have just what you need.

```
#!/bin/bash


############################
##
## Local Permissioning script for setting local administrative groups
## for system and ARD admin access.
## Uses dseditgroup to modify the active systems group membership. As
## Such, it can only operate on the active system volume.
##
## Written by Beau Hunter
## beauh@mac.com
##
##########################################################

declare -x version=08310901
export PATH="/usr/bin:/bin:/usr/sbin:/sbin"

## vars
## localAdminGroup: specify network group to provide local admin access to
declare -x localAdminGroup="od_desktopadmins"

## setupLocalARDGroups: if '1', ard access groups
## will be created in local Directory Services
declare -x -i setupLocalARDGroups=1
```

```
## resetARD: if '1', ARD access will be configured
declare -x -i configARD=1

## resetARD: if '1', all ARD access privileges will be reset
declare -x -i resetARD=1

## ardAdminUser: the specified user will be have ARD admin access
declare -x ardAdminUser="hax_admin"

## ardAdminGroup: the specified group will be given ARD admin access
declare -x ardAdminGroup="mobo"

## ardInteractGroup: the specified group will be given ARD interact access
declare -x ardInteractGroup="monitors"

## static and system vars
declare -x scriptName=setNetworkAdminRights
declare -x theDate=$(date +'%Y%m%d')
declare -x -i isTiger="$(sw_vers | grep -c 10.4)"
declare -x -i isLeopard="$(sw_vers | grep -c 10.5)"
declare -x -i isSnowLeopard="$(sw_vers | grep -c 10.6)"
declare -x ARDVersion="$(defaults read ↵
/System/Library/CoreServices/RemoteManagement/ARDAgent.app/Contents/Info ↵
CFBundleShortVersionString)"
declare -x -i ARDMajorVersion="$(echo "$ARDVersion" | awk -F. '{print $1}')"
declare -x -i ARDMinorVersion="$(echo "$ARDVersion" | awk -F. '{print $2}')"

function getGUIDforGroup() {
    ## outputs a GUID for passed group name
    declare -x theGroupName="$1"
    declare -x GUID="$(/usr/bin/dscl /Search read /Groups/"$theGroupName" GeneratedUID | ↵
    awk '{print $2}')"
    if [ ! -z "$GUID" ]; then
        echo $GUID
    else
        logger -s -t "$scriptName" "Error! Could not determine GUID for group↵
        \"$theGroupName\""
        return 1
    fi
    return 0
}

if [ "$USER" != root ]; then
    echo "Must run as root user, exiting!!"
    exit 1
fi
```

```
if [ ! -z "$localAdminGroup" ]; then
    GUID=$(getGUIDforGroup "$localAdminGroup")
  if [ $? == 0 ]; then
    logger -s -t "$scriptName" "Nesting Directory Group: $localAdminGroup into local ↵
    Group: admin"
    /usr/sbin/dseditgroup -o edit -a "${localAdminGroup:?}" -t group admin
  else
    logger -s -t "$scriptName" "Error! Could not determine GUID for group ↵
    \"$localAdminGroup\""
  fi
fi

if [ $configARD -eq 1 ]; then
        if [ $setupLocalARDGroups -eq 1 ]; then
      if [ "$isSnowLeopard" -ge 1 ]; then
        ardAdminLocalGroup="com.apple.local.ard_admin"
        ardInteractLocalGroup="com.apple.local.ard_interact"
      else
        ardAdminLocalGroup="ard_admin"
        ardInteractLocalGroup="ard_interact"
      fi
        else
        ardAdminLocalGroup=$ardAdminGroup
      ardInteractLocalGroup=$ardInteractGroup
    fi

  ## Process our Admin Group
  if [ ! -z "$ardAdminGroup" ]; then
    GUID=$(getGUIDforGroup "$ardAdminGroup")
    if [ $? == 0 ]; then
        if [ $setupLocalARDGroups -eq 1 ]; then
        logger -s -t "$scriptName" "Nesting Directory Group: $ardAdminGroup into ↵
        local Group: $ardAdminLocalGroup"
        /usr/bin/dscl . read /Groups/$ardAdminLocalGroup &> /dev/null || ↵
        /usr/sbin/dseditgroup -o create -i 115 -g 2806364B-49F6-4F18-89F9-D159BB93B08C ↵
        $ardAdminLocalGroup
        /usr/sbin/dseditgroup -o edit -a "${ardAdminGroup:?}" -t group ↵
        $ardAdminLocalGroup
      fi
    else
      logger -s -t "$scriptName" "Error! Failed to create Local ARD Admin Group: ↵
      $ardAdminLocalGroup"
      errorCode=1
    fi
  fi
  ## Process our Interact Group
  if [ ! -z "$ardInteractGroup" ]; then
    GUID=$(getGUIDforGroup "$ardInteractGroup")
    if [ $? == 0 ]; then
        if [ $setupLocalARDGroups -eq 1 ]; then
                logger -s -t "$scriptName" "Nesting Directory Group: ↵
                $ardInteractGroup into local Group:$ardInteractLocalGroup"
```

```
            /usr/bin/dscl . read /Groups/"$ardInteractLocalGroup" &> /dev/null || ↵
            /usr/sbin/dseditgroup -o create -i 116 -g 2806364B-49F6-4F18-89F9-D159BB93B08D ↵
            "$ardInteractLocalGroup"
                /usr/sbin/dseditgroup -o edit -a "$ardInteractGroup" -t group ↵
            "$ardInteractLocalGroup"
            else
            ardInteractLocalGroup=$ardInteractGroup
        fi
    else
        logger -s -t "$scriptName" "Error! Failed to create Local ARD Interact Group"
        errorCode=2
    fi
fi
## Process our kickstart commands
kickstart="/System/Library/CoreServices/RemoteManagement/↵
ARDAgent.app/Contents/Resources/kickstart"
if [ $resetARD -eq 1 ]; then
        logger -s -t "$scriptName" "Resetting ARD permissions"
        "$kickstart" -uninstall -settings
        "$kickstart" -configure -access -off
fi
if [ ! -z "$ardAdminUser" ]; then
    id "$ardAdminUser" &> /dev/null
    if [ $? == 0 ]; then
        logger -s -t "$scriptName" "Setting ARD access for user \"$ardAdminUser\""
        "$kickstart" -configure -access -on -users "$ardAdminUser" -privs -all
    else
        logger -s -t "$scriptName" "Could not resolve user \"$ardAdminUser\""
        errorCode=3
    fi
fi

## reset Directory Services and flush cache
/usr/bin/dscacheutil -flushcache
/usr/bin/killall DirectoryService
sleep 2
id &> /dev/null

if ( [ ! -z "$ardAdminGroup" ] && [ ! -z "$ardInteractGroup" ] ); then
    logger -s -t "$scriptName" "Setting ARD access for groups ↵
    $ardAdminLocalGroup,$ardInteractLocalGroup"
elif [ ! -z "$ardAdminGroup" ]; then
    logger -s -t "$scriptName" "Setting ARD access for groups $ardAdminLocalGroup"
elif [ ! -z "$ardInteractGroup" ]; then
    logger -s -t "$scriptName" "Setting ARD access for groups $ardInteractLocalGroup"
fi
```

```
    if ( [ $ARDMajorVersion -eq 3 ] && [ $ARDMinorVersion -ge 3 ]); then
        logger -s -t "$scriptName" "Kickstart -configure -clientopts -setdirlogins -↵
        dirlogins yes -restart -agent"
        "$kickstart" -configure -clientopts -setdirlogins -dirlogins yes -restart -agent
    elif ( [ $ARDMajorVersion -eq 3 ] ) ; then
        logger -s -t "$scriptName" "Kickstart -configure -clientopts -setdirlogins -↵
        dirlogins yes -setdirgroups -dirgroups $ardAdminLocalGroup,$ardInteractLocalGroup ↵
        -restart -agent"
        "$kickstart" -configure -clientopts -setdirlogins -dirlogins yes -setdirgroups -↵
        dirgroups $ardAdminLocalGroup,$ardInteractLocalGroup -restart -agent
    else
        logger -s -t "$scriptName" "ARD Version: $ARDVersion not supported!"
        exit 5
    fi
fi
```

Allowing Local Users to Manage Printers

You can also provide administrative access to a number of granular functions within OS X by adding a user to the corresponding local group, rather than having a bunch of extraneous administrative users on your system. A great example is one of the ways to allow print queue management in OS X. The Managed Client framework (MCX) has the ability to allow a user to add a printer. The following script was largely created to address an issue with older OS X 10.5–based machines, where allowing users to modify printer lists via MCX was sometimes problematic. However, the script is useful to provide granular control to printing functions. Another way to allow a user to add printers and also let them manage queues is to add a user to the lpadmin group (the group historically used for managing "line printers" that now refers to all printers). The lpadmin group provides capabilities for numerous printing functions, such as resuming print queues, which is not available to standard users. Printing in OS X is supplied via CUPS, which provides granular access to numerous functions. The following script adds a specified Open Directory group into the local _lpadmin group, thereby granting directory users lpadmin rights:

```
#!/bin/sh

PATH=/bin:/sbin:/usr/bin:/usr/sbin

## only members of the following group will be given printer admin rights
declare -x printAdminGroup="staff"

## modifies cupsd.conf to NOT require admin group membership to add printers,
## mainly needed for early versions of 10.5 where the equivalent MCX function
## was unstable.
declare -x modifyCupsdDotConf=false

###### script usage vars, should need to make changes  beyond this point. ######
```

```
declare -x theDate=`date +'%m%d%y'`
declare -x version="20150721_20:03"
declare -x scriptTag="setPrinterAdminRights"

logger -s -t "$scriptTag" "Executing $0 v.$version…"

### Add printer admin  ###

## Make sure an admin group was specified
if [ -z "$printAdminGroup" ]; then
        logger -s -t "$scriptTag" "ERROR: No print admin group specified, exiting!"
        exit 1
fi

## Add specified admin group to local lpadmin group
logger -s -t "$scriptTag" "Adding $printAdminGroup to lpadmin group."
dseditgroup -o edit -a "$printAdminGroup" -t group lpadmin
addMemberReturnCode=$?
if [ $addMemberReturnCode == 0 ]; then
        logger -s -t "$scriptTag" "Successfully added $printAdminGroup to lpadmin"
else
        logger -s -t "$scriptTag" "Failed to add $printAdminGroup to lpadmin, returnCode: ↵
        $addMemberReturnCode"
fi

## modify our cupsd.conf file if applicable, this gives lpadmin permissions to add/modify ↵
printers
if [ ${modifyCupsdDotConf:?} == "true" ]; then
        logger -s -t "$scriptTag" "Granting group lpadmin rights to add printers in ↵
        cupsd.conf!"
        perl -00pe 's/(<Limit CUPS-Add-Modify-Printer.*?)(AuthType.*)(Require user)↵
        (\@SYSTEM$)(.*?<\/Limit>)/$1$3 \@SYSTEM \@lpadmin$5/ms' -i /etc/cups/cupsd.conf
else
        logger -s -t "$scriptTag" "cupsd.conf not being touched"
        killall cupsd
fi
```

Home Folder Permission Maintenance

If you maintain a large number of centralized home directories, you may want to periodically flush the filesystem structure on the system to guarantee proper access restrictions are in place. This can be useful, for instance, to protect files and folders that users add directly into the root of their home directory, often with global read access. Unwitting users can place sensitive data inside these folders, not realizing they are exposed to every user in the system. (User home folder structure was covered in depth in Chapter 7.)

The script listed in this section can be used to fix such permissions problems on home folders. The homeDirectories variable defines all root home folders on the machine in question and allows for a customizable depth. For instance, an institution might have two home folder sharepoints on an AFP server, say mapped to /studenthomes1 and

/studenthomes2. Inside these folders, each home folder might contain a list of subdirectories denoting the graduation year of a student, each of which contains user home directories. On top of all this, you have the local /Users sharepoint, which you will add to the system as an example. To address these three home folders, you would specify the following homeDirectories value like so:

```
homeDirectories="/studenthomes1:1,/studenthomes2:1,/Users:0"
```

Using these values, the script will iterate through each of the specified folders, repairing home folders for each user.

You can also use this script to employ ACLs for administrative access, perhaps for a group of users—supervisors—who need read/write access to all User home folders. Alternatively, you might want to give your filesystemadmins group access to all data on the share. This is specified via the aclGroups variable and allows you to indicate one of three access levels: fc (equivalent to a Full Control ACE), rw (equivalent to a Read/Write ACE), ro (equivalent to Read Only). (See Chapter 4 for more information on ACLs.) The desired access rights would be accomplished with the following aclGroups entry:

```
declare -x aclGroups="filesystemadmins:fc,supervisors:rw"
```

The script also has a variable removeOrphans that, when set to true, will remove any file or folder found at the specified home folder depth that is not associated with an active user in the system. This check will fail if the name of the folder is not equivalent to an active user's short name. This can be a handy function if you have a large number of users to manage and want to ensure that former users' folders are cleaned from the system.

By setting these variables to the desired values in the following script, you can ensure that these groups have the appropriate access to all user home folders and also that user data has complete confidentiality to the home folder's owner, outside of the ~/Public and ~/Sites directories. The script ensures that these folders have the appropriate access rights.

```sh
#!/bin/sh


##########  Home Directory Privilege Repair Script ####################
##   Written by Beau Hunter
##   beauh@mac.com
##
##   Script which automates the management of home directory permissions
##   It's typical usage is to ensure proper permissions on every user's
##   home directory. That is, mode 700 to all home folders except ~/Public
##   and ~/Sites. Additionally, if useACLs is set to true, then ACE's will
##   be pushed to each home directory for its respective user.
##
##   On top of this, you can specify global admin groups via the aclGroups
##   variable, in addition to a permission set to apply to each group.
##
##   The tool can be used to cleanup stale home
##   folders for non-existent users by placing the homes in an orphanage
##   folder.
##
######################################################################
```

```
PATH=/bin:/sbin:/usr/bin:/usr/sbin

## homeDirectories: Comma separated list of home roots, specify the
## depth via a colon. For instance, a standard
## OS X local home folder has user homes directly in
## /Users, thus I could specify a homeLoc of
## /Users:0. However, a depth of 0 is the default
## depth so it can be omitted.
declare -x homeDirectories="/testUsers:1"

declare -x repairPrivs=true
declare -x removeACLs=true
declare -x useACLs=true

## $aclGroups Groups sets an inherited ACL across $homeLoc, groups should be
## comma delimited. Access levels can be delimited with a colon,
## supported values are: "fc", "rw", and "ro". Default is rw.
## Example:
## aclGroups="admin:fc,powerusers:rw,rousers:ro"

declare -x aclGroups="admin:fc,staff:rw"
declare -x removeOrphans=true ## Remove non-user directories from the path.
declare -x orphanageName="orphanage" ## the name of the orphanage folder

#### int script vars, probably don't need to make changes beyond this point ####

declare -x date=`date +'%m%d%y'`
declare -x version="20080822_12:03"
declare -x scriptTag="$(basename "$0")"

logger -s -t "$scriptTag" "Executing script: $scriptTag v.$version"

function repairPrivs() {
        ## repair privileges on all items in a particular home folder
        ## expects home profiles based on users shortname.
        ## if the directory name is not resolvable as a user, we skip
        ## A directory path can be passed as a variable, otherwise
        ## executes based on PWD

    declare -x scriptTag="$scriptTag:repairPrivs()"

    if [ -n "$1" ]; then
        declare -x passedDirectory=$1
        if [ -d "$passedDirectory" ]; then
            cd "$passedDirectory"
        else
            logger -s -t "$scriptTag" "structureForOSX() passed directory: ↵
            \"$passedDirectory\" does not exist!"
            return 1
        fi
    fi

        logger -s -t "$scriptTag" "Validating users in \"$(pwd)\" for privilege repair"
```

```
IFS=$'\n'
for fileObject in `ls | grep -v .DS_Store | grep -v "$orphanageName" | egrep -v ↵
'^\.'`; do
        #logger -s -t "$scriptTag" "Validating $fileObject for priviledge repair"
        id "$fileObject" &> /dev/null
        if [ $? == 0 ]; then
                #logger -s -t "$scriptTag" " - validation passed, changing ↵
                permissions for $fileObject at `pwd`/$fileObject"
                logger -s -t "$scriptTag" " Validation passed for $fileObject, ↵
                changing permissions"

        else
                logger -s -t "$scriptTag" " Validation failed for '$fileObject', ↵
                it is an orphan "

                ## get our pwd and get our current directory. We
                ## mimic our structure in the orphanage, this script
                ## needs more facilities to handle depth properly.

                declare -x PWD="$(pwd)"

    if [ "$homeDepth" == 0 ]; then
        declare -x orphanDir="$homeLoc/$orphanageName"
    else
        declare -x orphanDir="$homeLoc/$orphanageName/$(basename "$PWD")"
    fi

                if [ "$removeOrphans" == true ]; then
                        logger -s -t "$scriptTag" " - Placing $fileObject in ↵
                        orphanage:$orphanDir!"
                        if [ ! -d "${orphanDir:?}" ]; then
                                mkdir -p "${orphanDir:?}"
                                if [ $? != 0 ]; then
                                        logger -s -t "$scriptTag" " - ERROR: ↵
                                        Could not create $orphanDir, not moving!"
                                        continue
                                fi
                        fi

                        mv "$fileObject" ${orphanDir:?}/
                        if [ $? != 0 ]; then
                                logger -s -t "$scriptTag" " - ERROR: ↵
                                Could not move user home \"$fileObject\" to orphanage!"
                        fi
                fi
                continue
        fi
```

```
            #echo chown -R "$fileObject":admin "$fileObject"
            chown -f -R "$fileObject":admin "$fileObject"
            if [ ${removeACLs:?} == "true" ]; then
                    #logger -s -t "$scriptTag" "  - removing ACL's"
                    chmod -f -R -N "$fileObject"
            fi

            ## Apply ACLs to the user dir, we do an explicit ACE at the user's home
            ## and then apply inherited ACLs to children.
            if [ ${useACLs:?} == "true" ]; then
                    logger -s -t "$scriptTag" "  - applying user ACL's"
                    chmod +a "$fileObject:allow:list,add_file,search,delete, ↵
add_subdirectory,delete_child,readattr,writeattr,readextattr,writeextattr, ↵
readsecurity,writesecurity,chown,file_inherit,directory_inherit" "$fileObject"
                    chmod -f -R +ai "$fileObject:allow:list,add_file,search,delete, ↵
add_subdirectory,delete_child,readattr,writeattr,readextattr,writeextattr, ↵
readsecurity,writesecurity,chown,file_inherit,directory_inherit" "$fileObject"/*
            fi

            chmod 755 "$fileObject"
            chmod -R 700 "$fileObject"/*
            if [ -d "$fileObject"/Sites ]; then
                    chmod -R 775 "$fileObject"/Sites
            fi
            if [ -d "$fileObject"/Public ]; then
                    chmod -R 775 "$fileObject"/Public
                    chmod -R 773 "$fileObject"/Public/Drop\ Box
            fi
    done
    ## if we were passed a directory, traverse out of it
    if [ -n "$passedDirectory" ]; then
        cd "$OLDPWD"
    fi
}  ## end repairPrivs()

function setACLForGroup() {
        ## passes $directory as first argument, $group as second argument, and $permissions
        ## this sets an explicit ACL at $directory, with all children receiving an ↵
        'inherited' ACL
        ## we accept several different permission types:
    ## "fc"(Full Control)
    ## "rw" (Read and Write)
    ## "ro" (Read Only)
    ## "append" (Append Only)

        declare -x directory=$1
        declare -x group=$2
        declare -x permissions=$3
        declare -x scriptTag="$scriptTag:setACLForGroup()"
```

```
logger -s -t "$scriptTag" "Attempting to apply: ACL to dir:$directory for group: ↵
$group with perms:$permissions"

    ## sanity check our directory
    if [ ! -d "$directory" ]; then
            logger -s -t "$scriptTag" " - ERROR: Could not apply ACL.. dir: ↵
            $directory does not exist!"
            return 1
    fi

    ## sanity check our group
    dscl /Search read /Groups/"$group" name &> /dev/null
    dsclCode=$?
    if [ $dsclCode != 0 ]; then
            logger -s -t "$scriptTag" " - ERROR: could not apply ACL.. group: ↵
            $group does not exist! dscl code: $dsclCode"
            return 2
    fi

    ## sanity check our permissions
    ##if ( [ "$permissions" != "fc" ] && [ "$permissions" != "rw" ] ↵
    && [ "$permissions" != "ro" ] ); then
    ##        logger -s -t "$scriptTag" "setACLForGroup() could not apply ↵
    ACL.. permissions:$permissions invalid, use 'fc'(Full Control), 'rw' (Read and Write), ↵
    'ro' (Read Only)!"
    ##        return 3
    ##fi

    ## deploy our ACL's
    case "$permissions" in
     fc) ace="allow:list,add_file,search,delete, ↵
     add_subdirectory,delete_child,readattr,writeattr,readextattr,writeextattr, ↵
     readsecurity,writesecurity,chown,file_inherit,directory_inherit";;
     rw) ace="allow:list,add_file,search,delete, ↵
     add_subdirectory,delete_child,readattr,writeattr,readextattr,writeextattr, ↵
     readsecurity,file_inherit,directory_inherit";;
     append) ace="allow:list,add_file,search,add_subdirectory, ↵
     readattr,writeattr,readextattr,writeextattr,readsecurity,file_inherit, ↵
     directory_inherit";;
     ro) ace="allow:list,search,readattr,readextattr, ↵
     readsecurity,file_inherit,directory_inherit";;
     *) logger -s -t "$scriptTag" "setACLForGroup() could not ↵
     apply ACL.. permissions:$permissions invalid!! defaulting to 'ro' (Read Only)!"
        ace="allow:list,search,readattr,readextattr, ↵
     readsecurity,file_inherit,directory_inherit"
        permissions="ro"
     ;;
esac

    logger -s -t "$scriptTag" " - applying ACL to dir:$directory for group: ↵
    $group with perms:$permissions"
```

```
    /bin/chmod +a "$group:$ace" "$directory"
        chmodCode1=$?
        if [ $? != 0 ]; then
                logger -s -t "$scriptTag" " - Failed applying ACL to
                top level of dir:$directory code:$chmodCode1… exiting!"
                return $chmodCode1
        fi

        /bin/chmod -f -R +ai "$group:$ace" "$directory"/*
        chmodCode2=$?
        if [ $? != 0 ]; then
                logger -s -t "$scriptTag" " - Failed applying ACL to dir:
                $directory code:$chmodCode2"
                return $chmodCode2
        fi

        return 0
} ## end setACLForGroup()

######### START ############
###########################

## Iterate through all of our specified homeDirectories.
OLDIFS=$IFS
IFS=','
for homeEntry in $homeDirectories; do
    ## check to ensure we have a good homeLoc
    homeLoc=$(echo $homeEntry | awk -F: '{print$1}')
    homeDepth=$(echo $homeEntry | awk -F: '/[0-9]/ {print$2}')

    if [ -z "$homeDepth" ]; then
        homeDepth=0
    fi
    if [ -d "${homeLoc:?}" ]; then
        cd "$homeLoc"
    else
        logger -s -t "$scriptTag" "Fatal error, $homeLoc is not a directory"
        errorOccured=true
    fi

    if [ $homeDepth == 0 ]; then
        if [ "$restructureHomes" == "true" ]; then
            logger -s -t "$scriptTag" "Restructuring home folders for $homeLoc"
            structureForOSX
        fi
        if [ "$repairPrivs" == "true" ]; then
            logger -s -t "$scriptTag" "Reparing Privileges for $homeLoc"
            repairPrivs
        fi
    else
        IFS=$OLDIFS
        for homeDir in `ls | grep -v "$orphanageName" | grep -v "Shared" |
        egrep -v "^\."`; do
```

```
            if [ -d "${homeLoc:?}/$homeDir" ]; then
                cd "$homeLoc/$homeDir"
            else
                continue
            fi
            if [ "$repairPrivs" == "true" ]; then
                logger -s -t "$scriptTag" "Reparing Privileges for $homeLoc/$homeDir"
                repairPrivs
            fi
            cd ..
        done
    fi


    ## Deploy our aclGroups to the root of the home directory
    if [ ! -z "$aclGroups" ]; then
        IFS=$'\,'
        for group in $aclGroups; do
            groupName=`printf "$group" | awk -F: '{print$1}'`
            groupRights=`printf "$group" | awk -F: '{print$2}'`
            setACLForGroup "$homeLoc" "$groupName" "$groupRights"
        done
    fi
done
```

Enabling the Software Firewall

The next script enables the application firewall in OS X, which should generally be done in all mass deployments where security is even a minimal concern. The script ends with exit 0, which you may have noticed in previous scripts as well. The script brings in positional parameters, setting them as variables (discussed in detail in Chapter 6). Then the paths for commands used in the script are declared, with more lines in the script dedicated to declaring variables than to the payload, a common occurrence.

```
#!/bin/bash
declare -x DSTROOT="$3"                 # Installation Volume of mount point.
declare -x SYSROOT="$4"                 # The root directory for the system.

declare -x PLIST="${DSTROOT}/Library/Preferences/com.apple.alf.plist"

declare -x defaults="/usr/bin/defaults"
declare -x plutil="/usr/bin/plutil"
declare -x chmod="/bin/chmod"
declare -x mv="/bin/mv"

"$defaults" write "${PLIST%.plist}" 'globalstate' -int 1 &&
echo "Plist Edited: ${PLIST}"
```

```
if $plutil "${PLIST:?}" >/dev/null ; then
        echo "Plist written successfully"
        $plutil -convert 'binary1' "${PLIST:?}"
        # Not needed , just for good measure
        $chmod +r "${PLIST:?}"
else
        "$mv" "${PLIST:?}" "${PLIST:?}.bad"
fi
exit 0
```

Furthermore, you can build on the logic just introduced. The following script will loop through all the local users on a system and alter the umask variable for each. Each section is documented accordingly; note the beginning, where variables from the positional parameters are mapped into paths for packages, mount points, and the system root. Having a custom system root allows the script to be run against a nonbooted drive, as would be common with a number of imaging workflows.

```
#!/bin/bash
# Standard Package Install Postional Parameters $1 $3 $4
declare -x PKGBUNDLE="$1"        #     Full path to the install package.
declare -x DSTROOT="$3"          #     Installation Volume of mount point.
declare -x SYSROOT="$4"          #     The root directory for the system.

# Command short hand
declare -x awk="/usr/bin/awk"
declare -x chown="/usr/sbin/chown"
declare -x chmod="/bin/chmod"
declare -x basename="/usr/bin/basename"
declare -x dirname="/usr/bin/dirname"
declare -x id="/usr/bin/id"
declare -x ls="/bin/ls"
declare -x plutil="/usr/bin/plutil"
declare -x sudo="/usr/bin/sudo"
declare -x whoami="/usr/bin/whoami"

# Run time varibles
declare -x SCRIPT="${0##*/}" ; SCRIPTNAME="${SCRIPT%%\.*}"
declare -x USER_TEMPLATE="$DSTROOT/System/Library/User Template/English.lproj"
declare -x FINDER_PREFS="$DSROOT/Library/Preferences/com.apple.finder.plist"

# User customized values, also use a file in the same directory <script>.conf
declare -ix UMASK=2
declare -x HOME_PATH="/Users"
# You could change this if you have an external Volume hosting homes
source "${PKGBUNDLE:?}/Contents/Resources/${SCRIPTNAME:-"$SCRIPT_NAME"}.conf"

#       As root is not covered in /Users/* set it here
if [ "$DSTROOT" = '/' ] ; then          #       If Installing on the startup disk
        echo "Setting umask for current user $($whoami):$UMASK"
        $defaults -g 'NSUmask' -int ${UMASK:?}
        #         -g means .GlobalPreferences.plist for the current user
fi
```

```
#      This sets the Finder umask, which is not done in umask Doctor AFAIK
echo "Setting Global umask for the Finder: $FINDER_PREF to $UMASK"
$defaults write ${FINDER_PREFS%.plist} 'umask' -int ${UMASK:?}


#       Loop through the homedirectorys in <Destination Volume>/Users/*
loopThroughHomes(){
OLD_IFS="$IFS" IFS=$'\n'
#      Reset the Field Sep to spaces don't hose us.
for USERHOME in "${DSTROOT}${HOME_PATH:-"/Users"}"/* ; do
# Start looping through the path on the destination Volume,defaults to /Users
       test -d "$USERHOME" || continue
               #       Skip anything thats not a directory
       test -d "$USERHOME/Library" || continue
               #       If the loop folder is missing a Library skip it
               #       This will skip Filevault, Shared, Deleted Users etc.


#      Setup the loop variables
declare USER_NAME="$($basename "$USERHOME")"
       #       Pull the username from /Users/<username>
       declare USER_PREF="$USERHOME/Library/Preferences/.GlobalPreferences.plist"
       #       The users Dot Global Preferences file
       declare -i NSUMASK=$($defaults read "$USER_PREF" 'NSUmask' 2>/dev/null)


       test ${NSUMASK:?} =${UMASK:?} && continue
       #       If value is already set or to craziness like 0 , then continue
echo "Processing: $USER: $USER_PREF"
echo "Preference file: $USER_PREF"
if [ "$DSTROOT" = '/' ] ; then
       #       if we are running on the active startup Volume
               $id "${USER_NAME:?}" &>/dev/null || continue
               #       Check if the user is valid via DS search policy
               #       Skip if the user's id lookup fails protects against del
$sudo -u "$USER" $defaults write ${USER_PREF%.plist} 'NSUmask' -int $UMASK
#       Actively set the Global preferences as the user to keep ownership
       echo "Configured $GLOBAL_PREF for $USER"
else
       declare OWNER_UID="$($ls -lnd "$USERHOME/Library" |
                                       $awk '/^d/{print $3;exit}')"
       #       If we can't rely on DirectoryService, then pull the parent UID
       $defaults write ${USER_PREF%.plist} 'NSUmask' -int ${UMASK:?}


       echo "Chaining ownership on $USER_PREF to UID:$OWNER_UID"
       $chown "${OWNER_UID:-0} ${USER_PREF:?}"
fi

done
IFS="$OLD_IFS" #       Reset our field separator
return 0
} # End loopThroughHomes()
```

```
# Validate plist syntax and ownership and move if they fail the tests
checkPlistFiles(){
declare PLISTS="$@" #  Read in all the given files in the PLISTS array
for PLIST in $PLISTS ; do
declare -i OWNER_UID="$($ls -lnd "$($dirname "$PLIST_CHECK")"|
                                    $awk '/^d/{print $3;exit}')"
declare -i PLIST_UID"$($ls -ln "$PLIST_CHECK"|
                                    $awk '/^d/{print $3;exit}')"
$plutil "${PLIST:?}" 1>/dev/null
done
return $?
} # End checkPlistFiles()


loopThroughHomes
checkPlistFiles
exit 0
```

Managing Items in ARD

Apple Remote Desktop has the ability to use a task server but not to share databases by default. You can import and export databases and copy information between computers manually from within ARD but not actually share databases. In com.apple.RemoteDesktop, there is an array called ComputerDatabase. This array lists all the items in the All Computers list within Remote Desktop. You can view a much less human-friendly output of all the hosts in All Computers by running the following command:

```
defaults read com.apple.RemoteDesktop ComputerDatabase
```

You can push an entry into the list by using the defaults command to write an item into that array in com.apple.RemoteDesktop. Here's a command to do so for a computer with a name of CharlesTest and an IP address of 10.10.10.10. Most of the other fields are extraneous and could probably be removed from the command, but it works:

```
defaults write com.apple.RemoteDesktop ComputerDatabase -array-add ' ↵
{ addedToDOC = 0;collectingAppUsage = 1;collectingUserAccounting = 1; ↵
docInfoUpToDate = 0;hostname = CharlesTest.local;name = "CharlesTest"; ↵
ncFlags = 0;networkAddress = "10.10.10.10";preferHostname = 0; ↵
showCursorForLegacy = 1;uuid = "C8F8966B-ED28-4221-CCE0-E1385D366717"; }'
```

You will need to restart the Remote Desktop services before you can see the new entry in the Remote Desktop application. You can just reboot, or you can restart using a pair of commands similar to the following:

```
launchctl stop `launchctl list | grep com.apple.RemoteDesktop | awk '{print $3}'`
launchctl stop `launchctl list | grep com.apple.RemoteDesktopAgent | awk '{print $3}'`
```

Disk Utilization

The df command is a great tool for checking the amount of free space on a disk (and the amount that's taken). df has a number of options for viewing the output and can even look at free iNodes and blocks rather than just showing free space. However, df is going to come up short if you're hunting for where all your free space went within a given volume.

For this, look to du, a great tool for checking disk utilization at the directory level. For example, the following command shows you how much space is being taken by each application in the /Applications directory:

```
du -d 1 /Applications/
```

Now run the command without the -d 1 parameters.

```
du /Applications/
```

The -d flag limits the depth that the command will traverse. By specifying 0, you'd see only the files in a given directory, whereas if you specify -d 2, you'll see the sizes of the child directories from the path you specified and their children (since that's two). You can go as deep as you want with the depth setting, but the data returned by the command can be too much at times. Also, it will take longer for the command to complete because it's calculating more data.

Some other flags that are useful are -x and -H. These will traverse mount points and symbolic links, respectively (both of which are not followed by default). This can help to keep your command's output limited to the host and volume of directories underneath the specified parent directory.

If you're interested in seeing way too much information, try just running the following:

```
du -a
```

If you suddenly have only 1KB of free space available, a series of du commands can turn up information about where all your data is in no time.

Network Setup

Networking on OS X can be automated. In many environments, system administrators will want to reorder the network interfaces to leverage wired connections over wireless when both are available. Therefore, we'll explain how to configure the interface and show how to automate this configuration from the command line so you can quickly deploy and then troubleshoot issues with this machine-specific part of your deployment.

Before getting started, it is important to note that there is a significant distinction in the nomenclature used in OS X for network *interfaces* (devices) versus network *services*. An interface is a physical network adapter. These are indicated by traditional UNIX names such as en0, en1, fw0, and so on. You can determine which is which in a variety of ways, such as using ifconfig or Network Utility from /Applications/Utilities. A network service, in this context, is an abstraction of a network interface. Each service will have a physical adapter, and a physical adapter can have multiple services, which is how, for example, you would go about assigning two IP addresses to a single physical adapter. Things can get even more confusing with bond interfaces, where you are virtualizing a service to spread across multiple interfaces, in which case multiple interfaces are represented as a single network service.

To get a list of the network services running on your machine, you can use the following command:

```
networksetup -listallnetworkservices
```

That command might return the following:

```
Ethernet
Airport
FireWire
```

There are about as many naming conventions for interfaces as there are actual interfaces. For the purposes of this example, we'll patch Ethernet into the network and rename it to WiredNetwork, using the networksetup command again, with the -renamenetworkservice option as follows:

```
networksetup -renamenetworkservice Ethernet WiredNetwork
```

While it's not required to rename your network services, people often do. As you can see, it's quick and easy and can save you a bunch of time in the future in terms of troubleshooting, remote support, and automation facilitation. Renaming is specific; the command looks for a pattern in the name and replaces it with a new pattern. So, built-in Ethernet would need to be enclosed in quotes, as in "Built-in Ethernet", and so forth. Now let's rename the other services to WirelessNetwork using the following command:

```
networksetup -renamenetworkservice AirPort WirelessNetwork
```

Next, you want to make sure that WiredNetwork is listed before WirelessNetwork. This will ensure that standard communications DNS, directory services, HTTP management traffic, and other unnecessary traffic default to the wired network. To start, let's look at what order the services are listed in. You'll use networksetup yet again, this time with the -listnetworkserviceorder option, as follows:

```
networksetup -listnetworkserviceorder
```

This should provide a listing similar to the following, though perhaps in a different order:

```
(1) WirelessNetwork
(Hardware Port: Ethernet, Device: en1)

(2) WiredNetwork
(Hardware Port: Ethernet, Device: en0)

(3) FireWire
(Hardware Port: FireWire, Device: fw0)
```

Here you see that `WirelessNetwork` is listed as the first item in the network service order. Because you actually want the `WiredNetwork` first, you'll reorder the services using the `networksetup` command with the `-ordernetworkservices` option. Using this option, you simply list each service in order, as you can see here:

```
networksetup -ordernetworkservices WiredNetwork WirelessNetwork FireWire
```

Notice that you include `FireWire` in the command. This is because you have to include all your network services for the command to execute successfully. Now you are actually going to disable the FireWire network service (when you do, the interface itself will still function) using the `-setnetworkserviceenabled` option of the `networksetup` command. Because the FireWire service is automatically named FireWire, you simply tell `networksetup` to `setnetworkserviceenabled` to off as follows:

```
networksetup -setnetworkserviceenabled FireWire off
```

You'll now configure the IPv4 settings for your two network interfaces. For example, `WiredNetwork` might be set up to use DHCP. In that case, there's not much configuration that needs to occur. While DHCP should be the default setting used with the controller, it would still be wise to specify it again anyway (just in case) using the next command, where `-setdhcp` is the option that enables DHCP for the `WiredNetwork` service.

```
networksetup -setdhcp WiredNetwork
```

While the `WiredNetwork` could be DHCP, in this case you'll set it as a static IP address of 10.100.1.11. The subnet mask will be 255.255.0.0, and the gateway will be 10.100.0.1. This is all sent to the service in one command, using the `-setmanual` option with `networksetup`. When you use this option, you use the `-setmanual` option followed by the name of the service to configure, then the IP address that will be given to the service, then the subnet, and finally the router (default gateway). In this case, the command is as follows:

```
networksetup -setmanual WiredNetwork 10.100.1.11 255.255.0.0 10.100.0.1
```

The wireless network is a bit more persnickety. As is typical, we will use DHCP, but you will also need to configure a number of proxy services. Use the following command to set the adapter to DHCP:

```
networksetup -setdhcp WirelessNetwork
```

To set the proxies, use a combination of two of the following proxy options per service:

- *setftpproxystate*: Enables the FTP proxy
- *setftpproxy*: Sets up a proxy for FTP
- *setwebproxystate*: Enables the web proxy
- *setwebproxy*: Sets up a proxy for web traffic
- *setsecurewebproxystate*: Enables the SSL proxy
- *setsecurewebproxy*: Sets a proxy for SSL traffic

- *setstreamingproxystate*: Enables the streaming proxy
- *setstreamingproxy*: Sets a proxy for streaming traffic
- *setgopherproxystate*: Enables the Gopher proxy (if you are using Gopher, please stay after class for a parent-teacher conference)
- *setgopherproxy*: Sets the Gopher proxy
- *setsocksfirewallproxystate*: Enables a socks firewall
- *setsocksfirewallproxy*: Sets up the socks firewall
- *setproxybypassdomains*: Defines the domains that the proxy will not be used for

To deploy a proxy setting, you'll use two commands, one to enable the option and the other to set it. For each proxy option that can be set, you will add the network service, a host name (or IP address), and a port number that the proxy will run on. Optionally you can then specify (still on the same line of the command) an authentication option (as either on or off) along with a username and password for each proxy service. For example, to set a web proxy for proxy.318.com that runs on port 8080 and requires authentication as username proxyserv with a password of Asimov, you would use the following commands:

```
networksetup -setwebproxystate on
networksetup -setwebproxy WirelessNetwork proxy.318.com 8080 on proxyserv Asimov
```

Now that you have the services configured, you need to assign name servers. To set up DNS, you will use the -setdnsservers option with networksetup. In this case, the DNS servers are 10.100.0.2 and 10.100.0.3. When using the -setdnsservers option, you simply list the primary name server, followed by the secondary name server and any tertiary name servers. DNS is used on WiredNetwork as WirelessNetwork picks up DNS from DHCP.

```
networksetup -setdnsservers WiredNetwork 10.100.0.2 10.100.0.3
```

At this point you're probably thinking to yourself that you could have done all this in the Network pane of System Preferences in about two minutes. Now, however, that you'll take all the commands you used in this example and put them into a shell script, replacing the actual IP addresses with positional parameters for the WiredNetwork and WirelessNetwork IP addresses so that you can send the script along with the IP address that it will receive to each workstation. The script would look something like this:

```
#!/bin/bash
networksetup -renamenetworkservice Ethernet WiredNetwork
networksetup -renamenetworkservice Ethernet2 WirelessNetwork
networksetup -ordernetworkservices WiredNetwork WirelessNetwork FireWire
networksetup -setnetworkserviceenabled FireWire off
networksetup -setmanual WiredNetwork $1 255.255.0.0 10.100.0.1
networksetup -setdnsservers WiredNetwork 10.100.0.2 10.100.0.3
networksetup -setmanual WirelessNetwork $2 255.255.255.0
networksetup -setwebproxystate on
networksetup -setwebproxy WirelessNetwork proxy.318.com 8080 on proxyserv Asimov
```

Now the script can be sent to each workstation. For this example, you'll call the script `setnetworkservices.sh`. To send an IP address for the `WiredNetwork` of 10.100.1.12 and an IP for the `WirelessNetwork` of 192.168.1.12, you would simply send the following command (including the path of course):

```
sudo setnetworkservices.sh 10.100.1.12 192.168.1.12
```

Then, to set up the next host using the same convention, you would use the following:

```
sudo setnetworkservices.sh 10.100.1.13 192.168.1.13
```

If you want to get a bit more complicated with the script, you could add some logic. For example, you might query for en0 and convert a service name to be used with en0 based on the interface to keep the script from failing because of someone having renamed the service in the past. Because a common issue during setup is to patch the wrong interfaces into the networks (in the case that there are two wired interfaces), you could also use the `ping` command to test each network to verify it is live and if not (`else`) go ahead and swap the IP settings and names. You might also turn every single setting into a variable to make it much more portable.

Finally, as you are updating this information, you are augmenting the `/Library/Preferences/SystemConfiguration/preferences.plist` file. While there are a variety of ways to edit this file directly, I wouldn't really suggest it because most adapters are referenced by MAC and have generated service IDs (for example `F8166C7E-CCFC-438C-98C6-CB05C7FA13E7`). It is far easier to simply use the `networksetup` tool than it is to use a file drop of the plist or to augment this file directly.

You can also use `networksetup` to import and export 802.1x profiles (and link them to certificates that you import from `pkcs12` into Keychain), which will ideally ease implementation burdens for environments with supported 802.1x setups. The second is that `networksetup` can now be used to manage a Baseboard Management Controller (BMC), which is the chip that enables ipmi/Lights-Out Management. The third new option is the addition of network locations control from within `networksetup`. This means that `networksetup` can now be used to configure basically the entire network stack.

You can also programmatically configure and control preferred wireless network settings from the command line. Arguments associated with this functionality are `-listpreferredwirelessnetworks`, `-addpreferredwirelessnetworkatindex`, `-removepreferredwirelessnetwork`, and `-removeallpreferredwirelessnetworks`. For instance, to add a preferred wireless network called Ansible with WPA2 personal security, you would use the following command:

```
sudo networksetup -addpreferredwirelessnetworkatindex Airport Ansible 1 WPA2 Secretp4$$
```

You can also manage location management to `networksetup`. Locations have always been pretty straightforward in the Network pane of System Preferences, and you can create and change locations programmatically. Simply use the `-getcurrentlocation` option to show you which location is active (if you haven't ever customized network locations, this should be Automatic). You can see all available locations (not just the active one) by using the `-listlocations` option. New locations can be created with the `-createlocation` argument followed by the name to be assigned to the location. By default, the default services will not be included in this location, so use the populate option to add them. As an alternative, you can add individual services manually via the –createnetworkservice option. If you were creating a new location called MyCo Location, with all network services populated, then your command would look something like the following:

```
networksetup -createlocation "MyCo Location" populate
```

To then make that location your active location, use the -switchtolocation option. For example, you could use the following to activate that location you just created:

```
networksetup -switchtolocation "MyCo Location"
```

To delete it if you did something wrong, use -deletelocation (to continue with the previous example).

```
networksetup -deletelocation "MyCo Location"
```

Power Management

Power management can most easily be managed via MCX or configuration profiles, as discussed in Chapter 7. However, there may be instances where you need to resort to scripting to deploy your power management settings, and you can use the pmset command-line utility to accomplish this. For starters, let's look at enabling the *wake-on magic packet*:

```
pmset -a womp 1
```

The -a indicates that the setting will apply to all settings modes for a computer. It will apply to the system when on battery, when you're plugged in, or when you are running on UPS backup power. You can change settings for only a specific state with the following flags, which fall into the first positional parameter:

- *-a:* All
- *-b:* Battery
- *-c:* Wall power
- *-u:* UPS

The next parameter you'll pass to the command is the option (argument) for that power setting that you would like to send. Here you can set the number of minutes before the display goes to sleep, the brightness at various power settings, and other options that have a direct effect on power behavior. These include the following:

- *acwake:* Wake when the system is connected to power; it's a 0 or 1.
- *autorestart:* Automatically restart when there's been a power loss (when the system is plugged in); use 0 or 1.
- *disksleep:* Number of minutes before the disk spins down.

- *displaysleep:* Number of minutes before the computer's monitor (signal to the monitor) goes to sleep.

- *dps:* Allows the CPU speed to dynamically change with power; 0 or 1.

- *halfdim:* Controls whether the display goes to half-brightness for the power setting in question; 0 or 1

- *lessbright:* Same as the previous one, just not as much.

- *lidwake:* Automatically wake the system when the lid is opened; 0 or 1.

- *powerbutton:* Allows the box to go to sleep if someone hits the power button. If it's disabled, the system will not go to sleep if someone hits the power button. This doesn't disable powering down by holding down that same power button; 0 or 1.

- *reduce:* Allows reduction of the CPU speed; 0 or 1.

- *ring:* Wake if someone calls the modem (but since the modern laptops don't have modems, likely not something you'll be using). It's an integer; 0 or 1.

- *sleep:* Number of minutes before the computer goes to sleep (but doesn't spin down the disk).

- *sms:* Controls whether you're using the Sudden Motion Sensor to stop the disk heads from locking down when the system gets jarred (G-force math is "kewl"). It's a Boolean thing; it's either on or off.

- *womp:* Explained previously.

In addition to these, you can also use `pmset` to get information with the `-g` flag. Using `-g` alone will net you all the available information, and there are other options to limit what it outputs. Just use `grep` for that.

There are also a number of options for managing SafeSleep (maintaining the system state in memory, using the argument `hibernatemode`) or UPS options (`haltvalue` for how much battery to trigger a shutdown and `halfafterfor` to spin the CPU to 50 percent of full). If you're trying to manage the system and you have a battery (such as a laptop plugged into a UPS), the settings will not be respected.

Just as in the System Preferences pane, you can also control scheduling for when the system sleeps, wakes, powers on, or shuts down. You can schedule these events by using the `schedule` and `repeat` arguments, which can be used to set one-time power events or repeated events, respectively. Options for each are `sleep`, `wake`, `poweron`, and `shutdown` in conjunction with using date, time, and weekdays. You can optionally provide a string name of the person setting the schedule for documentation purposes.

```
pmset schedule poweron "09/09/15 9:09:09"
pmset repeat shutdown MTWRF 21:00:00
```

There are also a few other options that you don't have in the GUI. These include `force`, which doesn't write settings to disk; `touch`, which reads currently enforced settings from the disk; `noidle`, which prevents idle sleep (and just spins the disk down when it's ready); and `sleepnow`, which puts the system to sleep right then. `sleepnow` is useful when you're troubleshooting why a system won't go to sleep.

Servers and Change Monitoring

At its most basic, you can use change control in OS X Server by leveraging the `serveradmin` command. You can use the `serveradmin` command with the settings option, as you did extensively in Chapter 5 to obtain information about settings and augment those settings in OS X Server on a per-server basis. However, you can also use the `serveradmin` command to report all the settings for all of its services. To do so, you use the following command:

```
serveradmin settings all
```

You can then pipe this information into a file. For example, the following command would copy the information from `serveradmin` into a text file in the `/scripts` directory of a system called `dailyservercheck`:

```
serveradmin settings all > /scripts/dailyservercheck
```

It is important to note that any changes made directly to a particular software package's configuration files will likely not be detected through this method, such as if a user modified the postfix service's configuration at `/etc/postfix/main.cf`. To monitor UNIX utilities such as these, Tripwire, a change monitoring solution both with open source and enterprise solutions available (`www.tripwire.org` and `www.tripwire.com`), is a better option. That being said, `serveradmin` is a great way to track changes made through standard Apple tools and therefore certainly does have a purpose.

Troubleshooting

Regardless of the specific debugging techniques you use (and there are about as many methods for debugging as there are programmers), there are a few general principles to keep in mind as you debug your scripts.

The first task in any debugging effort is to learn how to consistently reproduce the bug. If it takes more than a few steps to manually trigger the buggy behavior, consider writing a script to trigger it. You will be able to debug much more quickly this way.

As you are debugging, you will want to progressively narrow your scope. In many cases, this involves eliminating half the possibilities at each stage of troubleshooting. Analysis is the thoughtful consideration of a bug's likely point of origin, based on detailed knowledge of the codebase. In practice, you will probably use a combination of analysis and sheer brute force. A preliminary analysis will isolate the area of your code that is most likely to contain a given bug, and then reviewing all the code within that area will often help to locate it precisely.

Use debuggers, but don't spend an extended period of time getting the debuggers to work. Often, you step through a piece of code, statement by statement, only to find that you accidentally fixed the problem. Stepping through the code is invaluable because the more times you go through it, the more streamlined and commented it tends to become. Becoming more in tune with your code in this way can help to make you a better programmer.

If you are attempting to write scripts just for simple admin purposes and don't want to spend a lot of time debugging, use a search engine and see whether the specific portion of your script has been written before. In the course of writing this book, we found many of our scripts in an almost identical state on the Web. In some cases, there are a finite number of ways of writing a script, and if someone else has found the way to get the script to work, then learn from their work and build on it.

When trying to isolate a bug, you often want to change only one thing at a time. Debugging is a process where you make changes to code and then test to see whether you've fixed a bug. Then you make another change, test again, and so on, until the bug is fixed. At each iteration, make sure to change only one thing so that when the bug is fixed, you will know exactly what caused it. If you change several things at once, you risk including unnecessary changes in your fix, which may in some cases cause bugs themselves.

A trace statement is a console or log message that is inserted into a piece of code suspected of containing a bug and then generally removed once the bug has been found. Trace statements trace not only the path of execution through code but the changing state of program variables as execution progresses. Once you have found the bug, you may find it helpful to leave a few of the trace statements in the code, perhaps converting console messages into file-based logging messages to assist in future debugging.

If you're using a third-party server, database, or script, check all the components and you will often find a good amount of useful information about errors in the log files for each application or operating system. You may have to configure the component to log the sort of information you're interested in.

Sometimes, after you've been hunting a bug for long enough, you begin to despair of ever finding it. When this happens, it can be useful to start from scratch. Create a new script, and bring each function from your old script over one at a time, checking each portion thoroughly before integrating it into the new script. At times, it is also a good idea to break each portion of a script into a separate scripts of its own.

Research shows that bugs tend to cluster. When you encounter a new bug, think of the parts of the code where you have found bugs in the past and whether they could be involved with the current bug. At times, this is just that the functions you are working with may not be your strongest or that the code in general is just buggy, but experience tells that where there is one pesky bug, there are likely to be others.

One of the most obscure sources of bugs is from using incompatible versions of third-party libraries. It is also one of the last things to check when you've exhausted other debugging strategies. For example, if version 5.1 of some library has a dependency on version 1.4g of SSL or some other library but you install 1.4b instead, the results may be issues that are difficult or impossible to diagnose. Checking your documentation can help with this.

If all else fails, read the instructions. It's remarkable how often this simple step is skipped. In their rush to start programming with some class library or utility, some developers will adopt a trial-and-error approach to using, for example, a new Perl mod. If there is little or no documentation, this may be appropriate. It's possible that your bug results from misuse of the mod and the underlying code is failing to check that you have obeyed all the necessary preconditions for its use.

When a bug suddenly appears in functionality that has been working for some time, you should immediately wonder what has recently changed in the scripts or software that calls the scripts that might have caused the bug. This is where a version control system can be helpful, providing you with the ability to look at the change history of your code or re-creating successively older versions of the codebase until you get one in which the bug disappears. CVS and Subversion are both great examples of version control systems.

What may be multicausal problems are often troubleshot as a single-cause bug. When troubleshooting network issues and buggy scripts, it is often hardest to isolate issues that contain multiple errors. In fact, we often do not consider this until trying everything else. But they do happen, and if nothing else explains an issue, you should look for multiple bugs.

Normally you scrutinize the error messages you get carefully, hoping for a clue as to where to start your debugging efforts. But if you're not having any luck with that approach, remember that error messages can sometimes be misleading. Sometimes programmers don't put as much thought into the handling and reporting of error conditions as one would like, so it may be wise to avoid interpreting the error message too literally and to consider possibilities other than the ones that are specifically identified.

When you're really stuck on a bug, it can be helpful to grab another programmer and explain the bug to them. Also tell them the efforts you've made so far to hunt down its source. They may offer some helpful advice, but this is not what the technique is really about. It sometimes happens that in the course of explaining the problem to another person, you realize something about the bug you didn't think of before.

Many have noted that solutions come much easier after a period of intense concentration on the problem, followed by a period of rest. Another way to get a fresh look at a piece of code you've been staring at for too long is to print it out and review it. We read faster on paper than on the screen, so this may be why it's slightly easier to spot an error in printed code than displayed code.

After a time, you may notice that you are prone to writing particular kinds of bugs. If you can identify a consistent weakness like this, you can take preventative steps. If you have a code-review checklist, augment the checklist to include a check specifically for the type of bug you favor. Simply maintaining an awareness of your "favorite" defects can help reduce your tendency to inject them.

Further Reading

Pro Bash Programming: This chapter had a heavy focus on shell scripting because such scripts provide an accessible, powerful environment, which can be handled for numerous automations. *Pro Bash Programming* by Chris Johnson and Jayant Varma provides an excellent look into shell scripting. See www.apress.com/9781484201220.

Expert Shell Scripting: As you get more confident with Bash, you may look to do much more complex scripts. This book, by Ron Peters, will take you from intermediate to expert. See www.apress.com/9781430218418.

Beginning Perl, Third Edition: Perl is another command-line and scripting tool that can be used to automate almost anything in OS X. In this book, by James Lee, you will learn the basics of programming in Perl. This is often the next step when budding programmers outgrow the capabilities of Bash. See www.apress.com/9781590593912.

Pro Python: Python is another language that people like to try once they master the shell for OS X. Python has a number of options that can be leveraged with OS X. See www.apress.com/9781484203354.

Learn AppleScript: Some tasks can't be completed by shell and Python scripting. Some tasks need you to click GUI buttons, need deeper integration with Apple technologies such as Automator, and so on. Thus, it's a good idea to have a basic understanding of AppleScript, including when you should be using it and how to use it. See www.apress.com/9781430223610.

Virtualization

When faced with the ultimate goal of integrating OS X clients into the enterprise, the preferred focus should be to provide your OS X users with a native environment whenever possible. There are many benefits to this. Your users' lives will be better, which will make your life better. They will have a consistent user interface and a generally smoother experience.

While keeping users in a native environment is preferable, virtualization is a popular option when deploying Windows and Linux applications on OS X clients because there are always going to be environments where certain business-critical applications are platform dependent. When you have those one or two applications that are business critical to your organizations but the applications cannot be used natively for the Mac, virtualization is a popular way to deploy non-Apple platform solutions onto OS X. Deploying virtual environments is also a handy way to provide a fallback when transitioning a user base from a different platform. Having said that, it's important to keep in mind that when you deploy virtual machines, your mass deployment system is now no longer one machine; it includes the deployment and initial configuration of both your host operating system (the OS X operating system that will be housing your virtual machines) and the sum of all your guest operating systems (the operating system running on each of your virtual machines).

Each guest operating system will come with its own deployment considerations, system requirements, long-term management requirements, and, of course, licensing. Each of these costs adds up to reduce the business case for having OS X in the first place. Therefore, when possible, it is highly recommended to look at alternatives before deciding to deploy typical virtualization candidates such as Microsoft Windows to all your Macs. If you can streamline all your applications into items available for OS X, then your deployment will go much more smoothly. The paradigm shift to web-based applications that is occurring in most environments might help you in this regard. If you cannot, consider application publishing to a central server, using a tool such as Citrix, prior to considering whether to deploy a virtualization application en masse to your end users. If you are transitioning a user base to OS X from another platform, you may have the facilities and licensing already in place to support the former environment. In this case, you have all the pieces in place to deploy a relatively low-cost, historical window to your old environment—all provided through virtualization.

While the mass deployment of only a single operating system in many environments is difficult, this task is made wholly more difficult when you are deploying guest operating systems on top of this. Keep in mind that both operating systems need to be manageable using your patch management solution or may require two different patch management solutions. Each typically needs to have policies enforced, and each will need similar automation logic. They will also need twice the surface space. This sprawl magnifies the need for centralized management and can often lead to the need for a higher staff count to deal with support tickets.

OS X is a capable environment in that it plays well with others. If you are migrating from a UNIX environment, its native support for X11 will likely make you happy. Common applications available on Windows such as MIcrosoft Office and Lotus Notes are both natively supported. More and more business apps are turning into web applications, where the Mac is (usually) a first-rate citizen. However, the reality of the situation is that many purpose-built business apps are platform dependent in one way or another. Sometimes, there may be a native Mac client for your business app, but after testing, it proves to be unreliable and generally unsupported (or perhaps written by the CEO's 16-year-old son, but you did not hear that from us). In some cases, the OS X client may just simply be missing critical functionality. If you need to publish alternative platform applications to users that they can use offline, if you need to allow users to test software, or if you find some features of the OS X versions of certain packages to be lacking, then you will likely need to deploy Windows alongside OS X. If you find this reality staring at your face, you need to simply know that the process can work out great, provided that you follow a few specific steps. In this chapter, we will focus on explaining aspects of deployment that are unique to the virtualization environment for OS X, with a general focus toward Microsoft Windows as the guest OS. This will begin with VMware Fusion, Parallels Desktop, Boot Camp (not technically virtualization, but more on that later), and finally CrossOver Mac (an OS X native Wine implementation, which is a Windows API translation layer). We will explain how to deploy the Windows OS to OS X clients and will cover various aspects used to manage the guest operating system. Once the VM has been deployed, we will move into patch management of the guest operating system.

Boot Camp

Microsoft Windows can be deployed on a Mac using Boot Camp. Boot Camp will require the system be rebooted between each operating system switch and comes with a host of additional deployment considerations. The Mac doesn't natively support PXE booting and other traditional Windows deployment options; however, you can deploy Boot Camp by using DeployStudio, JAMF Software's Casper Suite, and a number of other solutions.

Thin Clients

Before moving into discussing how to deploy virtualization applications, it is never a bad idea to pose a simple but important question: "Why?" As we've discussed, deploying multiple operating systems per host can create a large amount of overhead in all facets of your infrastructure, thus increasing the total cost of ownership of your overall environment. Why not deploy applications instead of entire operating system environments? The entire provisioning process occurs faster, and upgrades happen centrally; thus, there is no need for additional infrastructure to support these operating systems.

One of the oldest and most stable thin client solutions with OS X is Citrix XenApp. XenApp can be used to publish a session, whether that session is an entire operating system environment or a single application. If you are considering deploying virtualization software to supply only a handful of non-native applications to your Mac users, consider XenApp as an alternative.

Microsoft also licensed XenApp technology to include Windows Server. This "Terminal Services" also fully supports a Remote Desktop Connection client for the Mac. You can download Microsoft Remote Desktop from the Mac App Store or use the open source CoRD at `http://cord.sourceforge.net`, which provides you with the ability to tap into multiple Windows Remote Desktop Protocol (RDP) sessions concurrently. Terminal Services is going to be less costly than XenApp but will also have fewer features and is best used when publishing an entire operating system environment, rather than a specific application.

The biggest drawback to a thin client environment is that access requires users to be online. This may or may not be detrimental to your user's productivity, but whether it is will generally be a pretty easy question to answer. With Wi-Fi showing up on flights around the country, high-speed cellular data networks, and a multitude of mobile devices supporting the Remote Desktop Protocol (including the iPhone), thin clients are becoming a more accessible solution.

> **Note**   In addition to publishing Windows environments for Mac users, you can also publish Mac environments for both Windows and Mac users with Aqua Connect. You can learn more about Aqua Connect at `www.aquaconnect.net`.

VMware

VMware provides an OS X native virtualization client, dubbed Fusion. VMware Fusion is a type 2 hypervisor, meaning that it runs on top of an existing operating system (OS X) as an application. Furthermore, the application currently requires an active user session, which definitely has implications when deploying in a server environment. In such a case, a type 1 hypervisor, or bare-metal hypervisor, is typically desirable in a server environment, allowing a system's virtualized operating systems to operate independently of each other. Where Fusion succeeds is desktop OS virtualization, such as Microsoft Windows.

The best way to deploy VMware Fusion to Mac clients is via an Apple Installer package. However, at first glance, the VMware Fusion installer is actually an application and not an Installer package. Never fear, there is in fact a native installer package; it's just hidden inside the application bundle's Library folder and named Deploy VMware Fusion.mpkg. As such, you can extract this package for mass deployment, without the Installer application, to deploy VMware Fusion along with a virtual machine file. Many environments will choose to customize the application installer. For more information about creating your own deployment package, see `http://kb.vmware.com/selfservice/microsites/microsite.do?cmd=displayKC&externalId=2058680`.

VMware Fusion in Monolithic Imaging

As described in Chapter 6, a monolithic image will contain all the items needed to deploy a workstation in a single image and will not typically rely on bolting any additional software. Adding VMware Fusion to a monolithic OS X image is a fairly straightforward process: you manually install VMware Fusion on your base image using a volume license. If you don't have a volume license, then you'll need a postflight script or package to deploy a new license on each client after they receive the initial software.

> **Note**   With any monolithic imaging solution, it is strongly recommended that you maintain a change log to track software that has been added or removed from your image. It is also recommended that you list any necessary automations and the utility they provide. Having a detailed change log becomes a key component to the ongoing management of almost any imaging scenario, but more so in a monolithic imaging environment.

To install VMware Fusion, begin by mounting the VMware Fusion disk image or launching the installation media that came with the software. Next, double-click the VMware Fusion prompt, as shown in Figure 9-1.

Figure 9-1. The VMware Fusion installation prompt

At the screen for the software license agreement, read the agreement carefully, and then click the Agee button, as in Figure 9-2.

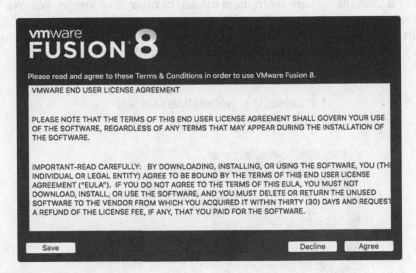

Figure 9-2. Software license agreement

At the next screen, enter a license. Here, you should enter your volume license master serial number (shown in Figure 9-3) and then click the Continue button. If you do not have a volume license serial number, you will need to enter a valid serial number, which will subsequently automate the replacement of a separate package.

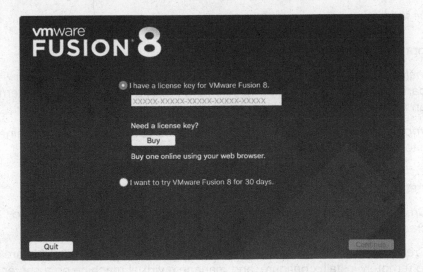

Figure 9-3. Licensing VMware Fusion

At the next screen, you will be prompted to install your first virtual machine. As shown in Figure 9-4, you can select "Install from disc or image," which creates a new virtual machine using a .iso disk image file, optical media, or other disk image. For example, if you download a Windows installer as an .iso file, you can mount this file and install a new virtual machine from that. You can also select "Import an existing PC," which allows you to migrate a Windows computer into a virtual machine running on a Mac.

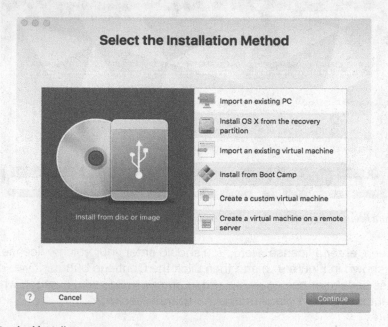

Figure 9-4. The standard install screen

Additional options include the following:

- *Install OS X from the recovery partition*: Allows you to use the recovery partition to download a Mac installer and install a new operating system on a virtual machine from that

- *Import an existing virtual machine*: Allows you to move a virtual machine into the VMware Fusion database

- *Install from Boot Camp*: Deploys a virtual machine from a Windows instance running on the computer now running VMware Fusion

- *Create a custom virtual machine*: Shows a list of operating systems to create a new virtual machine from

- *Create a virtual machine on a remote server*: Allows you to use VMware to remotely install, configure, and manage a virtual machine on a server

We will cover deploying virtual machines later in this chapter.

VMware Fusion with a Package-Based Deployment

VMware Fusion is distributed as a package installer that has been bundled inside an application bundle. They cleverly disguise the .app file with an installer icon, which is confusing to some administrators. When installing Fusion directly onto a client, you can deploy either package or run the application. However, when performing mass installations, installer packages are convenient. Extracting the actual .mpkg file will provide you with much better mass deployment options. When you are pushing out the .mpkg file, you will then be able to embed a license key in it.

> **Note**   It's worth mentioning before getting too much further that some snapshot tools such as JAMF Software's Composer include presets for automatically creating Apple Installer packages from the existing installation of VMware. These tools typically (by default) grab all files, including registration. That said, if you managed to get a volume license key from VMware, this tool may save you a little bit of time by bypassing some of the steps covered in this section.

To extract the package, you will first need to mount the latest VMware Fusion disk image that you can obtain from the VMware web site (you will typically want to make sure you are deploying the latest stable release of most software). Then, Control-click Install VMware Fusion to see the menu in Figure 9-5.

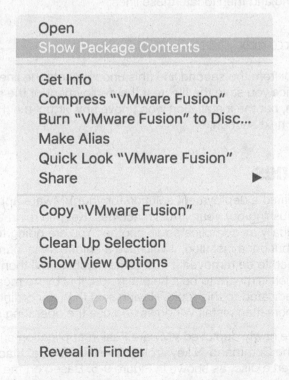

Figure 9-5. Menu shown while extracting the VMware Fusion package

Next, click Show Package Contents and then browse to the Contents folder followed by the Resources folder. Here you will find the `Install VMware Fusion.pkg` package, which is the actual package installer for Fusion. You can now copy `Install VMware Fusion.pkg` to another location, such as the desktop. Once you have completed preparing the package for deployment, you will want to store it in your package repository.

Assuming you have a volume license master serial, you will now want to customize the installation package to include the license and therefore fully automate the install. The license can be included inside the `Deploy VMware Fusion.mpkg` package so that when you go to deploy the package through Apple Remote Desktop or another patch management solution, the installer will not require the end user to enter a serial number—an annoyance that potentially prevents the installation from proceeding (depending on your deployment tool). To embed the license file, you will edit the contents of the package by placing the volume license master serial number into a file called `Deploy.ini` that is located in the `Deploy VMware Fusion.mpkg` package that you just extracted.

To get started, right-click or Control-click the `VMware Fusion.app` package and then click Show Package Contents. Open the Contents folder and then copy the `Deploy VMware Fusion.mpkg` file from the Library folder of this package to your desktop.

From here, you'll view the contents of the `Deploy VMware Fusion.mpkg` file in the same way that you viewed the contents of the `VMware Fusion.app` file, by right-clicking or Control-clicking the Apple Installer package and then clicking Show Package Contents. Then, navigate to the `Contents` directory and then the `OOFusion_Deployment_Items` directory. Here, you'll see a file called `Deploy.ini`. Open it using your favorite plain-text editor such as TextEdit, TextWrangler, vi, or nano and then locate these lines:

```
[Volume License]
# key = AAAAA-BBBBB-CCCCC-DDDDD-EEEEE
```

Delete the hash symbol from the second line (this uncomments the line) and replace the key with the actual key. Once you save the file, test the deployment of the package. This will deploy VMware Fusion, but the installation won't have any virtual machines as of yet. That's what we'll cover in the next section.

Virtual Machines

Now that you have created a deployment solution for your VMware application, it's time to focus attention on pushing out your virtual machines. Keep in mind that deploying any operating system is equally as complicated as another. You are going to install a virtual machine of Windows, but once installed, it will have a unique serial number and other unique information that will need to be removed if that same machine will then be deployed en masse. While this section is meant to be a helpful guide, it is by no means a replacement for books and software dedicated to this topic. Having said that, according to your task, you may need to do little more than install Windows and use the operating system.

To get started, open the newly deployed VMware Fusion application and select New from the File menu (or use the Command-N keystroke). The New Virtual Machine Assistant will now ask you to insert a disc, as shown in Figure 9-6. Based on the contents of the disc, the assistant will install an operating system. Go ahead and insert your installation media and complete the Create a New Virtual Machine Wizard, which installs Windows along with the required VMware drivers.

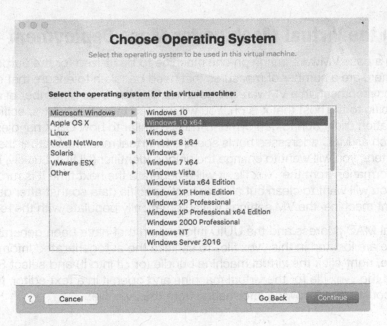

Figure 9-6. *Creating a new virtual machine*

When creating virtual machines, you have a number of options for optimizing performance. The default VMware Fusion settings are good for a number of environments, but you should also thoroughly test the performance of your virtual machines and tweak other settings as needed. For instance, in certain environments, guest OS performance may be paramount, and settings would then be weighted toward the guest OS in terms of RAM allocation and processor priority.

Next, determine whether you want to deploy the guest operating system's third-party software along with the OS in the virtual machine or as separate packages. If you choose to install all business software into the VM file directly, you may end up pushing out a rather bloated file. However, the abstraction provided in the virtual machine file provides the near equivalent of a block transfer, so it is often desirable to deploy as much software as possible in the VM file right from the start. If you instead choose not to embed your software in the VM file and opt rather to deploy it through other means after the fact, then you will likely end up building custom installers and further complicating the environment. As with choosing a deployment methodology with OS X, you will want to determine what methodology to take with your Windows virtual machine fleet. There are arguments for either side, but typically it is best left to the incumbent methodology being used for your physical Windows desktops, provided you have one.

Following the initial installation of the virtual machine and any third party add-ons, you will want to manage the systems similarly. If you have an existing solution in place, then it is likely best to continue using it. If not, then consider a solution such as Microsoft's System

Center Configuration Manager (SCCM), LANdesk, or other patch management solutions. At a minimum, you will likely want to leverage Microsoft's Windows Software Update Server (WSUS) to cache updates to the Microsoft products installed on your virtual machines.

Preparing the Virtual Machine for Mass Deployment

When building a base VMware image on one machine to be utilized for the purposes of mass deployment, there are a number of measures that need be taken to ensure that each client has a unique environment. In a VMware image's .vmx file, there are a number of attributes, which are specific to the host that it is on. You will want to tailor this host-specific information to each destination client during deployment. This is similar to how OS X handles ByHost information such as MAC addresses but is specific to virtual machines rather than physical hosts. For starters, you will want to change the unique identifier (UUID). Luckily, if you simply remove the information from the .vmx file, it will regenerate the next time it is run. Thus, prior to deployment, you will want to clean out all your host-specific data so that after deployment to a different client machine, the VM settings will automatically populate with the relevant data.

Both the virtual MAC address and the UUID information that have been generated for a virtual machine are located in this .vmx file. To sanitize the autogenerated information for a virtual machine, right-click the virtual machine bundle (or cd into it) and select Show Package Contents. Find the .vmx file for the virtual machine and open it in a text editor. Next, remove the lines that contain the following information from the .vmx file:

```
uuid.bios =
uuid.location =
ethernet0.addressType =
ethernet0.generatedAddress =
ethernet0.generatedAddressOffset =
```

You will now want to remove any information about Shared and Mirrored folders since those can potentially use paths that no longer exist on a host. To do so, open the .vmx file again and look for a line that is similar to the following:

```
sharedFolder1.hostPath = "/Users/cedge/Documents"
```

Change the information between the quotation marks to a tilde (~).

```
sharedFolder1.hostPath = "~/Documents"
```

Once you have made these changes to the virtual machine, do not power on this VM. If you power on the VM, the settings will be reset to user-specific settings and will need to be changed again. Thus, prior to this step, you will want to make sure that the VM host OS is configured fully to your liking. Make sure that any customized settings or software has been installed. Once the host OS is set up, you will need to normalize the software install. Similar to the previous cleanup of the .vmx file, Windows has a cleanup process that it must do in order to be suited for deployment to other machines.

Once you are satisfied with everything, clean up the appropriate values in the .vmx file and then copy the virtual machine to another host. Once it's copied, you can attempt to open the virtual machine. It should automatically re-create the preceding variables. If so, then the original virtual machine is ready for deployment (assuming the operating system resident on it is ready as well).

You can use VMware to automatically run a script, thus allowing you to rename a guest operating system or automate the binding process.

Virtual Machine Deployment

In addition to deploying VMware Fusion, nearly every organization that leverages virtualization will also want to deploy the virtual machines that contain a guest OS. The virtual machines themselves are stored as .vmware bundle files, and while you might think deploying would be as easy as copying these files to workstations, there are a few other steps involved to make for a great user experience.

As with many other solutions throughout this book, we're going to leverage a package to show how to deploy a virtual machine (more on packages in Chapter 6), which for the purpose of this example will be running Windows 10. We'll use Composer because it's an easy tool for such a task.

Go ahead and open Composer, found by default in the /Applications/Casper Suite directory. Upon launching Composer, you will see a sheet titled "Choose a method to create your package." Click the Cancel button, and you should see an empty package screen, shown in Figure 9-7.

Figure 9-7. Composer

Next, switch to the Finder and drag the VMBundle into the SOURCES section of the Composer screen. This creates a new package entry in SOURCES. As shown in Figure 9-8, you can then look at each directory to see the raw files and define where they'll be placed when the package is installed.

Figure 9-8. Viewing the contents of your package

Here you'll see that the files that make up the virtual machine are .vmdk files. Click Build as PKG (shown in Figure 9-9) to select a location for the package to be saved.

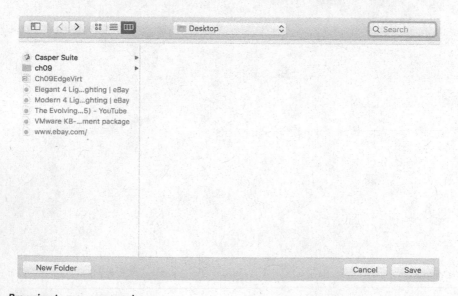

Figure 9-9. Browsing to save your package

You can also add scripts that can run before or after the payload for your package gets installed. To do so, right-click or Control-click the Scripts entry in the package and then click Add Shell Script. Here, click "postflight," shown in Figure 9-10.

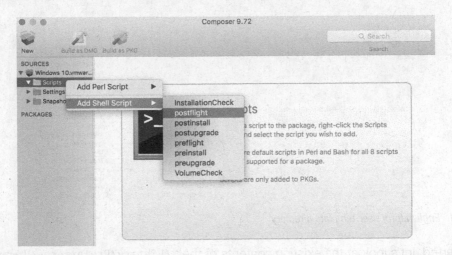

Figure 9-10. Adding scripts to your package

One appropriate automation for fresh installations is to disable the welcome screen. To do so, you would use the following command:

```
defaults write /Users/cedge/Library/Preferences/com.vmware.fusion↵
  VMWelcomeScreenViewed_2.0 -bool yes
```

> **Tip**   The `defaults write` command needs the absolute path, or it will write to the active user domain, and if it is being run during imaging, it could have unintended consequences. However, it is also not practical to deploy user-centric settings on a base image because it is unlikely that user home folders will be populated with data at this time. For this reason, it is best to deploy these settings via a system such as MCX or profiles, as discussed in Chapter 7.

Populating the Virtual Machine List

Another automation as a postflight for the package might be to populate the virtual machine library. Once your virtual machine has been placed in the target directory by the package, then you can use the `defaults` command (which is also described in Chapter 6) to populate the listing of virtual machines on clients. If you are deploying only a single virtual machine to each client, then you can copy the `com.vmware.fusion.plist` property list file to each user's home directory, which is stored in the `~/Library/Preferences/` directory. You can also add the file to the `English.lproj User Template` directory, as shown in Figure 9-11, to add it for all users of a given host.

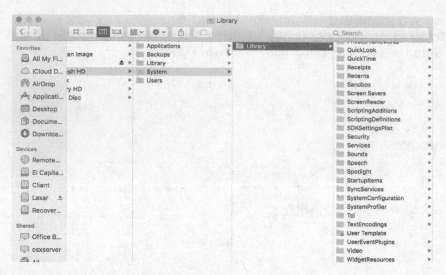

Figure 9-11. English.lproj User Template directory

To get started, let's look at the existing contents of the ~/Library/Preferences/VMware Fusion/preferences file in com.vmware.fusionStartMenu.

```
defaults read com.vmware.fusionStartMenu
```

The list of virtual machines available in the virtual machine list is stored in the fusionStartMenuVmList key, which is an array of machine names and paths. You can query for a listing of the machines that are currently available to the virtual machine library by reading the VMFavoritesListDefaults2 key alone.

```
defaults read com.vmware.fusionStartMenu fusionStartMenuVmList
```

Next, you'll use the array-add defaults option to add a virtual machine called Windows 10 to the virtual machine list, assuming it has a local path of ~/Documents/win.vmwarevm.

```
defaults write com.vmware.fusionStartMenu fusionStartMenuVmList -array-add
'{name = "Windows 10";cachePath="~/Documents/win.vmwarevm/startMenu.plist";}'
```

> **Note**   Rather than use the array-add option, you could have added a whole listing of virtual machines if you were deploying multiple .vmware VM bundles by using the -array option.

Assuming that the virtual machine list is your final customization to the package, once the postflight script is added, then you can build the package again. Once it's saved, you can deploy the package to test by using your mass deployment package or by leveraging a variety of patch management solutions such as Apple Remote Desktop or Casper Suite.

Tip We recommend pushing out only one virtual machine per package and then using the `array-add defaults` option per virtual machine to populate the Virtual Machine Library list.

Parallels

VMware Fusion is only one of a number of virtualization tools available for OS X. Parallels Desktop is another and is also a type 2 hypervisor, running as an application inside OS X. Parallels Desktop is available at www.parallels.com. As with Fusion, you will want to obtain a volume license for Parallels Desktop prior to leveraging the mass deployment options we illustrate through the remainder of this section. To get started, first download the Parallels Desktop .dmg from the Parallels web site.

Parallels Desktop on a Monolithic Image

Installing Parallels Desktop on an image that will be deployed monolithically is fairly straightforward. Open the .dmg file that you obtained from Parallels, and you will see the standard installation screen. Double-click the package, as shown in Figure 9-12, to start the installation.

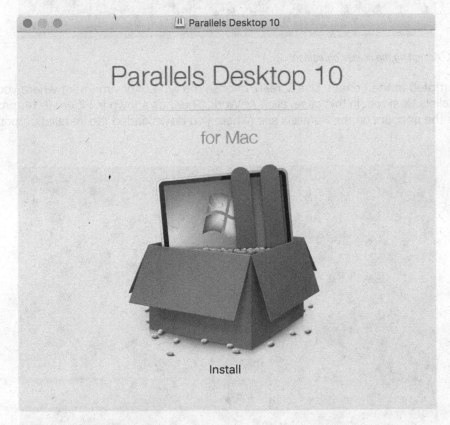

Figure 9-12. The standard installation screen

The package will then check the Parallels site for updates and verify that the computer meets the minimum requirements. Provided there are no updates and that the computer does indeed meet those minimums, you will next see the software license agreement. After you accept the license agreement, click the Accept button, as shown in Figure 9-13, and then enter the username and password to authenticate the Parallels Desktop installer.

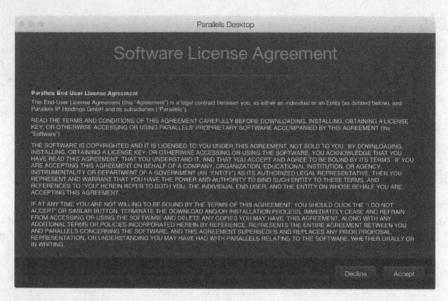

Figure 9-13. Accepting the license agreement

When prompted at the Primary Use screen, choose the type of environment where you'll be using Parallels Desktop. In this case, click At Work. Then, as shown in Figure 9-14, provide the details for the account on the Parallels site (where you downloaded the installation package).

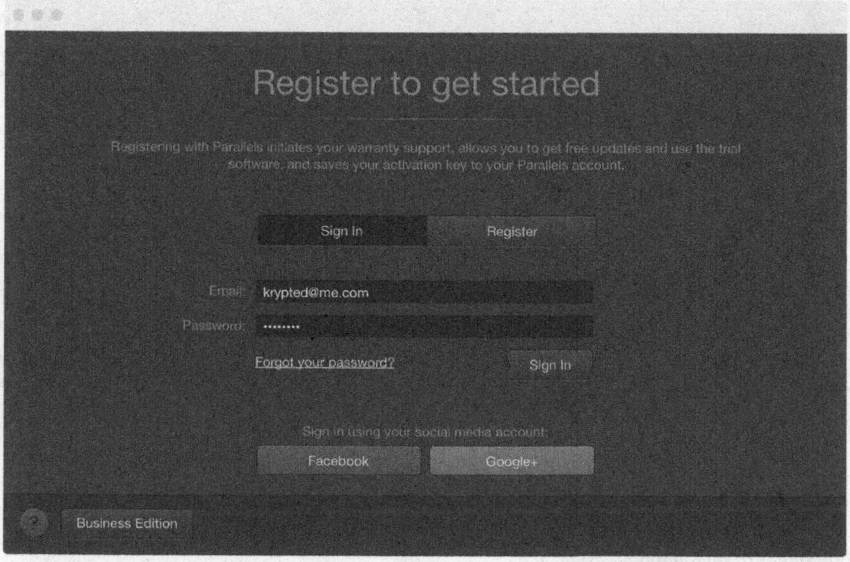

Figure 9-14. Entering registration information

You can then use Parallels, which includes the same tasks described previously in this chapter for VMware: install virtual machines, access Windows and other installations in virtual machines, and so on.

Virtual Machine Deployment

Within Parallels Desktop you can easily invoke the Virtual Machine Assistant, used to create new virtual machine instances. To do so, open Parallels Desktop and then click New from the File menu. At the New Virtual Machine screen, you will be able to install a new virtual machine (for example, from an .iso or installation media) or migrate a machine from a desktop. For the purposes of this example, click the button "Install Windows or another OS from a DVD or image file," as shown in Figure 9-15.

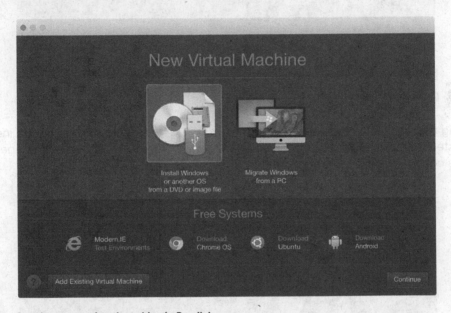

Figure 9-15. Creating a new virtual machine in Parallels

At the Parallels Wizard, you will be prompted to select the type of media that you will use to install an operating system on your virtual machine. This might be a DVD, an image file, or a USB drive, as shown in Figure 9-16.

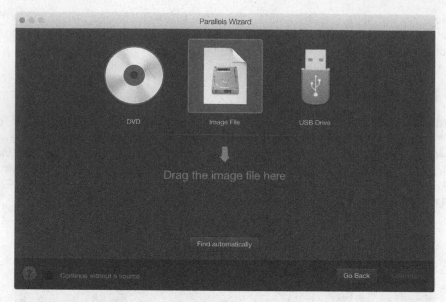

Figure 9-16. *Choosing the media type*

Next, drag the installation media on top of the arrow. The operating system you're installing is then listed in the Parallels Wizard, as you can see in Figure 9-17. Provided the operating system is correct, click the Continue button.

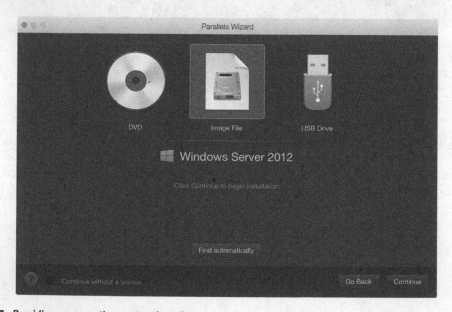

Figure 9-17. *Providing an operating system installer*

The installer then reads the installation media and presents you with options to automate the installation. In Figure 9-18, notice that you can provide the serial number and installation type for Windows Server 2012. Once entered, click the Continue button. If you don't yet have a product key, uncheck the "This version requires a product key" option and then click the Continue button.

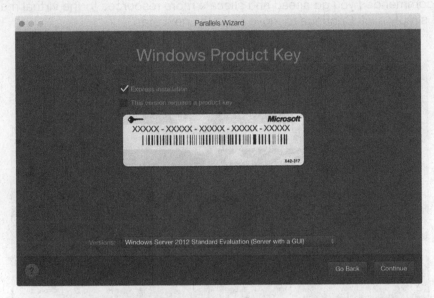

Figure 9-18. The express Windows installation screen

Virtual machines have a number of different options to optimize their performance. However, the options often fall into a few different categories. Since we're showing how to install a server, we'll select the Software Development option and then click Continue (Figure 9-19).

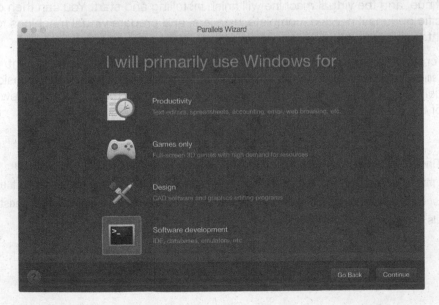

Figure 9-19. Choosing how you'll use the virtual machine

At the Virtual Machine Configuration screen, provide a name and location for the virtual machine, as shown in Figure 9-20. Enter the name and company name and provide a path for the virtual machine. You can then click the Configure button to increase the available RAM for the virtual machine and provision more than one processor if you so want. If you will be running more than an application or two or if the applications are fairly resource intensive, then it's recommended you go ahead and allocate more resources to the virtual machine. Otherwise, simply click Continue to move on to the next step.

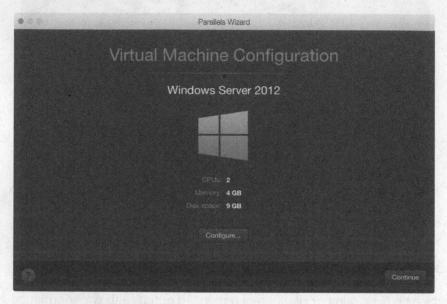

Figure 9-20. Browsing to the Parallels folder

Click Continue, and the virtual machine will finish installing and start. You can then configure more specific options if needed, complete installers, and prepare virtual machines for mass deployment.

Once you create the virtual computer, you can use Terminal to cd into the resultant <machinename>.pvm that makes up your Parallels virtual machine. When you are inside the file—in much the same way that you did in VMware earlier—you will be able to view the contents of the config.pvs file.

> **Tip**   Once it's installed, you will typically want to install the Parallels Tools software onto the virtual machine. This will allow for integration between the OS X host operating system and the guest operating system that you have just installed. This can be accomplished by selecting Install Parallels Tools from the Parallels Desktop VM menu when the guest OS is booted.

The `config.pvs` file is the settings file for each virtual machine. As with Vmware, the virtual machine that you see through the Finder is in fact a bundle, with a number of files inside of it. Parallels Desktop has a fair number of settings in the `.pvs` file, organized by keys. There are multiple UUID keys and a number nested within the Network Adapter key that will need to be changed if you were to mass deploy your virtual machine, although it doesn't have to be that complicated, as we will illustrate in the upcoming section.

Automating the Parallels Installation

Parallels provides a solution to mass deploy its software. To leverage the Parallels best practice to push out Parallels Desktop using a package, go to `http://download.parallels.com/desktop/tools/pd-autodeploy.zip` and download the Autodeploy package. The Autodeploy package will copy the application and virtual machine files for you and regenerate the unique identification information, similar to how you did manually for VMware Fusion earlier in the section "Preparing the Virtual Machine for Mass Deployment."

Once you have downloaded the package, right-click it and select Show Package Contents, as you did earlier with VMware Fusion. From here, browse to the `Parallels` folder and find the `deploy.cfg` file, as shown in Figure 9-21. By altering this file, you will provide the `Parallels Desktop Autodeploy.pkg` file with the serial number to use in an installation.

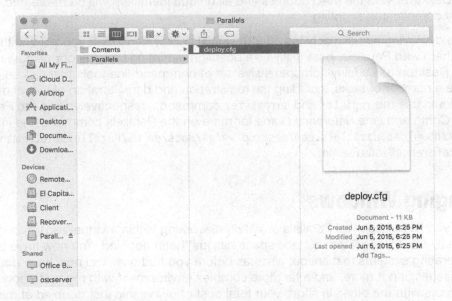

Figure 9-21. Browsing to the Parallels folder

You will then need to place the `Parallels Desktop.dmg` file that contains the original package into the Parallels folder as well, which will complete the automated installation of Parallels.

As you are considering automating the deployment of the Parallels software, it is worth noting that there are two property lists that control the application's global behavior across various virtual machines. These are `com.parallels.Parallels Desktop.plist` and `com.parallels.desktop.console.plist`, both in the `~/Library/Preferences` directory. (These are included with an installation, whether it is the Autodeploy or the standard installer.) The `com.parallels.Parallels Desktop.plist` file controls screen settings, update preferences, application toolbars, and the Virtual Machine Assistant. The `com.parallels.desktop.console.plist` controls last-used directories. You can now push out the Autodeploy package to automate the installation of the Parallels application.

Automated Virtual Machine Deployment

While we covered pushing out the application itself in the previous section, we have not yet covered how to push out virtual machines. To do so, you would first normalize the Windows installation, as we did with VMware Fusion virtual machines (and described in the section "Preparing the Virtual Machine for Mass Deployment" later in this chapter). Once it's normalized, again right-click or Control-click the `Parallels Desktop Autodeploy.pkg` file and select Show Package Contents. Next, copy the virtual machine bundle from the current location into the Parallels folder of the package, where you previously edited the `deploy.cfg` file.

Upon installation of the `Parallels Desktop Autodeploy.pkg` package, the `.pvm` file will now be copied into the user's `~/Documents/Parallels` directory by default. You can now leverage your mass deployment solution (DeployStudio) or your package management solution (Apple Remote Desktop), and the MAC address and all unique identifiers will be re-created without using any complicated scripting.

If you are deploying virtual machines after the initial deployment, then you will want to register them with Parallels, potentially as a postflight scripting task to your package. Parallels Desktop has a fairly comprehensive set of command-line tools that can be used to automate a number of tasks, including the registration and deregistration of virtual machines (which would use the `register` and `unregister` commands, respectively). See the *Parallels Desktop Command Line Reference Guide* for more on the Parallels command-line interface at `http://download.parallels.com/desktop/v9/ga/docs/en_US/Parallels%20Command%20Line%20Reference%20Guide.pdf`.

Managing Windows

Whether you have deployed Parallels or VMware, working within a virtualized environment means that your management surface space has just been doubled. You now have two or more operating systems to manage, whereas before you had one. You now have double the security issues, if not more, and a far more complex environment with regard to how each part interacts with the other. In short, your total cost of ownership just doubled at minimum! But while your management costs just shot up, they can be kept in check. In the following sections, you'll look at various ways to automate deployment and patch management to stay a lucid systems administrator.

Sysprep

Similar to deploying OS X, you will want to perform a number of automations on each virtual machine. As previously mentioned, each Microsoft Windows computer needs to be normalized, meaning it will need a unique identifier (SID) and a unique computer name. This means that two computers, whether physical or virtual, should not share an identifier, or else they have problems, for example, binding to Active Directory. Other automations often include renaming hosts and, of course, binding machines into Active Directory. The two primary methods for these automations are Sysprep or using custom scripts that typically call Sysprep. For many tasks, such as removing machine-specific information and renaming hosts, it will be difficult to justify custom scripting because Sysprep has much of the functionality required unless your organization's needs require logic that is beyond the basic Sysprep functionality.

Scripting Virtual Machine Automations in OS X

If you run a script at first boot, you can use the registry in combination with the Startup Items for an administrative user. A combination of the AutoAdminLogon, DefaultUserName, and DefaultPassword keys can be used in the HKEY_LOCAL_ MACHINE\SOFTWARE\Microsoft\ Windows NT\CurrentVersion\Winlogon path of the registry to enable automatic logon for the virtual machine. After your automations have completed, you will want to edit the same registry keys, remove the DefaultUserName and DefaultPassword contents, and disable the AutoAdminLogon key.

You can also run a script by passing the script into a command from your virtualization software. For example, you could leverage the vmrun command to initiate a Visual Basic script as part of an automation. If you have a script that will bind to Active Directory, then you can create a postflight script in your package or leverage a tool, such as Apple Remote Desktop, to send a script through VMware Fusion to your virtual machine and your guest operating system. Assuming the username of an administrator is administrator with a password of SECRETPASSWORD and a path to the Visual Basic script in the c:\scripts\bind.vbs file of the host, an example of this command is as follows:

```
vmrun -T fusion -gu administrator -gp 'SECRETPASSWORD' runScriptInGuest "/VMs/Windows 10.
vmwarevm/Windows 10.vmx" cscript.exe "c:\scripts\bind.vbs"
```

> **Note** You cannot run DOS batch files using vmrun.

You can run the vmrun command in /Library/Application Support/VMware Fusion/. You can run the command with no arguments to see pretty thorough documentation on the tool. To give a quick rundown of the previous command, the -T flag designates the host type (in this case VMware Fusion). The -gu command and -gp flags designate the guest host credentials. For this command to succeed, an OS X user must be logged in, and the virtual machine will need to be running. VMware Fusion can also use a Boot Camp partition as its guest OS. For Boot Camp–based virtual machines, Fusion stores the `.vmx` file in `~/Library/Application Support/VMware Fusion/Virtual Machines/Boot Camp`. Use the following command to find output the full path to a user's `Boot Camp` `.vmx` file:

```
find /Users/*/Library/Application\ Support/VMware\ Fusion/Virtual\ Machines/Boot\↵
Camp/ -name "*.vmx"
```

Policies and Open Directory

Group Policies use the registry to define where to pull a policy file from. If a preference manifest in OS X (described in more detail in Chapter 7) is a container of settings, then a Group Policy object is similar in that a file is created, and the unique identification of that file is located in Active Directory. These files are stored in the Group Policy Template (GPT) subdirectory of the SYSVOL folder, a directory created by default on all Windows Server domain controllers.

> **Note**   You can also use the Group Policy Object Editor on a host and apply the policies directly to that system in your virtual machine, which would then apply to virtual machines that are created based on the initial virtual machine; however, you should use SYSVOL because you will be able to centrally manage policies.

To create Group Policy objects, log into a Windows Server instance (if you are in an Active Directory environment) or a Windows XP computer (if you are applying the policy on the local computer). Click Start and then Run, and at the Run dialog enter gpedit.msc. The resulting window will show you two types of policies, as shown in Figure 9-22, for the Local Computer: Computer Configuration and User Configuration. These control computer-based settings and user-based settings, respectively.

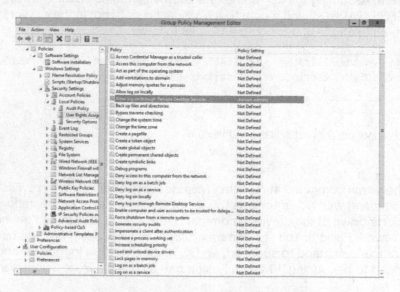

Figure 9-22. Local Computer: Computer Configuration and User Configuration policies

Computer Configurations

The Computer Configuration options mostly have to do with rights management. Here you can define which users or groups are capable of performing certain types of tasks and policies that span multiple users.

User Configurations

The User Configuration options are far more granular. Here you can configure various components of Windows, control applications (such as some of the previous Windows Update settings), and customize user environments (including settings pertaining to the Desktop, My Documents, Start menu, and the taskbar, such as whether the user has an option to open a Run dialog).

Other Virtualization Solutions

Up to this point we have focused on VMware and Parallels. The primary reason is that most enterprises are going to want to pay for support and are not typically considering free and open source software for deployment en masse. However, there are two stand-out applications that can be used in place of VMware and Parallels that can help to keep TCO numbers in check.

The first is VirtualBox by Sun Microsystems. VirtualBox, like VMware, is cross platform. It can run on practically any operating system, and virtual machines can be traded between hosts. VirtualBox comes in a package and can therefore be mass deployed with little fanfare. VirtualBox does not come with some of the slick additional features that VMware or Parallels has, but it is capable of running most operating systems as guests and is a solution that can be deployed inexpensively. For more on VirtualBox, see Chapter 10.

Another free solution is Q, which can be obtained from www.kju-app.org. Q comes in an .app bundle and can be copied to client computers as a payload of a package. Both Q and VirtualBox can have virtual machines deployed alongside the applications themselves in a package or using a separate package, as we did previously with VMware and Parallels.

Managing VMs and Boot Camp Through GPOs

One problem with introducing virtual machines into a mixed platform is that you are also introducing additional complexity. If you are already running Active Directory, then likely you will have bound your Macs into the directory, as described in Chapter 3. When you introduce virtual machines onto these machines, then you'll be binding the virtual host into AD as well. Suddenly, you have two computer objects per machine. If you have Boot Camp partitions not utilized by virtual machines, then this OS instance will also have its own computer record. How do you organize all of these? First, the naming convention on your OS hosts is paramount to be able to properly differentiate between the respective OS instances. One good practice is to use specialized prefixes or suffixes. For instance, the OS X environment may be jdoe-lt-0435. For this box, the VM instance's computer name might be called jdoe-lt-0435-vm, and its Boot Camp partition might be jdoe-lt-0435-bc.

Unless you are using a third-party integration tool, such as Centrify or Quest, or have extended your Active Directory schema for OS X support, then the computer object for your primary OS X instance isn't much good for management on your virtual machine. Its existence is without doubt a requirement, but any GPOs that would normally be applied to a Windows OS are promptly ignored. Because of this, either you can organize your OS X objects right next to your virtual machine objects or you can create purpose-specific Computer containers for each purpose: Computers, Macs, MacVM, and Boot Camp. Using purpose-specific containers is typically recommended for a number of reasons. First, in large environments it just helps organizationally. Most importantly, it provides a way to target each specific environment for GPO management.

There are certainly circumstances where you might want to target only specific VM instances, or perhaps only Boot Camp computers. For instance, both Parallels and VMware have options to redirect a user's home profile to local folders on the OS X file system. This is similar to a basic redirection-deployed GPO, but instead of pointing a user's folders to a network share, you point them to the file system on the host OS. This way, when you go to My Desktop on your Windows guest OS, you see the same items as you would when you go to your OS X Desktop folder. However, if you deploy GPOs by redirecting a user's My Desktop or My Documents folder to their network profile, those GPOs will conflict with the VM software's redirection, causing unpredictable results. The goal in this scenario would be to terminate redirections specifically on OS X virtual machine instances.

However, document redirection is a User policy, so computer objects do not have dominion to manage (or prevent) them. Luckily, Active Directory provides a function called User Group policy loopback. When linked to an OU, the User Policy application can be directly affected by User Policy GPOs applied to an OU containing computer records. Normally, only the user's Group Policy objects determine which user settings apply. However, if User Group policy loopback is enabled, when a user logs on to this computer, the computer's Policy objects determine which set of User Policy objects are applied. This will effectively allow you to block the inheritance of user folder redirection policies through the use of computer OUs (see Figure 9-23).

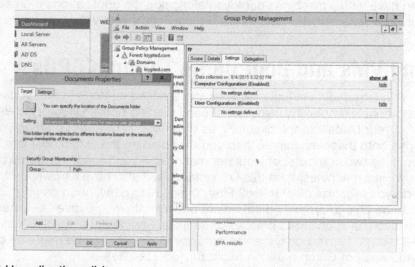

Figure 9-23. Folder redirection policies

Configuring your laptops in this way, by allowing your virtual machines to utilize local storage, has numerous benefits. First, the barrier between the host OS and the guest OS becomes less of a mental challenge when both have access to the same data. This means your users will have less difficulty in comprehending the dual OS workflow. Second, it allows for the utilization of OS X–based home directory syncing, which will ensure that both OS X– and Windows-altered documents in the user's home folder will get synchronized to the home directory server. This is particularly handy if your users will move back and forth between wired desktops and wireless laptops.

Through the use of OS X network home folders, Windows My Desktop and My Document GPO redirects, and OS X mobile syncing on laptops, you can provide a completely seamless cross-platform existence. When the user logs into a wired lab Mac, he will have access to his data. If he then logs into his directory-integrated laptop, syncing will ensure any changes made from the lab Mac show up on the laptop. The user then opens up a Windows VM on his laptop and modifies some documents.

The OS X host will eventually sync that data back to his home directory store as well. Perhaps next, that user logs into a laptop running Boot Camp or even hardware PCs. All changes made on the laptop are right there present on the desktop, and any changes will be saved back up through the chain.

This integration will be highly desirable in a large cross-platform environment. It will help to reduce end user confusion because they will no longer have to worry about which computer and OS their important data was last left on. It will provide the ability to transition between OSs with minimal burden on the user to understand the complexity that must go on behind the scenes.

Antivirus

Finally, consider the virus. The Mac (according to the commercials you see on television and in real life as well) is rarely harmed by malware. But Microsoft Windows, not so much. Therefore, make sure you have planned for viral infestations on all your computers. Whether you choose to use a solution such as Symantec's EndPoint Protection or a free solution, such as AVG (http://free.avg.com) or ClamWin (www.clamwin.com), it is important to run some form of antivirus to keep your environment free from threats. We won't go into further detail on antivirus solutions here because we assume most enterprises have robust antivirus solutions in place for the Windows platform.

## Chapter 10

Free and Open Source Tools for Mac Admins

Running an enterprise costs money. Depending on upper-level management's point of view, the Information Technology department is either a valued contributor to the company's success or a necessary evil. Sales is frequently the golden child of an organization because it is regarded as the "money maker" and "profiteer." It generates income. Departments such as IT take away from the bottom line. They repeatedly ask for resources—expensive resources—to store data, automate processes, and provide this thing called "security," which no one ever really sees. IT directors often have to re-justify their budgets when asked, "Didn't we just give you money for that five years ago?"

A second strike for the IT department is its support of "nonstandard" hardware and platforms such as Mac computers and OS X. A company would be able to save a lot of money if it could keep everything the same, right? One platform, one operating system, and one set of standard software for everyone. After all, those Macs are only here to do graphics, and the company can buy two or three PCs for the cost of one Mac. Just like IT, Macs cost money. They don't make money.

Dollar signs often cloud upper management's perception of IT's role in an organization and its cost to support employees. Interestingly, this isn't about how much IT costs but rather that IT doesn't generate revenue. Only Sales generates revenue. Everything else is an expense. When the market is down and the company is losing money (or not generating as much money as stakeholders would like), management cuts expenses. As Mac administrators, we have little control over this process.

We do have control over what we spend to support our users on the Mac platform. This is where commercial versus open source and free software come into play. Organizations build entire infrastructures on open source and free software products, redirecting the earnings toward IT support staff, other systems using commercial software, and maybe even the company's bottom line. It's not easy to do, but Mac administrators are one of the best IT groups poised to make this work.

In this chapter, we will cover whether building an environment around open source and free software is right for you and your company. Does it really save money? What are the costs of bringing your own support? We will examine why licensing is important when evaluating these tools for your environment and what you should know when you click that Agree button on behalf of everyone in your organization. And we will examine many tools for making your job as a Mac administrator easier or more productive.

Commercial vs. Free vs. Open Source Tools

Building a partial or entire support infrastructure around commercial or noncommercial software offers advantages and disadvantages. Weigh the value of commercial, open source, and free tools in your organization. The pros and cons of commercial tools compared to open source and free tools are generally polar opposites of each other.

Commercial Software

Commercial software's primary advantage is future support. Support means product updates to fix bugs and improve security, e-mail, and/or phone support for using the product and maybe even the ear of a responsive developer who listens for your needs in the product and implements feature requests. Most important, however, a commercial software developer has monetary incentive to continue improving the product. The livelihood of small software companies is dependent on responsiveness to customers and keeping them happy.

Of course, commercial software's primary disadvantage is it costs money, and good support may hinge on the amount of money you spend. A software developer is more likely to address a minor bug that affects hundreds or thousands of users than fix a major bug that impacts only your five users. Conversely, if you've licensed software for hundreds or thousands of seats, you have greater impact on the future development of the software.

Commercial software also comes with limited legal liability and control on behalf of the developer. That means judicial systems won't hold developers accountable if their software fails because of a bug and causes your company to lose its money. However, the company does have some legal recourse if a developer failed to disclose an alternate purpose for its software such as collecting sensitive information and feeding that quietly to an Internet server. It also means the developer has the right to embed a kill-switch in the software to prevent your use. Whether justified or not, the developer may have control to disrupt your company's workflows. That becomes a risk.

Here are the pros of commercial software:

- Paid software comes with developer support.

- Paid software comes with limited legal liability.

- More investment with the developer generally means more responsiveness from the developer.

Here are the cons of commercial software:

- It costs money (nominal or substantial).

- The developer maintains centralized control over the codebase.

- The developer maintains control over use of its product in your environment both legally and sometimes operationally via activation or kill-switches.

Open Source Software

Open source tools don't have an up-front cost, which is great for administrators with strapped budgets. And open source projects allow peer review, which means anyone can see the source code. Anyone in the community can contribute to a project to identify bugs and coding mistakes and verify the code doesn't contain malicious software. Also, anyone in the open source community can contribute code to a project or fork it to make another project. This offers administrators the advantage of starting with someone else's work to make their own solutions. Because open source software is developed by the community, the direction of the projects is also set by the community and often customized to the needs of that community.

While some commercial developers may require activation and paid annual subscriptions to continue using their products, open source software is decentralized, and your use of it is perpetual at the time of download. Decentralized code eliminates the risk of an outside entity having any control over a workflow function that's crucial to your company.

A disadvantage of open source software is that developers may offer their products as-is and totally on a whim. They develop their software on their timeline (often as time permits) and have no incentive to add features or fix bugs apart from their own sense of contribution to the community. Also, the licensing for a project may hinder a company's development by requiring it to release derivative works used in its commercial environment back to the community.

> **Note** Wait, can't you do anything you want with open source software? That depends on how the developer has licensed it to you. We'll touch on that in the section "I'm Not a Lawyer, but I Play One in IT" later in this chapter.

Here are the pros of open source software:

- There is no cost to use the software in most environments.

- The source code is available to everyone to review and improve.

- There is no centralized control over the codebase.

Here are the cons of open source software:

- Development is often at the whim of the developer and community. This can be a pro as well, as various members of the community can customize the software, allowing the software to appeal to the greatest number of people possible.

- Administrators may need to rely on the community for support.

- Licensing may deter development for commercial use.

Free Software

Free software? As in free lunch? Software developers may choose to give away their product for a few reasons. Or rather, they may choose not to require payment for you to use their product.

Like the analogy of giving away a razor to sell the blades, some companies will release their product for anyone to use freely as an enticement to purchase other software or support services. Similar to games with in-app purchases, the free version of the software may be exactly what you need, and the commercial plug-ins, add-ins, extensions, or services may be overkill. However, you have the option to start with a base product and build something more customized for your environment or can pay someone for support *if* you need help.

Commercial developers may release a product as a trial and expect you to honor their request to pay for the software if you continue using it. Originally called *shareware*, this software is technically *not* free. While these developers may not actively pursue collecting payment from individual users, they retain the option to pursue legal recourse if they discover organizations are using their products for profit.

And some developers are just plain generous. Members of the open source community may release a compiled project based on one of their open source projects. This is generally a courtesy to community members who are not developers and do not know how to use development tools to compile their own versions of the software. Or maybe they're not developers but fellow administrators who have chosen to give back to the community by releasing into the public domain some source code or a script they have written to solve a problem.

Beware of free software that requires you to provide personal information such as location or application usage on a regular basis. Although you may perceive the requirement as innocuous, the developer collecting the data may really be aggregating your data to learn more about your organization specifically or use it to sell to third parties.

Here are the pros of free software:

- "Free" may really mean free.

- It allows use of the software on a trial basis without any risk.

Here are the cons of free software:

- Free software may be limited and released as an enticement to purchase additional software or services.

- Trial software eventually may require payment (morally and legally) if you continue using it.

- Free software may be an enticement to collect sensitive information.

I'm Not a Lawyer, but I Play One in IT

This is the most important section of the chapter. Read it!

Almost every commercial software license agreement includes the phrase, "The software is licensed, not sold." That's means the end user is purchasing the legal right to *use* the software but has made no legal claim to deconstruct, reassemble, reproduce, or resell the software. This is similar to the legal disclaimers by the Motion Picture Industry Association of America (MPIAA) to customers purchasing DVDs or streaming movies online. The developer owns the copyright to the code and sells only the permission to use the compiled version of the software.

While open source software means the source code is available to the public, that doesn't mean the public can do just anything with it. Open source software still includes a license for use. Using the source code means accepting the developer's conditions for use. That may mean you are free to take the code and modify it any way you want for your company to make a profit. Or it may mean you legally have to return your own version of the source code to the public if you redistribute your derivative version of the code.

When evaluating software, don't consider the up-front cost as your total cost to use the software. Software is licensed, and the license dictates how and whether your company can legally use the software without legal liability.

Open Source Licenses

You, as an administrator, are the first line of defense with regard to the legal use of software in your organization. If you are asked to install any open source software, review the license first. The code is probably released under one of a handful of available open source licenses that lawyers have reviewed and refined. Become familiar with these types of licenses. Verify with your organization's legal team which licenses they deem acceptable and which licenses they deem as risks to the business.

Why do developers license open source software if they're releasing it for free to the general public? Licensing is just a subtopic of the broader Open Source Definition (http://opensource.org/docs/osd), which stipulates the terms of distribution for open source software.

- Free redistribution
- Source code
- Derived works

- Integrity of the author's source code

- No discrimination against people or groups

- No discrimination against fields of endeavor

- Distribution of license

- License must not be specific to a product

- License must not restrict other software

- License must be technology-neutral

Note that licensing accounts for nearly half of the Open Source Definition. Licensing allows open source software to be freely used, modified, and shared. It prevents someone from taking a developer's work released freely to the public, claiming copyright, and then preventing anyone else from using the software or charging for use of the software.

Let's review some of the more popular open source licenses.

Apache License 2.0

- *Site*: www.apache.org/foundation/license-faq.html

You are free to download software under this license for personal and commercial purposes and reuse it in your own products that you distribute. You must include all attributions to the original developers, including a copy of the Apache license.

Creative Commons

- *Site*: https://creativecommons.org/licenses/

Creative Commons includes six variations of licensing ranging from free use of the software with attribution to no modifications and no commercial uses allowed.

FreeBSD Copyright

- *Site*: https://www.freebsd.org/copyright/freebsd-license.html

The FreeBSD Copyright license isn't really a license per se but requires that any redistributed versions of the software contain the original copyright information. It makes no claims about who may use the software and for what purposes.

GNU General Public License, Version 3.0 (GPL-3.0)

- *Site*: www.gnu.org/licenses/gpl-faq.html

You are free to download software under this license for personal and commercial purposes and reuse it in your own products that you distribute. However, if you release a modified version to the public, you must make the modified source code available to the program's users under the GPL.

MIT License (MIT)

Massachusetts Institute of Technology ®

- *Site*: http://opensource.org/licenses/MIT

Similar to the FreeBSD license, the MIT license requires that all copies and substantial portions of the original code include the copyright and license information. It makes no claim about who may use the software and for what purposes.

Mozilla Public License 2.0

- *Site*: https://www.mozilla.org/MPL/2.0/FAQ.html

The MPL sits between the Apache license, which does not require modifications to be shared, and the GNU license, which does require modifications to be shared. Some publicly shared derivative works must be made open source.

> **Tip** Your organization's legal team should review all software licenses, especially commercial software licenses. Commercial license agreements are written to favor the software developer, not the customer. Open source licenses favor best practices when redistributing or modifying open source software. Your legal team can pre-approve open source licenses to make acquiring and using open source software easier.

Where to Find Free and Open Source Tools

Commercial software developers have the luxury of promoting their products. Most open source developers have no advertising or marketing budgets unless they are giving away the product to sell their services. Therefore, word of mouth in the Mac admin community is extremely important to spreading the word about new tools.

Where do Mac admins hang out and talk shop?

AFP548

- *Site*: https://www.afp548.com

AFP548 covers everything to do with Apple IT, from iOS to OS X. Its mission is to offer in-depth coverage, articles, and podcasts focusing on the latest developments in the Apple IT world and Mac admin community.

Contributors to AFP548 frequently post in-depth information and articles about open source projects.

Google

- *Site*: https://github.com/google/macops

Google developers maintain an unofficial repository of Macops tools developed for managing Macs in the enterprise. This is a collection of utilities, tools, and scripts for managing and tracking Google's fleet of Macintosh computers.

Homebrew

- *Site*: http://brew.sh

Homebrew bills itself as the missing package manager for OS X, installing the stuff you need that Apple didn't.

This project hosted on GitHub is based on Git and Ruby and takes care of installing all dependencies for an open source project. It handles the downloading and compiling of projects, making using open source on OS X easy.

JAMF Nation

- *Site*: https://jamfnation.jamfsoftware.com/

JAMF Nation is the support site for JAMF Software's Casper Suite, which is not open source; however, its forums are some of the busiest in the Mac admin community, and open source projects are commonly discussed here.

The site includes a third-party area devoted to specific applications where community members have contributed code for scripts, manifests, and extension attributes.

MacEnterprise Mailing List

 MacEnterprise

- *Site*: www.macenterprise.org/mailing-list

Penn State University hosts the MacEnterprise mailing list with a mission to provide an open and friendly technical exchange of information about enterprise deployment, integration, and maintenance of Macs. It's one of the oldest resources for Mac admins.

List members can subscribe to the list online and receive individual messages or digests. Anyone can view a read-only version of the list via Google Groups.

MacPorts

- *Site*: https://www.macports.org

The MacPorts project is an open source community initiative to design an easy-to-use system for compiling, installing, and upgrading either command-line, X11, or Aqua-based open source software on the OS X operating system.

Like Homebrew, MacPorts handles downloading and compiling projects, making them easy for the nondeveloper to access. It has nearly 25,000 ports in its tree.

Puppet

- *Site*: https://puppetlabs.com/puppet/puppet-open-source

Open Source Puppet is a configuration management solution that lets you define the state of your IT infrastructure, using the Puppet language. Open Source Puppet then automatically enforces the correct configuration to ensure the right services are up and running, on the right platforms.

The Puppet Forge is a resource with 3,000-plus modules—reusable, sharable, prewritten Puppet code for automating a large number of common admin tasks. Forge modules are created by Puppet Labs and by Puppet community members.

PSU MacAdmins

- Site: http://macadmins.psu.edu

Penn State University is also the host of the MacAdmins Conference, the premier East Coast conference for anyone who deploys and manages Macs and iOS devices.

The Resources Archive includes presentation slides and session videos from 2010 to today, and many of the presentations cover emerging open source projects as well as detailed guidance for using some of the more popular open source projects in the Mac enterprise.

University of Utah

- Site: https://github.com/univ-of-utah-marriott-library-apple

The University of Utah maintains a GitHub repository of scripts and management tools it has created for its own Mac administration needs.

Listing of Free and Open Source Tools

What are some of the more common open source tools Mac admins are using in their environments today? We cover some of them next, divided into these common Mac management categories:

- Management and inventory
- Coding and scripting
- Client tools
- Packaging
- Imaging
- Security and testing

Management and Inventory

Administration starts with a list of assets, both hardware and software. Knowing what you have to manage is simple in small environments of a few hundred devices. Keeping track of device models, licensing, and application versions is still challenging nonetheless. In large environments of several thousand hardware assets, each with its own set of software assets, management and inventory tools are paramount to maintaining stability.

Munki

- *Site*: `https://github.com/munki`
- *Purpose*: Software deployment and management

Munki is the most popular and well-known open source project in the Mac management arena and has helped spawn several other open source projects that complement its features. It and its creator Greg Neagle deserve special recognition for the impact they have had in both the enterprise and education.

Munki is a set of tools to manage software installs on OS X clients. It sounds simple, but the simplest tasks are often the most tedious and complex to manage. Good management ensures the right Mac has access to the right software titles such as Adobe Creative Cloud for graphic designers and Microsoft Excel for finance users. Management is not just about installing software but sometimes removing it too. Munki also handles patch management, keeping software up-to-date, by allowing users to control when updates install.

Adding to the complexity of what and when to install are software developers who package their products in standard and not-so-standard ways. Mozilla, for example, follows Apple's guidelines for drag-and-drop installation of Firefox and delivers its application in an OS X disk image file (`.dmg`). Microsoft uses Apple's native installer technology and delivers Office for Mac and its updates in Apple Installer's package format (`.pkg`). Adobe uses a proprietary installer for its Creative Cloud suite of products that's compatible with neither drag and drop nor Apple Installer tools. Munki is designed to work with all these software installation methods and even Apple's own software update service.

Software deployment is just one type of deployment Munki handles. Apple Installer packages also support scripts. That means Munki can deploy a security certificate file (`.cer`) to a Mac and use a postinstall script to install the certificate for one or all users. Also, Munki natively handles configuration profiles, which manage features such as FileVault encryption, Active Directory binding, Xsan client deployments, and application preferences. Finally, Munki runs scripts using nopkg packages, a method of storing a postinstall script without a package. Of course, it still supports installing a payload-free package with just a postinstall script to run administrative commands. A script does practically anything a user can do in the Finder and often more.

Munki takes the practice of software updates a step further by removing the need for the user to interact with the installer or even authenticate as an administrator. It provides the administrative credentials to OS X while giving the user control over when or if the updates get installed. Its Managed Software Center tool lets users run them immediately and additionally offers optional software installs (see Figure 10-1).

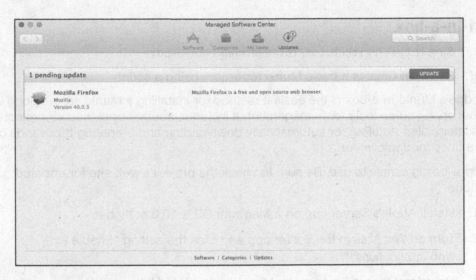

Figure 10-1. Munki Managed Software Center

The documentation for Munki (https://github.com/munki/munki/wiki) is thorough. It includes a walk-through Demonstration Setup for configuring a new server and preparing to serve clients, a guide for customizing the Managed Software Center for your organization, detailed and in-depth discussion for building complex Apple Installer packages, and numerous links to additional resources.

Munki's user community is strong and uses Google Groups mailing lists for discussion, support, and development. Before posting to any of the discussion groups, read the FAQs and posting guidelines and search for answers to your issue just in case someone else had the same question.

- *General Munki discussion*: https://groups.google.com/forum/#!forum/munki-discuss

- *MunkiAdmin*: https://groups.google.com/forum/#!forum/munkiadmin-dev

- *Munki-dev*: https://groups.google.com/forum/#!forum/munki-dev

- *MunkiReport*: https://groups.google.com/forum/#!forum/munkireport

- *MunkiWebAdmin*: https://groups.google.com/forum/#!forum/munki-web-admin

- *Sal*: https://groups.google.com/forum/#!forum/sal-discuss

- *Simian*: https://groups.google.com/forum/#!forum/simian-discuss

Now, let's look at some of the open source projects that complement Munki. Not all of these projects support just Munki. Some of them are useful stand-alone tools or useful in conjunction with other management systems.

Munki-in-a-box

- *Site*: https://github.com/tbridge/munki-in-a-box
- *Purpose*: Creates a basic Munki repository using a script

Tom Bridge's Munki-in-a-box is the easiest method for installing a Munki server along with additional open source tools for management. It includes another open source project we'll discuss later called AutoPkg for automatically downloading and preparing thousands of software titles for deployment.

Munki-in-a-box is simple to use. Be sure to check the project's web site for updated instructions.

1. Install Apple's Server app on a Mac with OS X 10.8 or higher.

2. Turn on Websites in the Server app and click the setting "Enable PHP web applications."

3. Download the zip file from the Munki-in-a-box GitHub repository.

4. Edit the script from the zip file to customize some details for your Munki server.

5. Open Terminal and run the script.

> **Tip**   To run the script in Terminal, use the cd command to "change directory" into the script's folder and then call the script from within the folder.
>
> ```
> admin $ cd /path/to/munki-in-a-box-master
> admin $ sudo ./munkiinabox.sh
> ```

The script takes care of downloading, installing, and configuring a basic Munki server; adding some example software packages such as Adobe Reader, Firefox, and TextWrangler; and preparing your server for the Demonstration Setup, which is part of Munki's introductory documentation.

Next, download and install the current official release of munki tools on a test client Mac:

https://github.com/munki/munki/releases

Proceed from here on your server with creating a client manifest and configuring your Munki client as described in the Demonstration Setup documentation:

https://github.com/munki/munki/wiki/Demonstration-Setup

MunkiWebAdmin

■ *Site*: https://github.com/munki/munkiwebadmin

■ *Purpose*: Adds a web console to Munki for easier administrative management

Administering a Munki server installation requires running command-line utilities and editing XML files. Greg Neagle created MunkiWebAdmin as a companion to Munki to provide a GUI interface in a web browser. MunkiWebAdmin is a mixture of various open source projects, each with its own set of dependencies.

The following instructions add MunkiWebAdmin to an existing Munki server running on OS X Server. Be sure to check the project's web site for updated instructions.

1. Open Terminal and run sudo easy_install virtualenv. This installs software you will use to create an isolated Python environment independent of your server's Python installation.

2. Assuming you installed your Munki repository into /Users/Shared, use the cd command to change directory to that location: cd /Users/Shared. You can choose to use a different directory. Keeping your Munki installations together just makes locating items easier.

3. Run virtualenv munkiwebadmin_env to create the virtual Python environment in a new munkiwebadmin_env folder.

4. Use the cd command to change directory into your munkiwebadmin_env folder: cd /Users/Shared/munkiwebadmin_env.

5. Run source bin/activate. Your prompt in Terminal should now look similar to (munkiwebadmin_env)bash-3.2$.

6. Run pip install django==1.5.1 to install Django, an open source web framework for creating database-driven web sites.

7. Run pip install django-wsgiserver==0.8.0beta to install the Web Server Gateway Interface, which acts as an interface between a web server and a web application.

8. Run git clone https://github.com/munki/munkiwebadmin/ munkiwebadmin to download MunkiWebAdmin's files from GitHub.

9. Run cd munkiwebadmin to change directory to the munkiwebadmin folder.

10. Run cp settings_template.py settings.py to copy the settings_template.py file to a settings.py file.

11. Use a plain-text editor such as Bare Bones Software's BBEdit or TextWrangler to edit the settings.py file.

12. Use your text editor's search feature to locate ADMIN and set its administrator name and e-mail address.

13. Search for TIME_ZONE and set the time zone.

14. Search for INSTALLED_APPS and uncomment (remove the # symbol) django_wsgiserver.

15. Search for MUNKI_REPO_DIR and enter the path to your Munki repository directory (by default /Users/Shared/munki_repo).

16. Save and close the settings.py file.

17. Return to Terminal and run python manage.py syncdb. This begins creating tables in a SQLite database.

18. When prompted to create a superuser account, enter yes and then provide a username and password. Remember these credentials.

19. In the Users & Groups pane of System Preferences, create a standard user account named munkiwebadmin. You will use this as a service account.

20. Run the following commands to prevent anyone from interactively using the account:

```
sudo dscl . create /Users/munkiwebadmin home /var/empty
sudo dscl . create /Users/munkiwebadmin passwd *
```

21. Run the following commands to create a munki group and add the munkiwebadmin account to it:

```
sudo dseditgroup -o create -n . munki
sudo dseditgroup -o edit -a munkiwebadmin -t user munki
```

22. Run the following commands to ensure the munki group has read-write access to the munkiwebadmin_env folder:

```
sudo chgrp -R munki /Users/Shared/munkiwebadmin_env
sudo chmod -R g+rw /Users/Shared/munkiwebadmin_env
```

23. Run the following commands to ensure the munki group also has read-write access to the munki_repo folder and its contents:

```
sudo chgrp -R munki /Users/Shared/munki_repo
sudo chmod -R g+rw /Users/Shared/munki_repo
```

24. Run the following commands to switch to your `munkiwebadmin` service account:

    ```
    sudo su
    su munkiwebadmin
    ```

25. Run `pwd` to verify you are still in the `/Users/Shared/munkiwebadmin-env/munkiwebadmin` folder. If not, run `cd /Users/Shared/munkiwebadmin-env/munkiwebadmin`.

26. Run `python manage.py runwsgiserver port=8000 host=0.0.0.0` to start `MunkiWebAdmin`.

27. After all that, the moment of truth! Open a web browser on your `MunkiWebAdmin` server and browse to `http://127.0.0.1:8000`. You should see the `MunkiWebAdmin` login page. Log in with the superuser name and password you created in step

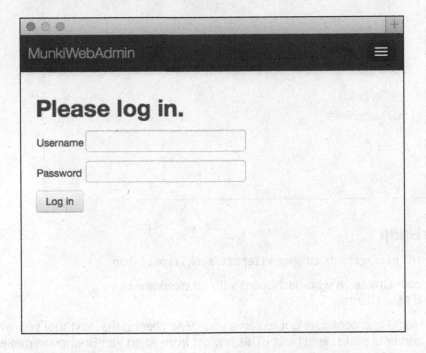

28. Click the Catalogs tab at the top of the window (you may need to expand your browser or click the menu list button in the upper-right corner) and then choose Testing from the Catalog pop-up menu. You should see a list of application titles installed when running Munki-in-a-box.

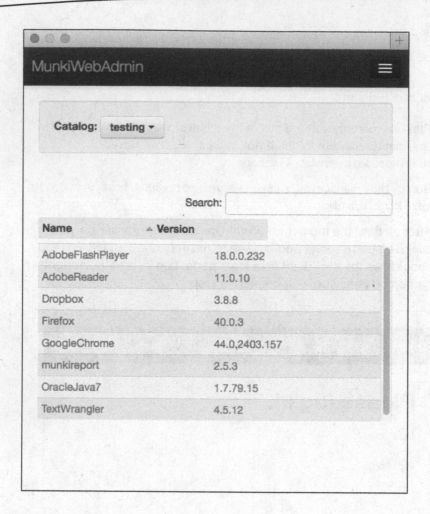

munkireport-php

■ *Site*: https://github.com/munkireport/munkireport-php

■ *Purpose*: Creates a web dashboard with an overview of Munki Mac clients

After installing Munki and configuring it to serve your Mac clients, the next tool you will use to extend your server is munkireport-php. This project from Arjen van Bochoven makes viewing the status of Mac computers easier by providing a graphical interface.

Installing and configuring munkireport-php requires a little knowledge about web servers. Assuming you have installed Munki on a dedicated OS X web server, these steps will guide you through the process. Be sure to check the project's web site for updated instructions.

1. Download the zip file from the munkireport-php GitHub repository onto your Munki server.

2. Extract the files from the unzipped folder and copy them to your web server's root directory.

3.   Duplicate the `config_default.php` file and rename the duplicate `config.php`.

4.   Launch a web browser either on the server or on another computer and visit the server's default web site at `http://server.example.com/`.

5.   Note the warning about no authentication information found. Enter a name and password to generate a hash for the first admin user. Click the Generate button.

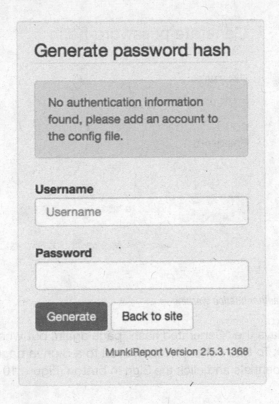

Figure 10-2. MunkiReport authentication warning

6.   Copy the generated hash to the clipboard (Figure 10-3).

Generated hash

Add this line to config.php:

`$auth_config['admin'] = '$P$BL98xOO/FgAxrDuQMGw23ITE8iGNMZQ`

Generate another   Back to site

Figure 10-3. MunkiReport generated hash

7. Open the `config.php` file with a text editor such as Bare Bones
    Software's BBEdit or TextWrangler and append the copied hash to
    the end of the file. Save the file.

8. Click your browser's Refresh button to refresh the page. The warning
    about no authentication information found should be gone. Enter your
    new credentials and click the Generate button again (Figure 10-4).

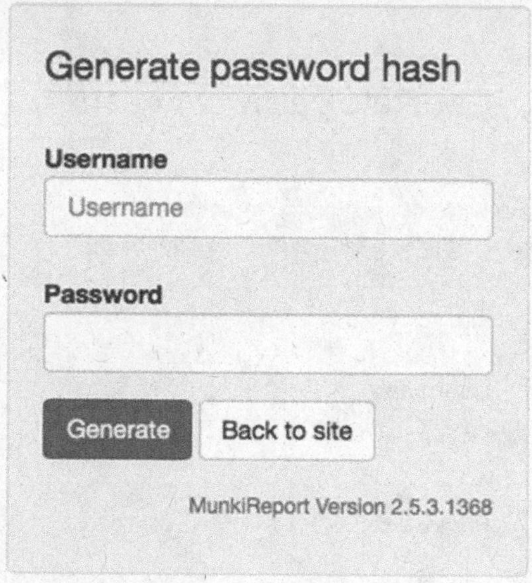

Figure 10-4. MunkiReport no authentication warning

9. The site displays the "Generated hash" page again, but when you
    click the Back To Site button, it returns you to a Sign In page. Enter
    your new credentials and click the Sign In button (Figure 10-5).

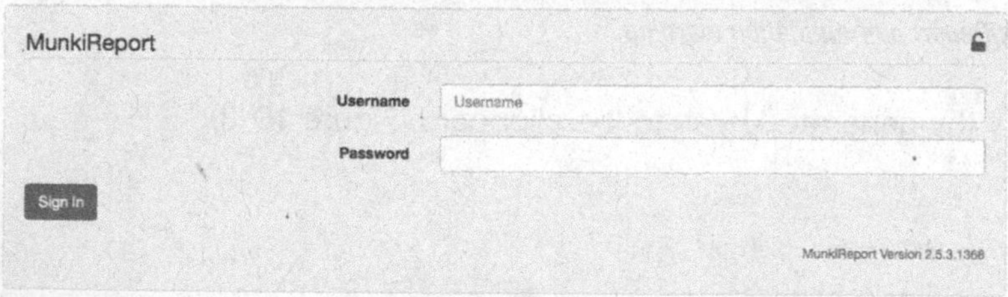

Figure 10-5. MunkiReport sign-in

At this point, MunkiReport displays an empty dashboard. You must configure your Mac
clients to connect to the server. Do this manually by running the following command in
Terminal on your first Mac client. Be sure to customize the server URL in the command.

```
sudo /bin/bash -c "$(curl -s http://example.com/index.php?/install)"
```

After running the command line on your Mac client, refresh your MunkiReport dashboard. It should now display one active client, as shown in Figure 10-6.

Figure 10-6. *MunkiReport one active client*

If this succeeds, add the command to a nopkg package in Munki or create a payload-free package with the command in the postinstall script and deploy to your Munki clients.

Select Clients from the Listings menu and click the name of your Mac client to display detailed information about the machine (Figure 10-7).

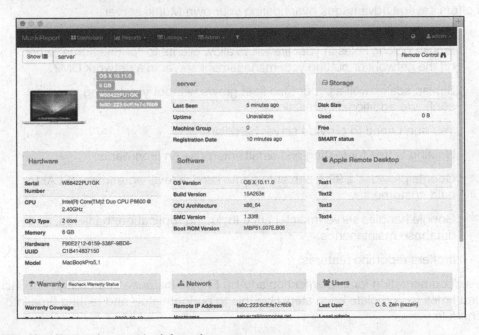

Figure 10-7. *MunkiReport view machine information*

If you have followed along and installed Munki, MunkiWebAdmin, and `munkireport-php`, then you should now have the beginnings of a robust Mac management system. You can automate software installs and OS X updates. You can run scripts and deploy configuration profiles to manage your Mac computers. Your users can help themselves to a library of optional software they may find useful to do their work. You can easily manage your Munki repository using a web browser. And you can view an elegant dashboard giving you inventory hardware, software, and configuration information about your Mac fleet.

Your investment in this entire system is only your time.

Let's take a quick look at another project in the Munki ecosystem.

Simian

- *Site*: `https://github.com/google/simian`

- *Purpose*: OS X software deployment solution from Google built on top of Munki

Simian is Munki in the cloud—specifically Google's App Engine cloud service. App Engine is a public web application hosting platform that runs entirely on Google's infrastructure. Simian offers several advantages over hosting your own Munki server.

- Cloud hosting means your management server is everywhere. It does not require poking holes in your firewall to allow clients to "phone home" when off the network or putting your management server in a network DMZ.

- Simian scales well as your Mac fleet grows without you having to configure additional installations.

- You don't need to provide server hardware.

- Hosting is free for testing and small enterprise environments.

- Google provides a 99.5 percent uptime service level agreement (SLA) for paid customers.

- Google handles server maintenance including replication, backups, and database maintenance.

- It offers reporting features.

Google's documentation for implementing an App Engine instance is thorough and includes estimated times to complete each step. Use this to budget setup and testing time into your schedule.

Like Munki, Simian uses Google Groups mailing lists for discussion and support.

- *Simian Discuss*: `https://groups.google.com/forum/#!forum/simian-discuss`

GLPI

- *Site*: www.glpi-project.org/spip.php?lang=en
- *Purpose*: IT asset management software

If you don't need the software management capabilities Munki offers but you do need to maintain a reliable inventory of assets including hardware, software, licenses, contracts, and more, then GLPI may be a good solution for you. It also includes a ticketing and documentation system to help you manage everything. GLPI is an extensible French open source project based on ITIL needs. Its full name in French is Gestion Libre de Parc Informatique, which translates roughly to Free IT and Asset Management Software.

GLPI is a multilanguage web application that stores its data in a MariaDB or MySQL database. It integrates with network directory services to control access to the application and control access to sensitive areas of the web site such as its centralized password database.

It offers plug-in support for extending its capabilities in 20 categories. The following are some of its available plug-ins:

- *OCS Inventory NG*: Automatically gathers and maintains inventory information from Linux, OS X, and Windows workstations and servers
- *Monitoring*: Uses SNMP to monitor assets for alerts such as printer maintenance needs
- *Relationships Inventory*: Enables linking assets together such as virtual machines to hosts
- *Databases Inventory*: Maintains an inventory of databases across an enterprise
- *Certificates Inventory*: Maintains an inventory of certificates across an enterprise
- *Racks/Bays Management*: Maintains a relationship of server hardware to physical location in racks in data centers

GLPI is platform agnostic using PHP.

The forums for discussion and support are mostly in French; however, they have forums specifically for English speakers too.

- *Forum GLPI-Project*: http://forum.glpi-project.org

Reposado

- *Site*: https://github.com/wdas/reposado
- *Purpose*: Software Update server for OS X that runs on Linux and Windows

Apple's Server app includes a Software Update service (SUS) for caching all system updates from Apple to serve them locally on a network. Its purpose is twofold.

- To eliminate Mac clients from consuming Internet bandwidth to get the same updates
- To allow an administrator to choose which updates he wants available to Mac workstations

However, the Server app runs only on OS X and Apple hardware, which means an administrator can't utilize its SUS utility in a Linux or Windows server environment. Reposado is a project that performs the same service for Mac clients but is platform agnostic. It runs on Linux, Windows, and even versions of OS X that may not normally serve updates to broader OS X versions.

Unique to Reposado is its ability to create "branches" of the Apple catalogs. For example, an administrator can direct a group of test Mac computers to a "testing" SUS URL to receive the latest updates while all other users receive only the tested and approved updates. And it can continue serving OS X updates superseded by newer updates until the administrator is ready to update clients.

Margarita

- *Site*: https://github.com/jessepeterson/margarita
- *Purpose*: Web interface to Reposado

Just as Munki requires the command line to administer its repository, Reposado also relies on command-line utilities for its administration. Jesse Peterson wrote Margarita to add a GUI front end to Reposado in a web browser. It's a quick-and-easy interface for listing and delisting software updates including branch catalogs.

Installation requires Flask, a Python web framework, and an existing Reposado server with its update catalogs initially synced. Administrators install Flask using the same easy_install command-line tool used with MunkiWebAdmin's installation. And like Reposado, Margarita is platform agnostic.

CauliflowerVest

- *Site*: https://github.com/google/cauliflowervest
- *Purpose*: FileVault 2 key escrow server

Funny name! CauliflowerVest is an anagram of FileVault Escrow. Justin McWilliams created this project to store FileVault 2 recovery keys for OS X 10.7 and higher and later expanded it to include support for BitLocker (Windows), LUKS (Linux), and Duplicity-encrypted rsync backups.

CauliflowerVest can do the following:

- Forcefully enable FileVault 2 encryption
- Automatically escrow recovery keys to a secure Google App Engine server
- Delegate secure access to recovery keys so that volumes may be unlocked or reverted

To FileVault encrypt Mac computers, CauliflowerVest requires Google App Engine and access to the csfde command-line tool to activate encryption. A GUI client starts the encryption, obtains the recovery key, and escrows it on the server.

Join the Google Groups mailing list for discussion and support.

- *cauliflowervest-discuss*: https://groups.google.com/forum/#!forum/cauliflowervest-discuss

Coding and Scripting

The most versatile tool for management is scripting. Most anything you can do in the GUI on one machine at a time, you can do en masse via command line or automatically. The following are some well-known and not so well-known free and open source tools for manipulating text including preference files and scripts.

TextWrangler

- *Site*: http://barebones.com/products/textwrangler/
- *Purpose*: Plain-text editor

TextWrangler is the first tool on the list because every Mac administrator needs to edit text files and needs a good, plain text editor. TextWrangler is a lighter and free version of its more powerful big brother, BBEdit.

Compared to Apple's built-in TextEdit application, TextWrangler makes viewing shell, Python, Perl, and other scripts easy with its syntax highlighting, line numbering, and page wrapping features. And while writing scripts, an administrator can run them from within the document to test and debug them. TextWrangler can open plist files without the need to convert them from binary to XML format and will prompt for administrator credentials when attempting to save a file to a location where the current user doesn't have permission to write.

Its Find/Replace capabilities are more than capable of changing all instances of *teh* to *the* in one file or across many files at once, but it shines with its ability to use regular expressions to find all instances of malformed IP addresses such as 192.268.12.22. It even includes a Compare Two Front Windows feature to highlight changes in long plist files where the only difference across hundreds of lines is a change in value for one key from 0 to 1.

Like a good pair of shoes, administrators will appreciate a good text editor like TextWrangler.

Atom

- *Site*: https://atom.io
- *Purpose*: Plain-text editor

This is a new text editor on the market, but unlike TextWrangler, which is a free application from a commercial vendor, Atom is open source. More than that, it's cross-platform, running on Linux, OS X, and Windows. Its developers tout it as a "hackable text editor for the 21st century."

Atom is extremely customizable with more than 800 themes to change its background color, syntax highlighting, and even cursor style. And the user can tweak those attributes even further, changing font, font size, line height, and line length. Practically every keyboard command is modifiable, and practically every important menu item and text navigation control has a keyboard command.

Packages are extensions to Atom, and with more than 2,500 available for download, Atom can do some pretty amazing things.

- Resolve Git conflicts
- Preview all open files (à la OS X's Exposé)
- Display a task board
- View and reuse clipboard history
- Integrate HipChat
- Run shell sessions
- Add syntax for more languages
- Format unformatted XML with line breaks and indents

If TextWrangler is an administrator's good pair of shoes, Atom is an administrator's Manolo Blahniks.

Freeformatter.com

- *Site*: `www.freeformatter.com`
- *Purpose*: Online tools for developers

Sometimes scripters need tools to clean up code, such as XML data in `.mobileconfig` files displayed as a string of text. Freeformatter.com has numerous tools to reformat text, validate code, minify code, and encode and decode code. Copy the unformatted text and paste it into the online formatter, and it returns properly indented text with correct line breaks. It also supports reformatting and validating common languages such as JSON, HTML, and SQL and even regular expressions.

This site is an at-hand resource for anyone who works with scripting languages, plists, XML, scripts, and other types of code.

ShellCheck.net

- *Site*: `www.shellcheck.net`
- *Purpose*: Online shell script code validator

Similar to Freeformatter.com, ShellCheck.net validates code. However, it validates only SH/Bash code and returns warnings for mistakes such as unused variables, Unicode quotes, and spaces in assignments as well as suggestions for improvements (Figure 10-8).

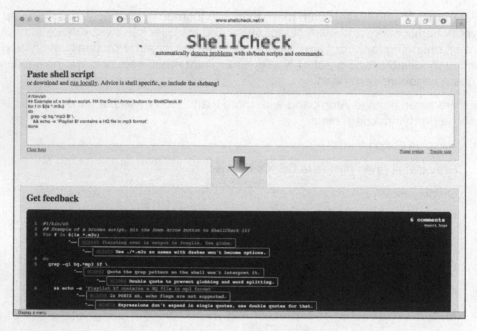

Figure 10-8.   ShellCheck.net examines code for errors and improvements

ExplainShell.com

- *Site*: http://explainshell.com

- *Purpose*: Dissects a line of shell commands and explains the commands or syntax

ExplainShell.com is a companion site to ShellCheck.net. If you're reviewing someone else's shell script or taking snippets from web sites with code you don't understand, you can paste it into Explain field, and the site explains each component of the command (Figure 10-9). For each item in the line, the site displays the corresponding man page entry.

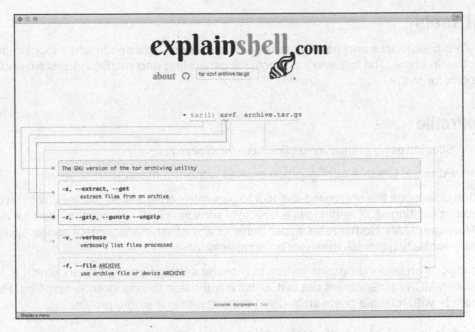

Figure 10-9. ExplainShell.com explains each component of a line of code

GitHub

- *Site*: https://desktop.github.com
- *Purpose*: GUI client for managing GitHub repositories

Most open source projects live in GitHub online repositories. It's free for individuals and a great way to share code across platforms and languages. Managing code across projects is not easy, but Git, a revision control system for tracking changes to code, at least eases the hassle of reviewing and updating constantly changing content that may affect usability. Managing all this at the command line gets confusing quickly.

GitHub makes a free application by the same name to facilitate check-ins, branches, and commits to code. Unlike the Git command line, the GitHub application is designed to work only with GitHub.com and not just any versioning system.

Client Tools

Well-crafted preferences and settings make a positive user experience when logging in to a Mac for the first time. The following are tools for generating and managing system and user preferences for Macs.

mcxToProfile

- *Site*: `https://github.com/timsutton/mcxToProfile`
- *Purpose*: Creates configuration profiles without a management server

Tim Sutton developed this command-line tool to generate configuration profiles (`.mobileconfig`) from plists or existing MCX settings in a directory services node without the need for Apple's Profile Manager, JAMF Software's Casper Suite, or any other management server system that would normally generate these for an administrator.

It also supports an undocumented feature to manage settings once or often, which is possible with MCX management but lost with the transition to configuration profiles. Running mcxToProfile with multiple plists embeds all the settings in a single profile.

```
./mcxToProfile.py --plist com.microsoft.office.plist --plist com.microsoft.autoupdate2.plist
--identifier Office2011Prefs --manage Once
```

launched

- *Site*: `http://launched.zerowidth.com`
- *Purpose*: Launchd agent and daemon generator

Launchd is Apple's alternative to cron. Like cron, it can run a command or script at specified times, but it also accepts events such as a file path changing or a disk mounting as triggers. Although launch agents and daemons are simple plist files, generating a correctly formatted file is tedious.

With the "launched" web site, an administrator enters details for a new plist file including triggers and commands and clicks the "Create .plist" button to view the plist code and optionally download the plist file.

outset

- *Site*: `https://github.com/chilcote/outset/`
- *Purpose*: Processes packages and scripts at first boot and user logins

If your Mac computers need to routinely run a series of startup scripts to reset user environments or computer variables, then making launchd plists may be burdensome and difficult to manage. And plists execute asynchronously, which means startup and login processes may not run in the same order every time.

Joseph Chilcote's outset is a set of two launchd items that call loose packages or scripts in individual folders at either startup or user login. To add more tasks to the startup and login processes, add new items to the appropriate folders. Outset handles the execution.

docutil

- *Site*: https://github.com/kcrawford/dockutil
- *Purpose*: Manages OS X Dock items

Users need the right tools to do their jobs, and a thoughtfully crafted Dock helps them find those tools. They need access to applications and their home folders, servers, and working directories. Kyle Crawford created dockutil to add, remove, and reorder dock items for users. It can also adjust dock settings to adjust the view of folders (grid, fan, list, or automatic), adjust the display of folders to show their contents or folder icons, and set folder sort order (name, date, or kind).

duti

- *Site*: http://duti.org/index.html
- *Purpose*: Sets default applications for document types and URL schemes

Enterprises often incorporate Macs into complex workflows that require consistent behaviors. If a workflow requires using the Firefox browser instead of Safari or using Microsoft Outlook instead of Apple's Mail application, Andrew Mortensen's duti can ensure the correct applications respond when opening a URL or new e-mail message.

The duti name means "default for UTI" or what Apple calls uniform type identifiers. Every file type such as an HTML page or Microsoft Word document has a UTI, and developers constantly create their own new UTIs. duti reads and applies UTI settings to pair applications with UTIs.

Firefox CCK2

- *Site*: https://mike.kaply.com/cck2/
- *Purpose*: Customizes and controls Firefox settings

Mike Kapley's Firefox Client Customization Kit (CCK) is for administrators to apply certain default application settings and enforce others. It manages practically every preference in Firefox's about:config settings page. This includes home pages, network proxy settings, hiding UI elements, software update settings, plug-ins, certificates, security, and many more options.

Download the latest CCK .xpi file and manually import it into Firefox using Tools ➤ Add-ons. Launch the wizard and follow it through its multitude of configurable settings. At the end of the process, you can create an autoconfig.zip file. Unzip the file and merge its contents into the Firefox application bundle itself starting in Firefox.app/Contents/Resources. Deploy your customized Firefox application normally. When any user launches Firefox, your customizations override the default settings.

Although Firefox CCK is free, premium support is not.

- *CCK2 Support*: http://cck2.freshdesk.com/support/discussions

Packaging

In 2003 NASA sent the Spirit and Opportunity rovers to Mars. To get them there, rocket scientists had to design a transport system that would survive the takeoff from Earth, a year's travel though the dead of space, and a bumpy landing on a planet no one had ever seen in person. How did they do it? Packaging!

Packaging is the art of assembling a payload of stuff and transporting it to a remote location safely and intact. A process at that remote location opens your package and follows your instructions to the letter about what it should do with its contents. A well-crafted package deploys perfectly even in the rockiest of environments. Our job as administrators is to ensure our packages with payloads of software, preference files, scripts, and other items travel, land safely, and deploy perfectly on systems we may never see in person.

AutoDMG

- *Site*: https://github.com/MagerValp/AutoDMG
- *Purpose*: Creates a deployable, never-booted, and cruft-free OS X package

Per Olofsson developed AutoDMG as the GUI successor to the command-line tool InstaDMG. On the project page he describes it as a tool that takes an OS X installer and builds a system image, suitable for deployment with DeployStudio or Absolute Manage. However, AutoDMG works with practically any popular Mac imaging tool. Its major advantage over capturing an image from an existing Mac is that it doesn't have to boot the system before capturing it. That means it contains no cruft such as user preferences, network settings, or caches. A cruft-free OS image is key to ensuring a reliable and repeatable OS deployment.

To build a cruft-free OS image, follow these steps:

1. Install AutoDMG on the same major OS version as your target OS. For example, you need to run AutoDMG on OS X 10.10 to build an OS 10.10 image. Minor OS version differences are OK.

2. Download the latest available OS installer app from the Mac App Store. While AutoDMG works with earlier versions of an OS, it requires the latest version for its feature to download and install system updates at the same time.

3. Launch AutoDMG. Its interface is simple and straightforward. Drag the .app OS installer into the top field. In a few seconds the app examines the OS version and checks for additional system update files from Apple. Available updates appear in the middle section of the app window. Click the Download button to include these updates. To forego the updates, disable Apply Updates.

4. Optionally, drag one or more Apple Installer package files into the Additional Software section at the bottom of the app window. This supports additional Apple software such as printer driver packages as well as third-party installers. AutoDMG will create a monolithic image with all the extra packages so long as they don't require installation to the current boot disk.

5. Click the Build button and choose a location for the new disk image. AutoDMG requires about three times the disk space as the final size of the image, which may be 6 GB to 8 GB or more, depending on the additional packages (Figure 10-10).

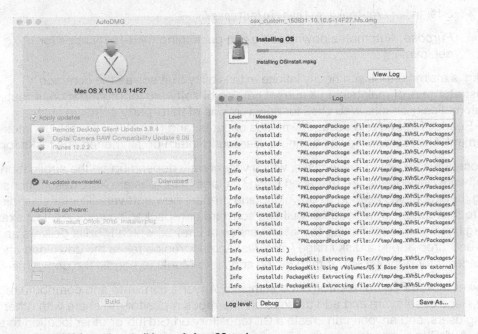

Figure 10-10. AutoDMG is ready to build a cruft-free OS package

Depending on the speed of the Mac running the application, building a package usually requires a minimum of 20 to 25 minutes and sometimes up to an hour or more.

Like its predecessor, AutoDMG also works via the command line for scripted or more automated image creation. The command line supports additional functionality such as templates to even further automate image creation.

createOSXinstallPkg

- *Site*: https://github.com/munki/createOSXinstallPkg
- *Purpose*: Creates a deployable OS X installer package

This project sounds similar to AutoDMG, and its purpose is similar: to deploy OS X. However, Greg Neagle's createOSXinstallPkg wraps Apple's Install OS X application (.app) in an Apple Installer package (.pkg) instead of deploying the OS directly. The advantage to this is an application deployment system such as Munki can push a new OS (upgrade) to a computer without having to erase the hard drive and without having to attend the installation.

This is especially useful for automated deployments such as school computer labs needing an OS upgrade or for self-help deployments where an OS X upgrade is offered as an optional software install for the user to initiate when ready.

Support for createOSXinstallPkg falls under the Munki umbrella of discussion groups.

AutoPkg

- *Site*: http://autopkg.github.io/autopkg/
- *Purpose*: Automates downloading and packaging third-party apps for deployment

AutoPkg is a simple tool with nearly infinite extensibility that solves the common administrator task of maintaining a current catalog of software for organization. It routinely and automatically checks web sites for new versions of third-party software such as Adobe Reader, Firefox, and Java; downloads updates; and repackages those updates for deployment if necessary. It's like having a year-round intern do all the tedious tasks for you.

The procedures for doing these tasks, which vary greatly depending on the application and software developers, are managed using "recipes." Recipes are XML descriptions for guiding the processes needed to download and prepare new software. Recipes handle where to find current downloads or building software or repackaging software. For example, AutoPkg has a recipe for finding the latest version of Firefox, which Mozilla delivers as a drag-and-drop app in a disk image (.dmg) file. Another recipe takes the download and repackages it for deployment. A third recipe adds it to Munki to handle the deployment.

The power of AutoPkg comes from its community. Anyone can write and contribute recipes for any piece of software and add those to an enormous repository to share with other AutoPkg users, and anyone can create a Git repository on GitHub or other location to share recipes. AutoPkg supports pulling recipes from multiple repositories.

Google Groups hosts its support and discussion list.

- *autopkg-discuss*: https://groups.google.com/forum/#!forum/autopkg-discuss

AutoPkgr

- *Site*: www.lindegroup.com/autopkgr
- *Purpose*: GUI application for installing and configuring AutoPkg

A common theme in the open source community is that projects written for the command line eventually find someone to write a GUI. The Linde Group contributes to the AutoPkg project with AutoPkgr.

AutoPkgr is for administrators who are not comfortable with the command line or who are not familiar with AutoPkg and want a quick and easy setup. It manages the same control and management of recipes, repositories, scheduling, and notifications but adds nearly instant setup with the click of a button (Figure 10-11).

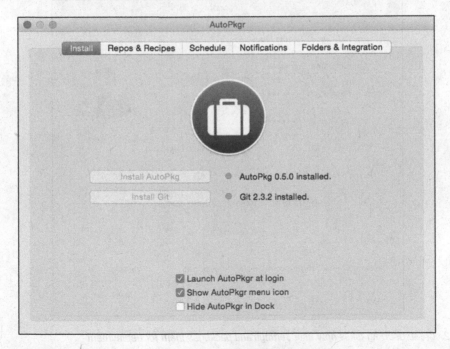

Figure 10-11. AutoPkgr installs AutoPkg and provides a GUI for easier management

CreateUserPkg

- *Site*: https://github.com/MagerValp/CreateUserPkg
- *Purpose*: Creates packages to deploy OS X user accounts

When preparing a Mac with a never-booted OS, you will need a process to create user accounts if you want to avoid Apple's Setup Assistant at first boot. Or you may need to quickly create an admin account on one or multiple Mac systems that you've just acquired and need to support. Olofsson's CreateUserPkg is a single-window application for creating admin or standard accounts along with names, passwords, user IDs, and pictures. The tool takes the information and generates an Apple Installer package (.pkg) compatible with most Mac software deployment systems such as Munki or Apple Remote Desktop (Figure 10-12).

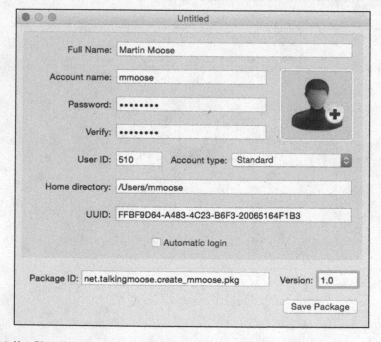

Figure 10-12. CreateUserPkg takes new user settings and packages them for deployment

Although CreateUserPkg lives on GitHub, its developer also makes it available in the Mac App Store so that you won't need to compile your own copy.

first-boot-pkg

- ■ *Site*: https://github.com/grahamgilbert/first-boot-pkg
- ■ *Purpose*: Installs packages at first boot

Graham Gilbert's `first-boot-pkg` project installs Apple Installer package files (.pkg) the first time a Mac boots. Its purpose is to install packages (including payload-free packages containing only postinstall scripts) that require installation to the currently booted drive. For example, no imaging solution to date binds a Mac to a directory service such as Active Directory or Open Directory during the imaging process. Binding requires the Mac be booted to its system first.

This project is independent of other package and deployment solutions, which means any solution that will deploy a package, such as AutoDMG, should accept packages created with first-boot-pkg.

Imaging

Henry Ford said, "Any customer can have a car painted any color that he wants so long as it is black." Mac admins typically don't have the luxury of saying anything like that. They prepare their fleets of Macs to meet the demands of their clients, which are diverse and complex across departments. Imaging is the assembly-line deployment of multiple Macs, and like an assembly line, imaging must be fast and efficient and reliably produce the same product every time.

DeployStudio

- ■ *Site*: www.deploystudio.com
- ■ *Purpose*: Imaging, deployment, and configuration for Mac systems

DeployStudio is the imaging workhorse of the free software community. If administrators are not using a paid solution for imaging their Macs, then they are more than likely using this.

While it is not a NetBoot server for booting Macs across a network, its Assistant utility produces a lightweight NetBoot image that runs nothing more than its Runtime application for deploying the assigned image. This makes it fast when preparing several machines at once. Its thin imaging approach to installing software one package at a time offers the flexibility of creating multiple workflows without having to prepare and store multiple monolithic images.

DeployStudio deploys not only operating system and software packages but system settings as well. It partitions drives, binds machines to directory services, ensures proper time syncing, checks for available software updates, and much more. When used in conjunction with other server systems such as Munki, DeployStudio can prepare machines and then hand them over to management when done.

The software and community support are free, but the developers do accept donations.

- *DeployStudio Forum*: www.deploystudio.com/Forums/index.php

Imagr

- *Site*: https://github.com/grahamgilbert/imagr/
- *Purpose*: Imaging and deployment for Mac systems

If you don't need DeployStudio's full-feature set or prefer something lighter, Imagr offers simple disk image restores and package installation at deployment. It is designed to run from a NetInstall environment created with AutoNBI.py; however, it also supports other NetBoot system such as Apple's Server app or JAMF Software's NetSUS utility. In addition to a NetBoot server and Python-enabled NetBoot or NetInstall set, Imagr requires a web server to host the workflow configuration that specifies the configuration for clients.

So, if DeployStudio is free and does more than Imagr, why not use that instead? Remember, "free" is not the same as "open source." DeployStudio is not open source, and its code is not publicly available for review. Also, it is an OS X–only application. Imagr is a community project that runs not only on OS X but on Linux too.

bsdpy and AutoNBI.py

- *Site*: https://bitbucket.org/bruienne/bsdpy and https://bitbucket.org/bruienne/autonbi/
- *Purpose*: NetBoot server implemented in Python

Don't have a NetBoot server to serve your DeployStudio NetBoot image or Imagr yet? Pepijn Bruienne developed bsdpy to offer the same functionality as Apple's NetBoot server without the reliance on OS X and Apple hardware. It is ideal for environments where the server infrastructure is non-Mac such as Linux or Windows. And it serves NetBoot Images (NBIs) created using OS X's System Image Utility.

For more granular customization of NBIs as part of larger workflows, AutoNBI.py takes a folder, Apple Installer application, or OS DMG and converts it automatically.

NetSUS

- *Site*: https://jamfnation.jamfsoftware.com/viewProduct.html?id=180
- *Purpose*: Combination Software Update service and NetBoot server

NetSUS is an alternative open source NetBoot (and Software Update service) server for virtualized environments. The SUS part of this dual-server system that runs on Linux is actually based on Reposado, mentioned earlier, and the NetBoot part of the server and development project from JAMF Software.

It includes a web interface for GUI management and offers both an installer version and an appliance OVA file for import into a virtualization server.

SuperDuper!

- Site: www.shirt-pocket.com/SuperDuper/SuperDuperDescription.html
- Purpose: OS X disk cloning

Migrating an entire system (applications, operating system, and user data) from one Mac to another requires a tool that understands the file system and can verify pre- and postmigration tasks. SuperDuper! handles full-disk cloning for free (with a paid version for copying specific directories and files). It also works while running live on the system it is cloning. That means an administrator can connect a new Mac booted into Target Disk Mode to an old Mac running SuperDuper! and still clone the booted system to the new machine. Additionally, it will clone into a disk image for archival purpose.

Security and Testing

Bender

- Site: http://robotcloud.screenstepslive.com/s/2459/m/5322/l/ 94467-bender-automated-backup-of-os-x-server-settings
- Purpose: OS X Server settings backup

Forget Computers, Ltd., makes this simple backup utility for OS X Server settings, which offers an homage to their favorite *Futurama* robot. Bender installs a launchd daemon and a script to automatically copy the Open Directory master and Postgres databases of all server services to a Backups folder at the root of the hard drive. In turn, Time Machine or any other backup solution will collect these files during system backups.

Restoring an Open Directory backup, all service backups, or individual backups to production is as easy as running one or two Terminal commands.

Suspicious Package

- *Site*: www.mothersruin.com/software/SuspiciousPackage/

- *Purpose*: Quick Look plug-in for viewing Apple Installer package contents

Apple's Quick Look technology makes viewing file contents as easy as tapping the spacebar. It's also extensible with plug-ins to view file types not natively supported by OS X. Mothers Ruin Software makes viewing the contents of Apple Installer packages (.pkg) before installing them possible using its free Quick Look plug-in.

Suspicious Package displays not only the files and folders a package installs but also script contents and the developer signing certificate (Figure 10-13).

Figure 10-13. Suspicious Package displays Apple Installer package contents

VirtualBox

- *Site*: https://www.virtualbox.org
- *Purpose*: Linux, OS X, and Windows virtualization

Software testing often requires testing on multiple systems. Oracle's open source VirtualBox project, an alternative to commercial virtualization software solutions such as Parallels and VMware, turns one Mac into one Mac plus another Mac, Linux, or Windows computer. Depending on your host Mac's hardware, VirtualBox lets you create a tiny network of computers. Take snapshots between changes to your virtual computer and roll back to an earlier snapshot in a few seconds if you damage your system or need a clean system without your changes.

VirtualBox also supports running on Linux, Solaris, and Windows, but Apple's licensing requires that any OS X virtual machines run on actual Apple hardware.

Docker

- *Site*: https://www.docker.com
- *Purpose*: Runs applications in containers independent of the host operating system

Docker uses containers to wrap software in a complete file system containing everything it needs to run including code, runtime, system tools, and system libraries. Containers are similar to lightweight virtual machines (VMs) that are portable between hosts, which means they will always run the same, regardless of the host environment. Whereas with a full VM a container runs its code on the host operating system and hardware but is isolated from everything. Containers are so quick and so lightweight that you can run many more containers than full VMs.

What can you run in a Docker container? A Munki repository. A Casper JAMF Software Server (JSS). A development or testing environment for open source projects. A web server. Minecraft. And you can run them side-by-side and isolated without them interfering with each other.

Apple Deployment Services

No Apple deployment is complete without considering how you will integrate with Apple's services. Apple provides a number of services used during large deployments. In some cases, these services are obviously good, and in other cases they can be a huge challenge because your security team will have big problems with these technologies. For example, Apple has a program used to purchase software in bulk and deploy that software to large numbers of devices concurrently. This is obviously a good thing in most cases. However, there are other services, such as iCloud Drive, that can be considered problematic from an information security perspective.

There is also a lot of misconception about what is required and what is not required to provide full support to large numbers of Apple devices. For example, while an Apple ID is required for a number of services, the Apple ID doesn't necessarily need a credit card associated with it to provide access to Apple's VPP program for a given Apple ID. This chapter addresses these misconceptions with Apple deployment programs so you can deploy the correct strategy with regard to Apple programs.

The Apple ID

Most devices are going to need an Apple ID. The Apple ID becomes the gateway to most of the services described throughout the remainder of this chapter. When doing large-scale deployments, you will not need to deploy an Apple ID for every single user. But it certainly helps if you do so. The Apple ID is a unique identifier provided by Apple, used to access a number of Apple services. This includes the most popular of these services: music purchased through iTunes. But it also includes iCloud, Messages, and the iBookstore.

Much of the security concern regarding Apple IDs arises from the fact that they can be used to access a computer or synchronize data to iCloud or iCloud Backup even after an OS X computer or iPhone has been wiped. This is more of a concern on iPhones and iPads, where wiping a device should provide a sense of security that the data on the device has been removed. While you can wipe an OS X device, there are far more ways to synchronize data with third-party services on a desktop operating system, and the concern around data security is lessened. A lot of software vendors now provide their software through the Mac

App Store. And until all of the Mobile Device Management (MDM) vendors support device-based Volume Purchasing Program (VPP) access, this will be pointed out as a flaw to that program. iOS 9 and OS X 10.11 bring device-based VPP, but at the time of the writing of this book, that feature has yet to be implemented by the main VPP vendors.

So, what can you do? MDM solutions do not report what Apple ID is being used to access software. However, you can use the `defaults` command to obtain information about Apple IDs in use on an OS X computer. You would do so by using `defaults` to read the global defaults domain. The following example uses the `grep` command to constrain the output to Apple IDs:

```
defaults rcad | grep AppleID
```

Today, most devices are going to need an Apple ID. The Apple ID becomes the gateway to most of the services described throughout the remainder of this chapter. The following is a list of Apple services that need an Apple ID:

- *App Store*: Buy apps on the iOS and Mac App Stores and have them automatically download to your devices.

- *Apple Developer programs*: Access beta copies of software and developer tools.

- *Apple Music*: Listen to music through Apple's music service, which uses a monthly fee rather than charging for each song.

- *Apple Music Radio*: Stream radio to your devices over the Apple Music Radio service.

- *Apple Online Store*: Purchase hardware and software through Apple.com.

- *Apple Retail services*: Access Concierge, Joint Venture, and programs, including the Apple Store app.

- *Apple Support Communities*: Access the Apple support site, ask questions, and answer any support requests you know the answer to.

- *Apple TV*: Access content purchased on Apple from an Apple TV and control the TV with the Remote app on an iOS device.

- *Back to My Mac*: Get remote access to a computer, even when that computer is using NAT behind a different firewall.

- *Device Enrollment Program (DEP)*: Automatically associate devices owned by an organization with a Mobile Device Management solution.

- *FaceTime*: Video conference with friends and family.

- *FileVault Key Escrow*: Keep the FileVault recovery key stored on a server.

- *Find My Friends*: Show the physical location of friends you have added using the Find My Friends app via GPS.

- *Find My Mac*: Show the physical location of your Apple devices using the iCloud web interface.

- *Game Center*: Access scores in apps that support Game Center integration for friends using the Game Center app.

- *iBooks Store*: Access books and other multimedia content on the Apple iBooks Store.

- *iChat*: Use a legacy chat system from 10.8 and older.

- *iCloud Calendars*: Set up the client for the Calendar app to work with an iCloud account.

- *iCloud Contacts*: Set up the client for the Contacts app to work with an iCloud account.

- *iCloud Drive*: Allow certain apps to write data into storage on iCloud servers.

- *iCloud Keychain*: Synchronize passwords and certificates between computers.

- *iCloud Mail*: Configure the Mail app to work with an iCloud account.

- *iCloud Photos*: Display the photo stream and integrate iCloud Photo Library with your Mac and allow for iCloud photo sharing.

- *iCloud Notes*: Synchronize notes created in the Notes app with an iCloud account.

- *iMessage*: Instant message with other iMessage users rather than using text messages.

- *iTunes Genius*: Track purchases on iTunes and find similar content to music in your library and purchase history.

- *iTunes Home Sharing*: Share data within apps such as iTunes and Photos from within a given local area network (LAN).

- *iTunes Match*: Access music that was ripped from CDs and other media.

- *iTunes Store*: Purchase music that can be downloaded and listened to offline.

- *iTunes U*: Access podcasts posted by educational institutions.

- *Handoff*: Show the same content on an iPhone or iOS device as on an OS X device if apps are built with Handoff support.

- *My Apple ID* (`http://appleid.apple.com`): Access information about an Apple ID and reset passwords and addresses for the Apple ID.

- *Volume Purchase Program*: Purchase applications in bulk and deploy those applications using codes, Apple IDs, or devices.

When doing large-scale deployments, you will not need to associate a credit card to an Apple ID. To remove a credit card from an Apple ID, open iTunes and click the e-mail address of your Apple ID. As you can see in Figure 11-1, click Account Info.

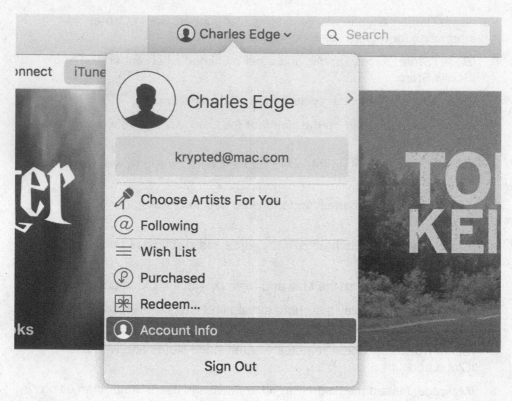

Figure 11-1. iTunes

Authenticate if required, and then from the Account Information screen, click Edit for the payment type (Figure 11-2).

Figure 11-2. The Account Information screen

From the Edit Payment Information screen (Figure 11-3), click the box for None.

Figure 11-3. The Edit Payment Information screen

Once you've removed a credit card from the Apple ID, users can still access VPP apps without fear of charging personal credit cards.

> **Note**   You can also use a script to set up an Apple ID. Owning a lot of Apple IDs is not a typical way to set up a large deployment, but it can work (the Volume Purchase Program is a much better solution). Should you need to do so, you can use the script from Enterpriseios.com at `http://enterpriseios.com/wiki/Apple_ID_Automation_Builder`.

iCloud

iCloud is Apple's cloud service. But iCloud has become more than just basic cloud services such as shared files and photos. iCloud also includes some pretty cool technologies, such as Find My Mac, which physically geolocates hardware that you might have misplaced. Viewing the iCloud preferences pane (Figure 11-4) in OS X shows the iCloud services used on a Mac.

Figure 11-4. The iCloud preferences pane

Click the Options button for iCloud Drive to bring up a list of applications on the computer that support saving data to an iCloud drive, shown in Figure 11-5.

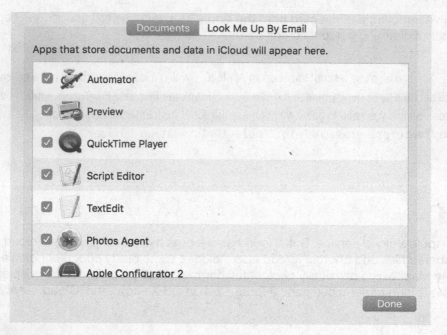

Figure 11-5. The iCloud Documents panel

This shows the potential security issue some see with iCloud. You can save files to a potentially unapproved iCloud account, without having the option to whitelist or blacklist the application that manages a cloud solution in question. This is why there's an option in many Mobile Device Management solutions to turn off iCloud, such as that shown in Figure 11-6. Here, you see the "Allow use of iCloud documents & data" option in Profile Manager, which disables the iCloud connection.

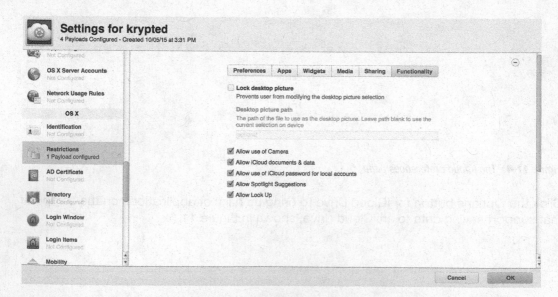

Figure 11-6. Disabling iCloud documents connection in Profile Manager

Administrators should try to preserve the Apple user experience as much as possible. Not only will this allow your deployment to continue to function even after Apple releases updates and upgrades, but it also allows how you handle your deployment to delight your users. By restricting only the parts of iCloud that an organization's security policy violates and trying to limit the services restricted, you are restricting as little as possible, providing as many options to users as possible.

The Mac App Store

Apple revolutionized the technology industry by building a mechanism for fast, safe, and scalable application distribution. This revolutionary approach to software distribution is known as the App Store. First introduced in iOS and later brought to OS X, the App Store became so big that Microsoft and other software vendors began following suit. Apple now touts how many apps are on the store in most of their special events about upcoming hardware, software, and other communications.

For the purposes of this book, we have focused on the deployment of apps through the VPP store, as well as through standard installation packages. You can also install apps manually, using the Mac App Store. If you buy an app through the Mac App Store, you will always see the app on your iCloud account. To view the apps owned by a given Apple ID, open the Mac App Store and click the Purchased icon in the toolbar. As you can see in Figure 11-7, you will then see all apps purchased using the Apple ID, including operating systems.

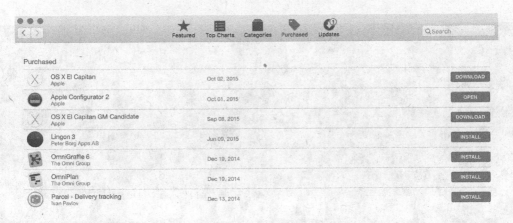

Figure 11-7. The Mac App Store

Note While you can't remove apps from an Apple ID, you can hide apps on each computer. If you buy an app on the App Store using a VPP account, the app can then be removed from the Apple ID.

To manually install an app from the Mac App Store, open the App Store and search for the app. Then click the app. As you can see in Figure 11-8, you will see an Install button. Click the Install button to start downloading the app.

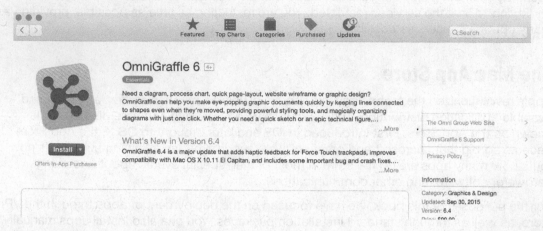

Figure 11-8. Installing an app using the App Store

The app will start downloading to the /Applications directory. Click the Launchpad icon in the Dock to see the status, as you can see in Figure 11-9.

Figure 11-9. Viewing app downloads in Launchpad

Once an app is downloaded, open the app to complete the setup. Once opened, you will likely see preferences appear in ~/Library/Preferences, but other than that, most apps should be self-contained and can easily be removed simply by dragging the app into the Trash at the far-right side of the Dock.

APNs

Apple Push Notification service (APNs) is a technology that sends information to iOS and OS X devices over an encrypted connection. The service receives notifications over a persistent connection and then alerts a user that there is information waiting. The app then pulls the information directly from the service that sent the notification rather than through the APNs servers at Apple.

APNs provides the basis of any Mobile Device Management solution. MDM is described further in Chapter 7, but for the purposes of this chapter, it's important to understand that almost any modern deployment of Mac systems needs devices to access APNs. To use APNs, you will need a number of ports open to Apple's push servers.

APNs runs over the following outgoing ports to Apple IP addresses:

- *TCP port 5223*: APNs
- *TCP port 2195*: Sends notifications to APNs
- *TCP port 2196*: The APNs feedback service
- *TCP port 443*: Wi-Fi fallback, when devices can't reach 5223

You can use the nc command to troubleshoot connectivity. For example, to establish a network connection with gateway.push.apple.com over port 2195, use nc, here with the –v and –w options:

```
/usr/bin/nc -v -w 15 gateway.push.apple.com 2195
```

To establish a network connection with feedback.push.apple.com over IPv4 only, use the -4 option.

```
/usr/bin/nc -v -4 feedback.push.apple.com 2196
```

Push notifications will need to work for a number of services, most notably for this book, including MDM commands.

DEP

Apple's Device Enrollment Program (DEP) is a program that allows a computer to automatically join an MDM solution. Strategically, DEP should be considered an important part of deployments because it allows for shipping boxes directly to ENC users without ever unwrapping them. An MDM solution can simply enroll devices and, if needed, deploy a binary onto OS X clients that allow administrators to then manage even more client systems.

Because DEP automatically enrolls clients into an MDM, the MDM is necessary. As you can see in Figure 11-10, when you purchase a device that has DEP enabled, you can configure the MDM server that the device will enroll into at setup time.

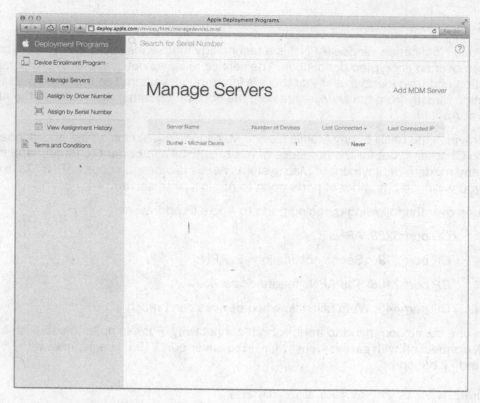

Figure 11-10. The Apple DEP portal

If MDM is configured and the MDM server is not available, an iOS device will not complete activation. In OS X you can still configure the computer, even when that computer can't access the MDM server or the Internet. If MDM is available, then you'll see the option to skip the configuration process for that device. At enrollment time, a user will need to provide a username and password to access the MDM service. This password then becomes how the MDM service will know which user is enrolling.

Once you provide credentials to the MDM solution, you'll be enrolled, as you can see in Figure 11-11.

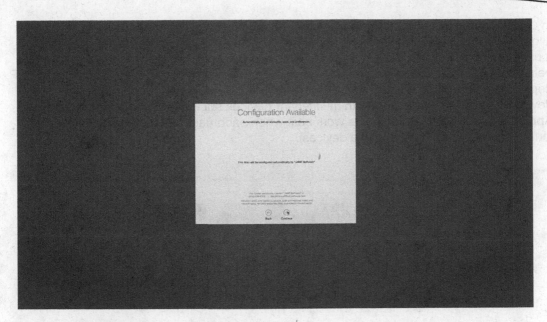

Figure 11-11. DEP enrollment

Once a user is enrolled, they will receive a confirmation that the device has been enrolled into an MDM service, and the device is then configured.

VPP

The Volume Purchase Program is a program that allows organizations to buy software en masse. Using a VPP account, an organization can use a credit card to buy hundreds or thousands of copies of an app and then push that app to a lot of different client computers. You then use that Apple ID with an MDM solution. That MDM solution manages sending apps through Apple to devices. Those apps can then be revoked from Apple IDs or devices.

The original VPP used a comma-separated value (CSV) file to deploy apps using redemption codes. Those codes resembled a gift card similar to what you'd receive if someone purchased a song for you on iTunes. This was great but led to the following challenges:

- Once codes were used, they could not be reused, leading to wasting a lot of otherwise valuable application installations.

- Codes were difficult to distribute except through an MDM solution.

- Support for iOS devices was added using Apple Configurator, but that required plugging devices into a Mac OS X computer.

Later, the ability to distribute apps using an Apple ID was added to VPP. This allowed administrators to send apps to Apple IDs rather than using spreadsheets. And even better, an app deployed to an Apple ID could then be revoked from that Apple ID and deployed to another user. This had a side benefit of providing the ability to remove the data that was inside the container of the app in iOS. In OS X, just being able to redistribute apps when there is turnover at an organization is enough.

In OS X 10.11 and higher, Apple has introduced device-based VPP (Figure 11-12). By allowing VPP to be tied to a device, administrators might not need Apple IDs. However, if a user has two or more devices, that user will need a license for each device rather than being able to reuse licenses on multiple devices, which can work with Apple ID–based VPP deployments. Each of these can work with a different deployment model. Typically device-based VPP works best with multitenant devices such as in school labs, whereas Apple ID–based VPP deployments work best when each user has their own device (and many will often have multiple devices).

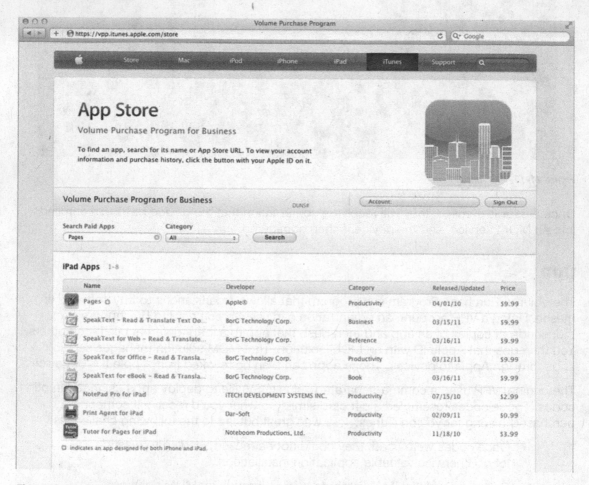

Figure 11-12. The VPP portal

Many apps provide the ability to purchase additional features inside an app. For example, if you use OmniGraffle, you can upgrade to OmniGraffle Pro using an in-app purchase. OS X and iOS app stores do not allow for in-app purchasing through the VPP. An in-app purchase will require a user to leverage an Apple ID and purchase those upgrades one by one.

In this chapter, we focused on the strategy of VPP. The technical aspects of using the VPP is covered further in Chapter 6.

Conclusion

We saved Apple services until the end of the book, mainly because every organization is going to have a different strategy for handling Apple IDs. Some will be concerned about security (and for some that's appropriate). Others will follow the Apple lead and leverage Apple services, but doing so as safely and scalable as possible.

Throughout this book, we've tried to preserve that consumer Apple experience that causes users within an enterprise to adopt the Apple platform. Restrict the experience and you risk backlash from users who were previously self-supporting themselves. Don't restrict the experience and you risk backlash from your information security team. What to do? As we mentioned when discussing iCloud, approach each service with an open mind and restrict elements of the operating system only when absolutely necessary. By preserving the user experience as much as your organization can, you will invariably have the happiest users. And you will likely have more job security.

Index

Get the eBook for only $5!

Why limit yourself?

Now you can take the weightless companion with you wherever you go and access your content on your PC, phone, tablet, or reader.

Since you've purchased this print book, we're happy to offer you the eBook in all 3 formats for just $5.

Convenient and fully searchable, the PDF version enables you to easily find and copy code—or perform examples by quickly toggling between instructions and applications. The MOBI format is ideal for your Kindle, while the ePUB can be utilized on a variety of mobile devices.

To learn more, go to www.apress.com/companion or contact support@apress.com.